THE TRANSFORMATION OF THE CLASSICAL HERITAGE

Peter Brown, General Editor

HOMER THE THEOLOGIAN

The Title Page of Chapman's *Odyssey* (1614?)

ROBERT LAMBERTON

HOMER
THE THEOLOGIAN

Neoplatonist Allegorical Reading
and the Growth of the Epic Tradition

UNIVERSITY OF CALIFORNIA PRESS
Berkeley • Los Angeles • London

University of California Press
Berkeley and Los Angeles, California

University of California Press, Ltd.
London, England

© 1986 by The Regents of the University of California

Library of Congress Cataloging in Publication Data

Lamberton, Robert.
Homer the theologian.

(Transformation of the classical heritage; 9)
Bibliography: p.
Includes index.
1. Homer—Religion and ethics.   2. Homer—Allegory and symbolism.
3. Religion in literature.   4. Allegory.   5. Neoplatonism.
6. Epic poetry—History and criticism.   I. Title.   II. Series.
PA4037.L32   1986   883'.01   85-1184
ISBN 0-520-05437-7 (alk. paper)

Printed in the United States of America

1   2   3   4   5   6   7   8   9

CONTENTS

PREFACE

The Homeric poems provide our earliest direct insights into the religious thought of the Greeks, and, with few interruptions, the presence of Homer in the Greek religious imagination, pagan and Christian, remained continuous until the decline of the Byzantine church in the late Middle Ages. Indeed, when we find Nikolaos Mesarites, a metropolitan of Ephesus early in the thirteenth century, describing a striding image of St. Paul in a mosaic at Constantinople with a phrase borrowed from a description of a Homeric hero (θέα μοι τοῦτον μακρὰ βιβῶντα) and borrowing from the Homeric chimaera the qualities to describe the teachings of the Apostles (τούτων αἱ διδαχαὶ πνέουσι μένος πυρός),[1] it is clear that for the Greeks not only the myths but the very diction of Homer never ceased to be a part of that highly charged realm of imaginative experience that is the province both of poets and of religious thinkers.

Nevertheless, the relationship of the Homeric poems to the various conceptions of divinity successively articulated in the Greek tradition between the sixth century B.C. and the Christian Middle Ages was never a comfortable one. It is surely one of the great and characteristic ironies of Greek intellectual history that, at the source of the tradition and at the dawn of Greek literacy, we find in full bloom a tradition of oral poetry apparently so utterly secularized, irreverent, and disillusioned that the gods could be used for comic relief. As has often been noted, Homer has a great deal in common with his Ionian compatriots of the sixth century, whose rationalism was to pave the way for the effective demythologizing of Greek metaphysical thought in the fifth and fourth.

1. G. J. M. Bartelink, "Homerismen in Nikolaos Mesarites' Beschreibung der

This study is concerned not with religious thought as such, but rather with a single phase of the history of the interaction of the Homeric poems with Greek ideas concerning the nature of reality and the divine: the reading of Homer by thinkers in the Platonic tradition from the second to the fifth century after Christ. The focus of attention is the problem of interpretation raised during that period by two important shifts in the cultural status of the Homeric poems. On the one hand, these interpreters strove to redeem the reputation of Homer as a bulwark of pagan Greek culture by demonstrating that his stories and the model of reality that could be deduced from them were in fact compatible with contemporary idealist thought. On the other hand, the more exoteric Platonists were simultaneously concerned to make use of Homer's prestige—to whose appeal no Greek could be immune—to bolster the doctrines of later Platonism.

This double impulse toward a redefinition of the meaning of the Homeric poems and their relationship to reality led to many formulations and exegeses that are not without an element of the absurd. When we learn from Proclus, for instance, that Proteus is an angelic mind (νοῦς τις ἀγγελικός) containing within himself the forms of all things that come to be and pass away, that Eidothea is a demonic soul (ψυχή τις . . . δαιμονία) joined to that divine intellect, and that seals are the mythoplasts' means of representing the flock of individual souls dependent on this particular divine "procession," there is no doubt that we are seeing the apparent meaning of the Homeric text distorted to the limit of recognition.[2]

However, the exegeses are by no means uniformly farfetched, and, more important, the demands made by them upon the text of the Homeric corpus represent a new departure in the context of ancient literary criticism.

We know relatively little of methods of interpreting literary texts in antiquity. G. M. A. Grube expresses the traditional view of the matter:

Much is absent from ancient criticism which we should expect to find there. The ancients seem to have felt that great writers were quite capable of expressing their meaning clearly to their audiences, directly, without intermediaries. There is very little in the ancient critics of any period about purpose or meaning, about imagery, symbolism, levels of meaning—these and other aspects of poetry which

---

Apostelkirche in Konstantinopel," p. 307.
   2. Proclus *In Rep.* 1.112–13.

are not easily subjected to intellectual analysis are nearly completely ignored.[3]

Nevertheless, it seems clear from a passage in the *Republic* that, by Plato's time, the whole of the *Iliad* and *Odyssey* had been interpreted allegorically,[4] and there is no doubt that explication of texts as well as myths formed part of the sophists' curriculum in the fifth century.[5] A papyrus from Derveni in Macedonia (still not adequately published) demonstrates that in an Orphic context, allegorical interpretation was applied to hexameter poetry as early as the middle of the fourth century.[6]

Grube's statement, then, must be qualified. The fact that we have very little literary exegesis from classical antiquity is *not* an indication that "the ancients . . . felt that great writers were quite capable of expressing their meaning . . . directly, without intermediaries." Intermediaries existed, but very little of their commentary comes down to us, because they were in many cases not primarily writers but oral teachers, and survive at all only by chance and usually at second hand in the scholia.

The process of interpretation and reinterpretation was, and is, continuous, constantly creating new images of the poet and of the meaning of the poems. Nevertheless, the surviving interpretive essays permit us to mark a watershed. Neither Heraclitus's *Homeric Allegories*[7] nor the essay on the life and works of Homer that comes down to us under Plutarch's name can be dated with precision, but they represent two widely divergent intellectual stances, the one hostile to Plato, the other eclectic but concerned with finding the sources of Platonic and Pythagorean thought (along with those of Stoic and Peripatetic thought) in Homer. Neither is committed to finding in Homer a single, fixed, and accurate account of reality.

3. G. M. A. Grube, "How Did the Greeks Look at Literature?" p. 99. See James A. Coulter, *The Literary Microcosm*, p. 22, on the "anti-allegorical bias" of most modern histories of ancient literary theory.

4. Ἥρας δὲ δεσμοὺς ὑπὸ υἱέος καὶ Ἡφαίστου ῥίψεις ὑπὸ πατρός, μέλλοντος τῇ μητρὶ τυπτομένῃ ἀμυνεῖν, καὶ θεομαχίας ὅσας Ὅμηρος πεποίηκεν οὐ παραδεκτέον εἰς τὴν πόλιν, οὔτ᾽ ἐν ὑπονοίαις πεποιημένας οὔτε ἄνευ ὑπονοιῶν (Plato *Rep.* 2.378d). Cf. Konrad Müller, "Allegorische Dichtererklärung," col. 17.

5. See N. J. Richardson, "Homeric Professors in the Age of the Sophists."

6. See S. G. Kapsomenos, "Ὁ ὀρφικὸς πάπυρος τῆς Θεσσαλονίκης." An unauthorized text of the papyrus was published in the *Zeitschrift für Papyrologie und Epigraphik* 47 (1982):1–12 in a new sequence following p. 300. For the most up-to-date discussion of the interpretation of the papyrus, see Jeffrey S. Rusten, "Interim Notes on the Papyrus from Derveni."

7. Throughout this study, the name Heraclitus will normally refer, not to the

These two works provide a background against which a focused image of Homer emerges, an image articulated by dogmatic Platonists and Neopythagoreans. This, to a large extent, was the tradition the Latin Middle Ages inherited, independent of the text of Homer, itself clothed in a forgotten language. The image finds its strongest medieval expression in Dante's portrait of Homer as the prince of poets, and the probability seems very great that the Neoplatonic exegesis of Homer and the model of the levels of meaning in literature for which Proclus is our primary source in antiquity may have had a profound, if indirect, influence on Dante's conception of his own work and his role in the development of the epic tradition.

Dante, moreover, is not the only major poet in whom the influence of this interpretive tradition may be perceived. The beginnings of deliberate and conscious allegorical poetry in the fourth, fifth, and sixth centuries after Christ appear to represent the transfer into the creative realm of the expectations with which allegorizing interpreters approached Homer and other early texts. The tradition of epic poetry was one of allegory, of masked meanings—or so the dominant tradition of interpretation claimed—and poets such as Prudentius and "Musaeus" seem to have created poems designed to be approached with exactly these expectations.

The history of the influence of the mystical-allegorical tradition beyond the Renaissance lies largely outside the scope of this study, but it is clear that Renaissance manuals of mythology tap medieval traditions, themselves ultimately reaching back to the Neoplatonists of late antiquity. After Ficino, the rediscovery of Plato, along with the Neoplatonist commentaries, again made available the philosophical basis of allegorical interpretation, and allegorizing interpretive texts regularly accompanied new editions of Homer down into the eighteenth century. Thomas Taylor, whose influence can be seen in Blake and the English Romantics, directed the attention of yet another generation of poets to the Neoplatonists and their habits of reading and interpretation.

As noted, the present study is concerned primarily with the evidence for the understanding of the meaning of the Homeric poems among the Platonists of late antiquity—the high period of mystical allegory, in which the figure of the visionary Homer and the scope of the allegorical meanings of his poems were fully developed and articulated. Neverthe-

---

sixth-century Ephesian philosopher, but to the author of a work on Homer that probably belongs to the first century after Christ.

less, since it is my purpose to portray a neglected and crucially important period of *transition* within the tradition of epic poetry (and, more
generally, of literature), considerable attention is paid to the proximal
end of that period and to the impact of the ancient Neoplatonists' reading of Homer on the Middle Ages.

The Neoplatonic allegorists refashioned Homer not by any interference with the text itself, but by exerting their influence on the other
factor in the equation of reading: the reader. In so doing, they pre-
disposed subsequent readers to expect, and so to discover, a certain
scope of meaning in early epics. Had they simply reshaped and reorga-
nized Homeric verses to convey their own teachings explicitly, their general effect would have been no greater than that of the Homeric *centones*
of the Gnostics. As it was, however, the effect of their refashioning of the
poems was far subtler and far more pervasive: it generated a *reading* of
the received text of Homer that was to become inseparable from the
meaning of that text for later generations.

ACKNOWLEDGMENTS

This study is a revision and expansion of my doctoral dissertation, "Homer the Theologian" (Yale, 1979). The teachers and colleagues who have helped are too numerous to list individually, but a few deserve special mention. Lowry Nelson, Jr., gave generously of his time, energy, and perceptions throughout the duration of the project, as did Jack Winkler. I am deeply indebted to both, not only for their judicious suggestions and advice, but for their constant encouragement. Their contributions have been so numerous that it would be impossible to acknowledge them as they occur. Others with whom I have discussed the project, in person or by letter, include C. J. Herington and A. H. Armstrong, both of whom gave me valuable ideas and helped me to develop a perspective on my material. Many friends and colleagues at the American School of Classical Studies in Athens also contributed in one way or another. Of these, David Jordan (with whom I shared many valuable and enjoyable hours over Plato) in particular contributed ideas and facts that have found their way, however distorted, into this study.

I must also thank Nancy Winter and the other librarians of the Blegen Library of the American School, as well as the librarians of the Ecole Française d'Athènes, the Deutsches Archäologisches Institut at Athens, the Gennadeion Library, and the Yale Classics Library, all of whom made me welcome and gave me generous assistance. During the year I devoted exclusively to the dissertation, I was supported by a doctoral fellowship from the Canada Council for the Arts.

I completed the revision of the study as a junior fellow of the Center for Hellenic Studies in Washington, D.C., with additional support from the Crake Foundation (Sackville, N.B., Canada). Like all of those who have had the pleasure and privilege of working at the center, I am deeply indebted to Bernard Knox and to the center's librarian, Jenö Platthy. The resources of Dumbarton Oaks, the Library of Congress, and the Georgetown University Library were also generously opened to me. My colleagues at the center in 1982–83 contributed greatly to the revision—often without knowing it—but among them Kathy Eden deserves special thanks for a wealth of suggestions and bibliography, as does James Lesher for sorting out the tangled skein of my ideas on several points.

To John Dillon, who read the book for the University of California Press, goes credit not only for numerous corrections and encouraging insights, but for suggestions that led to a substantial reorganization of the opening chapters.

The frontispiece was photographed from the copy of Chapman's *Odyssey* in the Gonzales Lodge Collection, Rare Book and Manuscript Library, Columbia University, and is published here with permission.

The jacket illustration is a detail of a drawing by Raphael in the Royal Library, Windsor Castle. Copyright reserved. Reproduced by gracious permission of Her Majesty Queen Elizabeth II.

Final preparation of the manuscript was completed in the stimulating atmosphere of the Society of Fellows in the Humanities, Columbia University, where my colleagues again contributed significantly to my work. Particular thanks are due to Larry Miller, who saved me from several errors in the subchapter on the Arabs, and to Peter Cowe of the Department of Middle Eastern Languages and Cultures, who gave generously of his time and expertise to help me with the passage of Philo's *De providentia* discussed in chapter 2A. At the University of California Press, Doris Kretschmer has nurtured the book with patient energy for several years. Her choice of readers has led to substantial improvements in the text.

Finally, my companion and former colleague Susan Rotroff has contributed many valuable ideas and suggestions, but above and beyond these it has been her constant help and encouragement that have made the work possible.

The Society of Fellows in the Humanities
Columbia University
May, 1985

ABBREVIATIONS

The following abbreviations are used in the text and in footnotes to designate reference works and series.

CHLGEMP   *The Cambridge History of Later Greek and Early Medieval Philosophy*, edited by A. H. Armstrong. Cambridge: Cambridge University Press, 1967.

D-K   *Die Fragmente der Vorsokratiker*, Greek text and German translation by Hermann Diels, 10th edition, edited by Walther Kranz. Berlin: Weidmann, 1960–61.

GCS   *Die griechischen christlichen Schriftsteller der ersten Jahrhunderte*, begun by the Kirchenväter–Commission der königlichen preussischen Akademie der Wissenschaften and continued by the Kommission für spätantike Religionsgeschichte der deutschen Akademie der Wissenschaften zu Berlin. Various editors. Leipzig: J. C. Hinrichs (succeeded after 1941 by Akademie-Verlag, Berlin), 1899–in progress.

KP   *Der kleine Pauly*, Lexikon der Antike auf der Grundlage von Paulys Realencyclopädie der classischen Altertumswissenschaft . . . , edited by Konrat Ziegler, Walter Sontheimer, and Hans Gertner. Stuttgart: Alfred Druckenmüller, 1964–75.

Lampe   *A Patristic Greek Lexicon*, edited by G. W. H. Lampe. Oxford: Oxford University Press, 1961.

LSJ   *A Greek-English Lexicon*, compiled by Henry George Liddell and Robert Scott, revised and augmented throughout by Sir Henry Stuart Jones, 9th edition, with supplement. Oxford: Oxford University Press, 1968.

PG   *Patrologiae cursus completus, series Graeca*, edited by J.-P. Migne. 162 vols. Paris: J.-P. Migne, 1857–66.

PL   *Patrologiae cursus completus, series Latina*, edited by J.-P. Migne. 221 vols. +4 vols. Paris: J.-P. Migne, 1844–64.

P-W   *Paulys Realencyclopädie der classischen Altertumswissenschaft*, new reworking begun by Georg Wissowa . . . . Munich: Alfred Druckenmüller (succeeded after 1940 by J. B. Metzler, Stuttgart), 1893–1974. References to P-W are based on the pattern used by John P. Murphy in his *Index to the Supplements and Supplemental Volumes of Pauly-Wissowa's R.E.* (Chicago: Ares, 1976), but his Roman numerals are replaced by Arabic numerals. The number of the volume is followed by "a" if the second series is meant, and the number of the half-volume (1 or 2) follows. Dates are also included.

Real. Ant. Chr.   *Reallexikon für Antike und Christentum*, edited by Theodor Klauser. Stuttgart: Anton Hiersemann, 1950–in progress.

SC   *Sources chrétiennes*, founded by Henri de Lubac and Jean Daniélou. Claude Mondésert, director. Various editors. Paris: Editions du Cerf, 1941–in progress.

I

The Divine Homer
and the Background of
Neoplatonic Allegory

A. HOMER'S PRETENSIONS

Our concern here will be to examine one among several traditions of the interpretation of Homer in antiquity: that characterized by the claims that Homer was a divine sage with revealed knowledge of the fate of souls and of the structure of reality, and that the *Iliad* and *Odyssey* are mystical allegories yielding information of this sort if properly read. It will be necessary to omit from discussion the larger part of the history of the interpretation of Homer in antiquity[1] in order to look specifically at the tradition closing that history and looking forward to the Middle Ages and Renaissance. Nevertheless it seems appropriate to begin by examining the earliest testimonia (including the Homeric texts themselves) providing insight into the prehistory and early history of the conception of Homer as a sage.

It has been customary among recent students of Homer to minimize the importance of the prophetic element in Homeric diction and, on the

---

1. This vast field was approached as a whole by Félix Buffière in *Les Mythes d'Homère et la pensée grecque*. His work, though anticipated to some extent by iconographical studies such as those of Franz Cumont, broke new ground and has remained the definitive treatment. Buffière's vast scholarship permitted him to sketch out a comprehensive history of the interaction between Homer and Greek philosophy. The debts of all subsequent work in this field to his study are very great. Of comparable importance, but more general in scope, is Jean Pépin's *Mythe et Allégorie: Les Origines grecques et les contestations judéo-chrétiennes*.

contrary, to emphasize the absence of any pretense to supernatural insight in the narrative voice. J. Tate sums up the negative evidence:

> Homer . . . does not claim to be "controlled" by a spirit not his own, or to utter oracles containing a manifold significance. . . . Nor does he claim the standing of a priest. . . . The Homeric claim to inspiration does not imply profound wisdom or even veracity.[2]

Tate's point is that the "divine" Homer of Plato, whom the Neopythagoreans and Neoplatonists systematically expanded (in isolation from the ironies and contradictions of the relevant passages of Plato) into a seer and sage, has no Homeric roots whatsoever. Tate does not place great weight on his own *argumentum ex silentio*, but at the same time he takes it for granted that any reasonable reader will agree with him. The Homeric narrative voice, though, is notoriously opaque with regard to its own identity and function, and Tate's argument does have decided weaknesses. For the sake of a full appreciation of the qualities of the poems, this commonly held view deserves to be examined and questioned.

No one will deny that direct access to information about a mode of existence beyond the human, about the fate of souls after death, and about events on the human plane but hidden from everyday perception is a possibility in the imaginative world of Homer. Revelation is the stock-in-trade of Homeric seers from Calchas to Theoclymenus and Tiresias, and direct, accurate perception of divine reality is commonly extended to the heroes themselves.[3] The contrast between human ignorance and divine omniscience is repeatedly drawn,[4] and the epiphanies that provide breakthroughs from perception on the human level to perception on the divine are among the most dramatic moments of the poems.

There is ample basis, then, on which to claim that the epics *contain* a complex model of perception in which the world of experience of ordinary mortals is seen as severely limited. The perceptions of the heroes remain similarly limited except for occasional moments of insight. Those of the seers differ from those of the other heroes only in degree: for

2. J. Tate, "On the History of Allegorism," p. 113.

3. The instances are so numerous and conspicuous as scarcely to require enumeration. In the *Odyssey*, Odysseus is repeatedly given privileged information by Athena. In the *Iliad*, her striking apparitions to Achilles at 1.194–222 and to Diomedes at 5.123–33 and 799–845, along with that of Apollo to Achilles at 22.7–20, all involve the imparting of privileged information, available only through the superhuman perceptions of a divinity.

4. E.g., in the line that opens Achilles' response to Thetis's questions at *Il.* 1.365.

them, epiphanies are the rule rather than the exception. The gods, whose experience otherwise in many respects resembles human experience, are omniscient, and though this principle is commonly incompatible with the demands of the narrative,[5] it is nevertheless repeatedly expressed and seems an integral part of Homeric theology.[6]

Where are we to place the bards in this hierarchy? It has been a commonplace of Homer criticism since antiquity that there is an element of self-portraiture in the bards of the *Odyssey*.[7] This principle extends to the *Iliad* as well, and the portrait of Achilles as amateur bard singing the κλέα ἀνδρῶν by his tent (*Il.* 9.189) is surely included to increase the prestige of the Homeric bard and the tradition of Homeric song. Without insisting, with Proclus, on the symbolic values of the portraits of the individual bards and their relationship to the various levels of poetry in the Homeric corpus, we may reasonably assume that we have, at least in Phemius and Demodocus, figures whom the Homeric tradition created in order to glorify its own self-acclaimed roots in the Heroic Age and to provide us, if not with a self-portrait, then at least with an ancestor-portrait of the founders of the Homeric line. The epithet "divine" applied to bards in the *Odyssey*[8] doubtless in part explains the application of the same epithet (θεῖος) to Homer by Plato, and the bardic performances depicted provide opportunities for numerous compliments that reflect upon the whole tradition of heroic song,[9] though focusing, it is true, rather on the capacity of the bards to delight the senses and the imagination than upon other "divine" qualities.

The characteristics of the *Odyssey* bards are not explicitly claimed by the Homeric narrative voice for itself, but the implication is very strong that the listener is expected to make the connection and to associate with the bard whose voice he is hearing the qualities of the bards whom that

5. E.g., the scene between Zeus and Hera at *Il.* 1.536–94, which is unthinkable if they are both truly omniscient. Pushing the concept to its logical conclusion, all dialogue between omniscient gods would be impossible or simply superfluous.

6. It is stated broadly in the formula θεοὶ δέ τε πάντα ἴσασιν, which occurs twice in the Proteus episode (*Od.* 4.379, 468). Vast knowledge leaping the boundaries of space and time is also characteristic of the Sirens (*Od.* 12.191). Achilles assumes that Thetis already knows what she has asked him to tell her at *Il.* 1.365, and Menelaus makes a similar assumption addressing Proteus at *Od.* 4.465.

7. E.g., Proclus *In Rep.* 1.193. See ch. 5D below.

8. θεῖος ἀοιδός and θεῖον ἀοιδόν occur twelve times in the *Odyssey* and θέσπιν ἀοιδόν once. The usage is foreign to the *Iliad*, where bards play little part.

9. E.g. *Od.* 8.44–45 and 478–81.

voice describes and impersonates. At one point, moreover, the narrative voice groans under the difficulty of the task and reminds us that super-human demands are being made upon it:

It is a hard thing for me to tell all this like a god.

ἀργαλέον δέ με ταῦτα θεὸν ὣς πάντ' ἀγορεῦσαι
(Il. 12.176)

A more complex, though largely tacit, claim to superhuman powers and knowledge can be found in the narrative voice's claims regarding its own performance. The salient characteristic of privileged knowledge in the context of Homeric psychology is the ability of the mind to move freely in time and space. The gods' knowledge is infinite because it extends into the past and into the future and is not limited to a single loca-tion or perspective. Normal human knowledge, however, extends only to that portion of the past the individual has experienced or been told about, and to that portion of the present currently within the grasp of the senses. Calchas the seer, however, is characterized as one

Who knew those things that were, those that were to be and those
    that had been before,

ὃς ᾔδη τά τ' ἐόντα, τά τ' ἐσσόμενα πρό τ' ἐόντα
(Il. 1.70)

and this is clearly the core of his claim to competence as a seer. The nar-rative voice, it is true, never makes explicit claims to share in this sort of privileged knowledge. It does, however, frequently request supernatural aid in order to comprehend or transmit the relevant information, and the invocation immediately preceding the catalogue of ships makes explicit the function of Homer's Muses:

Tell me now, Muses of Olympus—
for you are goddesses, here beside me, and know everything,
while we hear only reports and know nothing—
who were the leaders and chiefs of the Greeks?
For I could not remember them all and name them,
not if I had ten tongues in ten mouths,
an invincible voice and a heart of bronze,
unless the Olympian Muses, daughters of
aegis-bearing Zeus, remind me who came to Ilium.

Ἔσπετε νῦν μοι, Μοῦσαι 'Ολύμπια δώματ' ἔχουσαι—
ὑμεῖς γὰρ θεαί ἐστε, πάρεστέ τε, ἴστέ τε πάντα,
ἡμεῖς δὲ κλέος οἶον ἀκούομεν οὐδέ τι ἴδμεν—
οἵ τινες ἡγεμόνες Δαναῶν καὶ κοίρανοι ἦσαν·

πληθὺν δ' οὐκ ἂν ἐγὼ μυθήσομαι οὐδ' ὀνομήνω,
οὐδ' εἴ μοι δέκα μὲν γλῶσσαι, δέκα δὲ στόματ' εἶεν,
φωνὴ δ' ἄρρηκτος, χάλκεον δέ μοι ἦτορ ἐνείη,
εἰ μὴ 'Ολυμπιάδες Μοῦσαι, Διὸς αἰγιόχοιο
θυγατέρες, μνησαίαθ' ὅσοι ὑπὸ Ἴλιον ἦλθον·

(Il. 2.484–92)

Homer's humility, then, extends only to his own unaided voice. When aided by the Muses he can perform tasks of memory and song that go far beyond normal human limitations. Specifically, in this instance, he claims the ability to include within the scope of his song a vast and complex body of information about the past.[10]

Here, the invocation constitutes an inflated introduction to a set piece of exceptional complexity and the intention of the narrative voice seems to be to bring the magnificence of its own upcoming performance to the attention of the audience. In other instances, however, the narrative voice gratuitously destroys the dramatic coherence of a scene in order to impress us with its own broader perspective on the matters at hand, its ability to contemplate past and future, whereas the actors in the drama it relates cannot see beyond their immediate surroundings.

Thus, when Helen looks down on the Greek troops in the episode of the "View from the Wall," she mentions finally that she does not see her brothers Castor and Polydeuces, and conjectures that they may be absent because they are ashamed on her account. The narrative voice, however, closing the episode, observes:

Thus she spoke, but the fertile earth already held them fast,
back in Lacedaemonia, in their own land

Ὣς φάτο, τοὺς δ' ἤδη κάτεχεν φυσίζοος αἶα
ἐν Λακεδαίμονι αὖθι, φίλῃ ἐν πατρίδι γαίῃ.

(Il. 3.243–44)

The moment for the interruption is carefully chosen. We have been exposed for the last 180 lines to a complex dramatic situation the focus of which is discovery. One limited perception is played off against another: Priam's (rather unaccountable) ignorance, Helen's relatively great knowledge of the Greeks, and Antenor's limited, but complementary, knowl-

10. Hesiod (Theog. 36–38) adapts the description of Calchas's wisdom to describe that of the Muses:

. . . Μουσάων ἀρχώμεθα ταὶ Διὶ πατρὶ
ὑμνεῦσαι τέρπουσι μέγαν νόον ἐντὸς 'Ολύμπου,
εἴρουσαι τά τ' ἐόντα τά τ' ἐσσόμενα πρό τ' ἐόντα.

edge. The drama has been a drama of revelation in which we have been intensely conscious of the horizons of experience of each individual. This is the moment at which the narrative voice reveals something of the scope of its *own* knowledge, and the effect is one of a rapid alteration of perspective, analogous, perhaps, to a retreating zoom shot in the narrative vocabulary of cinema: we pass from an intense and claustrophobic dramatic situation, viewed from within, to a distant, ironic vantage point, which is that of the poet himself.

The particular instance we have examined relates to the past, and it is certainly true that the primary focus of the Homeric narrative voice's claims to privileged wisdom is retrospective. Homer is equally capable, however, of making such leaps to reveal some fact about the future, as when Patroclus has just requested of Achilles that he be allowed to lead the Myrmidons into battle and the narrative voice interjects, before Achilles can answer:

So the fool pleaded—he was asking
for his own foul death and doom.

Ὣς φάτο λισσόμενος μέγα νήπιος· ἦ γὰρ ἔμελλεν
οἷ αὐτῷ θάνατόν τε κακὸν καὶ κῆρα λιτέσθαι.
(*Il.* 16.46–47)

The effect is to emphasize the vast gap between the knowledge of past, present, and future available to the narrator and the limited knowledge of the actors in the drama. This gap generates the tragic irony characteristic of the narrative technique of the *Iliad*.[11] It necessarily involves the raising of the narrator to a level of perception for which the most obvious analogy is that of the gods. Thus the narrative voice does in some sense assimilate "divine" wisdom and adopt a privilege that implies such wisdom.

In the context of the implicit claims made by the Homeric narrative voice for its own powers and for the wisdom it taps, the descriptions of the *Odyssey* bards take on a new seriousness. Demodocus, in particular, the blind protégé of the Muse, is seen to enjoy that protection as more

---

11. There are numerous examples beyond those given here. The most frequent pattern is an interjection at the moment of an oath or prayer, in which the narrative voice indicates that what is prayed for or sworn will not be fulfilled. Cf. *Il.* 2.36 and 3.302. The narrative voice of the *Odyssey* seems far less concerned with this dramatic contrast, and in general the effect sought in the *Iliad*, with its cultivation of the brutal contrast between ignorance and knowledge, seems rooted in the far more bitter ironies of the military epic.

than an empty convention.[12] What appears to be simply insistence on the vastness of his repertory—

> for the god made him able to
> delight, however his heart might impel him to sing.

> τῷ γὰρ ῥα θεὸς πέρι δῶκεν ἀοιδὴν
> τέρπειν, ὅππῃ θυμὸς ἐποτρύνῃσιν ἀείδειν.
> (Od. 8.44–45)

—has overtones of an extraordinary power of the mind to move in space and time, along with the implication that Demodocus is "divine," not only in his power to delight, but also in his ability to exercise that power in casting his mind over a vast range of poetic material.[13] The only singers who make such claims explicitly in the poems are the Sirens:

> For we know all that the Trojans and Greeks
> suffered in Troy by the will of the gods.
> We know all that happens on the rich earth.

> ἴδμεν γάρ τοι πάνθ' ὅσ' ἐνὶ Τροίῃ εὐρείῃ
> Ἀργεῖοι Τρῶές τε θεῶν ἰότητι μόγησαν·
> ἴδμεν δ' ὅσσα γένηται ἐπὶ χθονὶ πουλυβοτείρῃ.
> (Od. 12.189–91)

The coincidence is far from gratuitous, and the Sirens resemble the Odyssey bards in other ways as well: they "bewitch" (θέλγουσιν, Od. 12.44) as Phemius's songs are called "bewitchings" (θελκτήρια, Od. 1.337). Thus they share both of the supernatural qualities attributed to the bards: the power of the mind to violate the normal limitations of space and time and the power to entrance their audience. The Sirens' claim to exceptional wisdom corresponds closely to the implicit claim of the Iliad poet, aided by his Muse, to universal knowledge of the Troy tale. By the time of Hadrian, the identification of Homer with his own Sirens must have been a commonplace, for in the Certamen (38) an oracle calls Homer himself an "ambrosial Siren" (ἀμβρόσιος Σειρήν). The evolution of Homer's Sirens—with the help of the quite different Sirens who generate the music of the celestial hemispheres in the myth of Er in

12. Cf. Od. 8.44–45, 61–63, 489–91.
13. See Od. 8.492–98 on the relationship of repertory to inspiration. The same claim may be implied in Penelope's line to Phemius, Φήμιε, πόλλα γὰρ ἄλλα βροτῶν θελκτήρια οἶδας, Od. 1.337. The idea expressed with reference to Demodocus (Od. 8.45) that his mind was able to move freely from song to song is brought up by Telemachus at Od. 1.346–47 with a moral thrust: Telemachus insists that Phemius must be allowed free choice of his song.

Plato's *Republic*—into symbols of the divine order in the universe[14] is an important part of the evolution of the claims for Homeric wisdom from esthetic convention to cultural and philosophical mythmaking.

This, then, is the range of Homeric singers to whom we can turn for self-portraits of the creator of the *Iliad* and *Odyssey*. But there is one other Homeric teller of tales whom a part of the later tradition was able to identify with Homer: Tiresias. Though there is no surviving evidence of the assimilation of Homer to Tiresias in antiquity, the engraving that appears on the title page of Chapman's *Odyssey* is unlikely to represent an invention of the early seventeenth century. This plate (see frontispiece) has often been reprinted,[15] but its contents and importance do not seem to have been examined, though Allardyce Nicoll describes it briefly and notes that a figure of Homer stands in the center.[16] There is little doubt that the figure is, in fact, Homer. The head, with blind eyes turned to heaven, illustrates a tradition, at least as old as Proclus,[17] that made of the myth of Homer's blindness a metaphor for transcendent vision. It is virtually the same head that appears on the title page of Chapman's *Iliad* and is there explicitly labeled "Homer."[18] The Homer of the *Odyssey* title page is, however, someone else as well. He is surrounded on all sides by ghosts, whose outlines are dotted. His is fully drawn, and the epithet over his head, *solus sapit hic homo*, along with that of the ghosts, *reliqui vero umbrae moventur*, clearly constitutes a paraphrase of Circe's description of Tiresias:

> Even in death, Persephone granted to him alone the use of his wisdom, but the others are shadows that flit around.
>
> τῷ καὶ τεθνηῶτι νόον πόρε Περσεφόνεια
> οἴῳ πεπνῦσθαι· τοὶ δὲ σκιαὶ ἀΐσσουσιν.
>
> (*Od.* 10.494–95)

In the foreground sit Athena and Odysseus, the latter looking up at Homer/Tiresias in response to the goddess, who is pointing upward.

The profile of Dante from Raphael's *Parnassus* is certainly the inspiration for the most clearly defined of the ghosts contemplating Homer, and the scene as a whole includes elements both of the *Odyssey* and of the

14. See Pierre Boyancé, "Les Muses et l'harmonie des sphères."

15. E.g., as frontispiece to George deF. Lord, *Homeric Renaissance*, and to the second volume of the Bollingen edition of *Chapman's Homer*, edited by Allardyce Nicoll (see "Works Cited: Ancient Authors").

16. *Chapman's Homer*, ed. Nicoll, vol. 2, p. xii.

17. Proclus *In Rep.* 1.193–94.

18. See *Chapman's Homer*, ed. Nicoll, vol. 1, frontispiece.

Divine Comedy.[19] Raphael's fresco is the principal source both of composition and of detail, but the scene has been moved from Parnassus back to the underworld. The ghosts swarming around Homer/Tiresias and crowned with laurel must surely be equated with the crowd of poets of the fourth canto of the *Inferno*, rather than those of the fresco. Homer is presented in the form of Tiresias as a seer and the founder of the poetic tradition. Though the literary conceit of visiting Homer in Hades is at least as old as Plato,[20] the vision of him surrounded by the other poets, all of whom look up to him as their leader, is Dantesque—or, rather, Dante and Raphael are the proximal sources that have most influenced the artist of the title page. The concept of Homer as the focus of a literary court in the other world has been traced to the Pythagoreans,[21] and Lucian was able to parody it in the second century, leaving little doubt that such a figure was taken seriously a millennium before Dante.[22] The notion of the assimilation of this vision of Homer to his own creation Tiresias, the one ghost able to provide true information about past, present, and future, may likewise have had a long history antedating Chapman. The iconography of the title-page clearly belongs to the Renaissance, and the baroque style of the engraving, with its aggressive and exaggerated classicism, is a reminder of its distance from classical antiquity—yet, as the examples above have shown, the possibility of a Homeric self-portrait in the form of a seer rather than a bard is not out of the question.

This survey of the claims, implicit and explicit, of the Homeric narrative voice to privileged knowledge has provided us with a range of possibilities and the rudiments of a historical outline. The widespread myth of Homer's blindness is probably an indication that, even before the classical period, the description of the blind bard Demodocus was read as a Homeric self-portrait. The bard of the *Hymn to Apollo* who describes himself as a blind man (*Hymn* 3.172) provides attractive support for this interpretation. By Proclus's time, the perception of the *Odyssey*

19. The Raphael drawing of Dante juxtaposed with a Homer of the Hellenistic "blind" type (actually drawn from the recently discovered Laocoön group), reproduced as frontispiece to Hugo Rahner, *Griechische Mythen in christlicher Deutung*, and on the jacket of this volume, is a study for the great Vatican fresco of Parnassus.

20. Plato *Ap.* 41a.

21. "L'immortalité, conçue comme une récompense de la science, devait nécessairement créer un paradis d'intellectuels." Franz Cumont, *Recherches sur le symbolisme funéraire des Romains*, p. 315.

22. Luc. *Ver. hist.* 2.14–16.

bards as Homeric self-portraits had become an apparent commonplace of interpretation. With Proclus, and perhaps earlier, those multiple portraits became metaphors for multiple levels of meaning in the poems. In the form in which it reaches us,[23] the assimilation of Homer's voice to that of the Sirens may be no more than a lovely, but fanciful, Hellenistic conceit, but it implies a history of interpretation that had already identified Homer's voice with the limitless knowledge of his Muses, and had seen the connection between that composite figure and the Sirens. Finally, the assimilation of Homer to Tiresias, though we glimpse it only in the context of the declining northern European Renaissance, casts some light on a lost portion of the history of the interpretation of the *Iliad* and *Odyssey* that had made of their poet a prophetic figure only dimly foreshadowed in the ancient critical tradition before the Neoplatonists.

B. INTERPRETATION, ALLEGORY, AND THE CRITICS OF HOMER

The interpretive tradition that made of Homer a theologian and, beyond that, a sage providing access to privileged information about the fate of souls and the structure of the universe has, in the past, been studied primarily by students of philosophy and of religion. The goal of the present study, however, is to examine that tradition's contribution to the history of literature. It represents, on the one hand, a substantial part of the neglected interpretive, non-formalist aspect of ancient literary criticism. Perhaps more important still, after the text of the *Iliad* and *Odyssey* had become inaccessible, this interpretive tradition, as transmitted piecemeal through the philosophers, provided the Latin Middle Ages with an image of the *kind* of poet Homer was. Its importance for the history of literature is thus both direct and indirect, and it has information to yield concerning ancient habits of reading and interpretation, as well as about medieval attitudes toward the poet, who was revered as the founder of the tradition but no longer read.

In examining the origins of this tradition of reading, we must bear in mind that our concept of a corpus of European literature with its origins in archaic Greece is a modern construct. At least in the period previous to the fourth century B.C., the problems of reading and interpretation could not be solved in terms of a body of material comparable to what we

23. See Plutarch *Quaest. conv.* 9.14.6 145d–e, and *Certamen* 38.

are accustomed to call "literature." Each preserved text had an identity of its own and a claim to truth, historicity, or beauty that was unique and not easily compared with the claims of other texts. Formal criteria provided convenient and seductive categories, of course, and the idea of a competition (essentially a dramatized comparison) of Homer and Hesiod is far older than the third-century papyrus that preserves part of an early *Certamen*.[24] Homer, in any case, remained a discrete category of experience to a degree that may be difficult for us to appreciate, and an understanding of Homer—of *what* as well as *how* the *Iliad* and *Odyssey* communicated—could not easily be compared to the understanding of other literature.

The uniqueness of antiquity's response to Homer may be traced to a number of factors closely bound up with unique qualities of the text itself. It was, first of all, a body of material manifestly conceived with the primary goal of entertainment (if we may use so unpretentious a term for the relationship between the bard and the audience of whose imagination and emotions he took possession). At the same time it was a text that spoke constantly about the gods and that enjoyed the prestige of enormous antiquity. These two qualities of the text demanded a response that was to some extent divided. Homer is clearly innocent of the characteristic scruples expressed by Herodotus with regard to "speaking of divine things,"[25] and his freedom in this regard must have been disturbing to Greek piety even independently of such philosophical reactions as that of Xenophanes. Again by Herodotus's account, Homer and Hesiod were the very first poets, and that "the most ancient is the most revered"[26] was a pervasive principle in Greek culture. The *Iliad* and *Odyssey* were thus inevitably placed in a position of very great honor and inspired an awe that must sometimes have jarred uncomfortably against the response demanded by such passages as the deception of Zeus and the song of Ares and Aphrodite.[27] If Homer demanded laughter—even bawdy laughter—tradition demanded that this response someh~~ ~~ made compatible with the dignity of the divi~~

24. See Homer (OCT) vol. 5, p. 225 *Scholarship*, p. 11) traces the tradition bacl
25. τῶν δὲ εἴνεκεν ἀνεῖται τὰ θηρία ἱρ⌐ τὰ θεῖα πρήγματα, τὰ ἐγὼ φεύγω μάλιστ⌐
26. τιμιώτατον μὲν γὰρ τὸ πρεσβύτατο⌐
27. Ps.-Plutarch (*De vit. Hom.* 214) lis⌐ though one is not quite sure he does not si⌐ ter is mentioned. In any case, he is more s⌐ tators to the humor in Homer.

text itself by virtue of its antiquity. Finally, much of the "theological" material other than the *Iliad* and *Odyssey* that the tradition transmitted was indeed deliberately obscure and oblique. The most obvious examples were the hexameter oracles in which the gods expressed themselves with characteristic coyness, constantly saying one thing and meaning something quite different. The impulse to resolve the contradictory responses demanded by text and tradition through the imposition on the poetry of Homer of a structure of meaning analogous to that of the oracles must be far older than the surviving interpretive texts can demonstrate.[28]

Many of the apparently contradictory elements in the response of ancient "critics" to Homer thus have their roots in the impact of Homer on Greek society in a preliterate or protoliterate phase. There is no doubt that Homer was expounded and read in other ways from that reflected in the tradition of interpretation under examination here, but it is nevertheless true that the attitudes of the mystical allegorists are anticipated in contradictions that belong to a period before the *Iliad* and *Odyssey* could comfortably be included in a larger class approximating what we call "literature." The texts we shall examine belong to a period in which such a category did exist, but Homer continued to demand a unique response, which gave him a special status. He had to be read both as "literature" and as something more. It is primarily that nebulous secondary element that will occupy our attention, but we would be mistaken to assume that a more down-to-earth response to the poems could not coexist with mystical allegory and with extraordinary claims for the authority of Homer. Indeed, the juxtaposition of such attitudes as those of the allegorists, who were willing to leap far beyond the text to discover its "true" meaning, with the sort of sensitivity to the text that we demand of a modern critic is a characteristic paradox of the interpretive literature.

Alongside the problems of the identification of "literature" in the Greek tradition, and of the relationship of the *Iliad* and *Odyssey* to that category of experience, stands that of the identity and role of the critic in antiquity.[29] Here again we find no clear one-to-one equivalent, no identi-

28. The Derveni papyrus (bibliography in Preface, n. 6, above) of the fourth century B.C. contains Orphic texts with allegorical commentary. The *Iliad* (24.527–?) is quoted to explain (incorrectly) an expression in the Orphic poem, and it is ? that the author feels that Orpheus was sufficiently close to Homer for Ho- ? be useful in illuminating his language.

?n the evolution of the terms φιλόλογος, γραμματικός, κριτικός, and ? equivalents, see Sandys, *History of Classical Scholarship*, vol. 1, pp. 4– ? describes Longinus as a "critic" (*Vit. Plot.* 20.1–2).

fiable role in early Greek society corresponding to that of the critic in our own. With Rudolph Pfeiffer, we should, perhaps, conceive of the poets themselves and the rhapsodes (including such philosopher-poets as Xenophanes) as the first interpreters of poetry, succeeded in the fifth century by the sophists.[30]

In the Hellenistic age the term γραμματικός takes on a meaning that may include at least a part of the function of the modern critic, and in Cicero and other Roman authors both *grammaticus* and *literatus* can refer to *interpretes poëtarum*.[31] The κριτικός, or *criticus*, likewise engaged in literary scholarship, and these terms seem simply to designate a *grammaticus* of a higher degree of distinction. It is difficult, however, to determine whether these designations implied interpretive skills in the modern sense, or rather the ability to expound grammatical points. In a valuable sketch of modes of interpretation, Seneca portrays the *grammaticus futurus* commenting on Virgil's *fugit inreparabile tempus* (*Georg.* 3.284) by pointing out other instances of Virgil's use of *fugit* to talk about the passage of time,[32] and then shows him commenting on another passage by citing instances of Virgil's characteristic use of the epithet *tristis* with the noun *senectus*.[33] In the same passage, Seneca illustrates the sort of comment that might be offered by a philosophically inclined reader,[34] and what emerges is a sensitive, serious paraphrase and elaboration of the meaning of the verses, incorporating a rich sense of their human content. In short, the philosopher and not the *grammaticus* appears here in the role of the modern critic.

It seems to have been generally true in antiquity that exegesis was the province of the educator, and specifically of the philosophical educator.[35] Only infrequently was such exegesis given an importance that implied a pretense to permanence, and so only infrequently has it entered the preserved literature, beyond the scholia. Methods of reading and interpretation were doubtless varied: the Stoa favored allegorical exegesis and passed that taste on to later Platonism and to the tradition under examination here, though we have no reason to believe that Stoics or Platonists

30. Pfeiffer, *History of Classical Scholarship*, pp. 8–12, 16–36, and 43–45.
31. Sandys, *History of Classical Scholarship*, vol. 1, pp. 7–9.
32. Sen. *Epist.* 8.24.
33. Sen. *Epist.* 8.28–29.
34. . . . *ille, qui ad philosophiam spectat* (Sen. *Epist.* 8.24–25).
35. See N. J. Richardson, "Homeric Professors in the Age of the Sophists" for a summary of the evidence for the use of allegorizing commentary on Homer by the sophists of the fifth century.

invariably approached all myths and texts as allegorical, or that what we can learn of their response to Homer from the surviving bits of ancient exegesis constituted their entire response, or even their normal response, to the poems.[36]

The available evidence suggests that modes of response to the poems that seem contradictory to us remained complementary in the eyes of the philosophical traditions of late antiquity, and that no clear distinction was made between reading Homer as "literature" and reading him as scripture. The philosphers, moreover, are more likely to offer us insights into methods of reading and interpretation in antiquity than those whose training was specifically grammatical or rhetorical.

In practice, each of the authors under consideration faced the problem of defining a tradition of his own. Philosophical training naturally provided a model. If one studied under a Platonist, one would be exposed to a predictable body of philosophical literature, though its exact contents might vary from teacher to teacher and from school to school. Similarly, all of these writers contemplate the past and its written artifacts in terms of specific traditions. Porphyry and Proclus are, of course, Platonic philosophers, and their attitudes toward the literature of the past are colored by the canon progressively developed by that school. Of all the authors discussed here, Numenius was probably the most radical in terms of his personal and creative redefinition of the tradition on which he drew.[37] But common to all is the effort to define the field of useful writings from the past and so to create for themselves a context, canon, or tradition. Their criteria are never stylistic: they are interested in literature as a source of truth, and they are all, to a greater or lesser extent, in search of what we might call a body of scripture rather than a literature.

Thus, when Ps.-Plutarch makes Homer the founder of the whole sphere of human (i.e., Greek) discourse, he is claiming Homer to be the source of Greek literature broadly defined to include science, rhetoric, history, philosophy, and, rather incidentally, comedy, tragedy, and other poetry. There does exist for him, then, an extremely broad concept of "literature," but it is so general that he needs no word for it, and, inscriptions and fortuitously preserved ephemera aside, it comprises the collective verbal artifacts transmitted in writing from the past.

Perhaps the most important distinction our authors make within this

36. Pfeiffer, *History of Classical Scholarship*, p. 237.
37. See ch. 2B below.

vast field is the one Heinrich Dörrie singled out in Plotinus,[38] that between works that contain some eternally valid truth and those that do not. The latter category, including the relatively recent poets and dramatists, may be used for decoration or to illustrate a point, but the discussion of the meaning of these authors would be superfluous. For the former category, however, interpretation is essential, and the nature of the verbal artifact and its relationship to the truth it reflects must be defined.

Thus for each of our "critics" there exists a category of literature for which, were they to give it any attention at all, the formalistic criteria often said to constitute the whole of ancient literary criticism might well be the relevant ones. Discussion of the meaning of such texts would, in any case, be of minor importance. In practice, however, they focus their critical talents on the other category, the literature in which they see the possibility of discovering some enduring truth. The elucidation and articulation of such truths constitute the impetus of interpretation.

The need to articulate the truth thought to be contained in the *Iliad* and *Odyssey* can be traced to two primary motives: the desire of the interpreters to use the prestige of the Homeric poems to support their own views and the desire to defend Homer against his detractors.

If we conceive the interpretive tradition to have its origins in the sixth century B.C., whether in Pythagorean circles or elsewhere,[39] then the desire to tap Homer's prestige probably came earlier than the desire to defend him.[40] This suggests that Homer was already something of a θεολόγος in the sixth century (though the word itself may be an anachronism), or at the very least that he was viewed as an authoritative source of information, a possibility that should not be too surprising in the light of Herodotus's testimony.[41]

Much of the interpretive literature that comes down to us is, however, concerned with the defense of Homer against his detractors. It is this "defensive" tradition that Porphyry traces back to Theagenes of Rhegium, ca. 525 B.C.[42] Defensive interpretive efforts must then have been first stimulated by such critiques as that of Xenophanes of Colophon, and

38. See ch. 5D, with n. 59, below.

39. See Pfeiffer, *History of Classical Scholarship*, p. 12, on Pherecydes and the sixth-century sources of allegorism, and ch. 1D below.

40. The primacy of "positive" over "defensive" allegory was convincingly maintained by J. Tate, "Plato and Allegorical Interpretation," p. 142. See also his "On the History of Allegorism," p. 105.

41. Herod. *Hist.* 2.53–54, discussed ch. 1C below.

42. See ch. 1D below.

at an early date the philosophical reaction against the anthropomorphic gods of Homer and Hesiod may have produced defensive interpretations relating to the nature of the poetic utterance and its structure of meaning.[43]

In the history of the reading of Homer, however, one critique—that of Socrates in Plato's *Republic*—stands out above all others, both for its devastating condemnation of the poet and for its influence on subsequent readers.[44] This critique is central to the concerns of Heraclitus (the author of the *Homeric Allegories*), who condemns Plato severely and insists on the superiority of Homer, and to those of Proclus, whose extended consideration of Homer was focused on a reconciliation of the poet and the philosopher. The attempt at reconciliation goes back at least to Telephus of Pergamon and Numenius in the second century after Christ, and must have been an issue of some importance to any Platonist who wished to place Homer alongside Plato in the canon of authors who might provide a glimpse of the truth. This tendency to emphasize the spiritual and cosmological authority of Homer (and of the other θεολόγοι) is a growing trend in Platonism under the Roman Empire—in part, no doubt, because of a need to offer an authoritative scripture able to bear comparison with the scriptures of the increasingly threatening Christian tradition.[45] It is significant that, for his part, Augustine was able wholeheartedly to praise Plato's banishing of the poets.[46]

Since the Platonic critique was so important to later Platonists, it will be useful to review its major points briefly here. The context in the *Republic* in which Socrates first comments on Homer is the discussion of the education of the guardians of the state. Admitting the necessity of stories (myths) for the education of the young, Socrates asserts (*Rep.* 2.377b–c) that they must be carefully controlled by the state and that most of those currently in circulation (i.e., the myths of Homer and Hesiod) must be rejected. They are to be rejected not simply because they are lies—it is explicitly accepted that all myths are lies that contain a kernel of truth (377a)—but because they are *ugly* lies.[47] Ugly lies are said to be lies that

---

43. Diogenes Laertius (2.46) mentions a critic of Homer antedating Xenophanes and said to be contemporary with the poet himself.

44. See Stefan Weinstock, "Die platonische Homerkritik und seine Nachwirkung," and Eric Havelock, *Preface to Plato*, ch. 1.

45. Moses the allegorical θεολόγος of Philo (*De vit. Mos.* 2.115) foreshadows Homer the allegorical θεολόγος of the Neoplatonists. See ch. 1C below.

46. See August. *Civ. Dei* 2.14.

47. . . . ἐάν τις μὴ καλῶς ψεύδηται. *Rep.* 2.377d.

distort that about which they speak, just as a bad painter distorts his subject (377e). The preeminent example chosen is Hesiod's treatment of Ouranos and Kronos (377e–378a). Each offensive myth mentioned is viewed in terms of its potential educational impact on the guardians. The myth of Ouranos and Kronos will encourage the young to punish their fathers (378b), and stories of the gods fighting with one another and plotting among themselves will encourage them to believe that internal strife in a society is an acceptable state of affairs (378c–e).

The only solution is to abolish all the existing myths and have new ones made up according to certain basic principles ($\tau\acute{v}\pi o\iota$) set by the lawmakers (379a–c). The first example of a $\tau\acute{v}\pi o\varsigma$ is the principle that god is not responsible for evil (379c–380c). Both the jars of Zeus (*Il.* 24.527–33) and the attribution of responsibility for Pandarus's treachery to Athena and Zeus (*Il.* 4.30–104) are rejected as violating this $\tau\acute{v}\pi o\varsigma$ (379d–e). The second $\tau\acute{v}\pi o\varsigma$ requires that the divine be immutable and, as a corollary, that the gods by nature never deceive men (380d–383a). This entails the rejection of several offending Homeric passages: the assertion by one of the suitors in the *Odyssey* (17.483–87) that gods travel among men in disguise (381d), the "falsehoods about Proteus and Thetis" (*Od.* 4.351–592) (381d),[48] and the false dream sent by Zeus to Agamemnon (*Il.* 2.1–34) (383a).

At the beginning of book 3 it is emphasized that these $\tau\acute{v}\pi o\iota$ when exemplified in myths should have beneficial effects on the young. Specifically, they should make the young honor the gods and their parents and take their friendships seriously (386a). Now the problem is approached from the opposite direction. We start from a quality we wish to instill, in this case bravery ($\dot{\alpha}\nu\delta\rho\varepsilon\acute{\iota}\alpha$), and ask what sort of stories will produce it. Clearly, they will be stories that will cause the listeners *not* to fear death, and on this score all the mumbo jumbo in Homer about the sufferings of ghosts must go (386a–387b).[49] A Homer who portrays death negatively is unfit for the ears of free men (387b). It is also important that the citizens bear misfortune with a stiff upper lip (387e). To be

48. Thetis undergoes no transformations in Homer, but (as Jowett and Campbell point out in their edition of the *Republic* (*ad. loc.*, vol. 3, p. 105), a fragment of Sophocles' *Troilus* (fr. 561 Nauck) indicates that she was commonly said by the poets to have performed changes of shape to escape her marriage to Peleus.

49. The verses specifically rejected are *Il.* 16.856–57, 20.64–65, 23.103–4, and *Od.* 10.495, 489–91, and 24.6–9, but it is clear that their exclusion implies the excision of most of the content of the *Odyssey nekyias* and of much of the moral core of the *Iliad*.

excised on this score are Achilles' mourning (*Il.* 24.9–21), Priam rolling about in the dung of his courtyard (*Il.* 22.414), Thetis lamenting her fate (*Il.* 18.54), and even Zeus's moments of sadness (*Il.* 22.168, 16.433), along with other portrayals of good men or gods overcome by emotion (388a–d)—even by laughter (*Il.* 1.599) (389a). A few passages in which Homer portrays restraint are praised (389e), but Achilles' insults to Agamemnon (*Il.* 1.225–32) are rejected, along with praise of feasting in the *Odyssey* (*Od.* 9.5–11, 12.342), the entire episode of Hera's deception of Zeus (*Il.* 14.153–351), and the song of Ares and Aphrodite (*Od.* 8.266–366) (389e–390c).

The profit motive must be removed from the embassy to Achilles in book 9 of the *Iliad*, and Achilles may accept neither Agamemnon's nor Priam's gifts (390d–e). Various excesses of Achilles—his threat to Apollo at *Il.* 22.15, his fighting with the river god and going back on his promise to the Spercheios by giving his shorn hair to Patroclus's pyre, his treatment of the corpse of Hector and the human sacrifice at Patroclus' funeral—are branded "not to be believed (οὐ πειστέον)" (391a–b). Further strictures are laid on the moral content of acceptable stories about men (392a–c), but Homer is not directly involved in this discussion. A few pages later, however, the description of the universal poet able to imitate anything, who if he visits Plato's state will be honored profusely and immediately deported (398a), foreshadows the more sinister discussion in book 10.

Plato returns to Homer in book 10 in the context of general observations on mimetic art, of which Homer is said to be the founder (595b). The model of art-as-imitation developed here is familiar and need not be examined in detail. As Proclus and other Platonists realized, however, the blanket rejection of virtually all art forms as mimetic—and, as such, far removed from reality—is inconsistent with the conception of inspired (if irresponsible) poetry articulated in the *Phaedrus*. Yet, for purposes of this discussion, there seems to be no way out: Homer is to be banished along with the other artists on the grounds that they are merely generators of images "at the third remove from truth" (τρίτος ἀπὸ τῆς ἀληθείας) (599d). He is interrogated and found wanting because he did not (like Pythagoras) found a school, and because there is no further evidence that he had in his own time, or has now, any power to make men better (599d–600e). Stripped of their attractive poetic form, the poems are found to have no usable content (601b). Their appeal is to the emotions and not to reason, and their incitement to indulge in emotion is undesirable (602–607). One listens to them only at the risk of disturbing one's internal balance (608a–b).

This critique did much to shape the thinking of the later Platonists with regard to Homer. Clearly, the thrust of Socrates' arguments is a moral thrust from beginning to end, and esthetics are at issue only to the extent that they impinge upon moral issues. It is probably no coincidence that the passages singled out for condemnation include several of exceptionally rich and evocative language, such as the deception of Zeus and the song of Ares and Aphrodite. It is an unspoken corollary of the esthetics of book 10 of the *Republic* that the *better* a poem is (in terms of its appeal to the imagination and the emotions), the *worse* it is (in terms of its impact on one's internal order). The passages are rejected most obviously for the reason that they attribute to the gods motives and actions incompatible with Socrates' τύποι, but secondarily and implicitly because they are exceptionally attractive episodes.

The critique, then, invites response that will defend Homer first of all on the moral plane and secondarily on the esthetic plane. A defense on the level of esthetics will have to be compatible with the Platonic model of reality articulated in the *Republic*, with its absolute and transcendent realm of forms that constitute the "true" reality, situated beyond the material universe. On this score alone, any pre-Platonic approach to Homer (whether Pythagorean or other) will prove inadequate, for the simple reason that this model of reality begins with Plato. In the surviving literature, a complete defense on the esthetic level is to be found only in Proclus, but the central concepts on which that defense is built are anticipated by Numenius and Porphyry.

The passages rejected on moral grounds are most easily defended on those same moral grounds, by reasoning from the text of Homer and reaching conclusions different from those reached by Socrates. Thus the first tools of defensive commentators will be paraphrase and interpretation. The moral issues are in some cases far less obvious than Socrates would have them, and it is not beyond the powers of dialectical reasoning, for instance, to reduce to a minimum the responsibility of Athena for the crime of Pandarus.[50] In such discussions, one is often reminded of the tendentious and playful sophistic tours de force by which, for instance, Helen was demonstrated to be innocent of causing the Trojan War.[51] There was, by the time of the Neoplatonists, a long tradition of turning the moral world of Homer upside down, for a variety of reasons, both rhetorical and philosophical.

It is the second alternative open to the defender of Homer that will be

---

50. Cf. Proclus *In Rep.* 1.100–106.
51. E.g., Gorgias's *Encomium on Helen*.

of greatest concern in the present study, the mode of interpretation that we are accustomed to call "allegorical" in the context of antiquity. There is a general failure in antiquity to make a clear distinction between allegorical expression and allegorical interpretation. What we call "allegorical interpretation" in this context normally takes the form of a claim that an author has expressed himself "allegorically" in a given passage. This is summed up in the scholiasts' frequently repeated, compressed observation, "He says allegorically . . ." (ἀλληγορικῶς λέγει . . .), by which they indicate that the passage in question says one thing, viewed superficially, but *means* another (ἄλλα ἀγορεύει). There is never any suggestion that the goal of the commentator is anything but the elucidation of the intention or meaning (διάνοια) of the author. Neither does the interpreter normally feel compelled to justify his claim that the text under consideration "says other things" than the obvious. His goal is to *find* the hidden meanings, the correspondences that carry the thrust of the text beyond the explicit. Once he has asserted their existence, he rarely feels the need to provide a theoretical substructure for his claims. If such a substructure is implied, it is often no more than the idea that a prestigious author is incapable of an incoherent or otherwise unacceptable statement, and that an offensive surface is thus a hint that a secondary meaning lurks beyond.

Thus our modern associations with "allegory" as an element of critical vocabulary are not particularly useful in this context. The ancient usage is broader and more difficult to define. The word has a specific definition in the sphere of rhetoric,[52] but that definition has little relevance to the phenomenon under consideration here. A model of poetic expression in which multiple levels of meaning are possible exists at least as early as Plato. Ancient "critics" would normally make no distinction of kind between the observation that Homer *says* "Hera" but *means* "mist" (ἀήρ)—i.e., that Homer is allegorical in the modern sense—and the observation that Homer *says* that Athena tricked Pandarus into acting in a cowardly manner, but *means* only that he was a weak and cowardly character from whom such action was to be expected.

"Allegorical interpretation," then, can comprehend virtually the whole of what we call "interpretation," beyond mere parsing. Grube's claim that the Greek critics assumed that works of literature were able to communicate without intermediaries[53] is thus in a sense justified—there

52. Ps.-Plutarch (*De vit. Hom.* 70) offers a definition linking it to irony and sarcasm.
53. See Preface, with n. 3, above.

does seem to be general agreement on the existence of a level of meaning that is obvious and often sufficient. There is also general agreement, however, that texts such as those of Homer "say other things" than the obvious (i.e., that they speak ἀλληγορικῶς), and that failure to apprehend one or more of these "other" meanings may often lead to failure to comprehend the author's full intention in the text.

The process of interpretation, thus conceived, clearly engages the reader in an active role. There are limits set by the text itself, and the Neoplatonists do not follow the Stoic lead that would seem explicitly to sanction the idea that the reader, not the text, determines the field of reference, and hence the scope of the meaning.[54] Ultimately, however, all interpretation will prove unsatisfactory if we accept the model articulated by Socrates in the *Protagoras*[55] and give in to his final frustration that we can never directly interrogate the author and thus can have no hope of testing our conclusions about the actual meaning of a text that is conceived of as coextensive with the meaning (that is, the intention) of its author. Other models are, however, possible—increasingly so when a text is no longer considered as a normal human utterance but as a piece of scripture, an utterance of a privileged sort that, whatever the frustrations and inadequacies of the process, *must* be interrogated for the sake of the important truths it is thought to contain.

It is difficult to say whether there was ever a time when the *Iliad* and *Odyssey* were *not* viewed as possessing this potential to reveal meanings beyond the obvious. What is demonstrable, however, is that the tradition of interpretation cultivated by the Neoplationists generated a model of the meaning of these poems—and of the structure of that meaning—that departed extraordinarily from the most obvious meaning, transforming the poems into revelations concerning the nature of the universe and the fate of souls. Since they never abandoned the idea that the meanings they

54. Plutarch (*De aud. po.* 34b) mentions with approval Chrysippus's observation that "what is good in a work must be transferred and carried over to similar things" (ὅτι δεῖ μετάγειν καὶ διαβιβάζειν ἐπὶ τὰ ὁμοειδῆ τὸ χρήσιμον). The examples given are trivial, and Chrysippus's remark *may* have been directed only toward the broader application of moral principles found in the poets. But the fact remains that Chrysippus was an allegorist, and the principle cited by Plutarch, however circumscribed its application, is perhaps the only point at which ancient literary theory bypasses the "intentional fallacy" and recognizes the active role of the reader in the creation of the meaning of the text. This role is expressed as the obligation on the reader's part to set the field of reference of the text and even to expand that field beyond what is given: ἐπὶ πλέον τῶν λεγομένων.

55. Plato *Prot.* 347e, discussed below in the Afterword.

found in the poems had been placed there deliberately by Homer, the image of the poet himself underwent a corresponding change. It is by a process such as this that the Homer antiquity saw reflected in Demodocus was transformed into the Homer of the title page of Chapman's *Odyssey*, assimilated to Tiresias.[56]

C. HOMER AS THEOLOGOS

That Homer, at least in Hellenistic usage, had virtually exclusive rights to the designation "the Poet" (ὁ ποιητής) is well known,[57] but when Porphyry casually refers to Homer as ὁ θεολόγος—a term commonly used to refer to Orpheus—we seem to be in touch with claims on Homer's behalf to excellence of quite a different sort. In fact, however, Porphyry is relying upon the context of his remark to make us understand which θεολόγος is meant, and the suggestion that Homer is the θεολόγος κατ' ἐξοχήν (i.e., "the Theologian") is but a gentle hint at most. Furthermore, the use of the word has good classical precedents that must be reviewed as background for the usage of the Neoplatonists.[58]

The earliest passage that prepares us for the application of the term θεολόγος to Homer is in Herodotus, who, though he does not in fact use the term,[59] nevertheless provides an enlightened fifth-century testimony to the relationship between Homer's poetry and information about the divine. He is making the point that Greek culture had only relatively recently absorbed the basic elements of religion:

> The Greeks later got this from the Pelasgians, and they were ignorant, so to speak, right up until yesterday or the day before about the origins of the individual gods and whether they were all eternal and what sort of shapes they had, for it is my belief that Homer and Hesiod were four hundred years older than myself and no more. These were the ones who provided the Greeks with an account of the origins of the gods and gave the gods their names and defined their honors and skills and indicated shapes for them. The poets who are

56. For a summary of ancient passages attributing magic powers to Homer, see Cumont, *Recherches*, pp. 4–8.

57. See A. M. Harmon, "The Poet κατ' ἐξοχήν," for a history of the usage.

58. Porph. *De ant.* 32. Cf. L. Ziehen, "θεολόγος," whom I have followed in part.

59. Neither θεολόγος nor θεολογία occurs in Herodotus.

said to have lived before these men in fact, in my opinion, lived after them.[60]

This peculiar conception of Homer as a source, a creator, at least in terms of the Greek tradition, rather than a transmitter of information, is rather unsatisfactory from our perspective. Herodotus seems to be recreating Homer in his own image—as many ancient critics were in fact to do—as a sort of ethnographic curiosity seeker who sought out foreign and august sources of wisdom, which he then brought home and presented to a Greek audience in a unique new Greek form. The extravagant author of the essay on Homer attributed to Plutarch would only have to forget the Pelasgians and the Egyptians in order to move from this conception of Homer's creative role to a vision of Homer as an absolute source, a purely creative imagination.

Plato, likewise, is innocent of the term θεολόγος, though in an important passage in the *Republic*, discussed above, he refers to θεολογία.[61] The point Socrates wants to make here is that the basic patterns the poets are to follow in their mythmaking are the concern of the city founders.[62] These are grouped under "the basic patterns of theology" (οἱ τύποι περὶ θεολογίας). He clearly conceives, then, that the earlier tradition allowed its poets to be creatively mythopoeic. Either they were not bound by any basic rules or patterns, or those they followed were mistaken. His desire to impose *correct* patterns and norms in order to ensure the educational value of the poetry produced is consistent with his general mistrust of poetic inspiration.[63]

Aristotle lists "theological philosophy" (θεολογική) among the types of "contemplative philosophy" (θεωρητικαί, *Metaph.* E 1026a19), and his reference to "those very ancient people who lived long before the pres-

60. παρὰ δὲ Πελασγῶν Ἕλληνες ἐδέξαντο ὕστερον. ὅθεν δὲ ἐγένοντο ἕκαστος τῶν θεῶν, εἴτε αἰεὶ ἦσαν πάντες, ὁκοῖοί τέ τινες τὰ εἴδεα, οὐκ ἠπιστέατο μέχρι οὗ πρώην τε καὶ χθὲς ὡς εἰπεῖν λόγῳ. Ἡσίοδον γὰρ καὶ Ὅμηρον ἡλικίην τετρακοσίοισι ἔτεσι δοκέω μευ πρεσβυτέρους γενέσθαι καὶ οὐ πλέοσι. οὗτοι δέ εἰσι οἱ ποιήσαντες θεογονίην Ἕλλησι καὶ τοῖσι θεοῖσι τὰς ἐπωνυμίας δόντες καὶ τιμάς τε καὶ τέχνας διελόντες καὶ εἴδεα αὐτῶν σημήναντες. οἱ δὲ πρότερον ποιηταὶ λεγόμενοι τούτων τῶν ἀνδρῶν γενέσθαι ὕστερον, ἔμοιγε δοκέειν, ἐγένοντο (Herod. *Hist.* 2.53–54).

61. *Rep.* 2.379a. The passage is also discussed by Victor Goldschmidt ("Théologia"), who works from it toward a prehistory of the term θεολογία.

62. οἰκισταῖς δὲ τοὺς μὲν τύπους προσήκει εἰδέναι ἐν οἷς δεῖ μυθολογεῖν τοὺς ποιητάς (*Rep.* 2.379a).

63. Cf. Weinstock, "Platonische Homerkritik," pp. 124–25, and Tate, "Plato and Allegorical Interpretation," pp. 147–51.

ent age and were the first to theologize"[64] probably does, as L. Ziehen asserts,[65] take us back to Homer and to the other early poets. The possibility should also be taken into account, however, that Aristotle may, in fact, be referring to the early interpreters of the poets rather than to the poets themselves, for θεολόγος was probably already ambiguous.[66] In general, Aristotle uses the term to speak of the early cosmologists as a class,[67] but by the time of Cicero, it was used comfortably for such interpretive writers on divine matters as the Euhemerists and even the grammarians. Clearly, these are authors who worked *from* the primary θεολόγοι and clarified the information on the divine transmitted through them. A passage from Strabo, quoted on page 26 below, indicates the necessary connection between theology as a field of philosophical inquiry and the myths and poems of the early tradition, which constituted the primary source material.

The distinction between "theologizing" by *writing* poetry in which information about the gods was presented in a more-or-less veiled form and "theologizing" by *interpreting* the poetry of the ancients in such a way as to bring out these meanings is, in fact, one that seems often to have been blurred in antiquity. From our perspective there is a world of difference between deliberate poetic allegory and the interpretation *as* allegory of existing poetry. By the fourth century, however, the verb θεολογέω and its complex of related words could refer to either activity.[68] Precisely the same divided usage is found in Porphyry over six centuries later.[69]

64. . . . τοὺς παμπαλαίους καὶ πολὺ πρὸ τῆς νῦν γενέσεως καὶ πρώτους θεολογήσαντες (*Metaph.* A 983b28–29).

65. Ziehen, "θεολόγος," col. 2031.

66. Cf. Ziehen, "θεολόγος." Particularly if we retain the words τῶν ποιητῶν in 983b, which were bracketed by Crist, it is tempting to believe that Aristotle has in mind the early interpreters, when he says about the "ancient people" just mentioned, Ὠκεανόν τε γὰρ καὶ Τηθὺν ἐποίησαν τῆς γενέσεως πατέρας, καὶ τὸν ὅρκον τῶν θεῶν ὕδωρ, τὴν καλουμένην ὑπ' αὐτῶν Στύγα τῶν ποιητῶν. Both the first statement and the second ("They made the oath of the gods 'water,' whereas the poets themselves said 'Styx.'") might well represent Aristotle's idea of early theologizing *from* the poets, since neither interpretation is obvious from the passages in question without further commentary. The verb ἐποίησαν itself, however, may be an indication that these "ancients" expressed themselves in poetic form.

67. See Ross's comments on *Metaph.* A 983b29.

68. Cf. Ziehen, "θεολόγος," cols. 2031–32.

69. See below, p. 29.

Both Herodotus and Plato clearly view the mythopoeic "theologiz-ing" of the poets as creative. Plato would go further and describe it as subjective and arbitrary. Neither suggests that the poets had any need to veil their teachings, or that the narrative surface of the poems is deliber-ately designed to be ambiguous or misleading. There is reason to believe that Plato had considerable sensitivity to the Homeric poems as complex verbal artifacts, but, unlike most later Greek philosophers, he is dis-inclined to make his points by appeal to earlier authority.[70] Parallel with this reluctance is Socrates' genuine hostility to confusing and disrupting the dialectical process by inserting discussions of poetic texts.[71] Plato is certainly aware of the possibilities opened up by the interpretation of epic according to "second meanings,"[72] yet he seldom feels the need to enter into that activity. The obvious reason for this is that Plato is himself mythopoeic: when he abandons dialectic to "theologize," he does so not by interpreting existing texts or stories but by generating new myths. In any case, neither of our important sources from the fifth and early fourth centuries emphasizes the complexity of the structure of meaning of the verbal artifact, though Plato acknowledges that his contempo-raries did so.[73]

It was no doubt in the early Stoa that the emphasis shifted, but the process must for the most part be reconstructed from relatively late evi-dence.[74] Along with the Stoa's emphasis on the poets went an impulse to interpret the received myths "allegorically." This is the context in which the impulse to understand the qualities of a poetic text by reference to things entirely outside that text became prevalent, along with an inclina-tion to view the myths as cryptic expressions of some further reality that the poets, for whatever reasons, chose to hint at rather than express di-rectly.[75] In the process, as Phillip DeLacy puts it, "poetic myth replaces philosophical example"[76] and is forced to fit broader referents than the poets intended. Chrysippus is explicit that "what is good in a poem

70. He nevertheless refers to Homer as an authority sufficiently often that Proclus is able to argue (*In Rep.* 1.163–72) that such appeal is characteristic.

71. Plato *Prot.* 347c–348a.

72. ἐν ὑπονοίαις (*Rep.* 2.378d).

73. Aside from the passage mentioned in n. 72 above, see the *Protagoras* (316d, discussed below) on poetry as a "screen" (πρόσχημα) for sophistry.

74. This evidence is assembled in Phillip DeLacy's excellent study, "Stoic Views of Poetry," which remains the definitive treatment of Stoic poetics.

75. Ibid., pp. 259, 267.

76. Ibid., p. 267.

must be interpreted as applying to things of the same kind beyond the limits of the poem."[77] Allegorical interpretation existed before the Stoics, but it was through their prestige that its influence became pervasive in Greek thought, culminating in such allegorical commentaries on Homer as those of Crates of Mallos and the other Pergamene grammarians, the rivals of Aristarchus and the Alexandrians. These commentaries reach us only in fragments, but the Heraclitus whose *Homeric Allegories* survives largely intact is their direct heir.[78] This shift of emphasis reflected in the Stoic attitude toward myth and poetry is a crucially important one for the development of the conception of the meaning of Homer that concerns us, yet properly speaking it forms only part of the prehistory of that conception.[79]

Returning to the evolution of the term θεολόγος and the related vocabulary, we find in Strabo, early in the first century A.D., a capsule summary of the Stoic conception of theology that had its roots in the fourth and third centuries B.C. He has just indicated in no uncertain terms that he himself dislikes myths:

> Every discussion of the gods [i.e., all theology] is built upon the examination of opinions and myths, since the ancients hinted at their physical perceptions about things and always added a mythic element to their discussions. It is not an easy thing to solve all the riddles correctly, but when the whole mass of mythically expressed material is placed before you, some of it in agreement and some in contradiction with the rest, then you might more easily be able to form from it an image of the truth.[80]

It is easy to see from this fascinating passage how the verb θεολογέω could simultaneously refer to the poets and to those who interpret them. The text is doubly valuable because Strabo professes himself hostile to

77. Ibid., p. 267. The source for Chrysippus's observation is Plutarch *De aud. po.* 34b. See n. 54 above for the text.

78. See Pfeiffer, *History of Classical Scholarship*, pp. 237–46.

79. Aside from DeLacy, cited above, see Buffière's extensive treatment of Stoicizing allegory of Homer, *Mythes d'Homère*, pp. 137–54, and passim.

80. πᾶς δὲ ὁ περὶ τῶν θεῶν λόγος ἀρχαίας ἐξετάζει δόξας καὶ μύθους, αἰνιττομένων τῶν παλαιῶν ἃς εἶχον ἐννοίας φυσικὰς περὶ τῶν πραγμάτων καὶ προστιθέντων ἀεὶ τοῖς λόγοις τὸν μῦθον. ἄπαντα μὲν οὖν τὰ αἰνίγματα λύειν ἐπ' ἀκριβὲς οὐ ῥάδιον, τοῦ δὲ πλήθους τῶν μυθευομένων ἐκτεθέντος εἰς τὸ μέσον, τῶν μὲν ὁμολογούντων ἀλλήλοις, τῶν δ' ἐναντιουμένων, εὐπορώτερον ἄν τις δύναιτο εἰκάζειν ἐξ αὐτῶν τἀληθές (*Geog.* 10.3.23 [C474]). The passage is cited in part by Ziehen, "θεολόγος," col. 2031. The attitude expressed is close to that of Plutarch (cf. Robert Flacelière, "La Théologie selon Plutarque").

the whole process. His is a practical and scientific intellect with no taste for ambiguities and contradictions.

This is not to say that he is bereft of literary sensitivity, or that the *Iliad* and *Odyssey* fall beneath his scorn when he describes himself as "not in the least a lover of myths."[81] He makes this clear in the first book of the *Geography*, where he extracts geographical information from Homer in an intelligent and sympathetic way, simultaneously rejecting interpretations of the poems that depart into allegory and demonstrating a strikingly modern critical acumen. The demands he makes upon the text are quite reasonable ones from our perspective, and he is refreshingly free of the conviction that Homer is omniscient.

In the passage quoted above, however, Strabo is specifically concerned with the recovery of "theological" information—a class of knowledge with which he is ill at ease. There are certain truths that can be approached only by an attack upon the forbidding mass of lies, half-truths, and contradictions bequeathed by antiquity, for these are the primary source material in the field of theology. The process of sifting the "opinions and myths" of the ancients—and particularly of Homer—for kernels of truth about the gods is as a whole, then, one undertaken not only by idle dreamers but by the most practical of men as well.

Porphyry is heir to the double meaning of the term θεολόγος and related vocabulary, but he is likewise heir to a somewhat different usage. This occurs as early as Aristotle and designates a body of poetry from which we might want to exclude Homer. It is clear from what has already been said that the θεολόγοι, from the fifth century B.C. on, are the early poets and their interpreters. But *which* poets? It is clear enough to us that there is a difference of kind between the *Iliad* and *Odyssey* on one hand and the *Theogony* on the other. The difference between the works that fit these two categories and the Orphic poems is even more striking. The word θεολόγος, in some of its earliest occurrences, seems more obviously appropriate to Orphic and mantic poets, and perhaps to Hesiod, than to Homer, and throughout the tradition ὁ θεολόγος, without explanation, is most likely to refer to Orpheus.

A fragment of Philolaus (a Pythagorean contemporary of Socrates) preserved by Clement of Alexandria and attested by Athenaeus, and perhaps even by Plato in the *Cratylus*, asserts: "The ancient theologians and seers bear witness that the soul has been yoked to the body as a pun-

---

81. ἥκιστα φιλομυθοῦντες, plural to agree with an "editorial we" (*Geog.* 10.3.23 [C474]).

ishment, and buried in it as in a tomb."[82] Philolaus is unique among the early "primary" sources for Pythagoreanism in that, at least in part, the surviving fragments attributed to him offer some evidence of the pre-Platonic traditions of Pythagoreanism.[83] Here, he links the θεολόγοι in question with μάντεις as witnesses to the relationship of soul and body. One might be inclined to assume that all of this must have absolutely nothing to do with Homer—indeed, poetry is unmentioned, not to say epic poetry. However, the implied etymology (σῶμα from σῆμα) became very much attached to Homer and was used to link the conception of the body as the "tomb" of the soul to the *Iliad*.[84] Even if it is not as early as the historical Philolaus, the fragment is unlikely to be post-Hellenistic, and the important point in the present context is that it links the θεολόγοι—quite possibly including Homer—with mantic poetry in support of a doctrine concerning the soul.

Aristotle also sometimes uses θεολόγος for the poets of the mystical traditions. "Hesiod and his school and all the theologians" (οἱ μὲν περὶ Ἡσίοδον καὶ πάντες ὅσοι θεολόγοι, *Metaph.* B 1000a9) may or may not include Homer. Here, Aristotle is merely bringing up a group of mythic creation accounts in order to reject them, and Homer, by reason of his subject matter, may well be spared. Likewise, the expression "the theologians who generate everything from night" (οἱ θεολόγοι οἱ ἐκ νυκτὸς γεννῶντες, *Metaph.* Λ 1071b27) again points directly to the Orphics, not to Homer.

That a distinction of kind had indeed been made in the fifth century between Homer and the Orphic poets (though Hesiod, because of the nature of his subject matter, might fall on either side of the line) is dramatically attested in the *Protagoras*, where the pompous sophist defends the hoary antiquity of his profession by insisting that there have always been sophists, but that the early practitioners of sophistry, "fearing the jealousy it provokes, made a screen and masked it, some with poetry,

82. μαρτυρέονται δὲ καὶ οἱ παλαιοὶ θεολόγοι τε καὶ μάντεις, ὡς διά τινας τιμωρίας ἁ ψυχὰ τῷ σώματι συνέζευκται καὶ καθάπερ ἐν σάματι τούτῳ τέθαπται (Philolaus fr. 14 D–K).

83. See Walter Burkert, *Lore and Science in Ancient Pythagoreanism*, pp. 218–38, for the evidence for the existence of Philolaus and for his authorship of an account of Pythagoreanism known to Aristotle.

84. This is one of the most frequently encountered of the etymological explanations of Homer that have been traced to Pythagoras. For the literature, see Delatte, *Littérature pythagoricienne*, p. 132, and for the later evolution of the (non-historic) etymology, C. J. de Vogel, "The Sōma-Sēma Formula: its Function in Plato and Plotinus Compared to Christian Writers."

like Homer, Hesiod, and Simonides, some with initiations and oracles: Orpheus, Musaeus and their associates."[85] The breakdown of categories such as these and the indiscriminate lumping of Homer with the rest of the early hexameter poets as θελόγοι with cosmological and mystical pretensions is one of the crucial developments in the history of the interpretation of Homer.[86]

Porphyry uses the term θεολόγος eight times in his essay on the cave of the nymphs in the *Odyssey*.[87] Six of these occurrences are in the plural and refer broadly and rather vaguely to the poetic and philosophical traditions.[88] The occurrences of the word in the singular refer specifically to Orpheus (*De ant.* 68.6) and to Homer (*De ant.* 78.15–16). A striking comparison to these instances of θεολόγος is found in Philo, who uses the term to refer to Moses in a context where, on the one hand, obscure symbolism is being discussed, and on the other, the very strong implication is that Moses is ὁ θεολόγος κατ' ἐξοχήν.[89] Though Porphyry does not make this claim for Homer, it is clear that his use of the term has affinities with that of Philo.

The development of this complex of words, then, is not at all what one might have expected. The earliest instances of θεολόγος point to an already ambiguous meaning spanning the semantic fields "poet" (with sometimes, but not always, the suggestion that allegorical mystical or

85. φοβουμένους τὸ ἐπαχθὲς αὐτῆς, πρόσχημα ποιεῖσθαι καὶ προκαλύπτεσθαι, τοὺς μὲν ποίησιν, οἷον Ὅμηρόν τε καὶ Ἡσίοδον καὶ Σιμωνίδην, τοὺς δὲ αὖ τελετάς τε καὶ χρησμῳδίας, τοὺς ἀμφί τε Ὀρφέα καὶ Μουσαῖον (Plato *Prot.* 316d).

86. Numenius, rather surprisingly, uses θεολόγος and θεολογία (fr. 23.5, 16) in a perfectly neutral way, referring simply to the Athenians' (and more specifically Euthyphro's) thoughts about the gods. Our word "theology" would be adequate to translate his θεολογία, whereas the word in Plato would require at least a footnote. Plotinus uses the word only once (*Enn.* 3.5.8.21), referring to "priests [ἱεροί] and theologians" who *interpret* myths in a certain way.

87. To look only at that essay constitutes an arbitrary sampling, but one with obvious relevance to the concerns of this study. Further analysis is rendered difficult by the absence of concordances to the works of Porphyry.

88. The θεολόγοι at *De ant.* 61.5, 66.24, and 77.22 could be virtually any poets, interpreters of poetry, or philosophers. Those of 71.17 must, on the evidence of Numenius, fr. 35, include Homer. Those of *De ant.* 62.10 refer back to the unknown author of a hymn to Apollo as well as Pythagoras, Empedocles, and Plato. Those of 76.23 are difficult to identify, though the Buffalo editors of the essay point to Pherecydes, fr. B6 D–K. All references to the essay are to page and line of Nauck's text.

89. Philo *De vit. Mos.* 2.115.

cosmological poetry is meant) and "interpreter of poetry." This ambiguity remains with the complex of words as they acquire a yet broader field of reference to include, along with virtually the whole of archaic poetry and its interpretation, an important branch of philosophy. For Porphyry, the philosophy in question is specifically the tradition of Platonic dogmatic theology inextricably bound up with "Pythagoreanism." Porphyry's location of Homer at the center of this field represents a substantial evolution of thought with regard to the author of the *Iliad* and the *Odyssey*, involving the loss of any perception of the difference of kind between his narrative poetry and the cosmological and mystical hexameters attached to the traditions labeled "Hesiod" and "Orpheus." That Porphyry, who was the first of the Neoplatonists to declare open war on the Christians, should thus treat Homer in somewhat the same way Philo had treated Moses suggests a defensive posture adopted by a fighter who knew his enemy well.

At the end of the ancient Neoplatonic tradition, with Proclus, Hermias, and then Olympiodorus, the complex of words retains much of its earlier meaning. Θεολογία can mean "theology" in the modern sense, a category of philosophy, with no hint of any connection with poetry.[90] Θεολογέω, at the same time, can refer to the poetic activities of the early hexameter poets, including Pisander[91] and Orpheus.[92] Proclus often uses this complex of words in his defense of Homer and likewise in the *Timaeus* commentary, where the θεολόγοι clearly include Homer.[93] Proclus appears to broaden the field of reference of the θεολογία complex to include still more mystical writings, with no apparent sense that, in his usage, the term suits Homer less and less well. In the commentary on Euclid, after quoting the *Chaldaean Oracles* and Orpheus in the context of a discussion of the circular movement within the universe and the "triadic god," he observes: "Thence have those who are wise and most initiated into the theological given him his name."[94] The unmentioned epithet in question is probably "trismegistos" and the reference would thus

90. E.g., Proclus *In Alc.* 317.18, where theology is contrasted with ethics.

91. δηλοῖ δὲ καὶ ὁ Πείσανδρος θεολογῶν τὰ κατὰ Κάδμου ἐν τῷ μύθῳ (Olymp. *In Phaed.* 172.3–4).

92. τοιαῦτα γὰρ περὶ αὐτοῦ καὶ ὁ Ὀρφεὺς ἐνδείκνυται περὶ τοῦ Φάνητος θεολογῶν (Proclus *In Tim.* 1.427.20).

93. See ch. 5D, with notes 63 and 64, below.

94. ἐντεῦθεν γὰρ αὐτῷ καὶ τὴν προσηγορίαν ἔθεντο οἱ σοφοὶ καὶ τῶν θεολογικῶν οἱ μυστικώτατοι (Proclus *In Euc.* 155.26–156.1).

be to the tradition that produced the Hermetic corpus.[95] There is little doubt that Homer remains central to the group Proclus qualified as the θεολόγοι, as attested by such expressions as "the ancient theology according to Homer," in the Euclid commentary.[96]

Hermias is the only author in the group in whom I have found the singular ὁ θεολόγος used in isolation to refer to Homer,[97] much in the manner of Porphyry. His understanding of the term does not differ conspicuously from that of his contemporary Proclus, and his θεολόγοι include all the early poets and a variety of other authors. He explicitly equates the procedure of the myths of Plato with that in use among the early θεολόγοι,[98] though he may, like Proclus, also be sensitive to important differences. When he refers to "the theologians and the inspired poets and Homer," the series appears to represent a centering process: the inspired poets are central to the group "theologians," and Homer in turn stands at their center.[99] Numerous other references make it clear that the group includes Orpheus, the Orphics, Hesiod, and Plato.[100] His understanding of the structure of meaning of early epic, along with the other material mentioned, may stand for that of all the late Platonists: "Mythology is a kind of theology," and the characteristic mistake of the uninitiated is "to fail to grasp with wisdom the intention of the mythoplasts, but rather to follow the apparent sense."[101]

D. THE PYTHAGOREANS

It is no doubt significant that our earliest indications of the existence of an allegorical understanding of Homer are associated with southern Italy and can be dated to a period very shortly after Pythagoreanism be-

95. See Morrow's notes to his translation of the commentary, ad loc.: p. 132, n. 129, and p. 38, n. 88.

96. ἡ παλαιὰ θεολογία . . . παρ᾽ Ὁμήρῳ (Proclus In Euc. 141.24–25).

97. In Phdr. 151.7, 11.

98. In Phdr. 233.21.

99. τοὺς θεολόγους καὶ τοὺς ἔνθους ποιητὰς καὶ Ὅμηρον (In Phdr. 77.10–11).

100. E.g., In Phdr. 154.15; 147.20; 148.18; 142.10, 14; 193.6.

101. (ἡ γὰρ μυθολογία θεολογία τίς ἐστιν). τὸ οὖν μὴ ἐμφρόνως περὶ τὴν μυθολογίαν ἀνεστράφθαι, τουτέστι τὸ μὴ ἐμφρόνως κατακρατῆσαι τῆς διανοίας τῶν μυθοπλαστῶν, ἀλλὰ τῷ φαινομένῳ ἔπεσθαι, ἁμάρτημά ἐστι περὶ μυθολογίαν (In Phdr. 73.18–21). Cf. Proclus In Rep. 1.176 on Socrates' "mistake" in the Phaedrus.

came established there. A Porphyrian scholion on the battle of the gods in *Iliad* 20[102] explains the battle as a physical, then a moral allegory, and continues: "This kind of answer [to those who attack Homer] is very old, dating from Theagenes of Rhegium, who was the first to write about Homer."[103] Several other ancient sources, none referring specifically to allegorical interpretation, confirm that Theagenes was an early Homer scholar and make it possible to fix his *floruit* around 525 B.C.[104] Among the modern scholars who have examined the problem, Armand Delatte[105] suspected Pythagorean influence on Theagenes, but Félix Buffière[106] was reluctant to believe that the Pythagoreans were concerned with the sort of physical allegory attributed to Theagenes by Porphyry. The most recent scholar to look into the question is Marcel Detienne,[107] whose conclusions are convincing. He argues that we have good reason to believe that Theagenes was a grammarian and hence unlikely to be the creator of the allegorical method. Furthermore, the Porphyrian scholion quoted above seems to attribute to Theagenes the simultaneous creation of both physical and moral allegory—an unlikely accomplishment for any one individual, much less a grammarian. Theagenes, Detienne concludes, was simply a grammarian who wrote on Homer and who may or may not have been influenced by the Pythagoreans who were undoubtedly present in Rhegium in his time: he simply mentioned the modes of interpretation he knew to be in use, which included physical and moral allegory. The important point to be gained from our meagre information on Theagenes is that both of these modes of allegory date from the period of the first Pythagoreans, ca. 525 B.C.

Given, then, that moral and physical allegory are at least as old as Pythagoreanism and that the contributions of Neopythagoreanism to the mystical allegorical interpretation of Homer articulated and transmitted by the Neoplatonists are quite substantial,[108] one must ask to

102. B scholion on *Il.* 20.67; *Schol. in Il.*, ed. Dindorf, vol. 4, p. 231; see Porph. *Quaest hom.*, ed. Schrader, vol. 1, pp. 240–41.

103. οὗτος μὲν οὖν τρόπος ἀπολογίας ἀρχαῖος ὢν πάνυ καὶ ἀπὸ Θεαγένους τοῦ Ῥηγίνου, ὃς πρῶτος ἔγραψε περὶ Ὁμήρου (Porph. *Quaest. hom.*, ed. Schrader, vol. 1, p. 241, lines 10–11).

104. If the attack on Homer goes back to the poet's own time, then the *apologia* for Homer must be of comparable age (see above, n. 43). On the dating of Theagenes, cf. Buffière, *Mythes d'Homère*, pp. 103–4.

105. Delatte, *Etudes sur la littérature pythagoricienne*, p. 115.

106. Buffière, *Mythes d'Homère*.

107. Detienne, *Homère, Hésiode, et Pythagore*, pp. 65–67.

108. See ch. 2B below on Numenius.

what extent the latter mode of exegesis may have depended on early Pythagorean interpretation. Buffière minimized the importance of early Pythagoreanism in the evolution of the allegorical tradition and placed great emphasis on the late second century—the period of Numenius—as the cradle of the mystical allegory of Homer, which for him is primarily Neoplatonic.[109] Other scholars have reacted strongly against his formulation, however, and have argued eloquently for the archaic roots of the mystical allegory of Homer in early Pythagoreanism.[110]

The tradition—or rather traditions—of ancient Pythagoreanism are notoriously difficult to reconstruct. The school's emphasis on secrecy prevented the general dissemination of a Pythagorean literature and favored the production of pseudepigrapha. The nature of the evidence is such that scholarly consensus on the content of the teaching of Pythagoras himself and of Pythagoreans before the time of Plato is a remote goal. In spite of this, substantial advances have been made in this century, and

109. Cf. Buffière in his edition of Heraclitus's *Allegories*, p. xxix: "l'exégèse mystique et pythagoricienne, dont on ne trouve aucune trace précise avant le temps de Plutarque." At the same time, he acknowledges the Pythagorean sources of Porphyry's essay on the cave of the nymphs (*Mythes d'Homère*, pp. 423–24), though it is clear he thinks of Neopythagoreanism as a phenomenon created by the second century after Christ.

110. In a study that appeared simultaneously with Buffière's, Jérôme Carcopino denounced the attribution to the Neoplatonists of the creation of mystical allegorical iconography and imagery relating to Homer: "Elles remontent tout au moins jusqu'aux gloses que, bien avant notre ère, des Pythagoriciens avaient rédigées" (*De Pythagore aux apôtres*, p. 199). Robert Flacelière, in an otherwise largely positive review of Buffière's work, questioned the late date for the beginnings of mystical allegory and remarked, "je croirais volontiers, pour ma part, que le pythagorisme du ve et du ive siècle avant J-C, aussi hostile que Platon à Homère, a pu, tout comme Platon lui-même, utiliser des vers d'Homère à ses propres fins" (*Revue des études grecques* 70 [1957], p. 261). He nevertheless went on to affirm that Buffière was no doubt correct in emphasizing the importance and originality of the Neoplatonic tradition of interpretation that begins with Porphyry and whose sources cannot be traced back with certainty beyond Numenius. Boyancé, introducing Detienne's study, is clearly referring to Buffière's work when he observes discreetly, "C'est à tort, croyons-nous avec M. Detienne, qu'un livre important, paru récemment, n'a pas accordé une attention suffisante a l'ancien pythagorisme" (Boyancé in *Homère, Hésiode et Pythagore*, p. 7). Finally, Detienne makes it clear throughout his *Homère, Hésiode et Pythagore* that he considers Buffière's emphasis wrong and that the mystical allegory of Homer, along with the other modes of allegory, had Pythagorean roots. He views these traditions as continuous from the sixth century B.C. to the end of paganism and beyond.

it is possible at least to propose a model to account for the development of Pythagoreanism and to examine the evidence for an early Pythagorean interpretation of Homer in its light.

Shortly after the pioneering work of Delatte,[111] the seminal study of Erich Frank appeared,[112] the thrust of which was to locate many of the discoveries of "scientific" Pythagoreanism in the early fourth century and to demonstrate the dependence of much of what has been transmitted as Pythagoreanism on Platonism, and, more specifically, on the generation of the successors of Plato, Speusippus and Xenocrates. Frank's focus was on the natural sciences, but Walter Burkert's more recent synthesis[113] has extended the same principles and concluded that much of what we have been accustomed to call Pythagoreanism is simply dogmatic Platonism, and that the Platonization of the Pythagorean tradition began far earlier than Eduard Zeller and the other historians of the last century dreamed:

> One might . . . define later Pythagoreanism as Platonism with the Socratic and dialectic element amputated. . . . Scholars have shown in different ways that Neoplatonism is quite closely dependent on the Old Academy, and "Pythagoreanism" too belongs in this category. It is also basically Platonism, existing at a time when Plato (as interpreted in Pythagorean fashion) had lost his position in the Academic school. Later, neo-Pythagoreanism converges, in the philosophical realm, with Neoplatonism.[114]

It is in the light of this understanding of Pythagorean tradition that any evidence for a pre-Platonic Pythagorean interpretation of Homer must be viewed.

111. *Littérature pythagoricienne* (1915).
112. Frank, *Plato und die sogenannten Pythagoreer*.
113. *Lore and Science in Ancient Pythagoreanism*, first (German) edition, 1962.
114. Burkert, *Lore and Science*, p. 96. For purposes of the present study, the embroiled question of whether the dogmatic Platonism expounded by the Neoplatonists can be traced to a secret teaching of Plato himself, or only to the generation of his successors, need not be answered. I have taken Letter 7 as an authentic document able to throw light on Plato's attitude toward the written word. This does not, however, imply a belief in a transmitted secret teaching traceable to Plato himself, and anyone disposed to believe that the existence of such a teaching is established should consult the sensitive and perceptive analysis of E. N. Tigerstedt in *Interpreting Plato*. Tigerstedt accepts, however, the principle that the Early Academy was dogmatic (p. 105) and the evidence assembled by Frank and Burkert makes it probable that much of what we receive as "Pythagoreanism" can be traced to that context.

What, then, is the evidence for an archaic Pythagorean exegesis of Homer? The testimonia that indicate a concern with Homer on the part of the early Pythagoreans were examined by Delatte[115] and have more recently been reviewed by Detienne.[116] The conclusions that may be reached are disappointing, and although it is highly probable that some of the dozens of interpretations of Homeric verses attributed to Pythagoras are in fact pre-Platonic, there is no single interpretive idea that can be dated with certainty to that period.

Most credible as early contributions are probably those "Pythagorean" interpretations that suggest a ritual use of the poems. Excerpts from Homer and Hesiod were sung for cathartic purposes, to "tranquilize" (καθημεροῦν) the soul.[117] Also credible is the attribution to early Pythagoreanism of a moralizing interpretation of the *Iliad* as a whole that made it the story of the disastrous consequences of the lack of self-control (ἀκρασία) of a single man (Paris).[118]

Overall, the significant thing that emerges from the testimonia is the emphasis that early Pythagoreanism placed on Homer and Hesiod, as revealed in the choice of these bodies of poetry for incantation over such more obvious choices as Orpheus and Musaeus.[119] In spite of the anecdote of Pythagoras's trip to Hades, where he is said to have seen Homer and Hesiod undergoing punishment for slandering the gods,[120] it does indeed seem that early Pythagoreanism was less hostile to the Homeric poems than were other religious and philosophical movements of the sixth century B.C. Both Porphyry and Iamblichus pass on the tradition that Pythagoras was the student of the Homeridae of Samos,[121] and there is little doubt that in early Pythagoreanism the *Iliad* and *Odyssey* were indeed used as sacred books—as sources of both magical incantations and moral exempla—at a time when Ionian thinkers such as Xenophanes were denouncing Homer as the representative of an outdated and misleading account of the divine. Pierre Boyancé has pointed out that an

115. Delatte, *Littérature pythagoricienne*, pp. 109–36.

116. Detienne, *Homère, Hésiode et Pythagore*. See also Boyancé, *Le Culte des Muses chez les philosophes grecs*, pp. 121–31.

117. Porph. *Vit. Pyth.* 32; cf. Iambl. *De vit. Pyth.* 111 and 113.

118. Iambl. *De vit. Pyth.* 42.

119. Cf. Boyancé, *Culte des Muses*, pp. 120–22.

120. Cf. Delatte, *Littérature pythagoricienne*, p. 109, n. 4, for numerous testimonia to the legend.

121. Porph. *Vit. Pyth.* 1.2; Iambl. *De vit. Pyth.* 9.11. Cf. Delatte, *Littérature pythagoricienne*, pp. 116–17 and Detienne, *Homère, Hésiode et Pythagore*, pp. 13–14.

attested cult of the Muses in early Pythagoreanism is an appropriate symbol of their bond with Homer.[122]

The relationship of this *use* of Homer in early Pythagoreanism to a transmitted Pythagorean *interpretation* of Homer is at best obscure. There is no evidence that a systematic early Pythagorean exegesis of Homer, in whole or in part, was ever committed to writing,[123] and the oral tradition is impossible to reconstruct.

It is nevertheless clear that, from an early period, Pythagoreanism was divided into two sects, one, commonly called the Akousmatikoi, that was more traditional and placed its emphasis on the original revelation and on ritual, and another, the Mathematikoi, that was mathematical and scientific in orientation.[124] The first of these sects was the vehicle for the transmission of many short sayings, or ἀκούσματα, which come down as an important element of Pythagoreanism, though generally it is impossible to date individual ἀκούσματα even approximately. Some ἀκούσματα have a Homeric flavor or are in some way relevant to Homer,[125] and it is quite possible that whatever elements might have survived of a primitive Pythagorean exegesis of Homer might have done so in this form. Some few shreds of Homer exegesis are also to be traced to Aristotle's account of Pythagoreanism, and others can be traced to various early sources that, though not unimpeachable, may well represent the early tradition of Pythagoreanism.

122. Boyancé, *Culte des Muses*, p. 241.

123. Diogenes Laertius's puzzling discussion of the numerous "simultaneous" Pythagorases (8.46–48) includes a "doctor who wrote about squill [or "Scylla" or "hernia"] and put together some things about Homer." (καὶ ἰατρὸν ἄλλον, τὰ περὶ σκίλλης [aliter σκύλλης, κίλλης, κήλης] γεγραφότα καί τινα περὶ Ὁμήρου συντεταγμένον.) The other Pythagorases mentioned all seem to have something to do with the traditions regarding the founder of the sect, and it is possible that we have in this observation a hint that such an early Pythagorean interpretive essay existed. The thread, however, is a weak one. The Derveni papyrus (see above, Preface, n. 6) demonstrates that interpretive material in a tradition closely related to the Pythagorean was available in written form by the early part of the fourth century B.C.

124. See Delatte, *Littérature pythagoricienne*, pp. 29–31, and Burkert, *Lore and Science*, pp. 193–206.

125. E.g., the ἄκουσμα that held that one must hold one's place in battle so as to be wounded only in the front (Iambl. *De vit. Pyth.* 18.85; cf. Burkert, *Lore and Science*, p. 172, with references). This is taken up by Ps.-Plutarch (*De vit. Hom.* 198) and shown to be illustrated in Homer, but there is no suggestion that the tradition was thought to be Pythagorean by the author of the essay.

Homer is credited by these Pythagoreanizing interpretations with having described the music of the spheres[126] and metempsychosis,[127] and having presented a personification of the monad in Proteus, "who contains the properties of all things just as the monad contains the combined energies of all the numbers."[128] He is said to have held such Pythagorean doctrines as the existence of a lunar paradise,[129] and his Sirens are transformed into the benevolent Sirens of the Pythagoreanizing myth of Er in the *Republic*.[130] This last instance is a striking one, illustrative of the central position of the dialogues of Plato in the establishment both of the canonical versions of "Pythagorean" myths and of the connections between those myths and Homer.

The use of the myths of Plato to explicate the myths of Homer and the idea that the two bodies of storytelling had like structures of meaning were perhaps the most important developments in the history of the reading of Homer in Platonic circles. The process at work in the early development of the interpretation of the myth of the Sirens was essentially the same as that which emerged more clearly in the second-century interpretation of the cave of the nymphs in the *Odyssey* by the Neopythagorean Numenius, whose "exegesis" of that passage was in all probability included entirely in a commentary on the myth of Er.[131]

In practice, the myths of Plato became central texts of a "primitive Pythagoreanism" that was little more than dogmatic Platonism disguised under the name of Pythagoras—a tradition rejected by the skeptical Academy, which Numenius attacked bitterly. Numenius would have fully assimilated the conception of Pythagoras and his doctrine elaborated by the successors of Plato. In proposing to demonstrate that the doctrines of Plato and Pythagoras were identical, he was simply restoring a primitive unity (though one with no necessary connection with Plato himself if we view dogmatic Platonism as the product of his suc-

126. Heraclit. *Quaest. hom.* 12.2–13.1. Cf. Delatte, *Littérature pythagoricienne*, p. 116.

127. *Schol in Il.*, ed. Erbse, vol. 4, pp. 310–11. Ps.-Plut. *De vit. Hom.* 122. Eust. *In Il.* 1090.31–33. Cf. Delatte, *Littérature pythagoricienne*, p. 127.

128. τὸν ἐν Αἰγύπτῳ ἥρωα τὰ πάντων ἰδιώματα περιέχοντα, ὡς ἐκείνη τὸ ἑκάστου ἀριθμοῦ συνέργημα (Iambl. *Theol. arith.* 7.20–23).

129. Porph. *ap. Stob. Ecl.* 1.41.61.

130. Plut. *Quaest. conv.* 9.14.6.145d–e. See also the *Certamen* (38) and the opening remarks in Eustathius's introduction to his commentary on the *Iliad* (translated by C. J. Herington in "Homer: a Byzantine Perspective").

131. See ch. 2B below.

cessors). In going beyond Pythagoras to demonstrate the same doctrine
in Homer, he may well have been working in a Pythagorean tradition as
old as the sixth century B.C., but which had been so radically reworked
in the fourth and third centuries that little, if any, of its pre-Platonic content was or is perceptible. Similarly, the interpretations of the passages
on the Sirens and on the arrows of Apollo that generated the music of the
sphere of the sun were doubtless articulated by thinkers—Plutarch is an
excellent case in point—thoroughly steeped in Platonism. Some, identifying their positions more emphatically with those of dogmatic Platonism, may, along with Numenius, have called themselves, or have been
called, Πυθαγόρειοι, but the myths of Plato loomed large among their
sources and there would have been little in their Pythagoreanism traceable to sources earlier than those myths.

Beyond the specific passages in the scholia and the surviving interpretive literature that have been claimed as illustrations of Pythagorean
influence on the early interpretation of Homer, there is the larger question of the sources of etymology as an interpretive tool.

Commentators on the meaning of the Homeric poems began early—
certainly before Plato's time—to focus upon individual words (whether
words of particular difficulty or simply words of particular importance)
and to explain them by analogy to words of similar sound. This was
done in a manner utterly devoid of historical perspective and without
any perception of the actual phonetic principles according to which
words evolve, and hence appears invariably arbitrary and naive. Nevertheless, it is a mode of explication as old as Homer himself.[132] Institu-
tionalized in the encyclopedic *Etymologiae* of Isidore of Seville (ca. 570–
636), moreover, it knew a tremendous vogue throughout the Middle
Ages.

Since its roots are demonstrably Homeric, there is little point in
searching elsewhere for the originator of this exegetic technique, but it
has nevertheless been suggested that the early Pythagoreans may have
made a substantial contribution to the considerable body of interpretation by etymology transmitted in the scholia and elsewhere. The *Cratylus* of Plato is the ancient work we might hope would throw light on
the question of the sources of pre-Platonic etymological thought, yet

---

132. See, among others, the passage on Odysseus's name (*Od.* 19.407–9),
which Homer derives from ὀδύσσομαι, providing a story to confirm the etymology, and that on Scylla, which he derives from σκύλαξ (*Od.* 12.85–86). Cf. also
Pfeiffer, *History of Classical Scholarship*, pp. 4–5, and references, p. 4, n. 5.

here, as so often, Plato is frustratingly vague regarding the background of the ideas he presents. In an important article Pierre Boyancé has analyzed the indications given for the source of the theory lying behind Socrates' etymological speculations in the *Cratylus*.[133] Using the principle asserted by Frank that only Aristotelian testimony about early Pythagoreanism is likely to reflect a tradition anterior to the Platonizing Pythagoreanism traceable to the generation of Speusippus, Boyancé arrives at the conclusion that it is authentic Pythagoreanism that we perceive dimly behind the position adopted ironically—and yet seriously—by Socrates, a position that includes the combination "d'une méthode d'exégèse des noms de dieux et d'une philosophie religieuse."[134] This idea is substantially developed by Detienne,[135] who places emphasis on Proclus's observation that Pythagoras shared the opinion, expressed by Cratylus in the dialogue, that names are established by an infallible nomothete and so correspond to the natures of things.[136] Proclus links this principle to Pythagoras by means of an ἄκουσμα representing the sage questioned by a disciple: "What is the wisest of beings? —Number. What is the second in wisdom? —He who established the names of things."[137] The same saying is reported in slightly different form by Iamblichus.[138]

Examined in isolation, however, the passage in Proclus is an excellent example of the kind of thought that later Neoplatonism attributed to Pythagoras. Proclus goes on to explain the ἄκουσμα:

> When [Pythagoras] speaks of the name-giver he hints at soul, which itself came to be from mind. With respect to things themselves soul is not primary, as mind is, but rather it contains images of them and detailed, essential λόγοι which are like statues of things themselves, just as names mimic the noetic forms that are numbers. And so being for all things comes from mind, which knows itself and is wise, while naming comes from soul mimicking mind. So, says Pythagoras, naming is not random but comes from that which contemplates mind and the nature of things and therefore names exist *by nature*.[139]

133. Boyancé, "La 'Doctrine d'Euthyphron' dans le *Cratyle*."
134. Boyancé, "Doctrine d'Euthyphron," p. 175.
135. Detienne, *Homère, Hésiode et Pythagore*, pp. 72–76.
136. Proclus *In Crat.* 16:5.25–6.19.
137. ἐρωτηθεὶς γοῦν Πυθαγόρας, τί σοφώτατον τῶν ὄντων· ἀριθμὸς ἔφη· τί δὲ δεύτερον εἰς σοφίαν; ὁ τὰ ὀνόματα τοῖς πράγμασι θέμενος (Proclus *In Crat.* 16:5.27–6.2).
138. Iambl. *De vit. Pyth.* 18.82.
139. διὰ δὲ τοῦ θεμένου τὰ ὀνόματα τὴν ψυχὴν ᾐνίττετο, ἥτις ἀπὸ νοῦ μὲν

The conception of ideal numbers expressed here is decidedly Platonic, not Pythagorean,[140] and the "hypostases" mind and soul belong to the vocabulary of Plotinian Neoplatonism. Yet Proclus claims to be expounding the thought of Pythagoras by explaining it in terms of thinking that postdated the historical Pythagoras by two to eight centuries. What for us can be nothing but a grotesque anachronism, however, was for him sound and time-honored philosophical method.[141]

The fact that the later Neoplatonists attributed an anachronistic conceptual model to Pythagoras does not, however, entirely obscure the fact that this ἄκουσμα gives us substantial reason to suspect that early Pythagoreanism understood there to be a real and explicable relationship between words and the things they represent, names and their sounds being keys to the essences of things.

The doxographic miscellany entitled *The Life and Poetry of Homer*, attributed to Plutarch, and in all probability belonging to the second century after Christ, throws considerable light on the relationship between Pythagoras and Homer as understood by late antiquity. The author's concern with Pythagoras is incidental to his larger, indeed megalomaniacal, plan to demonstrate that Homer is the source of all philosophy—and not simply of philosophy, but of rhetoric and of many other human skills as well.[142] Working in a heterogeneous tradition that doubtless owed much

---

ὑπέστη· καὶ αὐτὰ μὲν τὰ πράγματα οὐκ ἔστιν ὥσπερ ὁ νοῦς πρώτως, ἔχει δ᾽ αὐτῶν εἰκόνας καὶ λόγους οὐσιώδεις διεξοδικούς, οἷον ἀγάλματα τῶν ὄντων, ὥσπερ τὰ ὀνόματα ἀπομιμούμενα τὰ νοερὰ εἴδη τοὺς ἀριθμούς· τὸ μὲν οὖν εἶναι πᾶσιν ἀπὸ νοῦ τοῦ ἑαυτὸν γινώσκοντος καὶ σοφοῦ, τὸ δ᾽ ὀνομάζεσθαι ἀπὸ ψυχῆς τῆς νοῦν μιμουμένης. οὐκ ἄρα, φησὶ Πυθαγόρας, τοῦ τυχόντος ἐστὶ τὸ ὀνοματουργεῖν, ἀλλὰ τοῦ τὸν νοῦν ὁρῶντος καὶ φύσιν τῶν ὄντων· φύσει ἄρα τὰ ὀνόματα (Proclus *In Crat.* 16:6.10–19).

140. Cf. Burkert, *Lore and Science*, p. 27.

141. See ch. 5C below on Proclus's relationship to the literature of the past and specifically to Homer. The notion that Pythagoras and early Pythagoreanism recognized a non-material reality is universal in Neoplatonism from the time of Plotinus himself (*Enn.* 5.1.9) and can be traced still earlier to the second-century Neopythagoreans.

142. The idea was certainly not original with our author. It is implied in Socrates' attack on Homer's supposed ability to impart wisdom in all areas, in the *Ion*, and stated emphatically by Niceratos in Xenophon's *Symposium*: ἴστε γὰρ δήπου ὅτι Ὅμηρος ὁ σοφώτατος πεποίηκε σχεδὸν περὶ πάντων τῶν ἀνθρωπίνων. ὅστις ἂν οὖν ὑμῶν βούληται ἢ οἰκονομικὸς ἢ δημηγορικὸς ἢ στρατηγικὸς γενέσθαι ἢ ὅμοιος Ἀχιλλεῖ ἢ Αἴαντι ἢ Ὀδυσσεῖ, ἐμὲ θεραπευέτω. ἐγὼ γὰρ ταῦτα πάντα ἐπίσταμαι (Xen. *Symp.* 4.6). Socrates attributes this attitude to "certain people" at *Rep.* 598d.

to the Stoa, the author of the *Life* embraces a variety of doctrines and explicitly rejects very few. What we see at work in this text is the process by which Platonizing litterateurs of late antiquity—Plutarch himself is an outstanding example—incorporated much of the philosophical tradition into a matrix compatible with the thought of the successors of Plato in the Academy. The peculiarity of the *Life* is that the matrix is made co-extensive with the *Iliad* and *Odyssey* and their sphere of influence, and the roots of the entire tradition are located in the "enigmatic and mythic language"[143] of Homer. The author often indicates that Homer "hints at" (αἰνίττεται) various doctrines of later thinkers, and makes it clear that the poems are a vast encyclopedia with a complex, sometimes obscure, structure of meaning.

It is principally in the context of the discussion of souls that Ps.-Plutarch brings up Pythagoras, asserting that "of all the doctrines [concerning the soul], that of Pythagoras and Plato is the noblest, that the soul is immortal."[144]

For this author, as we shall see, there are certain doctrines that are specifically Pythagorean and others that are Platonic, though borrowed from, or at least shared with, Pythagoras.[145] The immortality of the soul is one of the latter, and though it doubtless does have pre-Platonic Pythagorean roots, as expressed by Ps.-Plutarch it represents a thoroughly Platonized Pythagoreanism.

Metensomatosis is introduced in the *Life* as a properly Pythagorean doctrine that "was not beyond the understanding of Homer."[146] The talking horses of Achilles and the old dog that recognizes Odysseus indicate that the souls of men and other animals are related, and the destruction of Odysseus's crew as punishment for killing the sacred cattle is viewed as a general indication that all animals are honored by the gods (*De vit. Hom.* 125). The subsequent passage (*De vit. Hom.* 126) on Circe as the symbol of the cycle of metensomatosis, to which "the thinking man" (ὁ . . . ἔμφρων ἀνήρ) Odysseus is immune, already suggests something more sophisticated and the patterns of the myths of Plato begin to be visible behind this hero who is liberated from reincarnation by the pos-

143. δι᾿ αἰνιγμάτων καὶ μυθικῶν λόγων . . . ἐμφαίνεται τὰ νοήματα (*De vit. Hom.* 92).

144. τὸ μὲν δὴ τῶν δογμάτων Πυθαγόρου καὶ Πλάτωνος γενναιότατόν ἐστι, τὸ εἶναι τὴν ψυχὴν ἀθάνατον (*De vit. Hom.* 122).

145. The idea of the dependence of Plato on Pythagoras is at least as old as Aristotle (*Metaph.* A 987a).

146. ἀλλ᾽ οὐδὲ τοῦτο τῆς Ὁμήρου διανοίας ἐκτός ἐστιν (*De vit. Hom.* 125).

session of reason (λόγος). The fact that λόγος is here identified with the Hermes of the myth likewise points back to the *Cratylus*, though this may be only the proximal source of the idea.[147] It points at the same time, however, to later developments of the same identification that lead, for example, to the identification, by the Naassenian Gnostics of the first and second centuries, of Hermes the Psychopomp (*Od.* 24.1–14) with the creative and redeeming λόγος—that is, with Christ.[148] In a fragment preserved in Stobaeus (*Ecl.* 1.41.60), Porphyry develops the allegory of Circe, making it clear that this "Pythagorean" tradition became part of the Neoplatonic reading of the passage.[149]

When Odysseus's descent to Hades is viewed as "separating soul from body,"[150] we have fully entered that bizarre realm of Platonized Pythagoreanism where the influence of the legend of Pythagoras's own temporary death and resurrection becomes indistinguishable from that of the similar story of Er in the *Republic*. From the present perspective, the important point, though, is that a comprehensive view of Odysseus the hero as a "thinking man," freed by reason from the round of reincarnation, a hero whose heroism consists precisely in the denial of existence on the material plane and the attainment of a higher state, exists here in isolation from doctrines of astral immortality and from elaborate demonologies. Whatever the later Neopythagorean and Neoplatonic contributions to the understanding of the poems, this core was already available for elaboration: a redefined Odysseus, far removed from the archaic Homeric hero and transformed by a complex and unrecoverable process into a hero of the denial of the flesh.

Finally, a word should be said about possible Pythagorean interpolations in the text of Homer. This is clearly not the place to reopen the question of the analysis of the Homeric text that dispersed the energies of so much of the classical scholarship of the nineteenth century. Suffice it to say that virtually every passage of Homer with a "Pythagorean" flavor has at one time or another been branded on internal evidence as "late." Burkert, who doubts that Pythagoreans ever were in a position to modify the received text, provides a list[151] that includes among other passages the larger part of the *nekyia* (the journey to the dead) of *Odyssey* 11

147. Cf. Buffière, *Mythes d'Homère*, pp. 289–90.

148. Carcopino, *De Pythagore aux apôtres*, pp. 180–82.

149. See ch. 3B below.

150. ὥσπερ ἐκλύων καὶ χωρίζων τὴν ψυχὴν ἀπὸ τοῦ σώματος (*De vit. Hom.* 126).

151. Burkert, *Lore and Science*, p. 279, n. 10.

as well as the second *nekyia* of *Odyssey* 24. Delatte[152] made a strong case for Pythagorean interference with the received text and pointed to evidence for a Pythagorean editorial team behind the Pisistratean recension. The question cannot be solved here and the most judicious attitude to adopt is a prudent doubt akin to Burkert's.

The evidence for early Pythagorean concern with Homer, then, is considerable, but evidence that demonstrates the early Pythagorean sources of the reading of the *Iliad* and *Odyssey* as mystical allegories is slim at best. Buffière's reluctance to believe that early Pythagoreanism was concerned with physical allegory does, however, seem unnecessary. Perhaps the most important lesson to be learned from this inquiry is that we should not insist too strongly on discrete categories of physical, moral, and mystical allegory. There is no reason to believe that the distinction was made in the classical period and the lines separating the categories are difficult to draw.

All the same, the chief aspects of the Neoplatonic tradition of interpretation as passed on to the Middle Ages are the ideas (1) that Homer was a sage who was acquainted with the fate of souls, and (2) that the model of the universe he articulated was characterized by an idealism compatible with the thought of Plotinus and the later Neoplatonists. The first of these aspects may well have had pre-Platonic Pythagorean roots, but the second cannot have done, for the simple reason that the concepts involved are, by Aristotle's testimony,[153] absent from pre-Platonic Pythagoreanism.

152. Delatte, *Littérature pythagoricienne*, pp. 134–36.
153. Arist. *Metaph.* A 989b29–990a32. Cf. Burkert, *Lore and Science*, p. 31.

II

Middle Platonism and the Interaction of Interpretive Traditions

A. PHILO OF ALEXANDRIA

The tradition of mystical allegorical commentary on Homer has survived in substantial form only in the writings of the Neoplatonists, but evidence from the first two and a half centuries of the Christian era—before the great synthesis of Plotinus, which marks the beginning of Neoplatonism proper—indicates that this period was a crucial one in the development of that tradition. Félix Buffière's insistence on the second century as the time of the birth of mystical allegory needs qualification, as the discussion of the role of the Pythagoreans has suggested, but this does not alter the fact that Numenius and Cronius, two second-century thinkers, are cited repeatedly as the sources for our earliest surviving essay in this mode, Porphyry's allegory of the cave of the nymphs in the *Odyssey*. The creative contribution of Numenius and his circle was doubtless substantial, but it in turn must be viewed against the background of developments in textual exegesis in Alexandria—developments concerned not with Homer but with the Hebrew scriptures.

It is clearly impossible to do justice to the riches of the Philonic corpus in the context of a study of this sort, and our problem is compounded by the fact that the sources of Philo's own thought, as well as the diffusion of his influence beyond the Jewish and Christian communities, are very imperfectly understood.[1]

---

1. The standard comprehensive treatment of Philo is still Emile Bréhier, *Les Idées philosophiques et religieuses de Philon d'Alexandrie*. For useful, brief, up-to-date summaries of his thought, see Henry Chadwick in CHLGEMP, pp. 137–57, and John Dillon, *Middle Platonists*, pp. 139–83.

Philo's death, ca. A.D. 50, falls at least a century before the *floruit* of Numenius in the tentative chronology we have adopted for the latter.[2] Clement of Alexandria, who must have been a younger contemporary of Numenius, and Origen the Christian, who, like Plotinus, studied under Ammonius Saccas, both show the influence of Philo.[3] He is dated by his role in a mission to Caligula in 39, which he himself describes and which Josephus, fifty to fifty-five years his junior, likewise mentions,[4] giving an indication that Philo was held in respect in the Alexandrian Jewish community during his own lifetime and that he was remembered as a philosopher a generation later.

Philo is known principally for his voluminous allegorical treatises on the Pentateuch, in which many of the habits of reading foreshadowed in the authors already discussed, but not fully developed in pagan contexts for several centuries, are systematically elaborated for the first time. Philo inherits the Stoic tradition of textual exegesis, already thoroughly Platonized, but paradoxically first preserved in substantial form *here*. The influence of Stoic elements incorporated into a Platonist matrix is perhaps stronger among the Alexandrians than elsewhere—a fact in part traceable to the influence of students of Antiochus of Ascalon, the tremendously influential Stoicizing Platonist who also taught Cicero and Varro.[5]

The specifically philosophical content of Philo's work and his overall debt to Stoicism need not concern us here, but one crucial issue—that of etymology—should occupy our attention for a moment. We have seen that there is some reason to accept the idea that the concept of an authoritative bestower of names, who guarantees a vital link between words and the things they designate, may go back to pre-Platonic Pythagoreanism.[6] Embodied in the *Cratylus*, at any rate, this idea formed the basis for later Stoic as well as Platonic speculation on etymology—or, more accurately, on syllabic and subsyllabic elements of words as keys to the relationships among words, and so among the things they designate.

This powerful analytical tool has already been associated with a Pythagorean ἄκουσμα attested by a variety of ancient authors, and that

2. Cf. KP s.v. Philon 10, vol. 4, col. 772, and see ch. 2B, below.
3. Colson and Whitaker in Philo vol. 1, p. xxi; KP vol. 4, cols. 774–75.
4. Joseph. *Antiq. Jud.* 18.259–60.
5. Dillon, *Middle Platonists*, pp. 142–45; on Antiochus and his influence, see also pp. 52–106, esp. 61–62.
6. See ch. 1D, above.

same ἄκουσμα is echoed repeatedly in Philo.[7] Here, it is Adam who is the "establisher of names" (Gen. 2.19) and thus the analytic tool finds its justification within the work to be analyzed. His assignment of names is described as a "work of wisdom and kingship" (σοφίας γὰρ καὶ βασιλείας τὸ ἔργον, De op. mundi 148), a phrase Pierre Boyancé has linked to a mysterious classification of levels of interpretation of words in Varro (De ling. Lat. 5.7–8), culminating in the fourth and highest level, ubi est adytum et initia regis.[8] Here again, the apparent common source for the terminology is Antiochus of Ascalon, who assured a place for a Stoicizing view of the building blocks of language (along with Stoic epistemology and Stoic physics) among the central concerns of Middle Platonism. Even in the context of ancient etymological speculation, Philo's application of analytic principles to words is a bit surprising when he explains Hebrew words according to Greek elements (e.g., the river Pheison from φείδεσθαι, Leg. alleg. 1.66).[9] Implied here, though, is no doubt the idea that Hebrew—which Philo would seem to have known hardly at all[10]—was the language of Adam, and hence the source of all subsequent languages, however far removed after the punishment of the builders of the tower of Babel. This idea surfaces repeatedly in Christian speculation about language and played an important role at least through the time of Isidore of Seville.

Before leaving general questions of the relationship of language to reality, mention should be made of a curious passage in Philo's Questions on Genesis (4.117).[11] Here the three basic phonetic building blocks of language—vowels, semivowels, and consonants—are compared respectively to mind, senses, and body, and the relationship of these elements of the human being is analyzed in terms of the relationship of the phonetic components of articulate speech. Although this unusual formula-

---

7. Quaest. in Gen. 1.20, Leg. alleg. 2.15, etc. See Pierre Boyancé, "Etymologie et théologie chez Varron," p. 109, n. 3, for five more passages in Philo that echo the ἄκουσμα.

8. Boyancé, "Etymologie et théologie chez Varron," pp. 107–15.

9. Dillon, Middle Platonists, pp. 181–82, cites this example.

10. Although most scholars loudly denounce Philo's ignorance of Hebrew, voices have been raised on the other side, most importantly Wolfson's. For a balanced view of the matter, including the significant caution that it is usually Rabbinists who claim that Philo did know Hebrew and Hellenists who claim he did not, see Samuel Sandmel, "Philo's Knowledge of Hebrew: the Present State of the Problem."

11. Dillon calls attention to this passage and points out its interest: Middle Platonists, p. 174, n. 2.

tion would seem to be unique for its time, it foreshadows later Platonists' concern with the macrocosm-microcosm relationship and ultimately with the literary text as microcosm.

Philo's exegetic theory and practice have been much discussed by students of Christian hermeneutics as well as by students of Jewish traditions of biblical interpretation.[12] The question of the sources of those techniques remains embroiled in the complexities of the problem of the dating and reliability of our sources on Jewish history and thought in the centuries just before Philo. There is no doubt, however, that Philo saw himself as one interpreter among many—he indicates as much in his many references to other interpreters, with whom he sometimes agrees and sometimes disagrees.[13] It has long been recognized that Philo's allegorical method derives ultimately from Greek thought, and specifically from the Stoic tradition of interpretation, itself eclectic and only fragmentarily attested before Philo's time, but resting primarily on the recognition in texts or myths of three levels of meaning—literal, ethical, and metaphysical.[14] To judge by the *Homeric Allegories* of Heraclitus, the third level of meaning in Stoic allegories often related not to the status of the soul and its relationship to the body, but rather to cosmology and the structure of the material universe, and we see already in Philo an increased concern with finding in texts a level of meaning having to do with the soul, a concern that is, of course, central to Neoplatonic allegory. By his own testimony, virtually every type of allegory offered by Philo is also, however, to be found among other interpreters of the scriptures known to him—that is, all types, including physical allegories and allegories of the soul, already existed in a Jewish context before Philo.[15] The question here, though, is not one of the ultimate sources of this allegorizing—it is doubtless all Greek and preeminently Stoic in origin— but simply one of date. It would seem that we are on the safest ground if

12. See in particular Jean Pépin in *Mythe et allégorie*, pp. 216–42, as well as his "Remarques sur la théorie de l'exégèse allégorique chez Philon." Also useful for an overview is Heinrich Dörrie, "Zur Methodik antiker Exegese." Irmgard Christiansen's *Die Technik der allegorischen Auslegungswissenschaft bei Philon von Alexandrien* offers an unusual and penetrating analysis, which treats allegorizing as "applied Platonic philosophy" (p. 13), exploring among other things the relationship of Philonic exegesis to the analytic techniques developed in Plato's *Sophist*.

13. For an analysis of these references, see David M. Hay, "Philo's References to Other Allegorists," to which I am indebted here.

14. Dillon, *Middle Platonists*, p. 142.

15. Hay, "Philo's References to Other Allegorists," esp. pp. 55–61.

we postulate no far-reaching originality of method or approach in Philo, but view him as the principal spokesman of a school of allegorists, a school Jean Pépin is no doubt correct in tracing to an impulse among Hellenizing Jews in Alexandria to give power and prestige to their own tradition and literature in the eyes of their Greek neighbors.[16]

The methods and vocabulary of Philo's exegesis are for the most part those of the earlier tradition of Homer commentary. He distinguishes emphatically between literal meaning (τὸ ῥητόν) and allegorical meanings (ἀλληγορίαι or ὑπόνοιαι).[17] He relies heavily as well on the verb αἰνίττομαι ("hint at," "indicate by means of symbols"), which from the time of Plato and before had been the principal verb used to designate the secondary meanings of texts and myths. Etymology, as already indicated, is broadly applied, especially to the explanation of the meaning of proper names, including toponyms. Philo is decidedly a pluralist, commonly elaborating multiple allegories based on a single passage.

It is puzzling to find that in spite of his frequent indications of his concern with, and knowledge of, pagan myth and his application to scripture of techniques unquestionably derivative from pagan exegesis, he nevertheless repeatedly denies that there is a mythic element in scripture. This contradiction—one of many in Philo—must be resolved by careful attention to the purpose of the writings in question. The essay entitled *The Confusion of Tongues* opens with a unique polemic against certain commentators who reduce scripture to the level of mythic accounts from other cultures—a procedure Philo denounces—and in *The Migration of Abraham* (89–93), certain allegorizers who have contempt for the Law are denounced. In spite of this, however, Philo consistently sides with allegorists against literalists (*De conf. ling.* 14).[18] When it is a question of maintaining the superiority of Judaic over gentile tradition, the μυθῶδες is viewed as empty of meaning and decidedly uncharacteristic of the former, but in less polemical contexts the suggestion is

16. Pépin, *Mythe et allégorie*, p. 231.

17. Pépin notes that Philo's use of these two important terms is slightly different from that described in an often quoted passage of Plutarch (*De aud. po.* 19). Plutarch, writing perhaps a century after Philo, indicates that in his time ἀλληγορία had simply supplanted ὑπόνοια, apparently meaning the same thing. In Philo, however, as Pépin argues, ὑπόνοια is not ἀλληγορία itself, but designates the basis and means of ἀλληγορία. (*Mythe et allégorie*, p. 234.) See note 25, below, for the suggestion that in the *De prov.* Philo may have linked the two terms together in what amounts to a hendiadys.

18. Cf. Pépin, "Remarques," pp. 144–46, and Hay, "Philo's References to Other Allegorists," pp. 47–49.

very strong that similar structures of meaning exist in both bodies of traditional literature.[19] Even when the *truth* of *Homeric* poetry is treated as dubious or unacceptable, that poetry is seen to have redeeming value. Philo says of the passage at *Od.* 17.485 describing how the gods travel among men, "This may not be a true song, but it is still advantageous and profitable."[20]

Philo's exegesis of scripture as such clearly lies beyond our concerns, but if Philo's substantial surviving works indeed represent the sort of evidence for the hermeneutics of Middle Platonism we have suggested, then given his extensive Greek learning,[21] and his overall receptiveness to Greek culture, we would expect to find here direct evidence for Homeric allegories. Although Philo's references and allusions to Homer are many and his quotations of Homer—generally not identified as such—are frequent,[22] the direct evidence for an allegorical understanding of the passages cited is slight. Most of his citations of Homer are purely rhetorical and decorative, and give little indication of what Philo may have thought the lines meant—if anything—beyond the literal. Nevertheless, as we shall see, the ghosts of familiar and unfamiliar allegories of Homer stand behind many passages of Philo.

In Philo's work *On Providence* we find explicit mention of the multiple levels of meaning in Homer and Hesiod, and of their importance. The context is a dialogue in which Philo's nephew Alexander attacks the idea of providence, and Philo defends it. In the course of his attack, Alexander offers some disparaging remarks about the obscenities and other crimes of Homer and Hesiod, elaborating his position rather colorfully out of commonplaces from Xenophanes and Plato. Philo's response (*De prov.* 2.40–41)[23] merits quotation *in extenso*:

19. Cf. Pépin, "Remarques," p. 146.

20. καὶ τάχα μὲν οὐκ ἀληθῶς, πάντως δὲ λυσιτελῶς καὶ συμφερόντως ᾄδεται (*De somn.* 1.233). The same passage is praised at *Quaest. in Gen.* 4.2.

21. On the extent of his knowledge of Greek literature, see Monique Alexandre, "La Culture profane chez Philon," pp. 107–13.

22. About forty are catalogued in the index of Colin and Wendland's edition of the *Works* of Philo, but the number of Homeric references is raised to near seventy in the index of the Loeb edition (including supplements). These include, however, a number of Homeric words whose status as actual Homeric echoes is highly questionable.

23. This work survives largely intact only in Armenian, and is usually cited from the translation of that text into Latin published by Aucher in 1822. The translation above began as a translation of that Latin (pp. 75–76), but Peter Cowe was kind enough to review it for me and to correct it in numerous places with

Philosopher, as you accuse the whole human race of ignorance on the basis of these things, you fail to realize that this is not the situation at all. For if the fame of Homer and Hesiod extends throughout the world, then the cause is the ideas contained in the events [*sententiae sub rebus comprehensae*], events of which there have been many recounters [*enarratores*] who wondered at them, and that were objects of wonder in their own time and remain so down to the present day. If they nevertheless seem to have offended in some passages, one should not blame them for this, but rather sing their praises for the great number of excellent ones with which they have produced benefit for life. . . .

I pass over the fact that the mythical element in poetry that you were just talking about contains no blasphemy against the gods, but is rather an indication of the allegorical meaning contained therein [*indicium inclusae physiologiae*]. Its mysteries must not be laid bare before the uninitiated, but in passing I shall give you a demonstration by way of example of some things that in some people's view are fabricated and fictitious, insofar as it is possible to establish a thesis according to the law, respecting at the same time the rule that it is not allowed that the mysteries be revealed to the uninitiated.[24]

If you apply the mythical story of Hephaestus to fire, and the account of Hera to air, and what is said about Hermes to reason, and in the same way that which is said of the others, following in order, in their theology, then in fact you will become a praiser of the poets you have just been condemning, so that you will realize that they alone have glorified the divine in a seemly manner. While you did not accept the principles of the allegories or hidden meanings [*regulas allegoriae aut sententiarum*],[25] then the same happened to you as to boys who out of ignorance pass by the paintings on boards [$\pi i \nu \alpha \kappa \epsilon \varsigma$?] of Apelles and are attached to the images stamped on little coins [$\dot{o}\beta o$-$\lambda o i$]—they admire the laughable and scorn that which deserves general acceptance.

---

reference to Aucher's Armenian text. To the extent that it faithfully represents the Armenian, the credit is Dr. Cowe's and not mine. He also pointed out to me several points at which the Greek original can be glimpsed through the Armenian. There seems to be no complete translation of the work into English, but Aucher's Latin has been translated into German (see "Works Cited: Ancient Authors").

24. Aucher identifies the Greek original in a fragment of Philo preserved in St. John Damascene: $o\dot{v}\ \theta \acute{\epsilon}\mu\iota\varsigma\ \tau\dot{\alpha}\ \acute{\iota}\epsilon\rho\dot{\alpha}\ \mu\upsilon\sigma\tau\acute{\eta}\rho\iota\alpha\ \dot{\epsilon}\kappa\lambda\alpha\lambda\epsilon\hat{\iota}\nu\ \dot{\alpha}\mu\upsilon\acute{\eta}\tau o\iota\varsigma$.

25. Dr. Cowe has pointed out to me that the word Aucher translates *sententia* here (*karceac^c*) is not the same as that represented by *sententia* in the first paragraph (*mitk^c n*). *Karcik^c* regularly represents $\delta\acute{o}\xi\alpha$, $\delta\acute{o}\kappa\eta\sigma\iota\varsigma$, $\dot{\upsilon}\pi\acute{o}\nu o\iota\alpha$, and $\delta\iota$-$\acute{\alpha}\lambda\eta\psi\iota\varsigma$ in translations from the Greek. I take it to represent $\dot{\upsilon}\pi\acute{o}\nu o\iota\alpha$ here, and the original phrase to be $\kappa\alpha\nu\acute{o}\nu\epsilon\varsigma$? $\dot{\alpha}\lambda\lambda\eta\gamma o\rho\acute{\iota}\alpha\varsigma\ \ddot{\eta}\ \dot{\upsilon}\pi o\nu o\iota\hat{\omega}\nu$.

This passage leaves little doubt that Philo was well acquainted with the standard Stoic allegories of Homeric myth, and of Greek myth in general. He clearly respected Homer not only as a poet,[26] but as a theologian as well. In *The Decalogue* (56), allegories of this sort are viewed from another perspective as mistaken deifications of parts of the material world (air *becoming* Hera, fire Hephaestus, and the hemispheres the ἑτερήμερος ζωή of the Dioscuri). This striking reversal again illustrates the multiple perspectives Philo adopts toward the complex levels of meaning in Greek myth. Likewise, again in the dialogue *On Providence* (2.66) when Alexander denounces the theological message of the claim that the brutal Cyclopes live at ease "trusting in the immortal gods," Philo responds that the Cyclopes are nothing but a mythical fabrication (πλάσμα μύθου) and then bursts into a hymn of praise for Greece, whose poor soil bore such rich intellects.

The vast majority of the Homeric words and phrases used by Philo are little more than poetic embellishments of the text. In discussing Numenius, we shall take time to look in more detail at this sort of use of Homer, which clearly was felt to be thoroughly compatible with allegorizing and with extraordinary claims for the meaning of the text. Setting aside such references in Philo, we are left with a small, but significant, sample of Homer citations that do bring along with them interesting claims regarding the meaning of the poems.

At only two points in the corpus of Philo have I found the claim that Homer "hints at" (αἰνίττεται) some meaning beyond the obvious. He hints at the doctrine that the pursuit of wealth is antithetical to virtue in his description of the virtuous Thracians (*Il.* 13.6–7; *De vit. cont.* 17), and, in describing Skylla as an ἀθάνατον κακόν, he hints that in fact it is folly (ἀφροσύνη) that is an "undying evil" (*Quod det. pot. insid. sol.* 178). This last phrase is evoked in two other passages as well,[27] always to complement discussion of the mark of Cain, by which an evil (Cain) was saved from death.

In general, however, Philo systematically applies Homeric phrases to a broader context than we would assume the poet intended and thus extends their meaning beyond the obvious. Once (*Quod omn. prob.* 31), Philo's language implies that this procedure is implicit in the structure of

26. The fact that he refers to Homer as ὁ μέγιστος καὶ δοκιμώτατος τῶν ποιητῶν (*De conf. ling.* 4) and elsewhere mentions him with respect guarantees at least this much.

27. *De fug. et inv.* 61; *Quaest. in Gen.* 1.76.

meaning of the poems. Homer calls kings "shepherds of the people," but "nature more specifically applies the title to the good" (ἡ δὲ φύσις τοῖς ἀγαθοῖς κυριώτερον τουτὶ τοὔνομα ἐπεφήμισεν). This might not at first sight appear to implicate the poem or its meaning, but in fact φυσιολογία in Philo is used to designate the allegorical level of meaning of texts, and what Philo describes here is probably the process by which the world impinges on the text and recreates the context of its meaning. Significantly, the same Homeric phrase is taken up elsewhere (De Jos. 2) and said to be an indication that Homer believed shepherding to be good training for kingship. A number of other Homeric phrases are transposed to new contexts. In the essay On Providence (2.3), the phrase πατὴρ ἀνδρῶν τε θεῶν τε is praised as illustrating the triple analogy, father : children :: king : city :: God : world. Similarly, when Homer says "let there be one king" (εἷς κοίρανος ἔστω, Il. 2.204), what he says is more appropriate to describing the relationship of God to the world (De conf. ling. 170); and when Homer says (of the Sun) that he sees and hears all (Il. 3.277, etc.), Philo, without comment on its original application, takes up the phrase and applies it to God (De Jos. 265). References of this sort are marginal in their evocation of an extended meaning within the poem itself, but anticipate the spiritualization of Homeric phrases in Plotinus—as does Philo's use of Od. 4.392 (from Eidothea's advice to Menelaus that Proteus can tell him

Whatever good and bad has been done at home

ὅττι τοι ἐν μεγάροισι κακόν τ᾽ ἀγαθόν τε τέτυκται)

to refer to self-contemplation (once by the νοῦς), with the goal of self-knowledge (De migr. 195; De somn. 1.57).

A few other passages evoke Homeric allegories known from other sources. In The Eternity of the World (127), citing the Homeric epithet χωλός ("lame") for Hephaestus, Philo echoes an allegory (also recorded in the scholia and traced by the scholiast to Heraclitus) that distinguished a celestial and a terrestrial ("lame") fire, the latter requiring fuel in contrast to the former. In Questions on Genesis (3.3), the Sirens are equated with the music of the spheres—an allegory clearly representing the conflation of Homeric and Platonic myth. In the same work, the Homeric division of the world into three parts (Il. 15.189) is juxtaposed with the Pythagoreans' assertion that the triad is the foundation of the being of this sublunary world (γένεσις) (Quaest. in Gen. 4.8).

The most interesting Homeric allegories in Philo, however, are undoubtedly those that lie just below the surface of his text. The suggestion has been made that several references in Philo to the (Stoic) λόγος as the cupbearer of God (e.g., *De somn.* 2.249) mask an otherwise unattested allegory that equated Ganymede with the λόγος.[28] There are also a number of passages suggesting that the allegorized Odysseus was known to Philo. In a passage in the essay *On Dreams* (2.70), Adam is said to have doomed himself to death by preferring the dyad (the created world symbolized by the tree) to the monad, here identified with the Creator. Philo then turns from description to prescription: "But as for yourself, pass 'out of the smoke and wave' [*Od.* 12.219] and flee the ridiculous concerns of mortal life as you would that frightful Charybdis and do not touch it even with the tip of your toe (as the saying is)."[29]

This can, of course, be read as a simple decorative elaboration, importing Homeric language and myth to enliven the injunction. As we shall see in discussing Numenius, however, there exists in Middle Platonism a developed allegory of Odysseus as rational man passing through the created sublunary universe (γένεσις) and returning to his celestial home. This theme is never explicitly tied to the Odysseus story in Philo, but passages such as the one just quoted strongly suggest that he was well acquainted with such an understanding of the *Odyssey*.[30]

The influence of Philo on the Alexandrian Christian Platonists, represented by Clement and Origen, is undeniable, and only the extent and importance of that influence are matters of dispute. Outside the Jewish and Christian communities, however, the influence of Philo has never been convincingly demonstrated. It nevertheless seems almost inconceivable that the walls between these intellectual communities should have been so high, or that a thinker such as Porphyry, who studied Christianity in order to combat it, should have ignored a thinker who from our perspective looms as large as Philo. Whatever the extent of his influence, however, Philo is of use to us primarily in that he *receives* the major intellectual currents of Middle Platonism and preserves an other-

28. This idea belongs to John Dillon, who supports it convincingly in "Ganymede as the Logos: Traces of a Forgotten Allegorization in Philo?"

29. ἀλλὰ σύ γε τοῦ μὲν καπνοῦ καὶ κύματος ἐκτὸς βαῖνε καὶ τὰς καταγελάστους τοῦ θνητοῦ βίου σπουδὰς ὡς τὴν φοβερὰν ἐκείνην χάρυβδιν ἀποδίδρασκε καὶ μηδὲ ἄκρῳ, τὸ τοῦ λόγου τοῦτο, ποδὸς δακτύλῳ ψαύσῃς (*De somn.* 2.70).

30. See Pierre Boyancé, "Echo des exégèses de la mythologie grecque chez Philon," pp. 169–73. In the same article, Boyancé pursues submerged evidence in Philo for several other Middle Platonic interpretive ideas, but the other material is not specifically Homeric.

wise unattested phase of that intellectual trend. That he passed these
concerns on to his Christian compatriots may well have had a decisive
effect on the history of Christian hermeneutics. That we are unable to
determine whether later pagan Platonists so much as read him may be
taken as an indication of a failure of communication of central importance to the intellectual history of late antiquity.[31]

B. NUMENIUS

The Uses of Literature

The earliest identifiable figure of importance in the history of the Neoplatonists' conception of the meaning of Homer is a shadowy and enigmatic Pythagorean of the mid- to late second century A.D.[32] Virtually
nothing is known of Numenius's life beyond the fact that he is connected
with Apamea in Syria and, less convincingly, with Rome.[33] Rudolf Beutler[34] was reluctant to date him any more precisely than the second century, but more recently, in support of the general tendency to place his
floruit at or shortly after mid-century, John Dillon is inclined to accept the
identification of his associate and probable near-contemporary Cronius
with the recipient of a work of Lucian datable to 165.[35] E. R. Dodds saw
"no chronological difficulty in supposing that Numenius was writing in
the time of Marcus [161–80] or even a little later."[36]

31. Sandmel's suggestion that Numenius spoke of Philo (*Philo of Alexandria*,
p. 4) is bewildering and unsupported by any of the fragments or testimonia collected by Leemans or Des Places. Numenius does mention Philo of Larissa (fr.
28), but this can hardly be what Sandmel had in mind.

32. After E. A. Leemans, *Studie over den Wijsgeer Numenius van Apamea, met
Uitgave der Fragmenten* (1937), the most useful contributions on Numenius are
the recent Budé edition of the *Fragments* by Des Places, whose numbering is
used here, P. Merlan's summary in CHLGEMP, pp. 96–106, and Dillon's in *The
Middle Platonists*, pp. 361–78. Also note E. R. Dodds, "Numenius and Ammonius," and on the specific problem of the relationship between Numenius and
Porphyry, J. H. Waszink, "Porphyrios und Numenios."

33. For Apamea, Porph. *Vit. Plot.* 17; *Suda* s.v. Νουμήνιος (1). For Rome, fr.
57. Cf. R. Beutler, "Numenios (9)," cols 664–65, and Dillon, *Middle Platonists*,
p. 361. Throughout Ch. 2B, "fr." is used, without further indication, to refer to
the fragments of Numenius.

34. Beutler, "Numenios," col. 665.

35. Dillon, *Middle Platonists*, p. 362.

36. Dodds, "Numenius and Ammonius," p. 11.

The works of Numenius are lost, with the exception of sixty fragments (including testimonia), preserved primarily in Eusebius, whose
method of direct quotation provides us with extensive passages that may
be taken to be the *ipsissima verba* of his source,[37] but also in a dozen other
authors, pagan and Christian, from Clement of Alexandria (150–ca. 215)
to John Lydus (sixth century). Most of the fragments not transmitted by
Eusebius make no claim to reproduce the exact words of Numenius, and
were classified by E. A. Leemans as testimonia. It is unfortunate, from
the point of view of the present study, that Numenius's contributions to
the allegorical interpretation of Homer are transmitted almost exclusively in Porphyry's essay on the cave of the nymphs in the *Odyssey*,[38]
which is itself the major source for the entire tradition of interpretation
of the passage. The fact that Porphyry does not quote Numenius directly
but refers to him repeatedly, along with Cronius, as the source of the
core of the allegory developed in his own essay makes it difficult to define the limits of Numenius's contribution with any precision, though
the importance of that contribution is unquestionable. From Porphyry's
testimony and from the fragments, it is possible, however, to reconstruct
something of Numenius's attitude toward Homer and more generally toward the literature of the past, and to gain an idea of the possible sources
of that attitude and of the scope of his application of allegorical methods
of interpretation.

Sixty fragments, varying in length from 3 to 361 lines, can hardly
form a satisfactory basis for assessing the readings, or even the borrowings, of an author, but a few points do emerge from an examination of
Numenius's use of previous writers. Initially striking are the divided
nature of his output and the two very different sorts of use of past literature that correspond to the two major divisions of his work.

Numenius was simultaneously a philosopher and a polemical historian of philosophy, and he would appear to have distinguished very
clearly between these two activities, both of which are well represented
in the surviving fragments. His primary contribution to the history of
philosophy was a work on the betrayal of Plato by his successors in the
Academy (Περὶ τῆς τῶν Ἀκαδημαϊκῶν πρὸς Πλάτωνα διαστάσεως),
shown by the fragments preserved by Eusebius to have been notable for
biting satire and a supple ingenuity in the manipulation of language for
comic effect. The following example will serve to illustrate the skillful

37. Cf. Des Places in Numenius, *Fragments*, p. 32.
38. Frs. 30, 31, 32, 60.

and ironic intermingling of levels of discourse characteristic of the work (leading John Dillon to proclaim Numenius and his contemporary Lucian two "island[s] of wit in [the] sea of bores" of the late second century):[39]

> At first, Mentor was the disciple of Carneades, but he did not succeed him. What happened was this: before Carneades died he caught Mentor in bed with his mistress. In order to grasp this, Carneades did not depend on "a credible impression," nor did he have to deal with the element of "incomprehensibility"—in fact, he had only to believe his own two eyes, and he dismissed Mentor from the school. For his part, Mentor went off and turned the force of his sophistry on Carneades, setting himself up as his rival and claiming that Carneades' doctrines themselves suffered from "incomprehensibility."[40]

Numenius produces his comic effects here by introducing lofty, technical philosophical jargon (πιθανὴ φαντασία) into what is essentially an obscene anecdote, and—less easily translated—by playing on the multiple meanings of καταλαμβάνω (=seize, grasp, catch—both intellectually and in the more obvious physical sense). He is clearly very sensitive to the expressive possibilities opened up by playing one sort of vocabulary off against another.

Numenius's discussion of the early history of the Academy is filled with examples of rhetorical sophistication and manipulation of tone comparable to the one given above. Rather surprisingly, it is in the context of this category of his work that Numenius makes most extensive use of the literature of the past, and specifically of Homer. The doctrinal arguments among the early Academicians and Stoics are inflated into mock-heroic warfare by means of complex borrowings and echoes of the *Iliad*:

> Arcesilaus and Zeno, with *henchmen* such as those just mentioned and arguments *mustered* on both sides, entirely forgot their common beginnings (they were both students of Polemon) *and, taking their stands and arming themselves, crashed ox-hide shields, crashed spears and rage of heroes armed with bronze. Bulging shields fell upon one another and a great roar went up from the murderous victors mixed with the howls of the dying* . . . Stoics. For the Academics went unscathed, and the Stoics,

---

39. Dillon, *Middle Platonists*, p. 379.

40. Καρνεάδου δὲ γίνεται γνώριμος Μέντωρ μὲν πρῶτον, οὐ μὴν διάδοχος· ἀλλ' ἔτι ζῶν Καρνεάδης ἐπὶ παλλακῇ μοιχὸν εὑρών, οὐχ ὑπὸ πιθανῆς φαντασίας οὐδ' ὡς μὴ κατειληφώς, ὡς δὲ μάλιστα πιστεύων τῇ ὄψει καὶ καταλαβὼν παρρητήσατο τῆς διατριβῆς. ὁ δ' ἀποστὰς ἀντεπισοφίστευε καὶ ἀντίτεχνος ἦν, ἐλέγχων αὐτοῦ τὴν ἐν τοῖς λόγοις ἀκαταληψίαν (fr. 27.61–67).

in their ignorance of their vulnerable points, were taken when their foundations were shaken from beneath them, unless they had some basis or first position from which to fight. Their first position was to accuse the Academics of not speaking "Platonically."[41]

The italicized words and sentences represent borrowings from or echoes of Homer. It is deceptive to print the passage as prose interrupted by a poetic quotation[42] because the actual situation is far more complex than this procedure would suggest. Numenius is not quoting Homer here: he is making a complex pastiche of Homer. The dactylic hexameter verse actually starts a bit earlier than Edouard des Places's arrangement of the text indicates, and continues longer. The core is a passage of the *Iliad* that occurs first in book 4 (446–51) at the beginning of the first major battle and recurs in book 8 (60–65). In other words, it is a stock description. Four and a half of the six lines appear in Numenius's prose just as they do in Homer, but they are introduced by a partly quoted and partly paraphrased line from book 12 (86), then interrupted first by another stock line (13.131=16.215) and later by the Iliadic *hapax* ἐδνοπάλιζεν from *Il.* 4.472, breaking the meter. They are followed by several phrases that drag on the pompous and parodic dactylic sing-song, using utterly unHomeric vocabulary.[43]

Unlike his contemporaries of the Second Sophistic, such as Maximus of Tyre,[44] who quote Homer extensively in their rhetorical exercises,

41. ὅ τε Ἀρκεσίλαος καὶ Ζήνων, ὑπὸ τοιούτων ἀρωγῶν, ἀμφοτέροις συμπολεμούντων λόγων, τῆς μὲν ἀρχῆς ὅθεν ἐκ Πολέμωνος ὡρμήθησαν ἐπιλανθάνονται, διαστάντες δέ γε καὶ σφέας αὐτοὺς ἀρτύναντες

σὺν δ᾽ ἔβαλον ῥινούς, σὺν δ᾽ ἔγχεα καὶ μένε᾽ ἀνδρῶν
χαλκεοθωρήκων· ἀτὰρ ἀσπίδες ὀμφαλόεσσαι
ἔπληντ᾽ ἀλλήλῃσι, πολὺς δ᾽ ὀρυμαγδὸς ὀρώρει.
ἀσπὶς ἄρ᾽ ἀσπίδ᾽ ἔρειδε, κόρυς κόρυν, ἄνερα δ᾽ ἀνὴρ
ἐδνοπάλιζεν.
ἔνθα δ᾽ ἅμ᾽ οἰμωγή τε καὶ εὐχωλὴ πέλεν ἀνδρῶν
ὀλλύντων τε καὶ ὀλλυμένων

τῶν Στοϊκῶν· οἱ Ἀκαδημαϊκοὶ γὰρ οὐκ ἐβάλλοντο ὑπ᾽ αὐτῶν, ἀγνοούμενοι ᾗ ἦσαν ἁλῶναι δυνατώτεροι. ἡλίσκοντο δὲ τῆς βάσεως αὐτοῖς σεισθείσης, εἰ μήτε ἀρχὴν ἔχοιεν μήτε μάχεσθαι ἀφορμήν. ἡ μὲν δὴ ἀρχὴ ἦν τὸ μὴ πλατωνικὰ λέγοντας αὐτοὺς ἐλέγξαι (fr. 25.83–99).

42. Cf. note 41 above, which respects Des Places's (and Leemans's) arrangement of the text.

43. οἱ Ἀκαδημαϊκοὶ γὰρ οὐκ ἐβάλλοντο ὑπ᾽ αὐτῶν opens with a roughly metrical parody of a Homeric hemistich, though the meter is soon lost.

44. See Jan Fredrik Kindstrand, *Homer in der zweiten Sophistik*, pp. 59–66.

Numenius *adapts* the vocabulary and style of Homer to his own needs, rising to a crescendo of Homeric bombast from which he eventually (but gradually) returns to his own more usual level of discourse. His technique has affinities with that of the *Batrachomyomachia* in that he juxtaposes his own decidedly non-heroic subject matter with the Homeric style and capitalizes on the distance between the heroic diction and the trivial disputes of the Academicians. Numenius also plays with the meter in subtle ways. He does not require full lines or, for that matter, complete sentences—his purpose is not to use Homer to support an argument or to display his own culture, but rather to exploit Homeric diction and its associations. If the line-ends are a bit confused and if the out-of-place ἐδνοπάλιζεν breaks the rules of the hexameter, still the dactylic rhythm is maintained and ἐδνοπάλιζεν does strengthen the Homeric flavor of the pastiche. After the last quoted hemistich, ὀλλύντων τε καὶ ὀλλυμένων, however, the words τῶν Στοϊκῶν *do* break the all-important rhythm, producing a "line" whose awkwardness reinforces the bathos of the descent from Homeric battle to Academic squabble.

As well as these and other *Iliad* citations and echoes, the fragments of the polemical history contain satiric hexameters borrowed from Ariston of Chios and from the *Silloi* of the Cynic Timon of Phlius,[45] an echo of Pindar,[46] and an anonymous tragic fragment.[47] These constitute the only true borrowings from earlier non-philosophical authors to be found in the surviving fragments of Numenius. The very strong suggestion is that Numenius knew a considerable body of poetry, including satiric poetry, and in this discrete section of his work could make excellent use of his culture, but that (with the exception of Homer) it was of no use to him when he was functioning not as an anecdotal historian but as a serious philosopher.

Numenius himself provides an observation on the sharp division of his activities into separate categories. Shortly after the passage of Homeric bombast cited above, he goes on to note that Zeno refrained from attacking Arcesilaus directly:

> Whether out of ignorance of Arcesilaus's theories or out of fear of the Stoics, he turned *from the great maw of bitter war* in another direction, on Plato. But I shall talk about the foul and irreverent fabrications of

45. Fr. 25, lines 21 and 6, respectively.
46. Fr. 25.151–52 echo *Isth.* 2.6.
47. Fr. 25.40 = *Trag. adesp.* 323 Nauck².

Zeno against Plato some other time, if I have leisure from philosophy, though I hope I never shall have the leisure—for this sort of thing, I mean—except as a diversion.[48]

Numenius explicitly characterizes as a game or "diversion" his witty, scandalmongering history, while the sphere of "philosophy," implicitly the serious pursuit of wisdom and truth, is kept quite separate. To these two spheres of activity correspond two very different literary styles, as well as different attitudes toward the literature of the past. The distinction itself demonstrates in an extreme form a divided approach to the cultural heritage that is visible also in Plotinus and Proclus.[49] The evidence of the satiric-historical fragments is admittedly scant, but it indicates a knowledge on Numenius's part of lyric and dramatic poetry, and beyond that of satiric poetry, that may have been considerable. Reinforced by the stylistic sophistication of the excerpts quoted, it is enough, in any case, to indicate that this Neopythagorean had a literary culture extending far beyond "sacred texts" and an ability to use that culture, whether to draw on it for quotation, to build a pastiche, or simply to provide him with models for the subtle and witty manipulation of the tone of his own discourse.

On the other hand, the fragments of Numenius's work *On the Good* (Περὶ τἀγαθοῦ) offer little hint of this culture but reveal another sphere of the writing of the past that Numenius knew well and approached in a significantly different manner. In the twenty-two fragments Des Places associates with this work, Numenius quotes or paraphrases Plato seven times, but there are no identifiable quotations from, or paraphrases of,

---

48. ἤτοι γὰρ ἀγνοίᾳ τῶν ἐκείνου ἢ δέει τῶν Στοϊκῶν

πολέμοιο μέγα στόμα πευκεδανοῖο

ἀπεστρέψατο ἄλλη, εἰς Πλάτωνα· ἀλλὰ καὶ περὶ μὲν τῶν Ζήνωνι εἰς Πλάτωνα κακῶς τε καὶ αἰδημόνως οὐδαμῶς νεωτερισθέντων εἰρήσεταί μοι αὖθίς ποτε, ἐὰν φιλοσοφίας σχολὴν ἀγάγω· μή ποτε μέντοι ἀγάγοιμι σχολὴν τοσαύτην, τούτου οὖν ἕνεκεν, εἰ μὴ ὑπὸ παιδιᾶς (fr. 25.126–32). Des Places's "si j'ai le loisir de philosopher" for ἐὰν φιλοσοφίας σχολὴν ἀγάγω is ambiguous and misleading, but the sense of the genitive after σχολή seems perfectly clear (cf. LSJ s.v. σχολή, I, 2). Numenius is *not* saying that he will return to this matter if his other concerns leave him time *for* philosophy, but just the opposite: he will return to his anecdotal history and fill in more details if he is not occupied by the more pressing demands of philosophy itself. The activity of the scandalmongering historian is one he clearly enjoys, but dismisses ultimately as a "game" (παιδιά).

49. See ch. 5D below at n. 59.

any other author. Beyond these, there are three references to Plato, one to Pythagoras, and one to Moses (or Musaeus).[50] Finally, the sources of the fragments attribute to Numenius in this work further references to Plato (several times), to Moses (three times), and to Jesus (once).[51]

There are no other significant bodies of fragments assignable to any single philosophical work of Numenius, but the sketchy picture provided here is adequate to the present purpose. The constant reference to Plato is not surprising, though the predominance of Plato over Pythagoras might seem odd in a thinker repeatedly designated as ὁ Πυθαγορεῖος.[52] The frequency of references to the Old Testament and the claim of acquaintance with the New Testament must be viewed in the light of the motives of the Christian apologists who preserved the fragments and provided the testimonia, but whatever distortion may arise from these sources, there can be no doubt that Numenius drew into his work material from the Jewish tradition. A direct quotation from Περὶ τἀγαθοῦ (in Eusebius) clarifies his motives and priorities:

> [With regard to theology] it will be necessary, after stating and drawing conclusions from the testimony of Plato, to go back and connect this testimony to the teachings of Pythagoras and then to call in those peoples that are held in high esteem, bringing forward their initiations and doctrines and their cults performed in a manner harmonious with Plato—those established by the Brahmans, the Jews, the Magi, and the Egyptians.[53]

50. On the confusion of Moses with Musaeus in fr. 9, or, more properly, the use of the name Μουσαῖος for the Jewish leader Moses (usually Μωσῆς), see Des Places *ad loc.*, fr. 9, n. 3 (p. 52). The problem is a puzzling one, and perhaps related to the development of the concept of Homer as a visionary sage. Another source cited by Eusebius in the same book of the *Preparatio evangelica* where the fragment of Numenius is preserved insists on the identification of Moses the Egyptian with the figure the Greeks call Μουσαῖος, who was the teacher of Orpheus. The ultimate source of the idea seems to be a Jewish historian Artapan, an Alexandrian of the second century B.C. Cf., on Homer and Moses, Jean Pépin, "Porphyre, exégète d'Homère," pp. 231–34.

51. Fr. 10a. Origen the Christian claims that Numenius "sets forth a story about Jesus without mentioning his name, and interprets it allegorically": ἐκτίθεται καὶ περὶ τοῦ Ἰησοῦ ἱστορίαν τινά, τὸ ὄνομα αὐτοῦ οὐ λέγων, καὶ τροπολογεῖ αὐτήν (fr. 10a = Orig. *Contra Cels.* 4.51).

52. E.g., frs. 1a, 5, 24, and 29. The imbalance in the references may well be a function of the Platonizing tradition that preserved the memory and the text of Numenius.

53. δεήσει εἰπόντα καὶ σημηνάμενον ταῖς μαρτυρίαις ταῖς Πλάτωνος ἀναχωρήσασθαι καὶ συνδήσασθαι τοῖς λόγοις τοῦ Πυθαγόρου, ἐπικαλέσασθαι δὲ τὰ

Plato, then, is a proximal witness to a truth earlier revealed to Pythagoras and expressed, perhaps less articulately, in the cult practices of certain non-Greeks. The attitude is one that is echoed repeatedly through the history of ancient Neoplatonism, but it is the influence of Numenius on Plotinus and, especially, on Porphyry that provides us with the earliest indication of its source within that school.[54] There is nothing new in Numenius's appeal to remote history for authoritative information; the innovation lies in the scope of the literature and the cultural source material he proposes to explore. This broad approach has led some scholars to assert that extensive "Eastern" influence can be seen in Numenius, though the more recent trend is to discredit these arguments and to point to Greek sources for many of the elements of his thought.[55]

It is clear that Numenius, in his role as philosopher, drew on a vast amount of earlier literature, Greek and non-Greek, in which he felt some direct revelation of absolute truth to be present. This category of writings has some overlap with the literature on which he drew in his role as historian, but it remains largely discrete. His use of this literature, or at any rate of some parts of it, was of a sort that is of particular interest in the present context. According to Origen the Christian, Numenius "did not shrink from using in his own writings the words of the [Jewish] prophets and treating them allegorically."[56] Origen has been cited above[57] using the same verb, τροπολογέω, to refer to the treatment of a New Testament story by Numenius. The verb occurs often in his writings but has virtually no existence in Greek outside the literature of Hellenizing Juda-

---

ἔθνη τὰ εὐδοκιμοῦντα, προσφερόμενον αὐτῶν τὰς τελετὰς καὶ δόγματα τάς τε ἱδρύσεις συντελουμένας Πλάτωνι ὁμολογουμένως, ὁπόσας Βραχμᾶνες καὶ Ἰουδαῖοι καὶ Μάγοι καὶ Αἰγύπτιοι διέθεντο (fr. 1a). As Merlan (CHLGEMP, p. 99) hints, this list is no more to be used as a basis for a claim of "orientalism" in Numenius than Diogenes Laertius's survey of the non-Greek roots of philosophy (1.1–2) is to be used to make an orientalizing thinker out of *him*.

54. Cf. Dillon, *Middle Platonists*, p. 378 and Des Places in Numenius, *Fragments*, pp. 22–23.

55. See esp. Dodds, "Numenius and Ammonius," for an attempt to define the "oriental element" in Numenius, and Henri-Charles Puech, "Numénius d'Apamée et les théologies orientales au second siècle," p. 754 (discussed below), on the belief on the part of some scholars that Numenius was a Jew.

56. οὐκ ὀκνήσας ἐν τῇ συγγραφῇ αὐτοῦ χρήσασθαι καὶ λόγοις προφητικοῖς καὶ τροπολογῆσαι αὐτούς (fr. 1b.6–8). On Origen's assessment of Numenius, see ch. 2C, below.

57. See n. 51 above.

ism and of Christianity.[58] There is no obvious difference in meaning between τροπολογέω and ἀλληγορέω, and a passage in which Origen uses
the two words together suggests that he makes little distinction between
them.[59] It seems quite unlikely that the word would have been used by
Numenius to refer to his own methodology, but the possibility that he
did use it cannot be eliminated. Whatever vocabulary he chose, however,
there can be no doubt that Numenius made use in his teachings of figu-
ratively or allegorically interpreted passages from the Old Testament and
possibly the New.

Porphyry provides us with an undoubted sample of this Old Testament explication when he mentions that the ancients "believed that souls
settled upon the water, which was 'god-inspired' as Numenius says,
adding that it is for this reason that the prophet said 'the Spirit of God
was moving over the face of the water.'"[60] It becomes clear in the re-
mainder of the passage that Numenius used Genesis 1.2 in association
with illustrations from the iconography of Egyptian religion and with
citations from Heraclitus to demonstrate that all these sources point to a
single truth about souls and their relationship to the material world. If
this was his manner of dealing with the literature of the Jews and the
iconography of the Egyptians, we may assume that he made similar use
of whatever Indian and Persian sources he had available. Here, however,
the sources that preserve the fragments are silent.

Numenius's approach to the literature he took to contain directly
revealed truth was not, however, limited to the search for *comparanda*
and the formulation of synthetic generalizations based upon multiple
sources. Perhaps the most revealing passage of Numenius for the light it
throws on his sophistication as a critic is the single fragment of the work
On the Secrets in Plato (Περὶ τῶν παρὰ Πλάτωνι ἀπορρήτων), fr. 23.
Numenius emerges here as the probable founder of a tradition of the in-

---

58. LSJ cites τροπολογέω in literature only for Aristeas—apparently the
Jewish historian of the second or early first century B.C. (cf. Franz Susemihl,
Geschichte der griechischen Litteratur in der Alexandrinerzeit, vol. 2, p. 651). Lampe
gives it extensive treatment, drawing most of his examples from Origen, but also
showing the word to have been in general use among the early Church Fathers.

59. κατηγορῶν τῆς Μωυσέως ἱστορίας αἰτιᾶται τοὺς τροπολογοῦντας καὶ ἀλ-
ληγοροῦντας αὐτήν (Orig. *Contra Cels.* 1.17). The subject is Celsus.

60. ἡγοῦντο γὰρ προσιζάνειν τῷ ὕδατι τὰς ψυχὰς θεοπνόῳ ὄντι, ὥς φησιν ὁ
Νουμήνιος, διὰ τοῦτο λέγων καὶ τὸν προφήτην εἰρηκέναι ἐμφέρεσθαι ἐπάνω τοῦ
ὕδατος θεοῦ πνεῦμα (fr. 30.3–6).

terpretation of the dramatic elements of the Platonic dialogues that survived at least until the end of Platonism in antiquity.[61]

Had he openly attacked the traditional stories that formed the core of the official religion, Numenius reasons, Plato would have given the Athenians reason to treat him as they had treated Socrates. His solution was to dramatize the critique in a cryptic dialogue:

> Since speaking the truth was more important to him than life itself, he saw that there was a way he could both live *and* speak the truth without risk: he made Euthyphro play the part of the Athenians—an arrogant twit and a remarkably bad theologian—and set Socrates against him in his usual character, confronting everyone he met just as he was accustomed to do.[62]

Eusebius, who transmits the fragment, has just quoted a passage from the *Euthyphro* and cites Numenius in the guise of commentary, introducing the citation with the pregnant remark, "Numenius clarifies the meaning [of Plato]."[63] It is often said that the Neoplatonic tradition of commentaries on the dialogues begins with Porphyry, in that sense the first scholastic. The method of teaching by commentary on existing texts was clearly much older,[64] however, and although we have no reason to believe that Numenius published commentaries on individual dialogues, nevertheless *On the Secrets in Plato* must have been made up of a series of commentaries on selected passages that posed specific problems—a procedure suggestive of the common approach to Homeric interpretation through a series of "problems" or "questions." This same work may, in fact, have included the commentary that Proclus indicates Numenius wrote on the myth of Er in the *Republic*,[65] and that commentary in turn

61. Cf. Dillon, *Middle Platonists*, p. 364.

62. ἐπεὶ δὲ ζῆν οὐκ ἂν προείλετο μᾶλλον ἢ ἀληθεύειν, ἑώρα δὲ ζῆν τε καὶ ἀληθεύειν ἀσφαλῶς δυνησόμενος, ἔθηκεν ἐν μὲν τῷ σχήματι τῶν Ἀθηναίων τὸν Εὐθύφρονα, ὄντα ἄνδρα ἀλαζόνα καὶ κοάλεμον καὶ εἴ τις ἄλλος θεολογεῖ κακῶς, αὐτὸν δὲ τὸν Σωκράτην ἐπ᾽ αὐτοῦ τε καὶ ἐν τῷ ἰδίῳ σχηματισμῷ ἐν ᾧπερ εἰωθότως ἤλεγχεν ἑκάστῳ προσομιλῶν (fr. 23.12–18). Cf., on Numenius's belief that the dialogues of Plato are cryptic, fr. 24.57–64.

63. Διασαφεῖ δὲ τὴν διάνοιαν ὁ Νουμήνιος (fr. 23.1).

64. Not only did the followers of Plato in the Academy teach by commentary on his works, but the Gnostics against whom Plotinus argued had their own commentary on the *Timaeus* (Puech, "Numénius d'Apamée," p. 778). There is some reason to believe that Posidonius (d. ca. 50 B.C.) wrote a commentary on the *Timaeus* (cf. Burkert, *Lore and Science*, p. 54, and n. 8 for references).

65. Proclus *In Rep.* 2.96.11.

was the probable original source of the core of the exegesis of *Odyssey* 13.102–12 transmitted by Porphyry.[66]

Whether or not this work contained the original version of the cave allegory, however, the fragment indicates a critical approach of an unprecedented sort. The dramatic form itself is conceived as an integral part of the structure of meaning of the work and examined for the light it can throw on the total meaning (the διάνοια, a word that, like English "meaning," combines the notions of thought and intention). The conclusion reached is rudimentary, even disappointingly obvious. It is clear enough that Numenius is correct to the extent that pretentious, muddleheaded Euthyphro represents the Athenian priestly establishment and, beyond that, the corresponding weaknesses of Athenian religion and religious thought. Numenius does not explicitly complete the equation: if Euthyphro "plays the part" of the Athenian people, then clearly Socrates on his side speaks for Plato. Here again, an approach that became basic to the later Platonic tradition is implicit in Numenius: when certain char-

66. Buffière realized that Numenius's goal in the original exegesis of the Homeric passage must have been the reconciliation of the Platonic and Homeric accounts of the fate of souls after death (*Mythes d'Homère*, pp. 442–44). Certainly the need of reconciliation was felt in his time. The *Suda* lexicon (s.v. Τήλεφος) attributes to the second-century grammarian Telephus of Pergamon a work entitled Περὶ τῆς Ὁμήρου καὶ Πλάτωνος συμφωνίας. Dillon (*Middle Platonists*, p. 364) believes Numenius's exegesis of Homer came from the commentary on the Myth of Er, mentioned by Proclus—an opinion that goes back at least to Puech ("Numénius d'Apamée," p. 748 and n. 2)—but for no obvious reason Dillon claims that this commentary "does seem to have been a separate work." Beutler ("Numenios," col. 678) considered it questionable whether it was a separate work or not. There seems to be no reason to believe that Numenius's exegesis of the *Republic* myth was a lengthy one, since we are told of no developed commentaries on dialogues or parts of dialogues, and it is tempting to believe that *On the Secrets in Plato* amounted to a collection of Numenius's most remarkable elucidations of exceptionally rich or exceptionally problematical passages in Plato. The fact that the one example we possess of the technique of interpretation used by Numenius in this work is rather unpretentious and far from the imaginative complexity of the cave allegory does not detract from this theory, since consistency of method is hardly to be expected. Both Porphyry's essay on the cave of the nymphs and Proclus's defense of Homer in his commentary on the *Republic* contain examples of the juxtaposition of widely different modes of exegesis and even of apparently mutually exclusive conclusions. An argument could also be made for *On the Good* as the source of the myth of Er commentary, which seems to follow the program laid out in fr. 1a of that work, but the same general program may have extended to *On the Secrets in Plato* as well.

acters speak in the dialogues—Proclus's list, for example, includes Parmenides, Socrates, and Timaeus—"then we take it that we are hearing the opinions of Plato."[67]

Though the results that we can measure directly are slight, Numenius's insistence on the expressive function of the total dialogue as a system of meaning may well lie behind the sophisticated attitudes toward the mimetic art of Plato developed by the later Neoplatonists.[68] These culminate in such formulations as an anonymous commentator's explanation of Plato's choice of the dialogue form: "He chose it, we say, because the dialogue is a kind of cosmos."[69] The commentator goes on to develop the analogy between the strata and hypostases of the Neoplatonic model of the cosmos and the characters, setting, style, manner, arguments, problem, and goal of the literary composition respectively.[70]

That Numenius interpreted the myth of Atlantis from the *Timaeus* and attached to it meanings that have little to do with the apparent intention of Plato's text emerges from a passage in Proclus's commentary on that dialogue (fr. 37). Numenius apparently explained the war between Athens and Atlantis as a battle between a superior group of souls, associated with Athena, and another group "concerned with generation" (γενεσιουργῶν) and consequently associated with Poseidon as the god presiding over γένεσις. To judge by Proclus's presentation of the interpretation, Numenius would appear to have taken this myth of Plato (and no doubt others as well) as a system of meaning comparable to the stories of Homer and to the symbols and doctrines of those non-Greek peoples whose value as sources of wisdom he asserted. It is difficult to say whether he made a distinction of kind between the mentality that produced the complex cryptic dramatic structures he apparently analyzed with some subtlety and the utterances of Egyptian priests and Greek bards.

67. τότε τῶν Πλάτωνος ἀκούειν ἡγούμεθα δογμάτων (Proclus *In Rep.* 1.110.16–17).

68. Cf. Proclus *In Rep.* 1.163–64 and James Coulter, *The Literary Microcosm*, pp. 101–3. Beutler ("Numenios," col. 668) lists Porphyry, Clement of Alexandria, Theodoret, and John Philoponus as authors echoing Numenius's belief that Plato "hints at second meanings" (αἰνίττεται).

69. λέγομεν τοίνυν ὅτι τοῦτο ἐποίησεν ἐπειδὴ ὁ διάλογος οἷον κόσμος ἐστίν (*Anonymous Prolegomena to Platonic Philosophy*, edited by L. G. Westerink, p. 152. Cited from Coulter, *Literary Microcosm*, p. 102 and p. 131).

70. See Coulter, *Literary Microcosm*, pp. 102–3.

Homer

As mentioned above, the evidence for Numenius's contribution to the exegesis of Homer comes exclusively from the Neoplatonists who used his interpretations, combined with others from sources that are sometimes revealed, sometimes not, to elaborate upon the meaning of various texts. Porphyry's essay on the cave of the nymphs is the most important source (frs. 30–33), followed by Macrobius's commentary on Scipio's dream in Cicero's *Republic* (fr. 34) and finally by Proclus's commentary on Plato's *Republic* (fr. 35). If we include Numenius himself, this chain extends from the time of Marcus Aurelius (or perhaps earlier) very nearly to that of Justinian, and the suggestion is very strong that Numenius's comparison and reconciliation of the views expressed by Homer and Plato on the fate of souls became an established (though not universally applauded) part of many later Platonists' understanding both of Plato's myth of Er (and with it even the parallel myth from the end of the *Republic* of Cicero) and of Homer's fiction.[71]

Although Porphyry's version is more attractive in that it integrates Numenius's explication of the myth into a broader examination of the Homeric passage, it is Proclus who appears to give the most complete account of what Numenius himself actually wrote on the subject. Furthermore, his overall tone of disapproval suggests that he is going through Numenius's exegesis point by point in order to give an account of its extravagances. The text is corrupt and the following translation avoids both the reconstruction offered by Buffière[72] and that of Festugière[73] in favor of a direct translation of the received text. A few Homeric phrases have been restored and the most problematical crux is indicated by a footnote.

Proclus is discussing the problem of locating the place of judgment described in the myth of Er in the *Republic* of Plato:

> Numenius says that this place is the center of the entire cosmos, and likewise of the earth, because it is at once in the middle of heaven and in the middle of the earth. There the judges sit and send off some souls to heaven, some to the region beneath the earth and to the rivers there. By "heaven" he means the sphere of the fixed stars, and he says there are two holes in this, Capricorn and Cancer, the one a

71. On the history of the exegesis of the cave of the nymphs and a possible pre-Numenian exegesis, see Appendix 4.
72. Buffière, *Mythes d'Homère*, p. 445, n. 23.
73. Cf. Des Places, *Fragments*, p. 86 (fr. 35, n. 6).

path down into γένεσις, the other a path of ascent, and the rivers under the earth he calls the planets, for he associates the rivers and even Tartarus with these, and introduces a further enormous fantasy with leapings of souls from the tropics to the solstices and returns from these back to the tropics—leapings that are all his own and that he transfers to these matters, stitching the Platonic utterances together with astrological concerns and these with the mysteries. He invokes the poem of Homer as a witness to the two chasms—not only when it calls

the one from the north a path for man to descend [*Od.* 13.110]

since Cancer brings to completion by advancing into Capricorn,[74] [and says]

the other, toward the south [is divine] [*Od.* 13.111, part],

through which it is impossible for men to [enter], for that path belongs exclusively to immortals [= paraphrase of *Od.* 13.111–12], since Capricorn, as it draws the souls upward, undoes their life in the human realm and accepts only the immortal and the divine—but also when it sings of

the gates of the sun and the people of dreams [*Od.* 24.12]

calling the two tropical signs the "gates of the sun" and the Milky Way the "people of dreams," as he claims. For he also says that Pythagoras in his obscure language called the Milky Way "Hades" and "a place of souls," for souls are crowded together there, whence among some peoples they pour libations of milk to the gods that cleanse souls, and when souls have just fallen into γένεσις milk is their first food. Furthermore, he claims that Plato, as mentioned, is describing the gates in speaking of the two "chasms" and that in describing the light that he calls the "bond of heaven" he is really referring to the Milky Way, into which souls ascend in twelve days from the place of the judges, for that place was in the center and, starting from there, the dodecad is completed in heaven. This consists of the center, the earth, water, air, the seven planets, and the fixed sphere itself. He claims the signs of the Tropics, the double chasms and the two gates are different only in name, and again that the Milky Way, the "light like a rainbow" and the "people of dreams" are all one—for the poet elsewhere compares disembodied souls to dreams. . . . But how could one accept the conflicts between this and what Plato himself has said? [*Proclus goes on to reject several points, including the conflation of the rivers of the underworld with the planetary spheres.*] Moreover, [Numenius] fills the Milky Way uniquely with souls that have gone up from here to heaven. [Plato] says that the fortunate souls do not go down to the underground

---

74. The implications of this bizarre and apparently corrupt sentence have led to various attempts at emendation.

place, while [Numenius] is forced to take them there first, if indeed it is necessary for every soul to go before the judges, and *then* to make them go to the heavenly place, where in fact the souls have their heavenly life.[75]

This outline of Numenius's ideas on the myth of Er, though it does not include all the supplementary details available in Porphyry and Ma-

75. Νουμήνιος μὲν γὰρ τὸ κέντρον εἶναί φησιν τοῦτον τοῦ τε κόσμου παντὸς καὶ τῆς γῆς, ὡς μεταξὺ μὲν ὂν τοῦ οὐρανοῦ, μεταξὺ δὲ καὶ τῆς γῆς. ἐν ᾧ καθῆσθαι τοὺς δικαστὰς καὶ παραπέμπειν τὰς μὲν εἰς οὐρανὸν τῶν ψυχῶν, τὰς δὲ εἰς τὸν ὑπὸ γῆς τόπον καὶ τοὺς ἐκεῖ ποταμούς· οὐρανὸν μὲν τὴν ἀπλανῆ λέγων καὶ ἐν ταύτῃ δύο χάσματα, τὸν αἰγόκερων καὶ τὸν καρκίνον, τοῦτον μὲν καθόδου χάσμα τῆς εἰς γένεσιν, ἀνόδου δὲ ἐκεῖνον, ποταμοὺς δὲ ὑπὸ γῆς τὰς πλανω-μένας (ἀνάγει γὰρ εἰς ταύτας τοὺς ποταμοὺς καὶ αὐτὸν τὸν Τάρταρον)· καὶ ἄλλην πολλὴν εἰσάγων τερατολογίαν, πηδήσεις τε ψυχῶν ἀπὸ τῶν τροπικῶν ἐπὶ τὰ ἰσημερινὰ καὶ ἀπὸ τούτων εἰς τὰ τροπικὰ καὶ μεταβάσεις, ἃς αὐτὸς πηδῶν ἐπὶ τὰ πράγματα μεταφέρει, καὶ συρράπτων τὰ Πλατωνικὰ ῥήματα τοῖς γε-νεθλιαλογικοῖς καὶ ταῦτα τοῖς τελεστικοῖς· μαρτυρούμενος τῶν δύο χασμάτων καὶ τὴν Ὁμήρου ποίησιν οὐ μόνον λέγουσαν τὰς πρὸς βορέαο καταιβατὰς ἀνθρώποισιν ὁδούς, ἐπείπερ ὁ καρκίνος εἰς †αἰγόκερων προσελθὼν ἀποτελεῖ· τὰς δὲ πρὸς νότον [εἶναι θειοτέρας], δι' ὧν οὐκ ἔστιν ἀνδράσιν [εἰσελθε]ῖν, ἀθανάτων δὲ μόνον ὁδοὺς αὐτὰς ὑπάρχειν· ὁ γὰρ αἰγόκερως ἀνάγων τὰς ψυχὰς λύει μὲν αὐτῶν τὴν ἐν ἀνδράσι ζωήν, μόνην δὲ τὴν ἀθάνατον εἰσδέχεται καὶ θείαν· οὐ ταῦτα δ' οὖν μόνον, ἀλλὰ καὶ ἡλίου πύλας ὑμνοῦσαν καὶ δῆμον ὀνεί-ρων, τὰ μὲν δύο τροπικὰ ζῴδια πύλας ἡλίου προσαγορεύσασαν, δῆμον δὲ ὀνείρων, ὥς φησιν ἐκεῖνος, τὸν γαλαξίαν. καὶ γὰρ τὸν Πυθαγόραν δι' ἀπορρήτων Ἅιδην τὸν γαλαξίαν καὶ τόπον ψυχῶν ἀποκαλεῖν, ὡς ἐκεῖ συνωθουμένων· διὸ παρά τισιν ἔθνεσιν γάλα σπένδεσθαι τοῖς θεοῖς τῶν ψυχῶν καθαρταῖς καὶ τῶν πεσουσῶν εἰς γένεσιν εἶναι γάλα τὴν πρώτην τροφήν. τὸν δὲ δὴ Πλάτωνα διὰ μὲν τῶν χασμάτων, ὡς εἴρηται, δηλοῦν τὰς δύο πύλας, διὰ δὲ τοῦ φωτός, ὃ δὴ σύνδεσμον εἶναι τοῦ οὐρανοῦ, τὸν γαλαξίαν· εἰς ὂν ἀνιέναι δι' ἡμερῶν δυοκαίδεκα τὰς ψυχὰς ἀπὸ τοῦ τόπου τῶν δικαστῶν· ἦν δὲ ὁ τόπος τὸ κέντρον. ἐντεῦθεν τοίνυν ἀρχομένην τὴν δυωδεκάδα τελευτᾶν εἰς τὸν οὐρανόν· ἐν ᾗ τὸ κέντρον εἶναι, τὴν γῆν, τὸ ὕδωρ, τὸν ἀέρα, τὰς ἑπτὰ πλανωμένας, αὐτὸν τὸν ἀπλανῆ κύκλον. εἶναι δ' οὖν τὰ τροπικὰ ζῴδια, τὰ χάσματα τὰ διπλᾶ, τὰς δύο πύλας ὀνόματι διαφέροντα μόνον, καὶ πάλιν τὸν γαλαξίαν, τὸ φῶς τὸ τῇ ἴριδι προσφερές, τὸν δῆμον τῶν ὀνείρων ταὐτόν. ὀνείροις γὰρ ἀπεικάζειν τὰς ἄνευ σωμάτων ψυχὰς καὶ ἄλλοθι τὸν ποιητήν. . . . [ἀλλὰ πῶς] ἄν τις ἀποδέξαιτο τὴν πρὸς τ[ὰς αὐτοῦ] τοῦ Πλάτωνος ῥήσεις αὐτοῦ διαφωνί[αν;]. . . . ὃ δὲ μόνον τὸν γαλαξίαν ἐκ τῶν ψυχῶν συμπληροῖ τῶν ἐντεῦθεν εἰς οὐρανὸν ἀναβεβηκυιῶν· καὶ ὁ μὲν τὰς εὐδαίμονας οὔ φησι χωρεῖν εἰς τὸν ὑποχθόνιον τόπον, ὃ δὲ ἄγειν ἀνα-γκάζεται πρῶτον εἰς ἐκεῖνον, εἴπερ πᾶσαν ψυχὴν εἰς τὸν δικαστὴν χωρεῖν πρῶτον δεῖ, ἔπειτα εἰς τὸν οὐράνιον τόπον ἀνελθεῖν, ὅπου γε διάγουσιν αἱ ψυχαὶ εὐδαιμόνως (Proclus *In Rep.* 2.128.26–130.14; 130.15–16; 131.8–14). The text is taken from Kroll, but is virtually the same as Numenius, fr. 35, as edited by Des Places.

crobius, is nevertheless a fairly strong indication that Numenius discussed the passage from Homer only casually, in the context of explicating Plato. The progress of the argument and the sequence of supporting and illuminating testimonia (Plato, astrology,[76] the mysteries, Homer, Pythagoras) and the focus on the harmony of the scattered revelations are reminiscent of the program for *On the Good* laid down in fr. 1a, where the search for the truth about the gods was to lead from Plato to Pythagoras and thence to the ritual and dogma of the Brahmans, Jews, Magi, and Egyptians.[77] Homer, then, would have been for Numenius a source of primitive revelation, comparable on the one hand with Pythagoras (who may have been seen by Numenius as a reincarnation of Homer, as he was by some Pythagoreans),[78] and on the other with the wisdom to be gleaned from the Old Testament, from Egypt, and from Persian astrology. There is no reason to believe that Numenius undertook a systematic exegesis of all or even part of the *Iliad* and *Odyssey*, but the Homeric corpus would appear to have bridged the chasm dividing his work: in the polemical history Homer was available for rhetorical pastiche, and in the serious philosophical works Homer provided a touchstone, a point of contact with a primitive revelation of the structure of reality and the fate of souls.

The attitude toward Homer that finds its fullest expression in Proclus is, then, already present in Numenius, though we have no basis for believing that Numenius articulated the complex theory of the Homeric text as a system of meaning that emerges in the later Neoplatonists. The essential point is that both perceived a single, absolute, static truth as having been revealed repeatedly and in different ways by a series of voices from the past—Homer, Pythagoras, and Plato among them. With

76. I.e., the wisdom of the "Magi" of fr. 1a (see n. 53 above).

77. Fr. 30, from Porphyry, follows a similar procedure, omitting Pythagoras, but explaining a doctrine by reference to the revelations of the Jews and the Egyptians.

78. Cf. Burkert, *Lore and Science*, p. 138, and Bailey's comments on Lucretius *De rer. nat.* 1.116, in vol. 2 of his edition, p. 619. Bailey bases a "complete" genealogy of the soul in question on Horace (*Odes* 1.28.9–13) and Persius (*Sat.* 6.10) and lists as the incarnations: (1) a peacock, (2) Euphorbus, (3) Homer, (4) Pythagoras, (5) Ennius. However "Pythagoras" was credited in the Hellenistic period with various attempts to define the poetic tradition by the mechanism of metensomatosis. Cf. Antipater of Sidon on Stesichorus:

οὗ, κατὰ Πυθαγόρεω φυσικὰν φάτιν, ἁ πρὶν Ὁμήρου
ψυχὰ ἐνὶ στέρνοις δεύτερον ᾠκίσατο.

Anth. Lyr. Gr. 7.75

his considerable rhetorical and literary acumen, Numenius clearly understood the subtleties of the various modes of discourse, but at the same time he looked *beyond* the rhetorical surface of certain texts, beyond their superficial meanings, for hints of new correspondences, new data to fill in the enigmatic coded picture of the absolute. There is a certain irony in the fact that Proclus, whose methods and attitudes in so many ways resemble those of Numenius, should be so intensely critical of his eclectic method here and should accuse him of introducing irrelevant astrological information and material from the mysteries. In the same work, Proclus himself, in fact, defends Homer against the Socratic attack by appeal to the mysteries.[79] There would seem to be some danger of being misled by Proclus's impatience here. He is not rejecting Numenius's method as a whole, but criticizing the passage at hand where certain elements—in particular the problem of the conflict of Numenius with Plato on the matter of the location of the place of judgment—present irreconcilable difficulties.[80]

As they emerge from Proclus's summary, the elements of the Numenian "interpretation" of the Homeric passages in question—the description of the cave of the nymphs at *Od.* 13.110–12 and the second *nekyia* at the opening of *Od.* 24—are the following:

1. The identification of the two gates of *Od.* 13.109–11 with:
    a. the two chasms of the myth of Er (though there is room for some confusion in the details of the comparison) (*Rep.* 10.614b8–c2)
    b. the astrological signs Cancer and Capricorn, taken respectively as the entrance and exit by which souls pass in and out of this world
    c. the "gates of the sun" of *Od.* 24.12
2. The identification of the "people of dreams" of *Od.* 24.12 with
    a. disembodied souls
    b. the Milky Way
    c. "the light that binds heaven" of *Rep.* 10.616c

The unavoidably Numenian elements supplementing these ideas preserved in Porphyry's essay on the cave of the nymphs are the claims that:

1. Homer refers—apparently at *Od.* 6.201—to certain souls as "wet," and means by this that they are in γένεσις (fr. 30)

79. Proclus *In Rep.* 1.110.21–112.12.
80. Cf., contra, Puech ("Numénius d'Apamée," p. 748), who paints a picture of blanket refutation and rejection of Numenius by the later Neoplatonists. There seems to be no doubt that his reputation was at its peak with Plotinus and Porphyry, but their prestige guaranteed the survival in later Neoplatonism of much that is Numenian.

2. The cave is an image and symbol of the cosmos (fr. 31)
3. Odysseus represents a man proceeding through the successive stages of γένεσις to regain his place among those who are beyond the material world; hence, for Homer as for Plato, water and waves were an image for the material world (fr. 33)

Several other points in Porphyry's essay are less securely linked to Numenius. The Pythagoreans, he tells us, used the name "Naiad Nymphs" for all souls descending into γένεσις, and also said that "souls cling to water." He then goes on to give what is explicitly Numenius's interpretation of Genesis 1.2 and the Egyptian iconography of gods riding on boats. There is no solid reason to believe that the connection of these ideas of Numenius with this particular passage of Homer existed before Porphyry, though it is quite likely that the connection was in fact made by Numenius himself (fr. 30).

The elaborate astrological summary and the *comparanda* from the rituals of the Romans and the Egyptians in fr. 31 may have come from Numenius's observations on the Homeric passage,[81] as may the discussion of the meaning of milk in rituals involving souls in fr. 32, but neither passage throws much light on his understanding of the meaning of the Homeric text itself, though they do provide further indication of the scope of Numenius's comparative approach.

Macrobius (fr. 34) does not mention Numenius by name, but Proclus's summary of Numenius's comments on the myth of Er, supplemented by the fragments from Porphyry, makes an ultimate Numenian source of Macrobius's ideas undeniable.[82] His discussion of the descent of souls *à propos* of Scipio's dream connects the account given there to the "divine wisdom of Homer" (*Homeri divina prudentia*) in the description of the cave, but vaguely refers the expression "gates of the sun" (*solis portas*, clearly the Ἡελίοιο πύλας of *Od*. 24.12) to the *physici*. He provides no further details of the specific relationship between the Homeric description that "represents" (*significat*) this transcendent reality and the reality itself.

The conclusion to which one is forced by the assembled unavoidably Numenian elements of the allegory is that Numenius's *response* to Homer was as divided as his *use* of Homer. There is a hint of close attention to

81. In the astrological material, however, one must suspect an interpolation. The argument at hand hardly necessitates a description and summary of the entire zodiac.
82. On this problem and others relating to the transmission of the allegory, see p. 270 below, and Appendix 4.

the text at fr. 31.24–26, where it is pointed out that the two gates are *not* attributed respectively to men and gods (θεοί) but to men and immortals (ἀθάνατοι), and that the latter term appropriately includes human souls. Nevertheless, this is one of the many points at which Porphyry switches from indirect to direct discourse in reporting Numenius's ideas, and I am inclined to believe that he is here offering his own observation and not that of Numenius. On the one hand, close attention to the text is else-where characteristic of Porphyry's essay; on the other, the point being made is one that may have bothered Porphyry more than it would have done Numenius—who, after all, was willing to identify human souls with the "spirit of God" (πνεῦμα θεοῦ) of Genesis 1.2 and with the "gods" (δαίμονες) of the Egyptians (fr. 30). Macrobius, relying on an ultimately Numenian source, claims that the "souls . . . [once disembodied] return to be counted among the gods" (*animae . . . in deorum numerum revertun-tur*), and Numenius's doctrines of the double soul (fr. 44) and of the in-corruptibility of the soul (fr. 29) leave room for virtual identification of individual human souls with gods. Porphyry, working from the basis of the more complex psychology of Plotinus,[83] may have been less likely to accept this identification uncritically, and so may have chosen to clarify the point by insisting upon the vocabulary of the passage.

In any case, this insistence on the meaning of ἀθάνατοι would be the only indication of close attention to the text in what remains of Nume-nius's strictly philosophical use of Homer. Elsewhere, he responds not to words or expressions but to *images* that catch the imagination: the gates of the sun, the people of dreams, the bizarre double cave; and then to elemental categories (here water and dampness). At the very least, Numenius stretched the puzzling διερός of *Od.* 6.201 into a claim that Homer associated "wetness" with the descent into γένεσις, and quite probably he made the connection mentioned above (pp. 70–71) and pro-vided Porphyry with the link between the dampness of the cave of the nymphs and its role as a symbol of the material world. He certainly be-lieved that Homer shared with Plato a basic association of the element of water with the material universe as opposed to the immaterial reality (fr. 33).

In fact, Numenius may well have been willing to change the text sub-tly to meet his needs, if indeed the substitution of πρὸς νότον for the usual πρὸς νότον of *Od.* 13.111 can be traced to him. The variant appears

83. In contrast to thinkers like Iamblichus, Plotinus did leave open the path for human souls to attain full participation in the divine. Cf. Dillon, *Middle Pla-tonists*, p. 219, on an interesting passage in Plutarch that anticipates this doctrine.

when the passage is quoted in Porphyry's essay and again in Proclus's paraphrase[84] and in both cases may come from Numenius.

In his search to define the constants in a series of literary statements regarding an elemental category, Numenius anticipates the activity of critics, such as Gaston Bachelard, who have tried to draw conclusions from the imagery of earth, air, fire, and water in a broad spectrum of literature. An obvious difference lies in the fact that Numenius believed in the absolute reality of the hidden archetype and viewed the various inspired utterances as ambiguous keys to it, whereas Bachelard's goal, the elucidation of the major lines of imagery, is far more humble. Both undertakings, though, share an impulse to define the meaning of the basic categories of the material world and both look beyond diction to search for meaning in images that express the relationship between the material and the human.

Sources

As mentioned above, Numenius is constantly referred to as a Pythagorean, and the evidence of the fragments (in spite of the predominance of references to Plato over references to Pythagoras) supports the epithet. It is extremely likely, then, that whatever use was made of Homer by earlier Pythagoreans was known to him, and it is surprising to find that very little that we know of his reading of Homer corresponds in any way to other interpretations passed down as Pythagorean. He is concerned, as the program of fr. 1a would lead one to expect, with establishing the concord of Pythagoras and Homer—that is, with demonstrating that the same truth is revealed by each, though in different terms. Proclus indicates that Numenius, in connection with his astrological elaboration on the cave of the nymphs, quoted Pythagoras as having used the expressions "Hades" and "place of souls" to refer to the Milky Way, "since souls gather together there."[85] The same doctrine is reflected in the version of Macrobius[86] and in that of Porphyry,[87] who attributes directly to

84. Proclus *In Rep.* 2.129.17.

85. καὶ γὰρ τὸν Πυθαγόραν δι᾽ ἀπορρήτων Ἅιδην τὸν γαλαξίαν καὶ τόπον ψυχῶν ἀποκαλεῖν, ὡς ἐκεῖ συνωθουμένων (fr. 35.26–28). For context, see n. 75 above.

86. Fr. 34.17–20. Macrobius here seems to conflate this idea with the related Pythagorean idea of the sublunary Hades. Cf. Burkert, *Lore and Science*, p. 367, and the references in his n. 93.

87. Fr. 32.6–9.

Pythagoras (without mention of Numenius) the doctrine that the Homeric "people of dreams" are souls gathered up into the Milky Way. This last doctrine is attributed by Proclus to Numenius (fr. 35.41–43). The question is simply whether (a) "Pythagoras," which is to say some pre-Numenian Pythagorean source, made the connection between the Homeric phrase and the Milky Way, and Numenius followed that source, or (b) the synthesis reported by Proclus is entirely the work of Numenius, who would thus independently have drawn together the Homeric image of the "people of dreams" (δῆμος ὀνείρων, Od. 24.12), the Platonic "column of light, like a rainbow" (φῶς . . . οἷον κίονα, μάλιστα τῇ ἴριδι προσφερῆ, Rep. 10.616b), and the Pythagorean equation of the Milky Way with Hades and its designation as a "place of souls" (τόπος ψυχῶν). In the latter case, Porphyry would loosely have attributed a Pythagorean doctrine, known to him through Numenius, to "Pythagoras" without giving credit to Numenius as its actual author. Since the sort of synthesis represented in Proclus's paraphrase of Numenius's commentary on the myth of Er seems characteristically Numenian—he clearly *was* concerned with establishing correspondences and wished to relate to Pythagorean principles elements from outside the received Pythagorean tradition—one is tempted to give Numenius full credit here (at Porphyry's expense) for making the reported connections, and to assume that no text of "Pythagoras" could be produced that referred to Homer in this context.

Whether or not Numenius is independent of earlier Pythagorean tradition in associating the Homeric δῆμος ὀνείρων with the Milky Way, the important point is that there is little beyond this to demonstrate that his reading of Homer was directly influenced by the treatment of Homer in Pythagorean tradition, however deeply colored by Pythagorean doctrine that reading may have been. Even if this element of the complex synthesis may be traceable to pre-Numenian Pythagoreanism, the arguments by which Armand Delatte[88] and Jérôme Carcopino[89] connect other parts of the exegesis transmitted by Porphyry to pre-Numenian Pythagorean tradition are based on little more than hypothesis. One viable possibility, though still not demonstrable, is influence in the form of a collection of traditional exegeses stemming from earlier Pythagoreanism. That such a tradition of interpretation existed can hardly be questioned. As I attempted to demonstrate in chapter 1, little of what may be

88. Delatte, Etudes sur la littérature pythagoricienne, p. 131.
89. Carcopino, De Pythagore aux apôtres, pp. 201–2.

called the "Pythagorean" interpretation of Homer is likely to predate
Plato, but much of it doubtless predates Numenius. The mechanism of
its transmission, however, remains a complete mystery.[90]

We remain in the dark with reference to Numenius's debts to earlier
Pythagoreanism in his exegesis of Homer in somewhat the same way that
we remain ignorant of Philo's debts to earlier Jewish tradition in his allegorical interpretation of the Old Testament. It seems highly unlikely,
however, that Numenius's approach to the relationship of Homer, Pythagoras, and Plato was entirely original with him. Much of what he says
could have its sources as early as the Old Academy. It is nevertheless clear
from his prestige and reputation that his grand synthesis was dynamic
and grasped the imaginations of many listeners and readers. Whether
his originality and personal creativity matched that dynamism remains a
frustrating and unsolved question.

The problem of the possible dependence of the exegetical thought of
Numenius on that of Philo is a doubly complex one. We have no evidence, on the one hand, that Philo's work was known or studied outside
the Jewish and, later, Christian communities. That Philo and the pagan
allegorists tap the same Stoic and Platonic traditions is universally accepted, and, given that their common background would explain all the
evident similarities between Philo's exegesis of the Old Testament and
the allegorical tradition of late paganism, and that no author in the pagan
tradition mentions Philo or his exegeses, it is nearly impossible to determine whether Philo did in fact have an influence outside the Jewish and
Christian communities.

Numenius would provide the perfect link; his knowledge of the Old
Testament is evident[91] and has led to the suggestion that he himself may
have been a Jew.[92] If Numenius not only had access to the literature of
Judaism but was himself a member of the thriving Jewish community of
second-century Apamea,[93] the probability that he was acquainted with
the allegorical method and writings of his Alexandrian predecessor
would be very great.

Unfortunately, however, there are no hard facts from which to work,
and few scholars have seen any positive reason to believe that Numenius
was a Jew. The fact that Origen applies the same verb, $\tau\rho o\pi o\lambda o\gamma\acute{e}\omega$, both

90. Cf. Delatte, *Littérature pythagoricienne*, p. 134.
91. Frs. 9, 10, 30, 56, and perhaps 13.
92. See Puech, "Numénius d'Apamée," p. 754.
93. See ibid., p. 750.

to Numenius's treatment of biblical stories[94] and to Philo's exegesis[95] is another tempting but inconclusive hint that the two were very close. It is possible to find striking *comparanda* in Philo for several images in the fragments of Numenius,[96] but in the absence of any demonstrable link between the two authors, they remain *comparanda* and nothing more.[97]

Conclusion

Before leaving Numenius, it should be asked whether any comprehensive theory of the relationship of language (and hence of literature) to reality can be deduced from the fragments. The emphasis on the mystery and ambiguity of texts and on the consequent necessity of explication for the understanding of the relationship of a text to the reality to which it refers emerges from the titles (e.g., Περὶ τῶν παρὰ Πλάτωνι ἀπορρήτων) as well as from the fragments and testimonia. Nothing indicates that Numenius approached this problem directly, however, and he may not have felt the need to articulate a conceptual framework for his activity in the form of a theory of the nature of the linguistic or literary sign.[98]

In a fragment from *On the Good*, there is, however, a hint that Numenius may have explored the meaning of language and its relationship to other phenomena:

—But what is being [τὸ ὄν]? Is it these four elements [στοιχεῖα], earth, fire, and the two in between? Are these themselves the things that are [τὰ ὄντα], either collectively [συλλήβδην] or individually?

94. Cf. notes 51 and 58 above.

95. Orig. *Contra Cels.* 5.55.

96. Cf. Des Places in Numenius, *Fragments*, fr. 2, n. 2, p. 104; fr. 4b, n. 4, p. 106.

97. Dillon, *Middle Platonists*, p. 144; cf. Pépin, "Porphyre, exégète d'Homère," p. 270, and Puech, "Numénius d'Apamée," p. 764 with n. 1, the latter for bibliography on scholars such as Guyot who positively affirmed an influence of Philo upon Numenius. For Sandmel's curious suggestion that Numenius actually mentioned Philo, see n. 31 above.

98. The statement (fr. 24.57–64) that Plato's writings were deliberately coded for political reasons has already been mentioned. In spite of the apparent similarity between Numenius's approach to the myths of Homer and his approach to the myths of Plato, this statement with regard to the dialogues seems to cover only that special case and *not* to provide a basis for constructing a general theory of meaning in literary texts.

—Come now, [How can you suggest this of] things that partake of γένεσις and change? Things that can be seen being born out of one another and undergoing change and having no real existence either as elements [στοιχεῖα] or as aggregates [συλλαβαί]?[99]

The hint is by no means obtrusive, but double meanings are extremely unlikely to be matters of chance in an author of Numenius's stylistic subtlety (one might even say preciosity). Karl Mras, the most recent editor of Eusebius, noted the word play and is followed by Des Places.[100]

Numenius's authoritative speaker builds on the ambiguity of the questioner's word στοιχεῖα (used since Plato for the "elements" of the universe and likewise for the primary sounds of Greek, its phonemes, and more loosely, for "letters" and the sounds they represent) and moves from the questioner's neutral adverb συλλήβδην "collectively," to the noun συλλαβή, which may refer, properly speaking, to any "collection" or "aggregate" but in practice had as early as Aeschylus been used primarily as a rough equivalent of its modern English descendant, "syllable."[101] Is this simply, as Mras put it, a "Witz"?

The implied metaphor suggests an equation that goes beyond the scope of a witticism: the elements of the material world are compared to the phonemes of a language, their compounds to aggregates of phonemes, or syllables. Syllables themselves are the building blocks of meaning in language, the beginnings of language as a structure of meaning.[102] If Numenius's authoritative speaker plays with the idea that language at its lower levels is organized like the cosmos, he surely suggests that the more complex structures are analogous as well, and that language as such provides a metaphor for the material world, itself the unstable, sublunary expression of a remote, permanent, and true reality.

99. ἀλλὰ τί δή ἐστι τὸ ὄν; ἄρα ταυτὶ τὰ στοιχεῖα τὰ τέσσαρα, ἡ γῆ καὶ τὸ πῦρ καὶ αἱ ἄλλαι δύο μεταξὺ φύσεις; ἄρα οὖν δὴ τὰ ὄντα ταῦτά ἐστιν, ἤτοι συλλήβδην ἢ καθ' ἕν γέ τι αὐτῶν;
καὶ πῶς, ἅ γέ ἐστι καὶ γενετὰ καὶ παλινάγρετα, εἴ γ' ἐστιν ὁρᾶν αὐτὰ ἐξ ἀλλήλων γιγνόμενα καὶ ἐπαλλασσόμενα καὶ μήτε στοιχεῖα ὑπάρχοντα μήτε συλλαβάς; (fr. 3.1–7).

100. Euseb. *Prep. ev.* 15.17.1, with Mras's note, vol. 2, p. 381, line 15: "ein Witz, der auf der Doppelbedeutung von στοιχεῖον (Element und Buchstabe) sowie auf der von συλλαβή (Zusammenfassung und Silbe) beruht." Cf. Des Places on fr. 3, n. 1, p. 105.

101. For both definitions and uses, see LSJ and Lampe.

102. In the *Cratylus* (389d–390a) Socrates envisions the συλλαβαί as the basic building blocks used by the nomothete in establishing the names of things.

C. CLEMENT AND ORIGEN

Although the chronology of the second- and third-century Platonists is
by no means firmly grounded, we may say with some certainty that the
careers of Clement and Origen roughly bridge the period between Numenius and Plotinus. This would make Clement a much younger contemporary of Numenius and not far distant in age from Ammonius Saccas, the teacher both of Plotinus and of Origen.[103]

Clement and Origen have a great deal in common with Philo and
Numenius, but as Christians they were alienated from these forerun-
ners, and the purpose of their writing is quite distinct. They will occupy
us here only to the extent that they throw light on attitudes toward Homer among philosophically inclined Christians at a time when the mystical allegorization of Homer was clearly becoming a characteristic part of
pagan Platonism.

The attitude of Clement toward Homer is far from simple, and indeed
appears fraught with contradictions. The influence of Philo's hermeneutics is everywhere apparent,[104] but Philo discussed only scripture, and
the status of the Homeric poems for Clement was not that of scripture
(though he cites the *Iliad* and the *Odyssey* over 240 times in his preserved
works). In Clement's view, Homer and the other early Greek poets, perceived as dependent on the Hebrew prophets, philosophized cryptically
in their poetry (δι' ὑπονοίας πολλὰ φιλοσοφοῦσιν).[105] Correct (that is,
Christian) doctrines were available to Homer, and some at least of his
mythic elaborations are viewed as shields for hidden, more acceptable,
truths. Nonetheless, Clement's attitude is far from the enthusiastic acceptance one might anticipate from some modern accounts.[106]

In his use of pagan culture, Clement has two central points, to which
he returns incessantly, and these are largely determinative of the picture
of Homer he presents. First and foremost, he is concerned to demonstrate the unworthiness—indeed, the nonexistence—of the pagan gods.

103. Ammonius Saccas must have had a long career, presiding over the education of Origen in the first decade of the third century and then over that of
Plotinus in the third. This is Dillon's chronology (*Middle Platonists*, p. 382).

104. See R. B. Tollinton, *Clement of Alexandria*, vol. 1, pp. 165–66, and vol. 2,
pp. 212–13, on Clement's debt to Philo, but note also Henri de Lubac's position
on the relationship between Philo and the Alexandrian Christian exegetes, discussed in ch. 6E below.

105. Clem. *Strom.* 5.4.24.1 = GCS 2.340.26.

106. See Hugo Rahner, *Griechische Mythen in christlicher Deutung*, pp. 243,
289.

Secondly, he wants to enhance the prestige of the Christian tradition and the texts on which it is based by showing that this same revelation penetrated, however dimly, to the most perceptive and authoritative of the pagans.

Taking the negative side first, in the *Protrepticus* of Clement we find a coherent portrait of Homer the poet, one clearly and rather surprisingly harkening back to Herodotus. Here again we find Homer the fashioner of gods (*Protrep.* 2.26.6), but now, of course, the purpose of the account is to discredit those gods and to undermine belief in them. The gods depicted by Homer were no gods at all—he himself calls them δαίμονες (*Protrep.* 4.55.4), insults them (*Protrep.* 7.76.1), and shows them to be wounded by mortals (*Protrep.* 2.36.1–2), committing adultery (*Protrep.* 4.59.1), and even acting as servants to mortals (*Protrep.* 2.35.2). Many of the offending passages are those singled out by Socrates, but the enumeration also seems occasionally to anticipate Proclus's somewhat expanded list of passages that must be explained through theurgy or allegory.[107]

The poet described in the *Protrepticus* is not himself in error, but the very nature of his account of the divine undermines belief—it is a poetic fantasy riddled with unacceptable notions. By contrast, the Homer of Clement's *Stromateis* (who is "said by most people to have been an Egyptian," *Strom.* 1.14.66.1) has glimmerings of truth. He erroneously claims that gods are perceptible to the human senses, and yet he simultaneously betrays a contradictory knowledge that this is *not* the case (*Strom.* 5.14.116–17 on *Il.* 22.8–10). He knows such doctrines as the sanctity of the seventh day (*Strom.* 5.14.107.3), the justice of God (*Strom.* 5.14.130), and the creation of man from clay (*Strom.* 5.14.99.4–6), and he even echoes Genesis on the separation of earth and water and the emergence of the dry land (*Strom.* 5.14.100.5 on *Il.* 14.206–7). Yet this Homer with his echoes of revealed truth remains essentially in darkness, a distant witness to the true revelation. He refers to Zeus as the "father of gods and men," but he is merely mouthing a formula, "knowing neither who the father is nor in what sense he is the father."[108]

These samples of Clement's treatment of Homer demonstrate that for this most Hellenizing, most receptive of the Fathers of the early Church,

---

107. A knowledge on Proclus's part of Clement's *Protrepticus* seems quite likely, and I do not doubt that a strong argument could be made that Proclus is responding indirectly to such critiques as this in his defense of Homer, though his ostensible and main goal is always to answer Socrates.

108. μὴ εἰδὼς τίς ὁ πατὴρ καὶ πῶς ὁ πατήρ (*Strom.* 6.17.151–52).

Homer was both an allegorical poet whose prestige might add to that of the Christian tradition and a participant in the revelation lying behind Christianity. But the limitations of Homer are crucially important. Homer perceived only dimly the truth of the revelation to the Jews. His poetic fictions are a "screen" ($\pi\alpha\rho\alpha\pi\acute{\epsilon}\tau\alpha\sigma\mu\alpha$): the term, so characteristic of Proclus, is used in Clement (*Strom.* 5.4.24.1) to refer to the poetry of Homer, Hesiod, Orpheus, Linus, and Musaeus. But that "screen" is misleading, false, and for all its beauty and ingenuity, Homer the allegorical poet, a visionary by heathen standards, is in fundamental points of doctrine profoundly wrong.

Clement is necessarily central to any understanding of the role of Homer in the thought of the early Christians, and although his Greek culture was certainly exceptional, and although the interpretive and philosophical traditions of Alexandria provided him with tools and attitudes not so readily accessible to Christians elsewhere, his combination of respect with criticism may be taken as typical. He saw in Homer an authoritative theological source for an inimical tradition who might be turned against that tradition and mustered to the new cause.

Origen, who appears to have learned much from Clement, nevertheless expresses a hostility to the pagans that contrasts markedly with Clement's own characteristic liberalism. The source of this may have been his experience of the persecutions of 202 in Alexandria (which Clement fled), but whatever its origin, it pervades his writings, and particularly the polemic *Against Celsus*, where allegorical interpretation of the obscenities of Homer and the other pagan theologians is denounced.[109] Still, the influence of Clement is inevitably felt. Homer is "the best of poets" ($\acute{o}$ $\tau\hat{\omega}\nu$ $\pi o\iota\eta\tau\hat{\omega}\nu$ $\acute{\alpha}\rho\iota\sigma\tau o\varsigma$, *Contra Cels.* 7.6), an author who may be taken as an authoritative source for the (benighted) pagan tradition, but Origen echoes Socrates' rejection of Homer and explicitly denies that Plato considered such poets inspired ($\acute{\epsilon}\nu\theta\epsilon o\iota$, *Contra Cels.* 4.36). Origen mentions the writings of an unnamed Pythagorean who wrote on the hidden doctrine of Homer and apparently used a complex demonology to explain some of the *Iliad*'s statements about the gods.[110] Since in other contexts he mentions Numenius several times with approval, it is tempting to identify the unnamed Pythagorean commentator as Numenius, but this identification remains far from certain. Numenius does, however, provide Origen with a valuable example of a pagan who

109. Origen *Contra Cels.* 6.42.
110. Origen *Contra Cels.* 7.6. On the identity of the Pythagorean, see Henry Chadwick's note *ad loc.* (*Origen: Contra Celsum*, p. 400, n. 2).

(in contrast to the "Epicurean" Celsus) read and studied the Hebrew and Christian scriptures and held them in respect "as writings that are allegorical and are not stupid" (ὡς περὶ τροπολογουμένων καὶ οὐ μωρῶν συγγραμμάτων, *Contra Cels.* 4.51). This is an interesting position, and one that in part anticipates Augustine. Origen and Augustine both find Pythagoreans and Platonists useful and, among the pagans, sympathetic. It is clear to Origen that, in Numenius's circle as in his own, to judge a piece of writing worthy of allegorical reading is to lend it dignity and importance—and he accepts this compliment to the scriptures. And yet, like Augustine, he is hostile to the defensive allegories of obscene myth, which he connects with the materialist Stoic/Epicurean tradition.

Origen is the only early Christian author known to me who makes explicit the analogy between the reading of Homer and the reading of the Gospels. He considers Homer to be largely historically accurate, but to incorporate fantastic elements that are to be interpreted allegorically. This sort of reading is simply a matter of open-mindedness for Origen, and he demands the same open-mindedness of pagan readers of the Gospels:

> He who approaches the stories [i.e., the Greek myths, including Homer's account of the Trojan War] generously and wishes to avoid being misled in reading them will decide which parts he will believe, and which he will interpret allegorically, searching out the intentions of the authors of such fictions, and which he will refuse to believe, and will consider simply as things written to please someone. And having said this, we have been speaking, in anticipation, about the whole story of Jesus in the Gospels. We do not urge the intelligent in the direction of simple and irrational faith, but wish to advise them that those who are going to read this story need to be generous in their approach and will require a great deal of insight and, if I may call it that, power of penetration into the meaning of the Scriptures in order that the intention with which each passage was written may be discovered.[111]

111. ἀλλ' ὁ εὐγνωμόνως ἐντυγχάνων ταῖς ἱστορίαις, καὶ βουλόμενος ἑαυτὸν τηρεῖν καὶ ἐν ἐκείναις ἀνεξαπάτητον, κρινεῖ, τίσι μὲν συγκαταθήσεται, τίνα δὲ τροπολογήσει, τὸ βούλευμα ἐρευνῶν τῶν ἀναπλασαμένων τὰ τοιάδε· καὶ τίσιν ἀπιστήσει, ὡς διὰ τὴν πρός τινας χάριν ἀναγεγραμμένοις. καὶ τοῦτο προλαβόντες δι' ὅλην τὴν φερομένην ἐν τοῖς Εὐαγγελίοις περὶ τοῦ Ἰησοῦ ἱστορίαν εἰρήκαμεν, οὐκ ἐπὶ ψιλὴν πίστιν καὶ ἄλογον τοὺς ἐντρεχεστέρους ἐκκαλούμενοι, ἀλλὰ βουλόμενοι παραστῆσαι, ὅτι εὐγνωμοσύνης χρεία τοῖς ἐντευξομένοις, καὶ πολλῆς ἐξετάσεως, καὶ (ἵν' οὕτως ὀνομάσω) εἰσόδου εἰς τὸ βούλημα τῶν γραψάντων, ἵν' εὑρεθῇ, ποίᾳ διανοίᾳ ἕκαστον γέγραπται (*Contra Cels.* 1.42 [end]; cf. ibid., 4.38, where the Genesis account of the origin of women is compared to Hesiod's).

The analogy between the reading of pagan mythic tales and the reading of the scriptures turns on the quality of εὐγνωμοσύνη (which I have translated as "generosity"), a right-mindedness that is also an openness to the text and a willingness to acknowledge levels of meaning within it, and at the same time to withdraw belief from that which is entirely unacceptable without rejecting the rest.

Origen stands at a considerable distance from Philo in his assessment of the Hebrew scriptures. For Origen, the literal meaning was at times unacceptable, with serious consequences for the credibility of the Jewish tradition.[112] He thus faced a problem precisely analogous to that of his younger pagan contemporary Porphyry with respect to Homer. The pagan exegesis of Homer and the Christian exegesis of scripture (and particularly the Hebrew scriptures) developed in parallel from this point, until several centuries later the author of the Dionysian corpus applied to the Hebrew scriptures precisely the methodology (based on precisely the same philosophical presuppositions) that his own pagan model, Proclus, had applied to the *Iliad* and *Odyssey*.[113]

112. See Chadwick in CHLGEMP, p. 183.

113. There are dozens of citations of Homer in *Against Celsus*, conveniently catalogued by Marcel Borret in the *Sources chrétiennes* edition. For the most part, they derive from Celsus and are of only secondary interest to Origen, but the quoted lines are often significantly embedded in Stoic allegories. For example, Zeus's words to Hera are the divine λόγοι addressed to matter (*Contra Cels.* 6.42). Still, one is impressed with a generous sense of the compatibility of the two traditions, if only a few essential corrections of Celsus's errors are made, including rearrangement for the "correct" historical sequence, which makes Moses older than Homer (*Contra Cels.* 6.43). Given the primacy of the Jewish tradition, Origen then quotes Homer's account of Calchas's privileged knowledge (*Il.* 1.70: ὃς ἤδει τά τ' ἐόντα. . . .) and attributes such knowledge to Moses (*Contra Cels.* 4.55). More characteristically, though, many lines are quoted in Celsus's own contexts only to be refuted. For example, Origen strikingly quotes two lines from Achilles' disillusioned speech in *Il.* 9 (319–20),

> ἐν δὲ ἰῇ τιμῇ ἠμὲν κακὸς ἠδὲ καὶ ἐσθλός·
> κάτθαν' ὁμῶς ὅ τ' ἀεργὸς ἀνὴρ ὅ τε πολλὰ ἐοργώς,

to *deny* their truth and assert that "in God" these things are not true (*Contra Cels.* 3.69).

III

Plotinian Neoplatonism

A. PLOTINUS

Language and Literature

Though the history of Neoplatonism starts, properly speaking, with Plotinus (205–70),[1] what we have called the Neoplatonic reading of Homer had its sources in habits of thought developed long before the third century and found full expression not in Plotinus himself but in Porphyry and then in the later Neoplatonists. Plotinus never mentions the name of Homer[2] and is very little concerned with interpretation of texts and myths from the poets. In the relatively sparse echoes of Homer and of other poetry in the *Enneads*, he does, however, make it clear that his knowledge of literature was substantial and his sensitivity to poetic language and imagery very great.[3] He likewise shows evidence of many of the attitudes that were to emerge more clearly in Porphyry and in the later Neoplatonists, including a willingness to see in the myths of the

1. Plotinus himself does not distinguish between his own thought and earlier Platonism, but the absence of major Platonic thinkers in the period immediately preceding his own, combined with his evident originality and the clear differences between Plotinian Platonism and the thought transmitted in the dialogues of Plato, make the term "Neoplatonism" a useful tool. Whatever the debts of the Neoplatonic reading of Homer to the Old Academy and to "Middle Platonism," it would be misleading to qualify simply as "Platonist" a tradition of textual interpretation of which there is scarcely a trace in Plato.

2. He designates Homer at three points, using the expression ὁ ποιητής once (*Enn.* 1.1.12.31) and twice referring vaguely to οἱ ποιηταί where the context makes it clear that Homer is meant (*Enn.* 5.5.8.6; 6.7.30.29).

3. See Vincenzo Cilento, "Mito e poesia nelle *Enneadi* di Plotino," the most important study of this aspect of Plotinus, but also note Jean Pépin, "Plotin et les

early poets complex structures of meaning expressing a reality far removed from the superficial sense.[4]

A summary of Plotinus's thought lies far beyond the scope of this
study, and so, a fortiori, does an examination of the sources of that
thought.[5] It should be noted, however, that no internal evidence will lead
us to the sources of Plotinus's attitude toward Homer, for the simple reason that Plotinus mentions by name no thinker more recent than Epicurus. Whatever the importance of preclassical and classical commentators in the early development of the idea of the structure and meaning of
the poems that we see elaborated among the Neoplatonists, the critical
stages of that development are postclassical and fall within the period of
over 500 years to which Plotinus does not acknowledge any debts.[6]

Porphyry supplements our knowledge of the proximal influences on
Plotinus, however, mentioning his period of study at Alexandria, along
with Erennius and Origen, under the mysterious Ammonius Saccas[7]
and offering a list of some of the authors Plotinus had read aloud for discussion during his lectures: Severus, Cronius, Numenius, Gaius, At-
ticus, Aspasius, Alexander, and Adrastus.[8] The last three are designated
Peripatetics and the first four names belong to second-century Platonists
and Pythagoreans. The striking name is, of course, that of Numenius,
and we know further from Porphyry that Plotinus's doctrines, at least to
outsiders, seemed so close to those of Numenius that he was accused of
plagiarism, with the result that Amelius wrote a treatise defending Plotinus against the charge.[9]

Finally, Porphyry quotes Longinus's opinion that Plotinus "submitted
the Pythagorean and Platonic principles, so it seems, to a clearer explanation than those before him, for not even the writings of Numenius,

---

mythes." To Pépin goes the credit for first systematically calling attention to the
extensive, if secondary, role of allegorized myth in the *Enneads*.

4. On Plotinus remembered as a thinker who understood the myths sym-
bolically, see Paul Henry, *Plotin et l'occident*, pp. 197–98.

5. The most useful modern general studies are those of A. H. Armstrong,
The Architecture of the Intelligible Universe in the Philosophy of Plotinus, and "Plotinus" in CHLGEMP, as well as J. M. Rist, *Plotinus: The Road to Reality*. R. T. Wallis
provides a valuable concise summary (*Neoplatonism*, ch. 3).

6. Epicurus died ca. 270 B.C. All of Plotinus's writings belong to the 250s and
260s of our era.

7. Porph. *Vit. Plot.* 3 (and cf. 14); on Ammonius, see Dodds, "Numenius and
Ammonius," pp. 24–32.

8. Porph. *Vit. Plot.* 14; on these figures, see Dillon, *Middle Platonists*.

9. Porph. *Vit. Plot.* 17.

Cronius, Moderatus, and Thrasyllus come close in precision to those of Plotinus on the same subjects."[10] None of these observations guarantees the influence of Numenius and Cronius on Plotinus's understanding of the meaning of the *Iliad* and *Odyssey*, but they do serve to establish that he was aware of these second-century interpretive efforts. It is quite possible that, if we knew more about the other second-century Platonists listed by Porphyry as included in the canon read in Plotinus's circle, we would discover that they also shared a tendency to elaborate upon the meanings of the revelations of the θεολόγοι. The fact that we again have good reason to suspect a second-century source for some of the attitudes in question does, however, add to the attractiveness of the theory that that period was crucial for the development of the conception of the meaning of Homer under consideration. The fact that Plotinus was an Egyptian, educated at Alexandria, might also point to a possible influence by Philo, but there is no substantial basis on which to claim such influence.[11]

In spite of the fact that Plotinus cannot be said to have made a substantial contribution to the history of the interpretation of Homer, an examination of his references to the *Iliad* and *Odyssey*, along with some discussion of his understanding of the structures of meaning of linguistic and literary signs, will be useful as background to later developments.

If we examine the language of Plotinus against the background of the language of Plato, the differences between the two thinkers on the level of expression appear so great at first that the profound dependence of Plotinus on Plato is obscured. The peculiar quality of the literary remains of Plato must, of course, be taken into consideration;[12] what we have is not his teaching, properly speaking, but a collection of formal compositions dramatizing that teaching, or some part thereof, in a manner that cultivates irony and ambiguity to such a degree that few dogmatic statements occur that are not elsewhere contradicted. Vast areas of central concern are passed over in silence or treated mythically rather than dialectically.

10. ὃς μὲν τὰς Πυθαγορείους ἀρχὰς καὶ Πλατωνικάς, ὡς ἐδόκει, πρὸς σαφέστεραν τῶν πρὸ αὐτοῦ καταστησάμενος ἐξήγησιν· οὐδὲ γὰρ ἐγγύς τι τὰ Νουμηνίου καὶ Κρονίου καὶ Μοδεράτου καὶ Θρασύλλου τοῖς Πλωτίνου περὶ τῶν αὐτῶν συγγράμμασιν εἰς ἀκρίβειαν (Porph. *Vit. Plot.* 20.71–76).

11. Cf. Armstrong, *Architecture of the Intelligible Universe*, pp. 70–74. Attempts have been made to link the λόγος doctrine of Plotinus to that of Philo by way of Numenius, and many studies have pointed to striking similarities between the two thinkers. Cf. Rist, *Plotinus*, p. 84.

12. Cf. E. N. Tigerstedt, *Interpreting Plato*, pp. 96–101.

The literary remains of Plotinus, on the other hand, appear approximately to reproduce his oral teachings and constitute essays in the modern sense of attempts to grasp and treat a given subject with some thoroughness. The primary difference lies in Plotinus's treatment of the areas Plato passes over in silence or treats mythically. Plotinus is not mythopoeic and thus that colorful possibility is eliminated. Neither does he mistrust language—written language—in the way Plato does, though he is intensely aware of the limitations of all language. His silences are never willed. Rather, he performs repeated assaults upon them. In R. T. Wallis's words, "In contrast to Plato, Plotinus's treatises exhaust the resources of language in endeavoring to attain successively closer approximations to what remains finally inexpressible."[13] The net effect is a prose so dense, elliptical, and difficult in its sinewy compression that Longinus, with perfect copies before him, was convinced that scribal carelessness had rendered them useless.[14] At the same time, however, this prose is rich in images of amazing beauty, which attempt to carry the reader over from the day-to-day experience of life to the experience of the essences or "hypostases" that for Plotinus were the true reality beyond the insubstantial and fragmented mask of the material universe.[15] Some of these images are apparently original, but some are borrowed, quite often from the imaginatively charged world of the *epea* of Homer and Hesiod.

To this extent, Plotinus's own use of language explains his relationship to the poetry of the past. Beyond this, however, his understanding of the relationship of language to reality can also throw some light on his contribution to later Platonic thought concerning the structures of meaning in language and literature.

The interrogation of the sounds of words for keys to the nature of the things they represent is not a central concern in the *Enneads*. Nevertheless, Plotinus makes it clear that the sounds of language—the Greek lan-

13. Wallis, *Neoplatonism*, p. 41. Cf. *Enn*. 6.9.3–4.

14. Porph. *Vit. Plot*. 19–20.

15. The procedure often lends to Plotinus's prose a power and beauty that draw him closer to Dante or Milton than to more obviously comparable authors. The magnificent simile of the fisherman's net in the sea (*Enn*. 4.3.9.38–48) illustrating the relationship of the material universe (the net) to soul (the sea) has perhaps its closest analogy in the similes of Milton, proceeding from the material and familiar to a statement about reality on a level at once abstract and removed from everyday experience. On Plotinus's imagery, see R. Ferwerda, *La Signification des images et des métaphores dans la pensée de Plotin*, passim, and esp. pp. 70, 75–76, 84, and 101. A comparable development of the simile in an author close to Plotinus's time may be found in Maximus of Tyre.

guage—are indeed bound up in the very structure of reality (*Enn.* 5.5.5), and he makes prominent use of several supposed etymologies. The most striking of these is the derivation of the name Κρόνος from κόρος, "satiety," and νοῦς, "mind,"[16] mentioned or alluded to on at least four occasions,[17] in support of Plotinus's radical interpretation of Hesiod's genealogical myth, discussed below.[18] It is striking that there was a Platonic precedent (*Crat.* 396b), however flippant, for an explanation of this name, but Plotinus appears to ignore that etymology entirely in favor of one that may well have been developed in Latin (*Saturnus* from *satur*) and thence translated into Greek.[19] Elsewhere, he alludes to etymologies from the *Cratylus* to explain δαίμων,[20] σῶμα,[21] οὐσία,[22] and Ἅδης,[23] and often plays on words and their sounds and meanings, drawing in etymologies from various sources.[24]

The relationship of the elements of the vocabulary of spoken language, however, constitutes a less suggestive sphere of inquiry for Plotinus than the role of language itself as a mediator between a spiritual and a physical reality. It is axiomatic for Plotinus that the order we observe in the material universe is the expression of a non-spatial, unchanging reality. An image used tentatively to express this relationship is that of the natural world as the mirror, itself devoid of form, of the ordering principles emanating from the higher realities of soul (ψυχή) and mind (νοῦς), beyond which lies the One (τὸ ἕν) (*Enn.* 1.1.8). This triadic structure, extending from the ultimate reality of the One to the unreality of matter, is described as a series of essences or hypostases, each in some sense recapitulating the hypostasis previous to it. It is language that provides the metaphor for the transitions, the process by which principles of order—λόγοι—pass from mind to soul and beyond soul into matter:

> For as the language [λόγος] spoken by the voice is an imitation [μί-μημα] of that in the soul, in the same way that one in the soul is an imitation of the one in the other [hypostasis, mind]; likewise, just as

16. Cf. Buffière, *Mythes d'Homère*, pp. 533–44.

17. *Enn.* 3.8.11.38–41; 5.1.4.8–10; 5.1.7.33–36; 5.9.8.8.

18. See pp. 104–6 below.

19. See Pierre Courcelle, *Les Lettres grecques en occident de Macrobe à Cassiodore*, pp. 162–63, and Cilento, "Mito e poesia," p. 253.

20. *Enn.* 6.7.6.32–33; *Crat.* 398b.6.

21. *Enn.* 4.4.22.33; 4.8.1.31; 5.9.5.46; *Crat.* 400c. Two of these passages connect σῶμα with σώζω, one with σῆμα.

22. *Enn.* 5.5.5.18–25; 6.2.8.7–8; *Crat.* 401c.

23. *Enn.* 6.4.16.37; *Crat.* 403a.

24. E.g., the meditation on Ἔρως in *Enn.* 3.5.3.

the language pronounced by the lips is fragmented [into words and sentences] in contrast to that in the soul, so is the one in the soul (which is the interpreter of that previous language) fragmented by comparison with the one that precedes it.[25]

This is a central passage for the λόγος doctrine of Plotinus, a doctrine that bears a considerable resemblance to ideas of Philo and is somewhat reminiscent of the λόγος doctrine of John the Evangelist. It provides a model that, by using the metaphor of human language to account for the relationships of the higher realities among themselves and to the world as we know it, establishes human utterance as a central fact within that complex structure and gives it enormous importance as a bridge, a manifestation or expression of a more perfect realm in the context of a more fragmented one. Though this model is not transferred explicitly to the evaluation of the structures of meaning within human utterance—to sentences, poems and the like—it nevertheless enhances the dignity of all human utterance and at least potentially provides a precedent for a view of certain kinds of human utterances as privileged and complex expressions of a higher reality.[26] The word λόγος in later Platonism can rarely be translated as "word" or "language" and yield satisfactory meaning.[27] The metaphorical and abstract senses, "reason principle," "principle of order," and so forth, entirely displace the root meaning. The great value of the passage just quoted, however, is its binding of that vast metaphorical structure securely to its basis in the relationship of the whole, entire, inarticulate λόγος of mind, imitated by the soul, with the fragmented, articulated λόγος that soul projects into the sense-world.

It is clear that the λόγοι take the form of articulate sounds (φωναί) only on this level and that reasoning (λογισμός) in the higher spheres will take some other form. "I certainly do not think we are to imagine souls when within the sphere of the intelligible using words," says Plotinus. "They would grasp [communications] from each other by [sponta-

---

25. ὡς γὰρ ὁ ἐν φωνῇ λόγος μίμημα τοῦ ἐν ψυχῇ, οὕτω καὶ ὁ ἐν ψυχῇ μίμημα τοῦ ἐν ἑτέρῳ. ὡς οὖν μεμερισμένος ὁ ἐν προφορᾷ πρὸς τὸν ἐν ψυχῇ, οὕτω καὶ ὁ ἐν ψυχῇ ἑρμηνεὺς ὢν ἐκείνου πρὸς τὸ πρὸ αὐτοῦ (Enn. 1.2.3.27–30).

26. See ch. 5B below.

27. The same statement could be made for the earlier history of the word λόγος, which had the fully developed (though secondary) meaning of "reason" by the fifth century B.C. What is characteristic of Neoplatonism is the new concept of the λόγος as mediator between hypostases (and later, between subdivisions of hypostases) and the explicit relationship of this λόγος to human speech.

neous, mutual] understanding, since even here in this world we can grasp many unspoken things through the eyes."[28]

This is exactly the process we see at work in Dante's *Paradiso* as articulate speech gradually becomes unnecessary and communication is increasingly accomplished by means of spontaneous understanding or telepathy. In this sense, the metaphor of speech is maintained at the higher levels at least to the extent that we imagine them as inhabited by individualized entities. Only the physical trappings of language—the articulated sounds—are excluded. The fact remains, however, that λόγοι issuing from mind would not be recognizable as language. Plotinus's demonology anticipates developments in later Neoplatonism when he asserts that in spite of the fact that at higher levels of reality speech becomes superfluous, "it is not illogical that δαίμονες and souls in the air should make use of speech, for such creatures are living beings."[29]

Leaving the metaphor of the λόγος to return to the complexities of human speech itself, one more point should be made regarding Plotinus's theoretical consideration of language. At the same time that he assaulted the necessary silences in the description of the higher realities, he also affirmed the inherent incapacity of human language to express truths about ultimate reality. In a magnificent passage—which can be read as an evocation of a scene in the *Odyssey*[30]—Plotinus asks first how any experience can be had of a reality beyond mind, and then rejects discursive understanding, which necessarily moves from point to point: "The same is true of discursive description [extended in time]. In that which is totally simple, what discursive description can there be?"[31] The contact with that reality is therefore ineffable: "One must trust that one

28. οὐδὲ δὴ φωναῖς, οἶμαι, χρῆσθαι νομιστέον ἐν μὲν τῷ νοητῷ οὔσας [sc. τὰς ψυχάς] . . . γινώσκοιεν δ' ἂν καὶ τὰ παρ' ἀλλήλων ἐν συνέσει. ἐπεὶ καὶ ἐνταῦθα πολλὰ σιωπώντων γινώσκοιμεν δι' ὀμμάτων (*Enn.* 4.3.18.13–20).

29. περὶ δὲ διαμόνων καὶ ψυχῶν ἐν ἀέρι φωνῇ χρῆσθαι οὐκ ἄτοπον· ζῷα γὰρ τοιάδε (*Enn.* 4.3.18.22–24).

30. Cilento, "Mito e poesia," p. 286, sees in *Enn.* 5.3.17.29–33 a reference to *Od.* 19.33–40, but this conclusion has apparently been rejected by Henry and Schwyzer, who omit this reference from their *index fontium*. In Plotinus, someone *summons* the illuminating deity—and this suggests some sort of theurgy—whereas in the *Odyssey* we hear only of Odysseus "contriving" the slaughter of the suitors with Athena (*Od.* 19.2) as preparation for her role as torchbearer. Some readers, though, would doubtless have perceived a Homeric echo here.

31. οὕτω γὰρ καὶ διέξοδος· ἐν δὲ πάντη ἁπλῷ διέξοδος τίς ἐστιν; (*Enn.* 5.3.17.24–25).

has seen it when the soul is suddenly illuminated, for this light is from it and casts illumination just as another deity did when called by a man into his house."[32]

This is the basis of the so-called "negative theology"—the affirmation of the incapacity of discursive language, because of the fragmentation inherent in its structure, to make any meaningful representation of the ultimate reality. There are, properly speaking, no statements that can be made concerning the One, no predicates that can be applied to it. For Plotinus, this includes even the predicate "exists." There are no λόγοι of the One, inasmuch as it is ultimately indifferent to the realities of which it is the source.[33] Yet there is a relationship (no longer a language because it has neither form nor content) requiring a new metaphor—that of illumination, of visual overload. It is visual experience without content that provides the metaphor for that final, ineffable moment. That metaphor was to have a long future, both among mystics and among poets.[34]

Homer

By my calculation there are in the works of Plotinus approximately twenty-eight passages, most of them very brief, in which some recognizable allusion is made to the content or language of the Homeric poems.[35] Four other passages allude to Hesiod[36] and will be discussed here for the light they can throw on Plotinus's attitude toward early poetry in general.

The decorative use of Homeric phrases and diction, frequent in later Greek prose and already encountered in a colorful form in Numenius, has a part in Plotinus's style as well. Unlike Numenius, Plotinus does not

32. τότε δὲ χρὴ ὡρακέναι πιστεύειν, ὅταν ἡ ψυχὴ ἐξαίφνης φῶς λάβῃ· τοῦτο γὰρ [τοῦτο τὸ φῶς] παρ' αὐτοῦ καὶ αὐτός· καὶ τότε χρὴ νομίζειν παρεῖναι, ὅταν ὥσπερ θεὸς ἄλλος [ὅταν] εἰς οἶκον καλοῦντός τινος ἐλθὼν φωτίσῃ (Enn. 5.3.17.28–32). I have taken the liberty of ignoring the gender of ἄλλος and ἐλθών in order to restore the reference to the Odyssey Cilento sees in the passage (see n. 30 above).

33. In Christian Neoplatonism, however, Christ becomes the λόγος of the supreme God. Cf. (on Marius Victorinus) Markus in CHLGEMP, pp. 333–34.

34. Cf. Cilento, "Mito e poesia," p. 263.

35. This list is based largely on the index fontium in the editio maior of Henry and Schwyzer's Plotinus, vol. 3, p. 446. They, however, exclude many of the passages discussed by Cilento, and I include some of these. One passage in Porphyry's "Life of Plotinus," in which Plotinus is portrayed quoting the Iliad, is also included.

36. All of these are in Henry and Schwyzer's index fontium.

make explicit quotations or adaptations of extended passages, but he does add depth and life to his prose through the use of Homeric words and phrases that may or may not evoke a specific episode in the epics. For the most part, these allusions imply no interpretive efforts on Plotinus's part, and neither do they tell us anything about what significance he attached to the passages in question. They do, however, provide cumulative evidence of Plotinus's knowledge of Homer[37] and of his sensitivity to Homeric thought and diction. Often the reference takes the form of a single word or short phrase inserted into an argument that may or may not make further use of Homer, though there is a tendency for Homeric echoes to be found in clusters, sometimes in the vicinity of a genuinely interpretive allusion.

The seventeen allusions that fall into this non-interpretive group break down roughly into those that evoke a specific passage or event in the *Iliad* or *Odyssey* and those that simply impart a Homeric flavor to the narrative, but these categories are extremely difficult to define with precision.[38]

37. It is true that most of the passages to which Plotinus alludes could be known to him through secondary sources and particularly through Plato. Cf. Schwyzer's comments on Cilento's "Mito e poesia," (discussion) p. 314. It is the subtlety with which Plotinus is able to weave Homeric echoes into his own thought and expression, rather than any specific citation or citations, that seems the best evidence for his personal knowledge of the *Iliad* and *Odyssey*, though Cilento (p. 277) is undoubtedly correct to emphasize that the citation by Plotinus (Porph. *Vit. Plot.* 15.17) of *Il.* 8.282, not available to him through Plato, is a proof of "la diretta lettura di Omero, da parte di Plotino." Looking forward, the currency of this "Life" in the fourth century may well explain the citation of the same verse in Gallus's exhortation to his brother Julian the Apostate, where the context suggests Plotinus (or Porphyry) as intermediary (publ. in the Loeb Julian, vol. 2, p. 614, line 2).

38. The following Plotinian passages seem to evoke the Homeric passages indicated: Porph. *Vit. Plot.* 15.17: *Il.* 8.282; *Enn.* 1.4.7.33: *Il.* 17.65; *Enn.* 3.7.11.7: *Il.* 16.113; *Enn.* 4.3.12.5: *Il.* 4.443; *Enn.* 4.7.8.36: *Od.* 10.555; *Enn.* 5.3.17.29–32: *Od.* 19.33–40; *Enn.* 6.1.27.19: *Od.* 4.417; *Enn.* 6.4.15.20–23: *Il.* 3.149. *Enn.* 4.3.12 constitutes an interesting example, because it is quoted by Augustine (*Civ. Dei* 9.10), and it seems clear that Augustine is unaware that *pater misericors mortalia illis vincla faciebat* (= Ζεὺς δὲ πατὴρ ἐλεήσας πονουμένας θνητὰ αὐτῶν τὰ δέσμα ποιῶν) is a complex echo of Plato *Symp.* 191b5, into which Plotinus has introduced a Homeric formula (Ζεὺς δὲ πατήρ) and then further enhanced the Homeric flavor of the passage by extending the dactylic rhythm in ἐλεήσας (though the combination is not Homeric). Henry and Schwyzer do not mention this Homeric echo. A special situation arises at *Enn.* 4.4.43.20–21, where the reference is to *Il.* 2.547, but the passage evoked, if any, must be the intermediate one that is clearly

The problem, of course, is that we cannot know just how slight an allusion would have been sufficient to evoke an entire passage, but Plotinus's aristocratic Roman audience doubtless had a considerable knowledge of the epics and knew many passages by heart. Some cases seem clear enough. When a Plotinian simile evokes the "elders of the city seated in assembly," (οἷον ἐκκλησίᾳ δημογερόντων καθημένων, Enn. 6.4.15.20) using Iliadic language that points specifically to the well-known passage at the beginning of the teichoscopia in which the Trojan elders are found sitting on the wall (ἧατο δημογέροντες ἐπὶ Σκαιῇσι πύλῃσι, Il. 3.149), the single word δημογερόντων is enough to evoke the entire passage.[39] It is striking here that the situation to which Plotinus alludes so subtly is one with an obvious relevance to the simile he is developing, where the major thrust is the contrast between the peaceful elders and the rowdy populace, prey to the appetites of the flesh. The assembly of elders in question is, in the Homeric passage, an oasis of peace and reason in the absurd and violent context of the war. Plotinus does not, however, develop the simile along the lines of the Homeric passage, though he does, in evoking the passage, take advantage not only of the richness of the Homeric diction but also of some of the qualities of the specific familiar situation to which he diverts his audience's memory. Allusions of this sort are not uncommon in Plotinus, and the use to which they are put is well illustrated by the case in point. Here, the elders and the populace are compared respectively to the divine element in man—the "soul sprung from the divine" (ἡ μὲν δὴ ἐκ τοῦ θείου ψυχή, Enn. 6.4.15.18–19)—and to the element more clearly associated with the flesh, and correspondingly closer to the disorderly material world in its behavior.[40] The Homeric image provides the base for the simile, but the development belongs entirely to Plotinus. The richly evocative quality of the Homeric language, combined with the recalled image, enhances the simile and gives it life.

Plotinus's source: Plato Alc. 1.132a5. The remaining non-interpretive allusions at Enn. 1.4.7.31–32; 1.6.5.14; 2.3.8.7; 3.8.11.32; 4.3.16.22–23; 4.6.3.13; 5.1.7.27; 6.5.10.21; and 6.6.8.11 do not seem to evoke the passages to which they are referred by Henry and Schwyzer, but simply to constitute non-specific Homeric echoes.

39. The word δημογέροντες in the plural occurs only here in the Homeric corpus and the one occurrence in the singular (Il. 11.372) need not concern us.

40. It is suggestive that this Homeric allusion and another at Enn. 4.3.27.7–13 (see pp. 101–2 below) occur in contexts where the doctrine of a divided soul, stated in an extreme form by Numenius, is prominent. It is quite possible that Plotinus was directly dependent on Numenius in some of his use of Homer.

At the other extreme of the non-interpretive class of allusions are such expressions as θάμβος δ' ἔχεν (*Enn.* 3.8.11.32), which is unmistakeably Homeric, but might allude to any of four passages in the *Iliad* and one in the *Odyssey*.[41] Here, it is the richness of the language, coupled in this instance with the very quality of "wonder" so characteristic of Homer, that is evoked.

These classes of Plotinian allusions to Homer correspond roughly to the first category we distinguished in Numenius's use of Homer; the major considerations are stylistic, and the meaning of the passages evoked does not become an issue. There is also, however, another category of Homeric allusions in the *Enneads*, nearly as large, where some effort of interpretation is involved,[42] though in many such passages the interpretation Plotinus gives to the words or to the myth to which he alludes is implicit or incidental to the point he is making.

We may first consider two marginal instances in which Plotinus makes use of Homeric images in such a way that an interpretive statement is implied but not developed. In *Enn.* 6.5, *On the Universal Entire Presence of τὸ ὄν*, Plotinus evokes the magnificent moment in book 1 of the *Iliad* when Athena restrains Achilles by grasping his hair from behind, so that his movement is arrested:

Achilles was astounded, turned around and immediately knew Pallas Athena—her eyes blazed terribly.

θάμβησεν δ' Ἀχιλεύς, μετὰ δ' ἐτράπετ', αὐτίκα δ' ἔγνω
Παλλάδ' Ἀθηναίην· δεινὼ δέ οἱ ὄσσε φάανθεν·

(Il. 1.199–200)

Apart from any implied interpretation of the passage, Plotinus's allusion is another good example of his use of Homeric evocations to provide richly imaginatively charged, yet anthropomorphized and immediately accessible, comparisons to help his reader grasp the spiritual experience he wants to communicate. In this instance he is working toward a statement concerning the individual's participation in, and identity with, τὸ ὄν. He has just asserted that "we and everything constitute a single en-

41. *Il.* 3.342, 4.79, 23.815, 24.482; cf. *Od.* 3.372.
42. I have classified the fifteen instances into (1) passages interpreting broad patterns or stories from Homer: *Enn.* 1.6.8.16 and 18; 3.3.5.42–43; 5.8.13.1–2; and 5.9.1.21; (2) passages interpreting Homeric expressions: *Enn.* 1.1.12.31; 4.3.27.7–13; 5.1.2.27; 5.5.3.20–22; 5.8.3.26; 5.8.4.1; 6.5.12.31–32; 6.7.30.28; and 6.9.7.23–24; and (3) marginally interpretive passages: *Enn.* 5.5.8.6 and 6.5.7.10–11.

tity,"[43] but that as long as we continue to focus our attention outside ourselves, we are like a creature with many faces surrounding a single brain, each face unaware of the others and of his identity with them.

> Were one able to be spun around, either by his own effort or through the good fortune of being yanked by Athena herself, he will find himself face-to-face with the god, with himself, and with the universe. He will not at first perceive what he sees as the universe, but when he finds that he is unable to locate and define himself and his limits, then, abandoning the definition of himself as something separate from the entire ὄν, he will enter the total universe without making a single move, but by remaining there, where the universe has its foundations.[44]

The unforgettable Homeric moment becomes a metaphor for the very experience the *Iliad* passage, with its archaic abruptness, endeavors to communicate. The difference is that that experience itself—the divine epiphany, the moment of revelation—has been redefined in terms of an ontology utterly foreign to Homer. The Homeric moment lends a physical presence to the abstract concept of Plotinus. It is an image combining physical immobility in a context of dynamic action with a violent wrenching of normal perceptions leading ultimately to the hero's redefinition of his own relationship to the world around him. This is the primary function of the image in Plotinus's essay, and the shift he demands—that we think in terms of turning our eyes not simply over our shoulders but within ourselves—is easily made.

Implied in Plotinus's use of the Homeric passage, however, is an important element in the earlier history of its interpretation. The Olympians as individual personalities are of little or no interest to Plotinus—Athena is not mentioned elsewhere in the *Enneads*—and this passage in particular had lent itself to interpretation along the familiar lines of the claim that Athena represents the restraining force of wisdom, reason, or mind, calming the impulsive emotions. The treatment of Athena as an essentially allegorical figure representing mind is probably Stoic in origin. With reference to the present passage, it is reflected in a scholion[45]

43. πάντα ἄρα ἐσμὲν ἕν (*Enn.* 6.5.7.8).

44. εἰ δέ τις ἐπιστραφῆναι δύναιτο ἢ παρ' αὐτοῦ ἢ τῆς Ἀθηνᾶς αὐτῆς εὐτυχήσας τῆς ἕλξεως, θεόν τε καὶ αὐτὸν καὶ τὸ πᾶν ὄψεται· ὄψεται δὲ τὰ μὲν πρῶτα οὐχ ὡς τὸ πᾶν, εἶτ' οὐκ ἔχων ὅπη αὐτὸν στήσας ὁριεῖ καὶ μέχρι τίνος αὐτός ἐστιν, ἀφεὶς περιγράφειν ἀπὸ τοῦ ὄντος ἅπαντος αὐτὸν εἰς ἅπαν τὸ πᾶν ἥξει προελθὼν οὐδαμοῦ, ἀλλ' αὐτοῦ μείνας, οὗ ἵδρυται τὸ πᾶν (*Enn.*6.5.7.11–17).

45. The T scholion on *Il.* 1.199–200; *Schol. in Il.*, ed. Erbse, vol. 1, p. 65, lines 44–45.

and in Eustathius.[46] To Plotinus and to his audience, it must have been immediately clear that the passage evoked represented not only a universally known and striking archaic image for a deeply felt spiritual breakthrough, but simultaneously also a complex image for the powers of mind—conceived as a universal acting upon individuals—over actions and events. It is against the background of this previous history of interpretation, which it implies and assumes, that this and other Plotinian evocations of Homeric passages should be viewed.

Bearing in mind the fact that in evoking a Homeric image, Plotinus is undoubtedly evoking a long history of interpretation as well, we may go on to another anomalous instance of Homeric allusion in the *Enneads*, which points to another implicit attitude lying behind Plotinus's use of Homer, and indeed behind all his statements regarding the physical universe. As already mentioned, this universe is for Plotinus merely the insubstantial expression of higher true realities. This is not to reduce it to the level of the utterly contemptible; in his tract against the Gnostics (*Enn.* 2.9) and elsewhere, Plotinus is explicit that the material cosmos, though teetering on the edge of nonexistence, is not to be viewed as inherently evil or the product of an evil creator. It is redeemed by the fact that it expresses higher realities. Implied in this attitude is the belief that the material universe itself constitutes a system of meaning, a language of symbols that, properly read, will yield a truth that transcends its physical substrate. We are close in spirit here to a Cotton Mather's search for transcendent meaning in the physical world and to an Ishmael interrogating the hieroglyphics on the whale's back. Any statement about this world may, on a higher plane, mask a statement about some true existent, not because of the nature of the statement, but because of the inherently symbolic structure of the universe to which it refers.

In his discussion of the relationship of the objects of cognition (τὰ νοητά) to mind (νοῦς) in *Enn.* 5.5, Plotinus characteristically evokes a Homeric image to serve as the basis for an assertion about non-spatial reality. Again, the central concept is immobility, and Plotinus is making the point he was making with reference to Athena and Achilles—that the experience of higher reality is attained not by physical displacement but by the journey inward:

> Thus one must not seek it out, but rather remain at peace until it makes its appearance, preparing oneself to contemplate it as the eye awaits the rising of the sun, which lifts itself above the horizon—"out of Ocean," the poets say—and delivers itself to the contemplation of

46. Eust. *In Il.*, *ad loc.*, 81–82 (vol. 1, p. 69).

the eye. But *this* reality, which the sun mimics, where will *it* rise from? What horizon will it lift itself over to make its appearance? [47]

This instance of Plotinian exploitation of an epic image is in many ways typical and can be read as entirely non-interpretive: its primary function is undoubtedly the placing of the imaginatively charged diction of Homer at the service of the intellectual and imaginative demands Plotinus places upon his audience, to provide a substantial and physical image of extraordinary scale and beauty *beyond* which Plotinus can strive to make his own point. Only the reminder that the sun—the physical sun in this physical universe—is the mimic, the imitation of a higher reality, implies anything further, but it *does* indicate, however subtly, that when the poets say, "the sun rose out of Ocean," they are describing a process that, because of the very nature of the world, and *not* because of the nature of their own imaginative act, mirrors the process by which νοῦς reaches the perception of mankind. Thus the poems as systems of meaning mimic the structure of meaning of the physical reality in which they participate, and there are indeed elements in their meaning that go beyond the intentions of the poets.

The remaining Plotinian allusions to the meaning of Homer's poetry break down into those that reflect upon the meaning of a Homeric word or phrase and those that explore the meaning of some broader aspect of the poems, some Homeric myth. The former category is somewhat larger, but most of the nine instances can be dismissed with only very few comments.

When Plotinus talks about the traditional gods, sometimes echoing Homeric language, he feels the need—as did most "theologians" in Greek pagan tradition—to make explicit the relationship between the traditional accounts and his own system. He never explores this relationship in detail, inasmuch as the traditional gods are of little use to him, yet the explicit elucidation of qualities attributed by Homer to the gods comes through at several points. In *Enn.* 5.8, *On Noetic Beauty*, Plotinus meditates upon the life of the gods: "They 'know everything' and what they know is not things of human concern but divine things that are properly

---

47. διὸ οὐ χρὴ διώκειν, ἀλλ' ἡσυχῇ μένειν, ἕως ἂν φανῇ, παρασκευάσαντα ἑαυτὸν θεατὴν εἶναι, ὥσπερ ὀφθαλμὸς ἀνατολὰς ἡλίου περιμένει· ὁ δὲ ὑπερφανεὶς τοῦ ὁρίζοντος—ἐξ ὠκεανοῦ φασιν οἱ ποιηταί—ἔδωκεν ἑαυτὸν θεάσασθαι τοῖς ὄμμασιν. οὑτοσὶ δέ, ὃν μιμεῖται ὁ ἥλιος, ὑπερσχήσει πόθεν; καὶ τί ὑπερβαλὼν φανήσεται; (*Enn.* 5.5.8.3–8).

their own, and all that νοῦς perceives."[48] This is clearly not the force of the Homeric claims for the universality of divine wisdom, which is taken to be a knowledge comparable to human wisdom but differing in scope because it is unbounded by time and space. What Plotinus is striving to communicate, however, is the hierarchy of states of consciousness that correspond to the hypostases. Homer's formulation is accurate, but requires interpretive elaboration. A few lines later another Homeric stock phrase is evoked and interpreted briefly but unmistakeably: "*There* is where 'living at ease' is."[49] The simple assertion that the Homeric cliché refers in fact to a realm other than the material—to an ἐκεῖ eternally distinct from the world of everyday experience ἐνταῦθα—though it could hardly be called an exercise in Homeric exegesis, still communicates clearly the way in which Homeric statements about the divine had evolved in later Platonism to adapt to an idealist cosmology with no apparent relevance to the world-model of the creators of the Homeric poems.

It is clear from another interpretive passage both that Plotinus considered Homeric anthropomorphism to be metaphorical and that he equated the structures of meaning of the Platonic myths with those of the early poets, including Homer. He is asking whether the concept of pleasure (ἡδονή) can have any relevance to experience on the level of νοῦς and concludes that this is true only in the sense that every activity, state, or existence can be either impeded or unimpeded, and that the latter situation is clearly more desirable and to be chosen over the former:

> It is because they consider this latter sort of state of the νοῦς more pleasant and preferable that they speak of it as having an element of pleasure mixed into it, for lack of an appropriate term, just as the poets use metaphorically the names of things we ourselves love and use expressions like "being drunk on nectar" and "feasting and banqueting" and "the father smiled" and thousands of other things of the sort.[50]

48. καὶ ἴσασι πάντα καὶ γινώσκουσιν οὐ τὰ ἀνθρώπεια, ἀλλὰ τὰ ἑαυτῶν τὰ θεῖα, καὶ ὅσα νοῦς ὁρᾷ (*Enn.* 5.8.3.26–27). Neither Cilento nor Henry and Schwyzer note the dependence of this phrase on the formula θεοὶ δέ τε πάντα ἴσασιν of *Od.* 4.379 and 468. Plotinus is doubtless again reaching to the Homeric formulation by way of intermediate thinkers—Henry and Schwyzer here cite Anaxagoras fr. B12 (D–K)—but it is unlikely that the Homeric echo is anything but deliberate.

49. καὶ γὰρ τὸ ρεῖα ζώειν ἐκεῖ (*Enn.* 5.8.4.1).

50. τὴν τοιαύτην τοῦ νοῦ κατάστασιν ἀσμενιστὴν καὶ αἱρετωτάτην εἶναι τιθέμενοι ἡδονῇ μεμίχθαι λέγουσιν ἀπορίᾳ οἰκείας προσηγορίας, οἷα ποιοῦσι καὶ τὰ ἄλλα ὀνόματα παρ' ἡμῖν ἀγαπώμενα μεταφέροντες, τὸ "μεθυσθεὶς ἐπὶ

They apply the terms metaphorically, "carrying over" (μεταφέροντες)[51] words that properly refer to human experience to talk about the experience of the gods. Thus when Homer's Zeus smiles (*Il.* 5.426=15.47), this constitutes a claim that the gods know pleasure, but only in the very narrowly limited sense just explained. The fact that "drunk on nectar" points *not* to the poets but to the myth of Diotima in the *Symposium* (203b5) seems unavoidably to indicate that Plotinus makes little distinction between the myths of Homer and those of Plato. Both poet and philosopher apparently use mythic language in the same way to hint at a higher reality.[52]

In the more complete Neoplatonic analysis of Homeric anthropomorphism that reaches us through Proclus, it becomes clear that much of what Homer says about the gods could be salvaged by imposing upon the Homeric myth the exegetical superstructure of a complex demonology. Proclus populated the universe with chains of spiritual, physical, and mixed beings extending from the νοῦς to the material world and found conveniently that certain Homeric statements about the gods that were objectionable with reference to noetic beings could acceptably be thought of as applying to lowly δαίμονες in their "processions."[53] The argument is at least as old as Apuleius, a contemporary of Numenius's.[54] Plotinus takes his place in the development of this approach to Homer's gods, distinguishing between the highest god, toward which the entire universe turns, and those other gods that appear to individuals: "These are the gods that 'wander through the cities in many disguises.'"[55] This verse from the *Odyssey* is, in a sense, a strange choice as a basis for the distinction, since Plato had specifically rejected the line.[56] Given the fact that Plotinus could not be unaware of Plato's judgment, we must conclude that this is an instance—however mild—of defensive interpreta-

---

τοῦ νέκταρος" καὶ "ἐπὶ δαῖτα καὶ ἑστίασιν" καὶ τὸ "μείδησε δὲ πατήρ" οἱ ποιηταὶ καὶ ἄλλα τοιαῦτα μυρία (*Enn.* 6.7.30.23–29).

51. The term is Aristotelian. See below, pp. 202–3.

52. The last example, "to feasting and banqueting," is likewise traced to Plato (*Phdr.* 247a8) by Henry and Schwyzer, and although the ultimate source of the image is Homeric, the familiar passage in the *Phaedrus* may well be the context Plotinus has in mind.

53. See ch. 5A and B below.

54. Cf. Aug. *Civ. Dei* 9.7.

55. ἀλλ' οὗτοι μὲν οἱ θεοί, ὅτι παντοῖοι τελέθοντες ἐπιστρωφῶσι τὰς πόλεις (*Enn.* 6.5.12.31–32).

56. *Rep.* 2.381d.

tion. Plotinus is anticipating the later Neoplatonic reconciliation of Homeric and Platonic statements about the gods by asserting that some Homeric statements apply properly only to certain lower classes of beings. This is to say that Homer's assertion remains essentially sound, though Plotinus, from his perspective, is able to make certain finer distinctions.

When he makes the point that there is continuity among the hypostases, Plotinus asserts that in the higher realm, the metaphor of kingship is a weak one, since a king (here) rules over creatures distinct from himself.

> But the king *there* is not a ruler over creatures separate and different from himself, but has the most just, the true kingship, rooted in the nature of things in that he is king of truth and by nature lord of his countless offspring and of a divine assembly and more justly called "king of a king" or "king of kings" or "father of gods," whom Zeus mimics even in this, unsated by the contemplation of his own father and looking beyond him to his father's father as an action accomplishing the existence of being.[57]

The juxtaposition of the familiar Old Testament epithet with the Homeric one is a hint that this may be one of the passages in which Plotinus followed Numenius closely.[58] At any rate, the method resembles that of Numenius, and the implication is that the cumulative evidence of the primitive revelations to be gleaned from such sources supports a certain conception of the divine.

In some instances Plato is clearly the intermediary in the spiritualization of a myth ultimately derived from Homer, as in the discussion of accomplishing the inward journey to revelation and returning to tell others: "Perhaps it was because he had such communion that Minos was called 'companion of Zeus,' and with this in his mind he established laws in its image, having been, so to speak, pumped full by contact with

57. ὁ δὲ ἐκεῖ βασιλεὺς οὐκ ἀλλοτρίων ἄρχων, ἀλλ᾽ ἔχων τὴν δικαιοτάτην καὶ φύσει ἀρχὴν καὶ τὴν ἀληθῆ βασιλείαν, ἅτε τῆς ἀληθείας βασιλεὺς καὶ ὢν κατὰ φύσιν κύριος τοῦ αὐτοῦ ἀθρόου γεννήματος καὶ θείου συντάγματος, βασιλεὺς βασιλέως καὶ βασιλέων καὶ πατὴρ δικαιότερον ἂν κληθεὶς θεῶν, ὃν ὁ Ζεὺς καὶ ταύτῃ ἐμιμήσατο τὴν τοῦ ἑαυτοῦ πατρὸς οὐκ ἀνασχόμενος θεωρίαν, ἀλλὰ τὴν τοῦ προπάτορος οἷον ἐνέργειαν εἰς ὑπόστασιν οὐσίας (Enn. 5.5.3.16–25).

58. The expression θεοὶ θεῶν that opens the speech of the demiurge in Plato's *Timaeus* (41a) may, however, provide an adequate precedent for Plotinus's language here without looking to the Hebrew scriptures. That passage of the *Timaeus* may in fact be the actual source for all of the three epithets.

the divine for the establishment of laws." [59] Plotinus's apparent source here is the *Minos*, especially 319a–320b, where Socrates examines in detail and analyzes the Homeric references to Minos; the myth is again evoked at the beginning of the *Laws*. Still, the Plotinian interpretation remains original to the extent that the spiritual discipline to which the myth is taken to refer is far more explicitly elaborated, and the myth that has served as a key to it emerges as a very crude representation at best.

The description of the physical universe previous to the arrival of soul borrows the Homeric phrase "hated of the gods" (τά τε στυγέουσι θεοί περ, *Il.* 20.65): "The [material] heavens have become a worthy thing when occupied by soul, having previously been a dead body, earth and water, or rather darkness of matter and nonexistence and, as someone says, 'what the gods hate.'" [60] The Homeric phrase occurs only to describe Hades and once again (in the Homeric *Hymn to Aphrodite* 246) to describe old age. In the Plotinian context, it functions here primarily as a decorative epithet to reinforce the assertion that matter deprived of soul is utter void. Yet there is, behind its use here, a kind of Plotinian anthropomorphism, a suggestion that, if there *were* gods in the epic sense, who could be thought of as hating something, what these gods would hate would not be the obvious human "ills"—death and old age—but the only *true* death, the condition of soulless matter, lying just beyond the limits of being. In a strange way, and certainly without intending it, Plotinus here opens up a possible line of defense of Homer against Plato's condemnation of him for the presentation of death as an evil, a defense that would seem somewhat less absurd against the backdrop of the later Neoplatonic conception of the Troy tale as a metaphor for the entry of souls into matter and their departure back to their true home. [61]

The discussions of Homer's description of Heracles in the first *nekyia* of the *Odyssey*,

> After him I noticed Heracles in all his strength—
> A mere image, for he himself [was] with the immortal gods . . .

59. οἵαν ἴσως καὶ Μίνως ποιούμενος ὀαριστὴς τοῦ Διὸς ἐφημίσθη εἶναι, ἧς μεμνημένος εἴδωλα αὐτῆς τοὺς νόμους ἐτίθει τῇ τοῦ θείου ἐπαφῇ εἰς νόμων πληρούμενος θέσιν (*Enn.* 6.9.7.23–26).

60. ἔσχε τε ἀξίαν οὐρανὸς ψυχῆς εἰσοικισθείσης ὢν πρὸ ψυχῆς σῶμα νεκρόν, γῇ καὶ ὕδωρ, μᾶλλον δὲ σκότος ὕλης καὶ μὴ ὂν καὶ ὃ στυγέουσιν οἱ θεοί, φησί τις (*Enn.* 5.1.2.24–27).

61. Cf. *Enn.* 5.1, quoted in n. 73 below, on the role of Rhea in the genealogical myth of the *Theogony*.

Τὸν δὲ μέτ᾽ εἰσενόησα βίην Ἡρακληείην,
εἴδωλον· αὐτὸς δὲ μετ᾽ ἀθανάτοισι θεοῖσι

(*Od.* 11.601–02)

fall between the elaborations of Homeric expressions and the interpretation of broader myths. The focus of concern is doubtless the myth, yet the words themselves take on special importance because of the problem of making sense of a single anomalous bit of information. The problem of Homer's ambivalence in the description of Heracles' soul had previously been noted by many commentators.[62] Cilento refers to the great temptation to extract doctrinal statements from Homer in support of such unusual Plotinian doctrines as that of the soul and its εἴδωλον,[63] and the earlier of the two discussions of this passage does stand out as a rather awkward attempt on Plotinus's part, if not to enlist the prestige of Homer, then at least to draw the Homeric passage and its meaning into line with his own thought.

In attempting to come to conclusions concerning the nature of the respective memories of the two aspects of the soul—the "more divine" soul and its expression in the universe—Plotinus evokes these lines and asserts, with very little foundation in the *Odyssey* as we have it, that Heracles' εἴδωλον is depicted as having a memory only of his most recent life on earth, in the persona of Heracles, whereas other souls, being entire, could perhaps add an element of moral judgment (δικαιοσύνη) inaccessible to him (*Enn.* 4.3.27).

The second discussion, from one of the essays of Plotinus's last year (*Enn.* 1.1), centers on the problem that we are told of sins, sufferings, expiations, and so forth on the part of the soul, and yet this is difficult to reconcile with a unified, eternal, and good soul. The problem is one that occupied him earlier in *Enn.* 4.4.16, where he expressed his desire to bring his own view into line with a traditional one, clearly Pythagorean: "For we have these things from those who in antiquity philosophized best concerning the soul and it is appropriate that we should try to make the present account harmonious, or at least non-contradictory, with that one."[64] Plotinus thus shrinks from contradicting the Pythagoreans, and

---

62. Cf. Ps.-Plutarch *De vit. Hom.* 123; also Plut. *De fac.* 944–45 and Dodds's comments on the relationship of the Plutarch essay to Plotinus's treatment of the passage, in Cilento, "Mito e poesia," (discussion) pp. 315–16.

63. Cilento, "Mito e poesia," p. 278.

64. ταῦτα γὰρ πάντα τῶν πάλαι περὶ ψυχῆς ἄριστα πεφιλοσοφηκότων παρειλήφαμεν, οἷς πειρᾶσθαι προσήκει σύμφωνον ἢ μὴ διάφωνόν γε ἐπιδεῖξαι τὸν νῦν προκείμενον λόγον (*Enn.* 6.4.16.4–7).

in this he echoes Numenius. It is striking that in his last treatment of the same problem, he attempts to rationalize the Homeric account of Heracles and does so by imposing a model reminiscent of the myth of Er in the *Republic*.

The εἴδωλον is the lower expression of the higher soul, but, being in contact with the material world, it is subject to error. It will ultimately cease to exist in the natural course of events, when the entire soul has again become absorbed in the contemplation of that which lies in its true home, "there" (ἐκεῖ). It is clear from the outset that the soul of Heracles is the only one in Homer's underworld that is described in a way compatible with Plotinus's model, which seems in turn to be based on the antithetical heavenly rewards and subterranean sufferings of the souls in the myth of Er. Neither Homeric nor Platonic myth can ultimately offer Plotinus an adequate account of this matter, and he thus bases his assertions on the Homeric anomaly, Heracles, participating simultaneously in the reward cycle and in the punishment cycle. The εἴδωλον Odysseus saw in Hades, Plotinus implies, will eventually wither away as the higher soul, already among the gods, forgets the experience of the material world. That Heracles should be so divided is particularly appropriate:

> The statement rapidly becomes credible when thus interpreted: Heracles was judged worthy to be a god, being possessed of practical virtue, on account of his goodness . . . but, because he was a man of action and not of contemplation, such that he might be entirely *there* [ἐκεῖ], he is above and there is yet something of him below.[65]

One is reminded of the soul in the myth of Er who made the wrong choice of a new life because he was spoiled for decision making by a cycle of reward obtained through a previous embodiment during which participation in a good society, and not contemplation or philosophy, made him worthy (*Rep.* 10.619c). The description of this soul in the *Republic* is immediately preceded by a sermon inserted by Socrates into the myth, the force of which is that philosophy is the only key to the correct choices, guaranteeing permanent reward (*Rep.* 10.618b–619b). The myth of Er seems to provide a source for the values as well as the model of the fate of souls that Plotinus imposes upon the Homeric account of Heracles. The "Pythagorean" punishments for erring souls are, if anything,

---

65. τάχα δ᾽ ἂν οὕτως πιθανὸς ὁ λόγος εἴη· ὅτι δὴ πρακτικὴν ἀρετὴν ἔχων Ἡρακλῆς καὶ ἀξιωθεὶς διὰ καλοκἀγαθίαν θεὸς εἶναι, ὅτι πρακτικός, ἀλλ᾽ οὐ θεωρητικὸς ἦν, ἵνα ἂν ὅλος ἦν ἐκεῖ, ἄνω τέ ἐστί τι αὐτοῦ καὶ κάτω (*Enn.* 1.1.12.35–39).

rather an embarrassment for Plotinus, and he is isolated from certain Platonists, as from most Christians, by his belief in the universal human potential for full union with the divine. The myth of Er is Plato's substitute for Homer's corrupting account of the sufferings of the dead. Though bound to both, Plotinus would clearly like to dispense with both. For him, the departure of the soul from the body can be nothing but a cause for rejoicing. The double soul that is so remarkable and idiosyncratic an element in the teaching of Numenius may well have provided Plotinus with the basis for a compromise. If so, the passages in question, with their seeming attempt to reconcile the Homeric and Platonic accounts, may well be traceable to a Numenian original.

Thus far we have been examining Plotinus's attitudes toward Homeric phrases and concepts, as well as to some details of myth that may be considered distinctively Homeric. The remaining Homeric allusions are to the broad lines of the story of the *Iliad* and *Odyssey*, and although there is no doubt that Plotinus approaches most of the material as distinctively Homeric, we have now passed beyond the level where evidence of close attention to the text makes it possible to assert that we are dealing with the interpretation of poetry and not simply of myth.

That Plotinus was capable of distorting a traditional myth into a form capable of bearing a meaning compatible with his model of reality is best illustrated by his treatment of myths that are properly Hesiodic and not Homeric.[66] The adaptation and interpretation of the Pandora story (*Enn.* 4.3.14) is, as Emile Bréhier noted, uncharacteristic of Plotinus, but it is at the same time in many ways typical of the imaginative expansions by which the tradition of allegorical interpretation enriched the inherited texts.[67] Zeus's malicious revenge on humanity fades entirely from the picture. Prometheus, identified with providence ($\pi\rho\acute{o}\nu o\iota\alpha$), is the creator of Pandora. She is herself a symbol of the material cosmos, endowed with so many blessings (gifts, $\delta\hat{\omega}\rho\alpha$) from the spiritual realm. If Epimetheus rejects Pandora, it is because contemplation (or perhaps afterthought) perceives that, given the choice, it is better to remain in the higher sphere and not to enter the material universe. Prometheus in chains is the creator locked in his own creation, but the story of his re-

66. The Pandora story as Plotinus recreates it is so far removed from Hesiod's account (*Works and Days* 60–89, *Theogony* 570–616) that one might question whether this was, in fact, his source. However, several echoes of Hesiod's actual words guarantee that *Works and Days* was at least among the sources on which Plotinus was drawing.

67. Plotinus, *Ennéades*, ed. Bréhier, vol. 4, p. 81, n. 2.

lease by Heracles likewise indicates that he has the potential of being freed from that creation. "This seems to be the sort of thing the myth is hinting at." [68]

Plotinus expresses some misgivings and hesitation about the interpretation, but his conclusion asserts his faith that the core is sound and that the story in question does indeed have the sort of meaning just elaborated: "Whatever one may think of these things, [the myth] does present the bestowing of gifts upon the cosmos and is in harmony with what we have said." [69] There is room, then, for a number of possibilities, and interpretation is far from an exact science.

The Hesiodic succession myth elaborated in the *Theogony* and only casually evoked in Homer (*Il.* 14.203–4) provided Plotinus with a mythic precedent for his breakdown of reality into the three "ruling hypostases." [70] The anthropomorphic representation of the One (τὸ ἕν) would constitute a grotesque paradox, and Plotinus avoids expressing this idea directly. It is implied, however, in the passage already quoted,[71] in which Zeus is envisioned contemplating not only his father but his grandfather as well. The significance of Kronos and Zeus is elaborated in the context of a historical survey highly suggestive of the method of Numenius, in which Plotinus proposes to demonstrate the sources of the doctrine of the three hypostases, first in "the mysteries and the myths," and then in Plato, Parmenides, and numerous other philosophers, concluding with the assertion that the ideas involved are Pythagorean as well (*Enn.* 5.1.7–9). The passage that concerns us opens with a decorative echo of Homer, itself simply a stylistic hint that the discussion is now to be extended to the sphere of heroic myth:

> This, then, is the generation of this νοῦς, and worthy of νοῦς in all its purity: it came to be [in the first place] from the first principle [i.e., τὸ ἕν], and when it had already come to be, it produced all those things that truly are: all the beauty of forms, all the noetic gods. It is full of those things that it produced and, as if it had swallowed them up

68. οἷον εἰκὸς καὶ τὸν μῦθον αἰνίττεσθαι (*Enn.* 4.3.14.5).

69. ταῦτα μὲν οὖν ὅπῃ τις δοξάζει, ἀλλ᾽ ὅτι ἐμφαίνει τὰ τῆς εἰς τὸν κόσμον δόσεως, καὶ προσᾴδει τοῖς λεγομένοις (*Enn.* 4.3.14.17–19).

70. Pierre Hadot has recently explored Plotinus's use of the Hesiodic creation myth ("Ouranos, Kronos, and Zeus in Plotinus' Treatise Against the Gnostics") and offered the most complete exploration to date of the Plotinian elaboration and adaptation of a single myth. See also Pépin, "Plotin et les mythes," pp. 21–27.

71. *Enn.* 5.5.3.16–25, quoted in n. 57 above.

again, contains them in itself lest they spill out into matter and be nursed by Rhea. Thus the mysteries and the myths about the gods say riddlingly[72] that Kronos, the wisest of the gods, shuts up again within himself that which he produces before the birth of Zeus, so that he is filled full and is νοῦς in its satiety [ἐν κόρῳ]. After this, they say that in its satiety, νοῦς produces Zeus, for νοῦς in its perfection produces ψυχή. [They are saying that] being perfect, it had to produce, and that it is impossible for such a force to remain unproductive.[73]

Thus Zeus represents soul, the lowest hypostasis, spilling over into matter. His father Kronos is mind, and his grandfather Ouranos is implicitly the transcendent first principle. This is the truth that the myths hint at and that the philosophical tradition has elaborated on a secondary level. This same myth is evoked at the end of the essay on noetic beauty (*Enn.* 5.8.12–13), where it is suggested that the binding of Kronos represents the unaltering transcendence of νοῦς, which leaves the governing of this world to its offspring, ψυχή. In this last instance, the best passage to consider as Plotinus's source may well (as Henry and

72. This seems the best translation of αἰνίττονται here. In the more frequent construction it is followed by the second, interpreted meaning as object. That is, "the myths *hint at* a certain doctrine or meaning." Both constructions can, however, be found in Plato.

73. ταύτης τοι γενεᾶς ὁ νοῦς οὗτος ἀξίας νοῦ τοῦ καθαρωτάτου μὴ ἄλλοθεν ἢ ἐκ τῆς πρώτης ἀρχῆς φῦναι, γενόμενον δὲ ἤδη τὰ ὄντα πάντα σὺν αὐτῷ γεννῆσαι, πᾶν μὲν τὸ τῶν ἰδεῶν κάλλος, πάντας δὲ θεοὺς νοητούς· πλήρη δὲ ὄντα ὧν ἐγέννησε καὶ ὥσπερ καταπιόντα πάλιν τῷ ἐν αὐτῷ ἔχειν μηδὲ ἐκπεσεῖν εἰς ὕλην μηδὲ τραφῆναι παρὰ τῇ Ῥέᾳ, ὡς τὰ μυστήρια καὶ οἱ μῦθοι οἱ περὶ θεῶν αἰνίττονται Κρόνον μὲν θεὸν σοφώτατον πρὸ τοῦ Δία γενέσθαι ἃ γεννᾷ πάλιν ἐν ἑαυτῷ ἔχειν, ᾗ καὶ πλήρης καὶ νοῦς ἐν κόρῳ· μετὰ δὲ ταῦτα φασι Δία γεννᾶν κόρον ἤδη ὄντα· ψυχὴν γὰρ γεννᾷ νοῦς, νοῦς ὢν τέλειος. καὶ γὰρ τέλειον ὄντα γεννᾶν ἔδει, καὶ μὴ δύναμιν οὖσαν τοσαύτην ἄγονον εἶναι (*Enn.* 5.1.7.27–38). On the text and its interpretation, see the important article by J. Igal, "La génesis de la inteligencia en un pasaje de las Eneades de Plotino (v, 1, 7, 4–35)," esp. pp. 155–57. In view of Igal's emendation (incorporated by Henry and Schwyzer in their *editio minor*) and his explanation, it seems likely that the received text and the earlier attempts of editors and translators to make sense of the first sentence have been troubled by the commonly retrospective force of οὗτος and by the Homeric lines echoed (*Il.* 6.211 and 20.241), where the force is emphatically retrospective. This is an indication that Plotinus can use Homeric echoes (sometimes, perhaps, drawn from Plato as intermediary) without evoking anything more than a certain style, a note of epic grandeur, with no thought of the original context. Close comparison with the Homeric original can even, as in this case, be misleading.

Schwyzer suggest) be the capsule summary at *Il.* 14.203–4, rather than Hesiod.

The myth here serves the function for Plotinus of providing a colorful and dynamic model of the hypostases and their relationships to one another. As Pierre Hadot has ingeniously pointed out, it also serves to focus Plotinus's attack on the rival Gnostic model, in which the world is viewed as the evil creation of an evil demiurge.[74] The Hesiodic model, with its violence minimized through Plotinus's emphasis on the simultaneity and necessity of the two revolts, nevertheless retains an inseparable sense of the superiority of the original ruler over the two rebels, whose sovereignty "is tainted at its root."[75]

This adaptation of the Homeric-Hesiodic account of the generations of the gods to his own triadic model of reality was probably Plotinus's most important contribution to the interpretation of myth. It did not become canonical, and many later Neoplatonists located the Olympians in the realm of νοῦς rather than ψυχή, but it provided a point of departure for later attempts at reconciliation of myth and idealist cosmology. Indeed, Plotinus himself is inconsistent and freely compares Zeus to νοῦς and even to the One, as Jean Pépin has noted.[76] Myth may be used to enliven Plotinus's exposition of his world-system, but the elements of myth remain subservient to that exposition and constitute a poetic language whose referents can be shifted as needed.

There is no indication in the *Enneads* that the meaning of the Troy tale as a whole, and of the *Iliad* in particular, was of any concern to Plotinus.[77] The *Odyssey*, however, provides him with several opportunities to reinforce his own points, and he makes it clear that he considers its stories to "hint at" meanings beyond the most obvious.

The only specific episodes mentioned are those of Circe and Calypso, between whom Plotinus makes no distinction. His presentation does, however, seem to pay particular attention to the position of the material in the *Odyssey* narrative, in that he emphasizes that it is Odysseus

74. P. Hadot, "Ouranos, Kronos, and Zeus," pp. 124, 133–34.
75. P. Hadot, "Ouranos, Kronos, and Zeus," p. 134.
76. Pépin, "Plotin et les mythes," p. 25.
77. The single explicit interpretation of an *Iliad* story (*Enn.* 3.3.5.42–43) is merely the evocation of a moral exemplum. Idomeneus, Plotinus points out (thinking perhaps of the *teichoscopia* in *Il.* 3.230–33), was not affected as Paris was by Helen's beauty. The point is utterly foreign to the Homeric narrative and tells us nothing about Plotinus's understanding of the meaning of the *Iliad*.

himself who tells the stories. The context is the discussion of the quest for τὸ καλόν and the necessity of first fleeing the obscurity of matter:

"Let us flee to our own land," one might better urge. What is this flight and how shall we be borne away? Just as Odysseus says he was delivered from a witch like Circe or Calypso, claiming—and I believe he hints at some further meaning—that it did not please him to stay, though there he enjoyed visual delights and was in the presence of enormous beauty on the level of the senses. Our land is that place from which we came and our father is there.[78]

The opening citation recalls situations in the *Iliad* (2.140, 9.27), but the crucial formula φίλην ἐς πατρίδα occurs nineteen times in the *Odyssey*, and the *Iliad* passages do not seem terribly important for the understanding of the use of the Homeric material here.

Odysseus has become explicitly a hero of the renunciation of the material world, along with the pleasures and beauties accessible to the senses, in favor of the transcendent, eternal beauty, and his *own* words in the narrative of books 9 through 12 are taken to constitute a symbolic structure hinting at further meanings. There is, of course, a particular appropriateness in the attribution: Odysseus is, in fact, the one Homeric character who habitually says one thing and means something quite different. The idea of placing emphasis on his creative storytelling and suggesting that he imposes upon it a complex structure of meaning seems, however, not to have been developed in antiquity.

This spiritualized Odysseus likewise appears in one of the earliest essays (*Enn.* 5.9), where Plotinus is distinguishing among three classes of men: those who do not attempt to rise above the physical, those who try but cannot, and the third class who succeed and arrive "there" (ἐκεῖ), "just as a man arrives in his well-governed land after a long journey."[79] Odysseus is not mentioned, but the mythic pattern of the return of the voyager has been adapted from the *Odyssey*. Here Odysseus has become a type, symbolic of the highest class of humanity: those who have, in Plotinus's sense, reached home.

---

78. φεύγωμεν δὴ φίλην ἐς πατρίδα, ἀληθέστερον ἄν τις παρακελεύοιτο. τίς οὖν ἡ φυγή; καὶ πῶς ἀναξόμεθα; οἷον ἀπὸ μάγου Κίρκης φησὶν ἢ Καλυψοῦς Ὀδυσσεὺς αἰνιττόμενος, δοκεῖ μοι, μεῖναι οὐκ ἀρεσθείς, καίτοι ἔχων ἡδονὰς δι᾽ ὀμμάτων καὶ κάλλει πολλῷ αἰσθητῷ συνών (*Enn.* 1.6.8.16–21).

79. ὥσπερ ἐκ πολλῆς πλάνης εἰς πατρίδα εὔνομον ἀφικόμενος ἄνθρωπος (*Enn.* 5.9.1.20–21).

B. PORPHYRY

Porphyry and Homer

It is to Porphyry, the disciple, editor, and friend of Plotinus, that we owe the single largely complete essay in the explication of a Homeric text—one might even say of a literary text—that survives from antiquity. Though the chronology of Porphyry's life has been reconstructed with care,[80] it is extremely difficult to locate his essay on the cave of the nymphs in the *Odyssey* within that chronology.

It has been traditional to attribute the essay to the latter part of Porphyry's career, later at any rate than 262, when he joined Plotinus's circle in Rome. We have few hard facts on which to rely and the thinking of the scholars who have examined the issue has been founded primarily on comparison of the essay with other works of Porphyry, and particularly with his *Homeric Questions*. Hermann Schrader, who assembled the remains of the latter work from the scholia where they are preserved, believed that the *Homeric Questions* belonged to an early period in Porphyry's career, antedating his association with Plotinus, and that the cave essay showed the influence of Plotinus's circle on Porphyry's thought and must therefore be later than 262.[81] Porphyry's modern biographer Joseph Bidez contented himself with repeating this judgment.[82] Both scholars emphasized the difference in method between the *Questions* and the essay and the absence, in the former, of mystical allegory of the Neoplatonic type.

It seems, however, that by restoring the order and balance of the opening of the essay, A. R. Sodano's recent edition of that portion of the *Questions* that survives intact likewise restores our perspective on Porphyry's understanding of his task.[83] Early in his introduction to the *Ho-*

---

80. See Joseph Bidez, *Vie de Porphyre*.

81. Porph. *Quaest. hom.*, ed. Schrader, vol. 1, p. 349.

82. Bidez, *Vie de Porphyre*, pp. 32–33. Pfeiffer, *History of Classical Scholarship*, p. 226, referring to Schrader and Bidez, likewise repeats this opinion as if it were demonstrable fact. Why W. Pötscher (*Porphyrius, Πρὸς Μαρκέλλαν*, p. 67) calls the essay a "Frühschrift" is unclear.

83. The text is buried in the back of Schrader's edition, p. 281, but stood at the head of the original essay. Schrader included more material by far than previous editors, but had in the process fragmented the portion surviving intact, relegating to obscurity much of the introductory and connecting material, left out by the scholiasts who were his major sources. Cf. Porph. *Quaest. hom.*, ed. Sodano, pp. xxiii–xxiv.

meric Questions, Porphyry explicitly puts off treatment of major Homeric problems to a more appropriate place: "I shall attempt . . . to defer the larger treatises on Homer to a time appropriate to their consideration, making the present work a sort of preliminary training for the Homeric 'contests'"[84]—that is, for debate over the meaning of Homer. The *Questions,* then, are to include only matters of limited scope, and specifically those where the Aristarchan principle that "Homer in many instances explains his *own* meaning" applies.[85]

The *Questions* are announced as an inquiry of a special sort with the specific goal of resolving Homeric problems by reference to other Homeric passages. A vast number of points can be thus resolved, and the fundamental methodology is unimpeachable. The real question, however, concerns the degree to which this methodology and the far less easily defended one revealed in the essay on the cave of the nymphs and in the fragments of Porphyry preserved in Stobaeus are mutually exclusive. The latter texts show the strong influence of Numenius and the mystical allegorical tradition of interpretation. In Numenius himself, however, we have noted the juxtaposition of two comparable and likewise apparently contradictory attitudes toward the text of Homer and its meaning, and we have absolutely no reason to believe that these two approaches belong to different phases of his career, separated in time. Our own inability to reconcile the two attitudes toward the text in Porphyry has its roots in the great hermeneutical revolution of the Reformation. Martin Luther's fundamental principle—*scriptura sui ipsius interpres*—is, after all, simply a distant echo of Aristarchus, and we have a tendency to transpose the modern conflict to the ancient context. We imagine Crates and the Stoic litterati at Pergamon (and later Proclus and the Platonists at Athens) in the role of the Vatican, championing tradition and its baggage of allegory as the only path to the meaning of Homer, while in Alexandria Aristarchus and the librarians, bathed in the harsh light of reason, pare away the accretions and painstakingly liberate the text from them. The evidence of the surviving interpretive literature does not support this vision of methodological conflict rooted in ideology. The differ-

84. πειράσομαι . . . τὰς μὲν μείζους εἰς Ὅμηρον πραγματείας ὑπερτιθέμενος εἰς καιρὸν σκέψεως τὸν προσήκοντα, ταυτὶ δὲ οἷον προγύμνασμα τῶν εἰς αὐτὸν ἀγώνων (Porph. *Quaest. hom.*, ed. Sodano, 1.22–28).

85. ὡς αὐτὸς μὲν ἑαυτὸν τὰ πολλὰ Ὅμηρος ἐξηγεῖται (Porph. *Quaest. hom.*, ed. Sodano, 1.12–14). Whether the principle as stated by Porphyry is taken directly from Aristarchus is questioned by Pfeiffer (*History of Classical Scholarship,* p. 227), who nevertheless admits that it is "not against his spirit."

ence between the schools, real enough in itself, is one of emphasis, and in Porphyry and Numenius we find no suggestion that sensitivity to the text on the level of language (and the ability to deal with such matters with an appropriate methodology) is incompatible with an understanding of the meaning of the text rooted in a tradition of allegorical interpretation. Caution is clearly prescribed, and we have, finally, no basis on which to claim that the *Questions* must belong to a different period from the essay.

Bidez's observation that the essay shares a great deal on the level of method with the early interpretive work on statues (Περὶ ἀγαλμάτων) [86] further suggests that Schrader's model may be unsound. As Bidez pointed out, fr. 1 of this work bears a close resemblance to Ps.-Plutarch (*De vit. Hom.* 113) in its discussion of the role of statues in representing for the senses that which in reality they cannot perceive. [87] The third fragment explicitly extends the principles of interpretation of statues to the interpretation of poetry about the gods. An Orphic fragment (fr. 123 Abel) is examined on the basis that the θεολόγοι who wrote the verses were creating an εἴκων of the god—an image with attributes like those of a statue and thus susceptible to explanation on the same basis. The remaining fragments examine the attributes and iconography of the Greek gods and then go on to a discussion of Egyptian iconography. [88]

If the work on statues is in fact early, we must conclude that Porphyry could probably have produced the essay on the cave of the nymphs at any point in his career—that is, at any period from the mid-250s until his death shortly after 300. It does not contradict, but rather complements, the *Questions*, and must surely constitute one of the "larger treatises" Porphyry promises in the introduction to that work.

The only help we have in situating either work, then, is the probability that the *Questions* belong to the period of Porphyry's association with Longinus, which must have begun in the 250s and extended to the time of his departure for Rome in 262. Even here, however, there is little to be said, since we know nothing of Longinus's understanding of the meaning of Homer, and a knowledge of his lost work *Was Homer a Philos-*

---

86. Bidez, *Vie de Porphyre*, p. 32, n. 3, and pp. 108–9. The fragments of Περὶ ἀγαλμάτων are published by Bidez in the same work, pp. 1–23 (Appendices).

87. Cf. Bidez, *Vie de Porphyre*, p. 1, note on fr. 1 (Appendices).

88. This is decidedly reminiscent of the comparative method of Numenius. The section of fr. 10 on the Egyptian sun-boat (p. 19, lines 7–12) recalls *De ant.* 10 (63.13–17), which is explicitly Numenian (= fr. 30.7–10).

opher? or a simple indication of the answer he proffered to the question posed in his title would be essential to the use of the evidence of Porphyry's association with Longinus to date either work.[89] The fact that a work with a similar title, "On the Philosophy of Homer,"[90] is attributed to Porphyry himself makes the problem even more interesting.

We do know, however, that when Porphyry arrived in Plotinus's circle, he had a reputation as a philologist,[91] and in the self-portrait in his "Life of Plotinus" we see him in that role as well as in that of poet (*Vit. Plot.* 15). Plotinus himself asked Porphyry to edit his writings (*Vit. Plot.* 7). The qualities of the man of letters, extending, according to the Alexandrian tradition, from meticulous philology to the writing of poetry, would surely have been qualities Porphyry acquired or perfected during his studies in Athens with Longinus, whom he himself calls "the preeminent critic of our time."[92] It is in part through Porphyry's praise that Longinus maintained his exalted reputation—so exalted that the essay "On the Sublime" was long attributed to him on little other basis. Little though we know of the true Longinus, however, it is clear that he and his circle cultivated a tradition of learning rooted in Platonism that made of their literary scholarship something substantially different in emphasis from that of the Alexandrians five centuries earlier. Porphyry need hardly have joined Plotinus's circle to be exposed to the teachings of Numenius and Cronius: Longinus himself pointed out that Plotinus had covered the same material as Numenius and the other Neopythagoreans.[93] It would not be surprising to find that the Athenian Platonists of the mid–third century, including Longinus, found in Homer the sort of meaning implied in Plotinus and developed by Porphyry in the essay on the cave of the nymphs. Neither is it beyond the realm of possibility that sometime in the years between 262 and 300, many of which he spent in relative seclusion, Porphyry should have found time, in spite of his undoubtedly increased philosophical activity, to exercise his mind on philological problems in Homer. The received dating, as Bidez implies, is en-

89. KP s.v. Longinos lists the titles Ἀπορήματα Ὁμηρικά, Προβλήματα Ὁμήρου καὶ λύσεις and Εἰ φιλόσοφος Ὅμηρος.

90. Περὶ τῆς Ὁμήρου φιλοσοφίας. Cf. Bidez, *Vie de Porphyre*, p. 70 (Appendices).

91. Cf. Porph. *Vit. Plot.* 16.14–18.

92. τοῦ καθ᾽ ἡμᾶς κριτικωτάτου γενομένου (Porph. *Vit. Plot.* 20.1–2).

93. Porph. *Vit. Plot.* 20. Cf. Dillon, *Middle Platonists*, pp. 362 and 385. See n. 10 above.

tirely hypothetical, and we can do little more than affirm, once again, a deeply divided response to Homer, corresponding to a deeply divided methodology of explication.[94]

Whatever the date of the *Homeric Questions*, the absence in them of the type of interpretation we are tracing makes them relatively unimportant from our standpoint. They participate in a tradition of commentary at least as old as Aristotle and had an enormous influence on the content of the Byzantine scholia, an influence that, even with Schrader's edition, has not been exhaustively explored.[95]

Several passages in the largely intact first book of the *Questions* strongly suggest the tone and method of Ps.-Plutarch in *The Life and Poetry of Homer*. After suggesting that Plato might appear to have been the first to assert that anger and suffering were mixtures of pleasure and pain, but that Homer had, in fact, seen this first and had thus "taught" Plato, Porphyry goes on, very much in the manner of Ps.-Plutarch (*De vit. Hom.* 130), to discuss the heart as the seat of emotion and *then* in a more characteristic manner to examine in detail the Homeric vocabulary relating to the emotions.[96] He likewise occasionally compares Homeric rhetorical devices to those used by the orators, and once mentions Pythagoras in the portion that survives intact.[97] To this extent he participates in the eclectic tradition represented by the Ps.-Plutarch essay, which he may well have known. For the most part, however, the *Questions* are neither so rhetorically oriented nor so exaggerated in their exaltation of Homer as *The Life and Poetry of Homer*. As the preface announces, they are content with the elucidation of minor, but often genu-

94. The internal evidence for dating is inconclusive. The *Homeric Questions* are addressed to one Anatolius, mentioned by Eunapius (*Vit. soph.* 457–58) as the teacher of Iamblichus during the period before the latter attached himself to Porphyry. (On this, however, see A. C. Lloyd in CHLGEMP, p. 295 and n. 4.) Thus he could easily have been the same age as Porphyry and the dedication is unhelpful. The essay on the cave of the nymphs has no dedication, though Nauck suggested that a formula of address might be restored to explain the fragmented syntax of the opening sentence. In this case, the name of the addressee would have been lost along with the opening words of the essay.

95. On the continuous tradition of works on "Homeric Questions" from Aristotle to Porphyry, see Pfeiffer, *History of Classical Scholarship*, pp. 67–70. On Schrader's contribution to scholarship on Porphyry's *Questions*, see Bidez, *Vie de Porphyre*, p. 33, n. 3.

96. Porph. *Quaest. hom.*, ed. Sodano, 68.8–83.16.

97. πολλὰ τοιαῦτα καὶ παρὰ τοῖς ῥήτορσι προοίμια ἐπιγράφεται πρὸς τοὺς θορύβους. Porph. *Quaest. hom.*, ed. Sodano, 114.16–18. On Pythagoras: 115.18.

inely difficult and puzzling, problems, and even here the underlying conviction that Homer was a philosopher is present.[98]

The exegetical principles Porphyry applied to the "larger" Homeric matters are suggested in a fragment from the lost work *The Styx* (Περὶ Στυγός), preserved in the doxographer Stobaeus:

> The poet's thought is not, as one might think, easily grasped, for all the ancients expressed matters concerning the gods and δαίμονες through riddles, but Homer went to even greater lengths to keep these things hidden and refrained from speaking of them directly but rather used those things he did say to reveal other things beyond their obvious meanings. Of those who have undertaken to develop and expound those things he expressed through secondary meanings, the Pythagorean Cronius seems to have accomplished the task most ably, but on the whole he fits extraneous material to the texts in question since he is unable to apply Homer's own, and he has not endeavored to accommodate his ideas to the poet's words but rather to accommodate the poet to his own ideas.[99]

Porphyry here reveals his mistrust of even the best interpreters and his simultaneous conviction that the model of the structure of meaning of the text of Homer on which those interpreters base their work is a valid one. The problem would seem to be insoluble. The author of these lines clearly has in mind the sound Aristarchan principle he stated at the beginning of the *Questions*: Homer is the best basis on which to elucidate Homer. Yet at the same time he accepts the idea that there are certain aspects of the meaning of Homer, certain truths contained in the *Iliad* and

98. ῥητέον δὲ ὅτι φιλοσοφεῖ Ὅμηρος (Porph. *Quaest. hom.*, ed. Schrader, 200 [*ad Il.* 15.13ff.]). Zeus's threatening reminder of the hanging of Hera has an unacceptable surface (διὰ ποίαν αἰτίαν οὕτως ἀσχήμως ὑβρίζει τὴν Ἥραν ὁ Ζεὺς διὰ θνητὸν Ἡρακλέα [;]), therefore "the answer is that Homer is philosophizing." Porphyry goes on to elucidate the passage with a Stoicizing physical allegory.

99. ἔστι δὲ ἡ τοῦ ποιητοῦ δόξα οὐχ ὡς ἄν τις νομίσειεν εὔληπτος. πάντες μὲν γὰρ οἱ παλαιοὶ τὰ περὶ τῶν θεῶν καὶ δαιμόνων δι᾽ αἰνιγμάτων ἐσήμηναν, Ὅμηρος δὲ καὶ μᾶλλον τὰ περὶ τούτων ἀπέκρυψε, τῷ μὴ προηγουμένως περὶ αὐτῶν διαλέγεσθαι, καταχρῆσθαι δὲ τοῖς λεγομένοις εἰς παράστασιν ἄλλων. τῶν γοῦν ἀναπτύσσειν ἐπιχειρησάντων τὰ δι᾽ ὑπονοίας παρ᾽ αὐτῷ λεγόμενα ἱκανώτατα δοκῶν ὁ Πυθαγόρειος Κρόνιος τοῦτ᾽ ἀπεργάσασθαι, ὅμως ἐν τοῖς πλείστοις ἄλλ᾽ ἄττα ἐφαρμόζει ταῖς τεθείσαις ὑποθέσεσι, τὰ Ὁμήρου μὴ δυνάμενος, οὐ τοῖς παρὰ τοῦ ποιητοῦ τὰς δόξας, τοῖς δὲ παρ᾽ αὐτοῦ προσάγειν τὸν ποιητὴν πεφιλοτίμηται (Stob. *Ecl.* 2.1.19). Cf. Phillip De Lacy, "Stoic Views of Poetry," pp. 259–60 on καταχρῆσθαι here and the figure catachresis (as in Ps.-Plut. *De vit. Hom.* 18).

Odyssey, that Homer deliberately refused to treat explicitly and that therefore must somehow be illuminated from without. It is no surprise that this careful and often plodding student of Homer left us with little in the way of elucidation of "major" Homeric problems. The only essay in that mode that survives is as profoundly divided, as dubious of its own methods, and as ambiguous in its conclusions as the paragraph quoted above might lead us to expect.

Before going on to examine the essay on the cave of the nymphs, however, it will be fruitful to consider the other fragments of Porphyry preserved in Stobaeus. They number over thirty, but few contain significant references to Homer. Another passage from *The Styx* contains a sensitive paraphrase and explanation of Anticleia's description of the dead (*Od.* 11.219–22). After quoting the lines Porphyry observes:

> The idea is that souls are like the images appearing in mirrors and on the surface of water that resemble us in every detail and mimic our movements but have no solid substance that can be grasped or touched. This is why he calls them "images of dead men" [βροτῶν εἴδωλα καμόντων, *Od.* 11.476, cf. 24.14].[100]

This is something more than the scholiasts give us but falls far short of a thorough analysis. In clarifying Homer's image, however, Porphyry displays his ability to enter imaginatively into the text and to convey his rich experience of it to the reader. There is nothing about his more extravagant allegorical interpretations that suggests that he was not always able, as in this example, to respond to the text in a humbler manner, free of the often nitpicking scholarship of the *Questions* and of the radical departures from the superficial meaning found in the essay on the cave of the nymphs.

Another passage from *The Styx* makes the claim that Homer envisioned three places where souls exist: this earth; the Elysian Field, where they go from this earth without dying, and hence must take their bodies along; and, finally, Hades, where they go after death and so without their bodies.[101] Porphyry schematizes Homer's Hades somewhat more

---

100. ὑποτίθεται γὰρ τὰς ψυχὰς τοῖς εἰδώλοις τοῖς ἐν τοῖς κατόπτροις φαινομένοις ὁμοίας καὶ τοῖς διὰ τῶν ὑδάτων συνισταμένοις, ἃ καθάπαξ ἡμῖν ἐξείκασται καὶ τὰς κινήσεις μιμεῖται, στερεμνιώδη δ᾽ ὑπόστασιν οὐδεμίαν ἔχει εἰς ἀντίληψιν καὶ ἀφήν· ὅθεν αὐτὰς βροτῶν εἴδωλα καμόντων λέγει (Stob. *Ecl.* 1.41.50 [p. 309, lines, 9–14]).

101. Stob. *Ecl.* 1.41.53. In another passage (Stob. *Ecl.* 1.41.61) Porphyry identifies Homer's Elysian Field with the portion of the moon illuminated by the sun, apparently explaining the proper noun Ἠλύσιον by way of the Homeric form of the aorist of ἔρχομαι ("go, move"), ἤλυθ——.

rigidly than the text justifies, maintaining that it contains concentric rings of beings: souls of women, souls of men, and finally gods at the center. Nevertheless, his description of the genuinely Homeric possibilities for souls is admirably accurate and entirely incompatible with the Numenian claims that dominate the essay on the cave of the nymphs, identifying the disembodied souls with the Homeric δῆμος ὀνείρων and the Milky Way. It is important to remember that Porphyry's vast knowledge of the *Iliad* and *Odyssey* placed formulations of this sort easily within his grasp. He was quite aware of the range of possibilities offered by the text, read *without* second meanings. When he offers us mystical or moral allegorical interpretations—his own or those he borrows from the second-century Neopythagoreans—we can never assume that he is unaware of the distance between the interpretations and what we may call a "normal" reading of the text. What most strikingly distinguishes his response from most modern readings, however, is that he apparently assumed that the *Iliad* and *Odyssey* could sustain multiple levels of meaning simultaneously and without contradiction.

Plato is not mentioned in the passages discussed thus far and it is impossible to say whether the problem of reconciling the *nekyia* with the myth of Er had become important for Porphyry when *The Styx* was written. He does use Plato to explain Homer in another passage from the same work (Stob. *Ecl.* 1.51.54), referring to the *Philebus* on the dependence of the imagination (φαντασία) on the memory (μνήμη) to explain the nature of the Homeric ghosts' experience of their former lives.

The most extensive interpretive piece from Porphyry preserved by Stobaeus comes to us without any indication as to which of Porphyry's lost works may have contained it. It focuses directly on cited texts from Homer in order to distil from them certain truths about the fate of souls, and as such imitates in miniature the structure of the essay on the cave of the nymphs:

> What Homer says about Circe contains an amazing view of things that concern the soul. He says:
>
>> Their heads and voices, their bristles and their bodies
>> were those of pigs, but their minds were solid, as before.
>>
>> [*Od.* 10.239–40]
>
> Clearly this myth is a riddle concealing what Pythagoras and Plato have said about the soul: that it is indestructible by nature and eternal, but not immune to experience and change, and that it undergoes change and transfer into other types of bodies when it goes through what we call "destruction" or "death." It then seeks out, in the pursuit of pleasure, that which is fitting and appropriate to it because it is

similar and its way of life is similar in character. At this point, by virtue of what each of us gains through education and philosophy, the
soul, remembering the good and repelled by shameful and illicit
pleasures, is able to prevail and watch itself carefully and take care
lest through inattention it be reborn as a beast and fall in love with a
body badly suited for virtue and impure, nurturing an uncultivated
and irrational nature and encouraging the appetitive and passionate
elements of the soul rather than the rational. Empedocles calls the
fate and nature that preside over this transformation a δαίμων

Wrapping souls in an alien tunic of flesh,
[fr. B126 (D–K)]

and giving them new clothes.

Homer, for his part, calls the cyclical progress and rotation of
metensomatosis "Circe," making her a child of the sun, which is constantly linking destruction with birth and birth back again with destruction and stringing them together. The island of Aiaia is both the
fate that awaits the dead and a place in the upper air. When they have
first fallen into it, the souls wander about disoriented and wail and
do not know where the west is

Or where the sun that lights mortal men goes beneath the earth.
[Od. 10.191]

The urge for pleasure makes them long for their accustomed way of
life in and through the flesh, and so they fall back into the witch's
brew of γένεσις,[102] which truly mixes and brews together the immortal and the mortal, the rational and the emotional, the Olympian and
the terrestrial. The souls are bewitched and softened by the pleasures
that lead them back again into γένεσις, and at this point they have
special need of great good fortune and self-restraint lest they follow
and give in to their worst parts and emotions and take on an accursed
and beastly life.

The "meeting of three roads" that is imagined as being among the
shades in Hades is actually in this world, in the three divisions of the
soul, the rational, the passionate, and the appetitive. Each path or division starts from the same source but leads to a life of a specific sort
appropriate to it. We are no longer talking about a myth or a poem
but about truth and a description of things as they are. The claim is
that those who are taken over and dominated by the appetitive part
of the soul, blossoming forth at the moment of transformation and
rebirth, enter the bodies of asses and animals of that sort to lead tur-

102. The word γένεσις is left untranslated here and elsewhere because it is a
technical term in later Platonism with no convenient English equivalent—least of
all its Latin equivalent genesis. It refers not just to birth or coming-to-be, but to
the entire cycle of coming-to-be and passing away that is the existence of the sublunary realm. Thomas Taylor at one point translates it expressively as "the humid
and flowing condition of a generative nature."

bulent lives made impure by love of pleasure and by gluttony. When a soul that has had its passionate part made completely savage by hardening contentiousness and murderous brutality stemming from some disagreement or enmity comes to its second birth, gloomy and full of fresh bitterness, it casts itself into the body of a wolf or a lion, projecting as it were this body as a defense for its ruling passion and fitting itself to it. Therefore where death is concerned, purity is just as important as in an initiation, and you must keep all base emotion from the soul, put all painful desire to sleep, and keep as far from the mind as possible all jealousy, ill will, and anger, as you leave the body.

Hermes with his golden staff—in reality, reason [λόγος]—meets the soul and clearly points the way to the good. He either bars the soul's way and prevents its reaching the witch's brew or, if it drinks, watches over it and keeps it as long as possible in a human form.[103]

103. τὰ δὲ παρ' Ὁμήρῳ περὶ τῆς Κίρκης λεγόμενα θαυμαστὴν ἔχει τῶν περὶ ψυχὴν θεωρίαν. λέγεται γὰρ οὕτως

οἳ δὲ συῶν μὲν ἔχον κεφαλὰς φωνήν τε τρίχας τε
καὶ δέμας· αὐτὰρ νοῦς ἦν ἔμπεδος ὡς τὸ πάρος περ.

ἔστι τοίνυν ὁ μῦθος αἴνιγμα τῶν περὶ ψυχῆς ὑπό τε Πυθαγόρου λεγομένων καὶ Πλάτωνος, ὡς ἄφθαρτος οὖσα καὶ ἀίδιος οὔ τι μὴν ἀπαθὴς οὐδὲ ἀμετάβλητος, ἐν ταῖς λεγομέναις φθοραῖς καὶ τελευταῖς μεταβολὴν ἴσχει καὶ μετακόσμησιν εἰς ἕτερα σωμάτων εἴδη, καθ' ἡδονὴν διώκουσα τὸ πρόσφορον καὶ οἰκεῖον ὁμοιότητι καὶ συνηθείᾳ βίου διαίτης· ἔνθα δὴ τὸ μετὰ παιδείας ἑκάστῳ καὶ φιλοσοφίας ὄφελος ἀναμνημονεύουσα τῶν καλῶν ἡ ψυχὴ καὶ δυσχεραίνουσα τὰς αἰσχρὰς καὶ παρανόμους ἡδονὰς δύναται κρατεῖν καὶ προσέχειν αὐτῇ καὶ φυλάττειν, μὴ λάθῃ θηρίον γενομένη καὶ στέρξασα σώματος οὐκ εὐφυοῦς οὐδὲ καθαροῦ πρὸς ἀρετὴν φύσιν ἄμουσον καὶ ἄλογον καὶ τὸ ἐπιθυμοῦν ἢ θυμούμενον μᾶλλον ἢ τὸ φρόνιμον αὔξοντος καὶ τρέφοντος. αὐτῆς γὰρ τῆς μετακοσμήσεως εἱμαρμένη καὶ φύσις ὑπὸ Ἐμπεδοκλέους δαίμων ἀνηγόρευται,

σαρκῶν ἀλλογνῶτι περιστέλλουσα χιτῶνι

καὶ μεταμπίσχουσα τὰς ψυχάς. Ὅμηρος δὲ τὴν ἐν κύκλῳ περίοδον καὶ περιφορὰν παλιγγενεσίας Κίρκην προσηγόρευκεν, ἡλίου παῖδα τοῦ πᾶσαν φθορὰν γενέσει καὶ γένεσιν αὖ πάλιν φθορᾷ συνάπτοντος ἀεὶ καὶ συνείροντος. Αἰαίη δὲ νῆσος ἡ δεχομένη τὸν ἀποθνήσκοντα μοῖρα καὶ χώρα τοῦ περιέχοντος, εἰς ἣν ἐμπεσοῦσαι πρῶτον αἱ ψυχαὶ πλανῶνται καὶ ξενοπαθοῦσι καὶ ὀλοφύρονται καὶ οὐκ ἴσασιν ὅπῃ ζόφος

οὐδ' ὅπῃ ἠέλιος φαεσίμβροτος εἶσ' ὑπὸ γαῖαν.

ποθοῦσαι δὲ καθ' ἡδονὰς τὴν συνήθη καὶ σύντροφον ἐν σαρκὶ καὶ μετὰ σαρκὸς δίαιταν ἐμπίπτουσιν αὖθις εἰς τὸν κυκεῶνα τῆς γενέσεως, μιγνύσης εἰς τὸ αὐτὸ καὶ κυκώσης ὡς ἀληθῶς ἀίδια καὶ θνητὰ καὶ φρόνιμα καὶ παθητὰ καὶ ὀλύμπια καὶ γηγενῆ, θελγόμεναι καὶ μαλασσόμεναι ταῖς ἀγούσαις αὖθις εἰς τὴν γένεσιν ἡδοναῖς, ἐν ᾧ δὴ μάλιστα πολλῆς μὲν εὐτυχίας αἱ ψυχαὶ δέονται πολλῆς δὲ σωφροσύνης, ὅπως μὴ τοῖς κακίστοις ἐπισπώμεναι καὶ συνενδοῦσαι μέρεσιν ἢ πάθεσιν αὐτῶν κακοδαίμονα καὶ θηριώδη βίον ἀμείψωσιν. ἡ γὰρ λεγομένη καὶ

This conception of Circe resembles one found in Ps.-Plutarch (*De vit. Hom.* 126), and if we can assume Ps.-Plutarch to be earlier than Porphyry, then we can say with some confidence that the essentials of the present analysis were traditional by the late third century.[104] The simple, unsupported assertion that the passage is an *αἴνιγμα* may itself be an indication that Porphyry did not expect his reader to be surprised at the revelation. In any event, the fact that Porphyry does not cite a source permits us to take these views to be his own, even though we have good reason to believe that they were not original with him.

The density of "Pythagorean" doctrine—including the citation of Empedocles—and the absence of any development of the reference to Plato are striking. In speaking of the crucial moment of choice for souls, the essential preparation for which is philosophy, Porphyry must have in mind the myth of Er, and especially Socrates' interruption within the myth (*Rep.* 10.618b–619c), where exactly this point is made. If he does not make the reference explicit, it may be in order to avoid the problem that would certainly be raised by the discrepancy between the immediate reincarnation described above and the thousand-year interval of punishment or reward between incarnations postulated in the myth of Er.

The myth developed by Porphyry out of the Homeric material is decidedly more attractive than the myth of Er, where the soul's choice of a new life is viewed as a clearheaded one, rather like the choice of a new

---

νομιζομένη τῶν ἐν ᾅδου τρίοδος ἐνταῦθά που τέτακται περὶ τὰ τῆς ψυχῆς σχιζομένη μέρη, τὸ λογιστικὸν καὶ θυμοειδὲς καὶ ἐπιθυμητικόν, ὧν ἕκαστον ἀρχὴν ἐξ αὑτοῦ καὶ ῥοπὴν ἐπὶ τὸν οἰκεῖον βίον ἐνδίδωσι. καὶ οὐκ ἔτι ταῦτα μῦθον οὐδὲ ποίησις, ἀλλ᾽ ἀλήθεια καὶ φυσικὸς λόγος. ὧν μὲν γὰρ ἐν τῇ μεταβολῇ καὶ γενέσει τὸ ἐπιθυμητικὸν ἐξανθοῦν ἐπικρατεῖ καὶ δυναστεύει, τούτοις εἰς ὀνώδη σώματα καὶ βίους θολεροὺς καὶ ἀκαθάρτους ὑπὸ φιληδονίας καὶ γαστριμαργίας φησὶ γενέσθαι τὴν μεταβολήν. ὅταν δὲ φιλονεικίαις σκληραῖς καὶ φονικαῖς ὠμότησιν ἔκ τινος διαφορᾶς ἢ δυσμενείας ἐξηγριωμένον ἔχουσα παντάπασιν ἡ ψυχὴ τὸ θυμοειδὲς εἰς δευτέραν γένεσιν ἀφίκηται, πλήρης οὖσα προσφάτου πικρίας καὶ βαρυφρόνης ἔρριψεν ἑαυτὴν εἰς λύκου φύσιν ἢ λέοντος, ὥσπερ ὄργανον ἀμυντικὸν τὸ σῶμα τῷ κρατοῦντι προϊεμένη πάθει καὶ περιαρμόσασα. διὸ δεῖ μάλιστα περὶ τὸν θάνατον ὥσπερ ἐν τελετῇ καθαρεύοντα παντὸς ἀπέχειν πάθους φαύλου τὴν ψυχήν, καὶ πᾶσαν ἐπιθυμίαν χαλεπὴν κοιμήσαντα, καὶ φθόνους καὶ δυσμενείας καὶ ὀργὰς ἀπωτάτω τιθέμενον τοῦ φρονοῦντος ἐκβαίνειν τοῦ σώματος. οὗτος ὁ χρυσόρραπις Ἑρμῆς ἀληθῶς ὁ λόγος ἐντυγχάνων καὶ δεικνύων ἐναργῶς τὸ καλὸν ἢ παντάπασιν εἴργει καὶ ἀπέχει τοῦ κυκεῶνος, ἢ πιοῦσαν ἐν ἀνθρωπίνῳ βίῳ καὶ ἤθει διαφυλάσσει πλεῖστον χρόνον, ὡς ἀνυστόν ἐστι (Stob. *Ecl.* 1.41.60).

104. On the comparison of these two texts, see Buffière, *Mythes d'Homère*, pp. 516–17.

suit, which may or may not still seem pleasing when the customer is out in the street. With Homer's help, Porphyry humanizes the story. The beautiful description of the anguish of the recently disembodied souls whose needs have not yet adapted to their altered state is reinforced by a line from the beginning of the Circe episode evoking the helplessness of Odysseus and his men faced with yet another unknown island. The entire episode, read as an allegory, becomes a substitute for the exhausted myth of the *nekyia*. It is a *nekyia* without punishments imposed by arbitrary and incomprehensible gods. The goal of Porphyry's elaboration from Homer is an understanding of the experience of the soul after death in terms of human truths that are observable in our own experience, our own motivations and weaknesses.

In Plato's myth, philosophy is necessary for the correct choice of a new life because the choice itself is a rational one and possibilities need to be intelligently weighed. In Porphyry's account, philosophy is the necessary preparation primarily because it is needed to subordinate the irrational parts of the soul to the rational. If philosophy fails, the choice will be made in a flash, by either the unbridled passions or the unbridled appetites, and the result will be disastrous. Only reason itself can ensure the attainment of the ultimate goal, the final liberation from the entire cycle of γένεσις.

Read sympathetically, then, this interpretive passage is something more than an extravagant exegesis. It responds to some of the needs already noted in Plotinus with regard to the traditional mythology and its interpretation. The claim that the Homeric passage itself is an αἴνιγμα is finally unimportant: Porphyry elaborates his account in the manner of Plotinus, exploiting the myths and language of Homer to communicate abstract truths. The use of Homer is somewhat more obtrusive than in Plotinus, but the reason for this undoubtedly lies in Porphyry's general inclination to refer to authority rather than develop his thoughts independently. What is superficially a scholarly exercise, uniting myths from Homer and Plato and exploiting the richness of Homer's language, achieves an unexpectedly human and moving synthesis.

The Cave of the Nymphs

At the head of the harbor is a slender-leaved olive
and nearby it a lovely and murky cave
sacred to the nymphs called Naiads.
Within are kraters and amphoras
of stone, where bees lay up stores of honey.

Inside, too, are massive stone looms and there the nymphs
weave sea-purple cloth, a wonder to see.
The water flows unceasingly. The cave has two gates,
the one from the north, a path for men to descend,
while the other, toward the south, is divine. Men do not
enter by this one, but it is rather a path for immortals.

αὐτὰρ ἐπὶ κρατὸς λιμένος τανύφυλλος ἐλαίη,
ἀγχόθι δ᾽ αὐτῆς ἄντρον ἐπήρατον ἠεροειδές,
ἱρὸν νυμφάων αἳ νηϊάδες καλέονται.
ἐν δὲ κρητῆρές τε καὶ ἀμφιφορῆες ἔασι
λάϊνοι· ἔνθα δ᾽ ἔπειτα τιθαιβώσσουσι μέλισσαι.
ἐν δ᾽ ἱστοὶ λίθεοι περιμήκεες, ἔνθα τε νύμφαι
φάρε᾽ ὑφαίνουσιν ἁλιπόρφυρα, θαῦμα ἰδέσθαι·
ἐν δ᾽ ὕδατ᾽ ἀενάοντα. δύω δέ τέ οἱ θύραι εἰσίν,
αἱ μὲν πρὸς Βορέαο καταιβαταὶ ἀνθρώποισιν,
αἱ δ᾽ αὖ πρὸς Νότου εἰσὶ θεώτεραι· οὐδέ τι κείνῃ
ἄνδρες ἐσέρχονται, ἀλλ᾽ ἀθανάτων ὁδός ἐστιν.
                                        (Od. 13.102–12)

This strange passage of the *Odyssey*, situated at the crucial moment of
Odysseus's magical return to Ithaca, has the distinction of being the subject of the earliest surviving interpretive critical essay in the European
tradition. If we think of Aristotle's *Poetics*, Horace's *Ars poetica*, and "Longinus" *On the Sublime* as the seminal works of ancient literary criticism,
it is primarily because of their vast influence. The interpretive tradition
in ancient criticism has not fared as well, and today is largely lost or ignored. If we ask ourselves what "literary criticism" has meant since the
eighteenth century, however, we must answer that it is an activity inseparable from interpretation. The critic preeminently mediates between
reader and text, and if we would discover the ancient precedents for this
activity, Porphyry has a better claim to our attention than Aristotle or
Horace.

Before examining the essay on the cave of the nymphs itself, a word
should be said about the problem of its internal contradictions and of the
implied contradictions in Porphyry's exegetical method. The most recent
scholar to examine the issue has been Jean Pépin, whose conclusions
help to clarify Porphyry's intentions and method.[105] Karl Praechter had
emphasized the contradictions within the essay and the incompatibility
of the various levels of interpretation offered by Porphyry.[106] He had ex-

105. Pépin, "Porphyre, exégète d'Homère."
106. Karl Praechter, "Richtungen und Schulen im Neuplatonismus." Cf.
Pépin, "Porphyre, exégète d'Homère," p. 243 and note.

plained this tendency in terms of Porphyry's attachment to ethics (and so to moral allegory, even when this was in contradiction with his other assertions about the meaning of the passage) and love of scholarship for its own sake. Pépin went one step further to suggest that, in spite of the apparent contradictions and of the perceptiveness of Praechter's observations, a subtle method lies behind the presentation of the mutually conflicting allegories, a "calculated pluralism" building out of sometimes discordant elements a cumulative interpretive statement with a coherence of its own.[107] This, surely, is closer to the truth. The contradictions within Porphyry's demands on the text are, I would argue, genuine, reflecting the doubts expressed in the first passage from *The Styx* discussed above. The fact that the interpretations offered do not always fit one another is, however, to be viewed in the light of earlier approaches to Homer. For an exegete who is committed to articulating the meaning of a text in all its richness, and who, having accepted the presence of a second level of meaning behind the first, is quite willing to multiply those levels, the fact that the various levels of meaning begin to enter into contradiction is relatively unimportant. All enhance the text.

There remains, throughout the essay, an unresolved dichotomy between the Porphyry who would make only the most reasonable and methodologically conservative demands upon the text of Homer and the Porphyry who is forced, by the nature of the text under discussion, to extend beyond that text the search for the key to its less obvious meanings. This description recalls the position of Strabo with regard to Homer and to the interpretation of myth,[108] and indeed at one extreme Porphyry is surprisingly close to the geographer's attitude. This affinity is reflected not only in Porphyry's demand that the description of the cave reflect a geographical and historical reality but, more intimately, in his choice of vocabulary.

At the beginning of the essay, after pointing out the problem of extracting the meaning of the text under consideration, Porphyry turns first to Cronius,[109] according to whom the geographers make no mention of such a cave as Homer describes. As we later learn, Porphyry is proud that he has looked more carefully than Cronius had and has discovered a geographer to corroborate Homer's account. For the moment, however, the paraphrase of Cronius continues, examining the possibility that Ho-

107. Pépin, "Porphyre, exégète d'Homère," pp. 243–49.
108. See ch. 1C above.
109. This is, of course, the same Cronius paid a backhanded compliment in the important fragment from Περὶ Στυγός discussed above.

mer "fabricated the cave out of poetic license": κατὰ ποιητικὴν ἐξουσίαν
(De ant. 55.17–18).[110] This expression, whether from Cronius or original
with Porphyry, is unequivocally pejorative here.

Though he never articulates the idea, Porphyry seems to admit two
possible modes of artistic creation, both of them mimetic. One is mimetic in the humble sense that it represents objects and events in this
world with more or less fidelity. Writing of this sort responds to the demands we make on the works of historians and geographers, demands
that Porphyry would also make upon the text of Homer. The second sort
of mimetic art, of a type not seriously explored before Plotinus,[111] leaps
the intermediary of the world of the senses and imitates a higher reality.
It remains, however, mimetic, determined by something outside itself.
The "poetic license" to which Porphyry casually refers here would not
produce art of the latter sort. Rather, it recalls Strabo's discussion of Homer's uneven reliability, where precisely the same definition occurs: "poetic license, which is a mixture of history, rhetoric, and myth."[112] The
liberty or "license" of Homer, for Strabo, is his mixing together of historically accurate descriptions with material of other sorts and leaving the
reader to distinguish among these elements.[113] Porphyry's use of the term
is slightly different. He seems to identify "poetic license" with all the
elements of Homer's poetry that are not historically sound. He goes on
to argue that if the passage in question is, in fact, an imaginative construct, it is an unconvincing, improbable one.

At the opposite pole from that of the critic who shies away from the

110. In text and notes, references to Porph. De ant. are to page and line of
Nauck's text, except in the summary in this chapter, where reference is to the
numbered sections.

111. On Plotinus's location of the beauty of art "on a level with the beauty of
nature as a way to the intelligible beauty," see Armstrong in CHLGEMP, pp.
232–34, with references. The Phaedrus provides a precedent but does not dimin-
ish the originality of Plotinus's esthetics.

112. See note 113, below.

113. Indeed, one has the strong impression here that either Cronius or Porphyry is echoing Strabo:

Str. Geog. 1.17.5–13:
εἰ δέ τινα μὴ συμφονεῖ, μεταβολὰς αἰτιᾶσθαι δεῖν ἢ καὶ
ποιητικὴν ἐξουσίαν, ἢ συνέστηκεν ἐξ ἱστορίας καὶ διαθέσεως
καὶ μύθου . . . [defined] . . . τὸ δὲ
πάντα πλάττειν οὐ πιθανόν, οὐδ᾽
Ὁμηρικόν.

De ant. 55.14–18:
ὅτι μὲν οὐ καθ᾽ ἱστορίαν παρει-
ληφὼς μνήμην τῶν παραδοθέντων
. . . ὅτι δὲ κατὰ ποιητικὴν ἐξουσίαν πλάσσων ἄντρον ἀπίθανος
ἦν. . . .

"poetic license" of Homer is the position, emerging gradually in the essay, of the critic who in every phrase of the Homeric passage finds new intimations of a truth that lies beyond the apparent meaning of the words. The effect is cumulative, and one has the impression that Porphyry is, by sheer weight of evidence, winning himself away from his skepticism in the direction of a genuine faith in the coherence of the passage as a statement of great complexity, neither historically mimetic *nor* mere "poetic license," but imitating a transcendent reality.

An important impulse in this transition from skeptical questioning to a vision of a rich and complex structure of meaning is an explicit urge to find—or to impose—order, an impulse that goes hand in hand with a repeatedly expressed horror of the possibility of randomness. It becomes increasingly clear that randomness (or chains of causality that escape him) are intolerable to Porphyry, whether in the poem—which could not have been composed "with what came to hand, randomly,"[114] or "according to some sort of chance,"[115]—or in the universe that is the archetype of the cave Homer describes: "The cosmos has not come into being in vain or randomly."[116] The element in the world that assures this order is divine purpose (φρόνησις), which negates randomness, just as "the theologian [i.e., Homer] indicates [in the olive tree and its placement] that the universe did not come into being spontaneously, the creation of irrational chance, but rather is the result of noetic nature and wisdom."[117]

The fact that, at the opening of his essay, Porphyry cites the entire eleven-line passage on which he intends to comment places the exegesis of the cave of the nymphs in a unique position in ancient criticism. The discussion sometimes departs conspicuously from the text, but it always returns sooner or later to Homer's *words*, and specifically to the series of internal problems apparently first raised by Cronius (*De ant.*, section 3). We are not dealing here with explication of a Homeric myth, but rather with that of a specific passage of a special sort, one so problematical that it cannot simply be paraphrased. Each phrase, each element of the description, must be interrogated separately in the attempt, first, to establish the structure of meaning—in this case, to establish that the superficial meaning cannot exhaust the significance of the passage—and then

114. τὸ πρόστυχον καὶ ὡς ἔτυχεν (Porph. *De ant.* 55.19). Cf. *De ant.* 57.18.

115. ἀπὸ τύχης τινός (Porph. *De ant.* 78.8).

116. ὁ κόσμος οὐκ εἰκῇ οὐδ' ὡς ἔτυχε γέγονεν (Porph. *De ant.* 78.11–12).

117. ὁ θεολόγος . . . σημαίνων δι' αὐτῆς ὡς οὐκ ἐξ αὐτοματισμοῦ τὸ ὅλον τοῦτο καὶ τύχης ἀλόγου ἔργον γέγονεν, ἀλλ' ὅτι φύσεως νοερᾶς καὶ σοφίας ἀποτέλεσμα (Porph. *De ant.* 78.16–19).

to explore the deeper meaning, to articulate it in all its richness. It is doubtful whether any other thinker in antiquity combined the philological skill and seriousness of Porphyry with a comparable desire to interrogate the meaning of the Homeric poems in all their implications.

The result bears more than a superficial resemblance to a modern essay in interpretation, though its emphasis on Homer as a source of information concerning prehistoric religion and on *comparanda* from various sorts of ritual make it appear a curiously unbalanced one. It is likewise an unavoidably naive explication. When Porphyry abandons his down-to-earth, Strabonic approach to the passage, he rapidly moves to the other pole of his critical perspective and begins to sound like a preacher elaborating on a text. Much of what should lie between these poles—between the philological-historical discussion and the assertion that the passage "hints at" a reality Homer refused to express directly—is missing.[118]

The first problem is to establish that the cave and its description do, in fact, "hint at" some further truth. Porphyry was by no means consistent in his thinking on the indications within a text that may steer the interpreter in the direction of identifying a secondary meaning. As Pépin points out, he rejected the allegorical reading of the Gospel of John 6.53 ("If you eat not of the flesh . . .") on the basis that the literal meaning was repulsive.[119] An unacceptable surface meaning would thus make a passage unacceptable as a candidate for interpretation on the level of secondary meanings. This may be a distant echo of Socrates' rejection of certain Hesiodic and Homeric myths "whether understood according to secondary meanings or not."[120] It is clear, in any case, that Porphyry reacts to Christian ritual cannibalism much in the same way Socrates is depicted as reacting to the myth of the castration of Ouranos—if the surface is unacceptable, it is superfluous to look behind it. The opposite position was, of course, one of the fundamental tenets of the defensive allegorists: an unacceptable surface was in fact a primary indicator that some deeper meaning was being expressed behind the screen.[121]

---

118. We know that texts from earlier philosophers were read aloud in Plotinus's circle as a basis for lectures or discussions (Porph. *Vit. Plot.* 14.10–14), and it is a distinct possibility that the methodology of Porphyry's exegesis of the description of the cave must be traced to that oral context.

119. Pépin, "Porphyre, exégète d'Homère," p. 236.

120. Plato *Rep.* 2.378d.

121. For a collection of ancient *loci* for this idea, see Pépin, "Porphyre, exégète d'Homère," pp. 252–56.

The attitude that Porphyry adopts at the beginning of the essay is closer to the second of the two just mentioned. He is dependent upon Cronius, whose testimony on this matter he later qualifies to such an extent that we are left with a serious problem in the logic of the demonstration that the passage is to be viewed as the vehicle of a profound statement. Cronius is credited with the observation that Homer described a cave dedicated to the nymphs on Ithaca that did not exist according to the geographers. On the basis that it was both geographically inaccurate and filled with obscurities that made it implausible as a purely imaginative creation, he concluded that the passage was allegorical (ἀλληγορεῖν), not an example of "poetic license" (Porph. *De ant.* 56.8).[122] The implication is that the surface is unacceptable (implausible) and so for that very reason the passage must contain some deeper meaning that will provide the missing links and restore harmony.

At this point, Porphyry interrupts Cronius to undercut him. Cronius, along with all the others who have approached the passage as a purely Homeric creation, has been careless. Porphyry's pride in his scholarship is all but audible: he has located a passage in the geographer Artemidorus of Ephesus (fl. ca. 100 B.C.) that, admittedly in the most general terms, describes the cave or at least attests its historical reality (*De ant.*, section 4). His conclusion is initially disarming. He has destroyed the logic of Cronius's demonstration that the passage is allegorical, only to attempt to restore it by claiming that it really makes no difference whether, in exploring the obscurities signalled by Cronius, we are exploring the poet's symbols or those of the people who consecrated the cave. In fact, to the extent that Homer is describing a historically and geographically authentic shrine of the nymphs, he is acting as intermediary for the wisdom of the ancients who, even before his own time, established the cult. This does not, of course, restore Cronius's logic. Porphyry leaves us in limbo: we do not know to what extent we are explicating a Homeric text with a complex structure of meaning and to what extent we are exploring the symbolism of a real shrine accurately described by Homer. The cave, in any case, is real.[123]

122. The word ἀλληγορέω, in the context of Porphyry's essay, seems to belong entirely to Cronius. It occurs only in this instance and once again (*De ant.* 57.20). Far more characteristic for Porphyry himself are forms of αἰνίττομαι (six times) and αἴνιγμα (twice), and particularly σύμβολον (eighteen times). The ὑπονοέω complex does not occur.

123. There seems to be little doubt that the description in Artemidorus—perhaps that in the *Odyssey* as well—refers to a cave in the bay of Polis on Ithaca,

Porphyry, one feels, would be happier if the description could be shown to be entirely accurate and historical. This would presumably remove any possibility that Homer has introduced some random, and therefore meaningless, element. Had the detailed description of the cave come from Pausanias, rather than Homer, much of Porphyry's commentary might have been no different.

The core of the essay is carefully contrived to avoid this problem and treats the elements of the description simply as data on early religion. Homer's intention is relegated to obscurity. We are apparently to assume that he is merely transmitting a description aspiring to photographic realism. It is only toward the end of the essay, and in particular in the discussion of the olive tree by the cave and in Porphyry's concluding remarks, that we unequivocally confront the problem of Homer's creative contribution and its significance, and there we find Porphyry making very remarkable claims for the scope and nature of Homer's intention.

The central part of the essay need occupy us only briefly. Much of the material is Numenian and has thus already been discussed.[124] After establishing the basic methodology sketched out above (section 4), Porphyry proceeds to discuss in general terms the symbolism of caves in "ancient" theology, asserting that they were consecrated to the cosmos. They were appropriate symbols for this purpose, able to be called both "murky" or "misty" ($\dot{\eta}\epsilon\rho o\epsilon\iota\delta\dot{\eta}\varsigma$) and "lovely" ($\dot{\epsilon}\pi\dot{\eta}\rho\alpha\tau o\varsigma$), despite the apparent contradiction, because of their nature and the possibility of viewing them from several perspectives (section 6). This passage is particularly interesting because it suggests that the juxtaposition of the adjectives in the line

and nearby it a lovely and murky cave

$$\dot{\alpha}\gamma\chi\acuteo\theta\iota\ \delta'\ \alpha\dot{v}\tau\hat{\eta}\varsigma\ \ddot{\alpha}\nu\tau\rho o\nu\ \dot{\epsilon}\pi\dot{\eta}\rho\alpha\tau o\nu\ \dot{\eta}\epsilon\rho o\epsilon\iota\delta\acute{\epsilon}\varsigma$$
$$(Od.\ 13.103),$$

was for Porphyry (as for Cronius before him) a paradox requiring resolution. In other words, the associations, negative and positive, of Homer's vocabulary are a key to the elucidation of meaning, at least to the extent

---

excavated by Sylvia Benton in the 1930s. See her "Excavations in Ithaca iii: the Cave of Polis," parts 1 and 2. The cave seems to have been associated with Odysseus at least from the Geometric period, and there are inscribed dedications to the nymphs beginning at least as early as the end of the third century B.C. Such a cult in Ithaca associated with Odysseus is likewise mentioned by Heliodorus (Eth. 5.22).

124. See ch. 2B above.

that the juxtaposition of a pejorative adjective with another having pleas-
ant associations triggers the response in these readers that the passage
requires further examination.

Porphyry's solution draws into the discussion of the text and its apparent contradictions the Neoplatonic model of perception postulating
that, just as the human being exists on multiple levels—soul in all its
complexity, and beyond soul, mind—so perception is possible on these
various levels. In terms of our everyday perceptions, the cave is "lovely";
that is, to our normal fragmented perceptions, it offers the pleasing spec-
tacle of form imposed on inert matter. We view it as participants in the
flux and disorder of this world and by means of the senses, which themselves are bound to matter. It thus intimates a higher reality—that of
form—and so gives us pleasure. At the same time, "seen from the point
of view of one who sees more deeply into it and penetrates it by the use
of mind," [125] it is "murky." That is, for the observer who has the perspective gained by the full realization of νοῦς, the adjective ἠεροειδής (with
its strongly pejorative cast) will be appropriate because, able to contemplate the forms themselves, he will see in the cave not matter beautified
by form but rather form obscured by matter.

The multiple valid perspectives and modes of perception implied by
such an epistemology are at the core of the Neoplatonists' perception of
meaning in the literary artifact, as indeed in any other object in the universe, or in the universe itself. [126] Porphyry's assertion of the existence of
numerous valid possibilities in the interpretation of a single text is thus
by no means evidence of a lack of clearly defined principles of interpretation, but rather a logical consequence of Neoplatonic psychology and
epistemology. [127]

The essay proceeds quite deliberately, considering the elements of the
passage phrase by phrase as they occur. The word that arrests Porphyry's
attention longest is, of course, "cave," which triggers an extensive recital
of material from various sources on caves as sanctuaries (sections 6–10),
which is gradually turned into an explanation of the specific appropriateness of caves to the Naiad Nymphs (sections 7–13), themselves identified with souls entering the material universe (sections 12–13). The
elucidation of the "symbols" seems to belong to the field of comparative

125. ἠεροειδὲς δὲ σκοποῦντι τὴν ὑποβάθραν αὐτοῦ καὶ εἰς αὐτὴν εἰσιόντι τῷ
νῷ (Porph. De ant. 59.23–25).
126. See ch. 5D, with n. 87, below, for Sallustius's observation that "the cosmos as well may be called a myth."
127. This model is applied systematically only in Proclus, where principles
merely implied in Porphyry are fully articulated. See ch. 5 below.

religion rather than that of literary criticism. By comparison with various cult practices, poetry, and customs, the stone kraters and amphoras, the stone looms, and the bees are thus found to be appropriate "symbols" for the soul-Naiads and their cult (sections 13–19). Porphyry then turns his attention to the final lines of the passage, describing the two openings of the cave.

The necessity of again citing part of the passage so that we may begin with a clear impression of exactly what Homer says reminds Porphyry of the problem of intention, which he had previously swept under the carpet. His only resolution, however, is to restate his assertion that the same structure of meaning is to be found both in the symbolism of religious cult and in the words of the poets: "We must now explore either the intention [βούλημα] of those who established the cult in the cave, if the poet is repeating historical fact, or his own riddle [αἴνιγμα], if the description is his own fabrication."[128]

Again Porphyry turns to Numenius and Cronius and evokes the identification, already discussed, of the gates with Cancer and Capricorn, and the "people of dreams" of *Odyssey* 24.12 with the Milky Way (sections 21–29). The density of comparative material throughout this passage is exceptionally great and both method and actual content owe a great deal to Numenius. Even beyond the astrological structure superimposed on the Homeric lines, Porphyry explores the specific appropriateness of a double cave to the physical universe, claiming that duality in all its manifestations corresponds to "otherness" (ἑτερότης), which is the source of the natural world. He does not actually mention the Platonic-Pythagorean dyad here, but the list of polar opposites characteristic of the universe is a clear evocation of the Pythagorean columns of opposites (sections 29–31).[129] The recital is arbitrarily cut short by the assertion that it has been sufficiently demonstrated that the two mouths of the cave are an image of the fundamental duality of the universe, and that the entire meaning of Homer's description of the cave has been plumbed.

128. ἕπεται τοίνυν ζητεῖν τὸ βούλημα εἴτε τῶν καθιδρυσαμένων, εἴπερ ἱστορίαν ὁ ποιητὴς ἀπαγγέλλει, ἢ αὐτοῦ γε τὸ αἴνιγμα εἴπερ αὐτοῦ πλάσμα τὸ διήγημα (Porph. *De ant.* 70.22–24). See p. 110 above for Porphyry's indications in the Περὶ ἀγαλμάτων that poetry about the gods may be read essentially the way statues may be "read." The εἰκόνες of the gods in stone and in words have analogous structures of meaning.

129. Cf. Geoffrey Kirk and J. E. Raven, *The Presocratic Philosophers*, pp. 236–42. The same pattern of thought is common to Syrianus and Proclus (see ch. 5E below).

The final section of the essay is the most interesting. Porphyry's discussion, though somewhat unbalanced, has been linear, proceeding methodically through the passage to the end. He has, however, kept something in reserve, the first verse, which he had passed over in silence:

At the head of the harbor is a slender-leaved olive.

αὐτὰρ ἐπὶ κρατὸς λιμένος τανύφυλλος ἐλαίη
(Od. 13.102)

This element in Homer's description is not part of the supposed dedication and cannot be referred to the wisdom of those who dedicated the cave. Again, Porphyry remains close to Homer's words. The "head" of the harbor was chosen for the olive tree, the symbol of Athena, who was born from the head of Zeus. The tree now emerges as the focus of the entire allegorical landscape. Given that the description of the cave itself is an allegory—whether Homeric or simply transmitted by Homer—representing the physical universe, the olive tree at the head of the harbor next to the cave itself represents divine purpose or wisdom (φρόνησις) that informs the universe and yet is something separate from it. This symbolic statement belongs to Homer, the θεολόγος, not to the hypothetical founders of the actual cult. A recital of symbolic qualities inherent in the olive follows, closing the ingeniously rearranged sequential discussion of the elements of the description (section 33).

The final three sections explore the broader myth that contains this allegorical landscape and pose the problem of the passage's relationship to its context. In view of the tendency of the surviving interpretive literature from antiquity to approach a given passage or problem with blinders and to treat it in utter isolation,[130] this in itself is striking evidence of Porphyry's perspective on his task. There is no longer any question of attributing to anyone but Homer the "wisdom" couched in the broader lines of the story. Porphyry's paraphrase of the episode of the hiding of the goods in the cave and the subsequent conversation between Odysseus and Athena (Od. 13.361–440) ignores the typically narrative-dramatic nature of Homer's exposition and transforms the whole passage into a didactic statement about the nature of man's spiritual progress, a statement that has the force of a command:

130. This is certainly true of Proclus (see ch. 5 below), and as already mentioned there was a continuous tradition of works with titles such as Ὁμηρικὰ προβλήματα and Ὁμηρικὰ ζητήματα extending from Aristotle to Porphyry and beyond, indicative of a tendency to treat specific problems or cruxes in isolation.

Homer says that all outward possessions must be deposited in this cave and that one must be stripped naked and take on the persona of a beggar and, having withered the body away and cast aside all that is superficial and turned away from the senses, take counsel with Athena, sitting with her beneath the roots of the olive, how he might cut away all the destructive passions of his soul.[131]

This is not, of course, what Homer says. It is what Homer describes, distilled into a moral imperative and fitted to a model of the universe and the nature of man that is not what we are accustomed to think of as Homeric.

The interpretation is not original with Porphyry and the tradition into which it fits is identified as that of Numenius and his circle (section 34). This is not to say that Numenius articulated the whole moral allegory Porphyry has just sketched out, but rather that he explained its central symbol: Odysseus as the symbol of man escaping the physical universe (the sea) to return, as Tiresias expressed it in his prophecy, to that place where there is not even any memory of the physical universe. The passage quoted above may well represent Porphyry's own reading; Numenius is introduced primarily to testify to the tradition of the interpretation of Odysseus's journey as a spiritual one.

The source of the second moral interpretation is less problematical: Porphyry presents it as explicitly his own. It complements the first and shares the metaphysical preconceptions that underlie it. The key—in characteristically Porphyrian scholarly manner—is provided by the statement (*Od.* 13.96) that the harbor where Odysseus was deposited belongs to Phorcys. This sea divinity, Porphyry reminds us, was the father of Thoosa, who in turn was the mother of the cyclops Polyphemus. Why does Homer bring this up here? He does so lest we forget Odysseus's original crime against "the gods of the sea and of matter" (ἁλίων καὶ ὑλικῶν θεῶν, *De ant.* 35).

More interesting than this claim that Odysseus's guilt is the thread that draws this part of the story into line with the tale of his wanderings is the interpretation of the Polyphemus episode that emerges here: "It was not in the nature of things for Odysseus simply to cast off this life of

131. εἰς τοῦτο τοίνυν φησὶν "Ομηρος δεῖν τὸ ἄντρον ἀποθέσθαι πᾶν τὸ ἔξωθεν κτῆμα, γυμνωθέντα δὲ καὶ προσαίτου σχῆμα περιθέμενον καὶ κάρψαντα τὸ σῶμα καὶ πᾶν περίττωμα ἀποβαλόντα καὶ τὰς αἰσθήσεις ἀποστραφέντα βουλεύεσθαι μετὰ τῆς Ἀθηνᾶς, καθεζόμενον σὺν αὐτῇ ὑπὸ πυθμένα ἐλαίας, ὅπως τὰ ἐπίβουλα τῆς ψυχῆς αὐτοῦ πάθη πάντα περικόψῃ (Porph. *De ant.* 79.12–19).

the senses by blinding it—an attempt to put an end to it abruptly."[132] The bungling, dimwitted, sensual giant of book 9, is, then, a projection into myth of the life of the senses—specifically of Odysseus's own life in this physical universe. The blinding of Polyphemus is a metaphor for suicide, an alternative denied the pilgrim by the gods that preside over this world. One cannot leave so easily. The life of the senses must be transcended not by violence but by contemplation. The path of violence is blocked and merely involves the pilgrim in an even more arduous ordeal of expiation in order to reach his "home." What is fascinating here is the transformation of an element of the myth entirely external to Odysseus into a projection of an aspect of his own spiritual life. The cyclops becomes a part of Odysseus—a part he wants desperately to escape—but his ineptitude in handling his escape at that early point in his career involves him in an arduous spiritual journey.

One cannot help thinking at this point of Porphyry's own intended suicide, which Plotinus was instrumental in preventing (*Vit. Plot.* 11). It seems highly probable that this particular internalization—the reading of the cyclops episode as a failed suicide—is one that had a very personal meaning for Porphyry. If there is an element of the essay that we may realistically think might be original and represent his *own* reading of the poem, this must be it.[133]

The conclusion of Porphyry's essay extends this principle of internalization of the action.[134] Porphyry describes the experience of Odysseus traveling off to the land where oars are unknown: he will travel "until he has become entirely free of the sea and stripped away his very experience of the sea and of matter, so that he thinks that an oar is a winnowing fan in his utter ignorance of the business of seafaring."[135] It is Odysseus's own ignorance that counts for Porphyry, and the details of Tiresias's

132. οὐ γὰρ ἦν ἁπλῶς τῆς αἰσθητικῆς ταύτης ἀπαλλαγῆναι ζωῆς τυφλώσαντα αὐτὴν καὶ καταργῆσαι συντόμως σπουδάσαντα (Porph. *De ant.* 80.11–13).

133. See my annotated translation of the essay (*Porphyry on the Cave of the Nymphs*), n. 28 (p. 42), and appendix, where Plotinus's brief essay on suicide (*Enn.* 1.9) is compared with the present passage.

134. We would lose this if we accepted the Buffalo editors' admittedly attractive ἐν ψυχαῖς ἀπείροις instead of the ἄπειρος adopted by Nauck at *De ant.* 80.20. The text is unavoidably corrupt at this point and the older emendation has the advantage of extending the exegetical method of the passage immediately preceding.

135. ὅταν παντελῶς ἔξαλος γένηται καὶ ἄπειρος θαλασσίων καὶ ἐνύλων ἔργων, ὡς πτύον εἶναι ἡγεῖσθαι τὴν κώπην διὰ τὴν τῶν ἐναλίων ὀργάνων καὶ ἔργων παντελῆ ἀπειρίαν (Porph. *De ant.* 80.20–81.1).

prophecy yield to the thrust of the interpreter's construction of the meaning of the passage. With an emphasis that may echo Plotinus on the forgetfulness of the higher soul once it has been reabsorbed in the contemplation of higher reality,[136] Porphyry insists that here again the myth has expressed in terms of a dramatized, fragmented development what is, in fact, a stage in the inner life of the soul.

The final paragraph defends these concluding general interpretations and insists that they are not "fanciful," though at the same time it implies contempt for another class of interpretations that is viewed as mere display of wit and ingenuity. The interpretations Porphyry has offered are justified by three factors: the wisdom of the ancients, the perfection of Homer, and the claim that "it is impossible that he should have successfully created the entire basis of the story without shaping that creation after some sort of truth."[137] This claim balances the ideas (presumably borrowed from Cronius) in the early paragraphs. It is simply not plausible that a *successful* poetic work could be produced by sheer "poetic license." The alternative that Porphyry seems to be offering is that Homer based his poems not on a physical or a historical reality but rather on transcendent realities—"truths" that govern the nature of his creation and its structure of meaning in ways that are far from obvious.

The unlikely coincidence of literary scholarship and Platonism that produced the essay on the cave of the nymphs has preserved a unique example of Neoplatonic attention to the meaning of a text rather than of a myth. Porphyry's internalization of the elements of the *Odyssey* story builds on a preexisting model of the meaning of that story but treats the relationship between text and meaning in a new way, or one not previously attested.

That the *Odyssey* was for Plotinus and his circle already a poem that, in subtly manipulated allegories, recounted a spiritual journey through a Platonized universe emerges in Porphyry's "Life of Plotinus" as well, in the oracle on the philosopher given to his disciple Amelius shortly after his death. It is no surprise that the hexameter oracle should contain echoes of Homeric lines.[138] One passage within the oracle, however, is

---

136. Plot. *Enn.* 4.3.27.

137. οὐ γὰρ ἐνῆν ἐπιτυχῶς πλάσσειν ὅλην ὑπόθεσιν μὴ ἀπό τινων ἀληθῶν μεταποιοῦντα τὸ πλάσμα (Porph. *De ant.* 81.6–8).

138. Henry and Schwyzer in their *index fontium* list nine verses containing Homeric material, but by using broader criteria the list could be lengthened substantially.

among the most convincing pieces of evidence demonstrating that by the late third century, the world of the *Iliad* and *Odyssey* had become a source of readily comprehensible metaphors for the progress of the soul. That is, the interpretation according to "secondary meanings" that made of Homer a seer and of his poems a spiritual allegory, current for centuries, had so completely entered the vocabulary of Greek culture—at least in Platonist circles—that no explanation was needed. The Homeric language and situations had entirely absorbed their new weight of meaning.

The oracle addresses Plotinus's soul:

Δαίμων—once a man, but now approaching
the holier lot of a δαίμων! The bond of human necessity
is broken and you are bursting out of the noisy chaos of the flesh,
powerful, using your wits to bring you to the shore of the seawashed
		headland,
far from the crowd of sinners, to walk the lovely path of a pure soul.

δαῖμον, ἄνερ τὸ πάροιθεν, ἀτὰρ νῦν δαίμονος αἴσῃ
θειοτέρῃ πελάων, ὅτ᾽ ἐλύσαο δεσμὸν ἀνάγκης
ἀνδρομένης, ῥεθέων δὲ πολυφλοίσβοιο κυδοιμοῦ
ῥωσάμενος πραπίδεσσιν ἐς ᾐόνα νηχύτου ἀκτῆς
νῆχε᾽ ἐπειγόμενος δήμου ἄπο νόσφιν ἀλιτρῶν
στηρίξαι καθαρῆς ψυχῆς εὐκαμπέα οἴμην.[139]

The metaphor is further extended and elaborated. It would have been superfluous to mention Odysseus by name, but the *Odyssey* to which the passage makes oblique reference was, in fact, an allegorical poem. The allegories it contained were placed in it not by the poets of the tradition that produced it but by a vigorous and obtrusive interpretive tradition that had corrected their oversight, an interpretive tradition that was as much a part of Platonism in late antiquity as the poems themselves.[140]

139. See Henry and Schwyzer's *editio maior* of Plotinus, vol. 1, p. 32, lines 23–38.
140. Many examples of the same image in Christian Platonism could be cited. See for instance the Eastern baptismal liturgy quoted by Hugo Rahner, "Das christliche Mysterium und die heidnischen Mysterien," p. 446: "Im dunklen Tale der Erde fährst du dahin wie auf einem Meer." Rahner draws the analogy to the Odysseus story without attempting to reconstruct the process of transmission to the Christian context.

C. JULIAN AND SALLUSTIUS

After the death of Porphyry, we hear little more of the disciples of Plotinus in Italy and the West, and the main stream of Platonic thought must be traced through Iamblichus (who taught in Syria during the first two decades of the fourth century) to the schools of Athens and Alexandria, which flourished in the fifth and sixth. The break between Porphyry and Iamblichus is significant in the history of Platonic thought from a number of points of view, and principally in the new prominence given to theurgy by Iamblichus and his followers. More important from our standpoint, however, is the almost complete lack of concern for the interpretation of early poetry that characterizes Iamblichus and his immediate circle.[141] This sort of exegetical interest will surface again as a central and worthy subject of philosophical inquiry only with Syrianus and Proclus in fifth-century Athens—no doubt "Iamblichans" themselves, as has recently been asserted,[142] but at the same time thinkers who made extraordinary demands of doctrinal coherence and compatibility on a heterogeneous literary tradition extending from Homer to Plato to the Chaldaean Oracles. It was this concern to demonstrate the unity of the tradition that led to the great synthesis of Platonic interpretation of Homer in Proclus, as well as to a renewal of a properly literary scholarship that would seem to be nearly absent from fourth-century Neoplatonism.

Two thinkers of this period do attract our attention, however, though the nature of their contribution itself suggests the degree to which Porphyry's interpretive zeal had, in fourth-century Platonist circles, been dispersed in other concerns. The essentials of a coherent and rather re-

141. Iamblichus's contribution to the exegesis of the Platonic dialogues and to the formulation of the principles that governed that exegesis was of the greatest importance. See Wallis, *Neoplatonism*, pp. 134–37, and Bent Dalsgaard Larsen, *Jamblique de Calchis, exégète et philosophe*, esp. pp. 429–62. As Wallis likewise asserts, however, Iamblichus was not concerned with the "piecemeal" exegesis cultivated by Porphyry. There are a few hints of Pythagorean use of Homer in his *Theologoumena arithmeticae*, but his other works yield little information on the development of the understanding of Homer. See B. Dalsgaard Larsen, "Jamblique dans la philosophie antique tardive," who observes (p. 7): "Il n'y a plus trace, chez Jamblique, d' exégèse homérique s'inscrivant dans la tradition de l'allégorie stoïcienne."

142. Garth Fowden, "The Pagan Holy Man in Late Antique Society," pp. 44–45. See the same insightful article, pp. 58–59, on the failure of the "Iamblichan sages" in Julian's circle.

served attitude toward myth, poetry, and Homer in particular as sources of truth emerge from the writings of Julian the Apostate (332–63).[143] In the tradition of Iamblichus, Julian on the whole shows relative indifference to the interpretation of early poetry. On the other hand, Julian's rhetorical use of Homer is frequent and widespread.[144] There are countless examples of decorative phrases and allusions, used in the manner of the rhetors of the imperial period to mark a point or simply to embellish the classicizing diction. Homer is likewise a rich source of exempla and *comparanda*, though these are not always used to his advantage.

The second panegyric on the emperor Constantius (*Or.* 2) offers the richest selection of such allusions, undertaking with characteristic bravado to demonstrate that in all the virtues Constantius outdid the heroes of the *Iliad*. At the time of the composition of the panegyric (between 355 and 359), the emperor had made Julian a Caesar and provided him with an army by means of which—willingly or unwillingly—he was to wrest away Constantius's empire within a few years. The heavy artifice of the rhetoric of the panegyrics, however, permits no irony to penetrate. The audience—assuming the discourse was in fact delivered—is offered a detailed comparison of the emperor with Agamemnon, Nestor, Odysseus, Hector, Achilles, and the other *Iliad* heroes, to whom he is shown to be superior in every particular. The striking point is that the rhetorical pretext leads Julian to emphasize the negative qualities of the heroes and their shortcomings. Agamemnon, for example, failed to honor Achilles, and Julian, adopting the persona of Achilles singing the κλέα ἀνδρῶν, asserts that Constantius has studied his Homer and would not make a similar mistake (50c). Likewise, Nestor's and Odysseus's failures are emphasized to underline the superiority of Constantius (75b–76b).[145]

In this context, Julian takes time to remind his audience that, in order

143. On the broader subject of Julian's relation to tradition, see Polymnia Athanassiadi-Fowden, *Julian and Hellenism*, and in particular her introduction (pp. 1–12) on Julian and the conflict of Hellenism and Christianity.

144. This is widely recognized, but little analyzed—see, for instance, W. C. Wright in the Loeb Julian, vol. 1, pp. xi–xii. Julian's use of Homer has also been frequently exaggerated and misunderstood. One cannot agree, for example, with T. M. Lindsay's assertion that "Julian quotes Homer as frequently and as fervently as a contemporary Christian does the Holy Scriptures" (*The Cambridge Medieval History*, vol. 1, p. 110).

145. Even exempla dear to the Neoplatonic allegorizing tradition are used negatively in Julian, in the familiar rhetorical manner. In *Ep.* 34 406b–407a, he evokes Proteus, "praised by Homer," only to observe, τῆς μὲν φύσεως αὐτὸν ἐπαινῶ, τῆς γνώμης δ' οὐκ ἄγαμαι.

to use them for Constantius's praise, he does not need to torture the
meaning of the poems as do certain contemptible exegetes who "cut up
the poems into convincing and possible assertions, starting from the
least hint of a second meaning [ὑπόνοια] and from very vague principles, and try to persuade us that these things are precisely what the
poets were trying to say." [146]

This skepticism with regard to interpretation by ὑπόνοιαι is, of course,
as old as Plato, and it goes hand in hand with a willingness to call Homer
"divine" (θεῖος, Or. 3 128b, Ep. 17 383d) and "inspired" (θεόληπτος,
Or. 4 149c), which likewise points to Plato. Julian's careful irony in using
these terms with regard to Homer is no doubt very close in spirit to the
attitude of Plato himself, though for somewhat different reasons. In
Julian's case, it seems based on a faith in the availability in the mysteries
of the direct testimony of the gods themselves, obviating the need to
make frequent appeal to ambiguous and frustrating poets for information about the divine.

That Julian had personal knowledge of the Iliad and Odyssey is unquestionable. In the Misopogon (351d–352b), he himself describes the
way in which his tutor Mardonius deflected him from real horse races to
the horse races in Homer, from real trees to the trees and landscapes of
the Odyssey: "There are many plants in Homer more lovely to hear about
than those one can see with one's eyes." [147]

The imaginative world of Homer was thus offered Julian as a more
desirable substitute for the real world, and he had fully entered into it.
The tradition of interpretation by ὑπόνοιαι was part of his education as
well, as his hostility indicates. That hostility, however, does not prevent
him from making claims for Homer as a theological authority. He re-
bukes an impious official—probably a Christian—for striking a priest
and thus indicating that he thinks of the punishment of the Greeks in
Iliad 1 for dishonoring Chryses as "mere fable" (μυθώδη, Ep. 62 450d).
He is violently contemptuous of teachers who interpret Homer and
Hesiod for their pupils and poison the children's minds by calling the
poets impious. He goes so far as to invite such teachers to go preach to
the "Galileans" and expend their exegetical talents on Matthew and

146. ἀναλύοντες ἐς λόγους πιθανοὺς καὶ ἐνδεχομένους τὰ πλάσματα ἐκ μι-
κρᾶς πάνυ τῆς ὑπονοίας ὁρμώμενοι καὶ ἀμυδρὰς λίαν παραλαβόντες τὰς ἀρχὰς
πειρῶνται ξυμπείθειν, ὡς δὴ ταῦτά γε αὐτὰ ἐκείνων ἐθελόντων λέγειν (Jul. Or. 2
74d–75a).
147. ἔστι γὰρ φυτὰ παρ' αὐτῷ πολλὰ τερπνότερα ἀκοῦσαι τῶν ὁρωμένων
(Jul. Misop. 351d).

Luke (*Ep.* 42 423a–b). There is a hint here that allegorical interpretation of texts in general is a mode of teaching Julian associates with the muddled vulgarizing of the Christians and excludes from his own purer religion.

He is skeptical of the general value of myth, which he views as pap for infantile minds. His aristocratic bias colors his approach to this commonplace: myths were generated to make truth accessible to souls that, in the language of the *Phaedo*, are just sprouting their wings (*Or.* 7 206d). Philosophers who have recourse to them are like physicians who are also slaves and so are reduced to the necessity of pampering their patients as they cure them (*Or.* 7 207d). This passage, though specifically directed against the offensive fables of the Cynics, holds to a lesser extent for the ancient poets as well. Julian's contempt does not reach so far, certainly, but his mistrust of fables does.

Though the great hymn to the sun (*Or.* 4) makes more generous use of Homer than Julian's other surviving writings, it also supplies us with the clearest statement of his misgivings about Homer as a source of truth. Homer and Hesiod are evoked in support of Julian's solar theology, primarily for purposes of supplying precedents for idiosyncratic associations of gods, and particularly for the association of the major gods with the sun. The poets' qualifications as witnesses are asserted in a tone that contrasts with the usual coolness: "This is not new at all but was previously held by the earliest of the poets, Homer and Hesiod, whether it was their opinion or whether like seers they were inspired with a frenzy for the truth by divine inspiration." [148]

The illustrations from Homer turn on standard elements familiar from other commentators: the word Ὑπερίων shows that Homer associated the visible sun with the higher sun(s) from which it emanates; Zeus's respect for Helios in the Odyssean episode of the cattle of the sun indicates the respect in which the sun was held. Finally, several physical allegories are evoked, based on the identification of Hera with "mist" (ἀήρ), by implication the antithesis of the sun and its penetrating light (136d–137b). The departure from Julian's usual method is short-lived. He abandons these allegories abruptly:

> But let us dismiss the poets' stories at this point. Along with the divine they contain a great deal that is merely human. Rather, to what

148. οὐδὲ νεαρὰ παντελῶς ἐστιν ἡ δόξα, προύλαβον δὲ αὐτὴν οἱ πρεσβύτατοι τῶν ποιητῶν, Ὅμηρός τε καὶ Ἡσίοδος, εἴτε καὶ νοοῦντες οὕτως εἴτε καὶ ἐπινοίᾳ θείᾳ καθάπερ οἱ μάντεις ἐνθουσιῶντες πρὸς τὴν ἀλήθειαν (Jul. *Or.* 4 136b).

the god himself seems to teach us both about himself and other things, let us go on to *that*.[149]

There is, then, more than one level to poetry of the sort Julian has been discussing, and more than one sort of truth. The problem had been formulated in similar terms, with a similar note of frustration, by Strabo,[150] and it was to be elaborated defensively with great ingenuity by Proclus.[151] If Julian does not, like Strabo, approach the problem of sorting through the "poetic license" of Homer with resignation, it is because he believes in a direct revelation that is far less ambiguous and more accessible. When, a few pages later, he argues that the information gleaned from the mysteries should be viewed not as "hypotheses" (ὑποθέσεις) but rather as "doctrines" (δόγματα), he has revealed the nature of that alternative: "They [sc., the priests in the mysteries] speak, having listened to the gods or to great δαίμονες."[152] In short, they have the poets' potential for direct perception of transcendent reality without the poets' ambiguities and human failings.

The enormous importance of the mysteries in Iamblichan Neoplatonism thus reduces the importance of the "scriptures" the *Iliad* and *Odyssey* had become earlier in the period of the confrontation of paganism with Christianity. In Julian we see an approach to the poems that owes little to the allegorical tradition, though it clearly needs to define itself with reference to that tradition. In asserting the value of the poems against Cynics and Christians, Julian is glorifying them as cultural monuments, not as scripture. His intense commitment to the integral coherence of Hellenism—to the necessary interrelation of religion, literature, and institutions—involved him in a problematic relationship to the texts themselves.[153] He himself is our best witness to the fact that the real conflict on the level of texts had become a conflict of interpretive communities. By explicitly barring Christians from teaching, and so from interpreting, Homer, he implicitly conceded the power of the interpretive community to shape the meaning of the poems. For him, a Christian Homer was worse than no Homer at all.

---

149. ἀλλὰ τὰ μὲν τῶν ποιητῶν χαίρειν ἐάσωμεν· ἔχει γὰρ μετὰ τοῦ θείου πολὺ καὶ τἀνθρώπινον· ἃ δὲ ἡμᾶς ἔοικεν αὐτὸς ὁ θεὸς διδάσκειν ὑπέρ τε αὐτοῦ καὶ τῶν ἄλλων, ἐκεῖνα ἤδη διέλθωμεν (Jul. *Or.* 4 137c).

150. See ch. 1C above.

151. See ch. 5D below.

152. οἱ μὲν γὰρ θεῶν ἢ δαιμόνων μεγάλων δή τινων ἀκούσαντές φασιν (Jul. *Or.* 4 148b).

153. On Julian's view of literary culture, see Athanassiadi-Fowden, *Julian and Hellenism*, pp. 122–24 and passim.

Julian himself emerges as the champion of a misconceived and un-examined literalism, an interpretive tradition existing only in fantasy, though shakily grounded in Socratic mistrust of interpretation (while committed in a fundamentally un-Socratic way to the educational use of Homer). He is by no means unique in his distrust of allegorists, but the combination of hostility toward other interpreters with his own mud-dling and impatient mode of explanation of texts marks him as a figure immersed in a conflict he only half understands. Christianized Helle-nism was well on its way to absorbing Homer into its cultural heritage, as Julian's contemporary Basil of Caesarea makes clear.[154] Julian's quixotic task, for which he was ill equipped, was in essence to rescue those texts from that interpretive community, but the community with which he would have replaced it had ceased to exist. Porphyry had been at heart a popularizer, and Julian is the very opposite. Moreover, it is reasonable to believe that, after Constantine, there was little need for new pagan popularizers. In its period of greatest activity, the mystical allegorical tradition tried to bond the content of Neoplatonism to the popular clas-sics of Greek culture. That endeavor had a very limited place in the brief pagan renaissance of the 360s, and when the tradition surfaces again with Proclus, its goals are academic and theoretical rather than practical.

An exception proving this rule can be found in the essay *Concerning the Gods and the Universe* of Sallustius. This popularizing manual from Julian's circle was indeed an attempt to communicate the basic truths of pagan Neoplatonism to a wide audience, and it does confront the prob-lem of the relationship of myth to truth. Nevertheless, Homer's name is never mentioned, and none of the stories discussed is specifically Ho-meric. Myth is treated in a way not incompatible with the attitude ex-pressed by Julian[155] and is brought in only to be dismissed in favor of direct (and therefore relatively abstract) statement of the basic truths of Neoplatonism.[156] Sallustius's popularization is thus quite different in its thrust from that of Porphyry in his exegesis of the symbolism of cult and of the early poets. Sallustius's primary goal is to state the difficult ab-stractions in the simplest possible form, not to relate them to received and authoritative mythic accounts.[157]

In spite of Sallustius's neglect of Homer, his chapters on myth will repay brief attention in view of the fact that some of the ideas on the

154. See ch. 6C below.
155. Cf. A. D. Nock in his edition of Sallustius, p. xlv.
156. The discussion of myth is in Sallust. *De diis* 3–4.
157. Porphyry had once taken a similar approach, in the work usually re-ferred to as *Sententiae ad intelligibilia ducentes*.

nature of myth to be found in them likewise appear a century later in Proclus's defense of Homer.

Sallustius begins his essay by stating the basic prerequisites for learning about the gods: the student must be educated and of good character and must accept certain universally held truths. Among these is the principle that "every god is good, immune to experience and emotion, and unchanging." [158] He should furthermore believe that "the essences of the gods never came to be . . . nor are they material . . . nor do they have spatial limits . . . nor are they separate from the first cause or from one another." [159] The string of negative assertions recalls the negative theology of Plotinus and his successors, but beyond that there is an echo of the prescriptions Socrates laid down in the *Republic* for the content of the new myths. [160] The conflict between this conception of the divine and the mythic accounts is obvious. Deities that possess the qualities enumerated here are qualitatively different from the gods of Homer and Hesiod. The implied conflict is so great that Sallustius's Neoplatonism sounds decidedly aniconic or even iconoclastic. It is this problem that inspires Sallustius to discuss myth and its relationship to the truth concerning the gods. His discussion is in effect a brief, but necessary, digression before he goes on to the more serious problem of stating the basic concepts about the gods directly.

The ancients, we are told, shied away from stating these facts directly and preferred to clothe them in myth. Sallustius mentions casually that one function of this procedure is to provide the listener, the student, with mental exercise: we are forced to inquire into the intention of the mythmakers, and are thus stimulated to mental activity. The divinity of myths is guaranteed by the fact that "the inspired poets and the best philosophers" [161] used them, as well as the founders of rituals and the gods themselves, expressing themselves in oracles.

The juxtaposition of the four classes of evidence to establish a presumption of validity again recalls the method of Numenius. Sallustius makes it clear that he views the myths of the poets in the same light as the myths of Plato, the stories associated with the mysteries, and the

158. ὅτι πᾶς θεὸς ἀγαθός, ὅτι ἀπαθής, ὅτι ἀμετάβλητος (Sallust. *De diis* 1; p. 2, lines 6–7 in Nock ed.).

159. αἱ τῶν θεῶν οὐσίαι οὐδὲ ἐγένοντο . . . οὐδὲ ἐκ σωμάτων εἰσὶ . . . οὐδὲ τόπῳ περιέχονται . . . οὐδὲ τῆς πρώτης αἰτίας ἢ ἀλλήλων χωρίζονται (Sallust. *De diis* 2; p. 2, lines 10–15 in Nock ed.).

160. See ch. 1B above.

161. τῶν ποιητῶν οἱ θεόληπτοι καὶ τῶν φιλοσόφων οἱ ἄριστοι (Sallust. *De diis* 3; p. 2, lines 22–23 in Nock ed.).

oracles. All must have comparable structures of meaning and mask the same ultimate truths. The relationship of myth to the divine can, to some extent, be explained. On the principle that like rejoices in like, the stories about the gods had to resemble them in order to please them. The mythoplasts, in representing the gods themselves, used complex statements built on the pairs of opposites *spoken/secret, revealed/unrevealed, manifest/hidden*. That is, each of their imitations has a surface meaning masking a hidden meaning intimately related to it. This structure of meaning is itself explained as an imitation of divine goodness, which functions on two levels. The gods provide benefits on the sense plane to all, but restrict the benefits on the level of νοῦς to the wise (τοῖς ἔμφροσιν); in imitation of them, the myths reveal the existence of the gods to everyone but restrict information regarding their true identities to those equipped for such knowledge.

The raw truth would produce only scorn in crude souls unprepared for it and would make the diligent lazy by failing to challenge them. Thus, by using the screen of myth, the mythoplasts shielded the truth from the scorn of the former and stimulated the latter to exploit the capacities of their minds (φιλοσοφεῖν). The immorality of some of the stories—adulteries, abuse of fathers, and so on—is part of the overall design, calling the alert student's attention to the complex structure of meaning through the strangeness and inappropriateness of the surface meaning.[162]

Sallustius divides all myths into five categories: those relating to the gods, to the nature of the universe, to the soul, to matter, and to more than one of these spheres (*De diis* 4). The category of theological myth is illustrated by the story of Kronos swallowing his children. "Since the god is noetic, and all νοῦς returns to itself [i.e., contemplates itself], the myth hints at the essence of the god."[163] The same myth, however, is also a myth relating to the nature of the universe and if we view it on the level of the gods' activities "with regard to the universe" (τὰς περὶ τὸν κόσμον ἐνεργείας), this level of meaning becomes central. In this interpretation, Kronos is "time" (χρόνος) and his children are the divisions of time, contained within the whole. Thus a single story has the potential of at least

162. Porphyry's ambiguous attitude on this matter has already been mentioned. Sallustius himself hedges to the extent of stating this idea by means of rhetorical questions, but there is little doubt that he adheres to the principle that an offensive surface meaning is an indication that some truth lies hidden beyond the screens (παρακαλύμματα) of the words.

163. ἐπειδὴ νοερὸς ὁ θεός, πᾶς δὲ νοῦς εἰς ἑαυτὸν ἐπιστρέφει τὴν οὐσίαν ὁ μῦθος αἰνίττεται τοῦ θεοῦ (Sallust. *De diis* 4; p. 4, lines 25–26 in Nock ed.).

four levels of meaning beyond the superficial. The model anticipates that elaborated for literature in Dante's famous letter to Can Grande and may not be unrelated to the somewhat earlier one to be found in Origen the Christian.[164] Sallustius does not, however, choose to insist upon the capacity of a given myth to be interpreted on all the levels. His categories suggest, rather, that the normal situation would be that in which a given myth would clothe a specific truth, belonging to one of the four classes. Nevertheless, the Kronos myth proves to be coherent on all levels.

Sallustius does not maintain a clear distinction between the deliberate allegory of the mythoplasts and the allegorical interpretation of the explicators. The relationship of the categories of myth (apparently reflecting the intentions of the mythoplasts) to the corresponding modes of interpretation (reflecting the multiple perspectives of the interpreters) remains undefined. The third type of myth—that on the level of soul—is not explored. We are told, however, that if we want to understand the Kronos myth in this mode, we should "focus on the activities of the soul itself, for the thoughts of our souls, even if they go forth to others, yet remain in those who bore them."[165] Kronos, then, can be read as soul itself, projecting its thoughts (νοήσεις) into the world, presumably in the form of λόγοι, and yet simultaneously retaining them within itself. This treatment of myth on the level of soul is frustratingly vague, particularly in view of the fact that, as we later learn, myths of this type, along with myths relating to the structure of the universe, are those suited to poetry.

Myths representing the parts of the physical universe as gods (earth as Isis, wine as Dionysus, and so forth) are dismissed as the lowest form, characteristic of the Egyptians. A brief explanation of the judgment of Paris as a "mixed" myth, with multiple levels of meaning, closes the enumeration of types. Thus the only examples actually presented have proven to be "mixed" myths.

Sallustius's categories imply the Neoplatonic model of reality as their prototype. Though he does not make the correspondences explicit, it is clear that Sallustius associates the highest level of myth with the tran-

164. See ch. 6E below.

165. ὁ δὲ ψυχικὸς τρόπος ἐστὶν αὐτῆς τῆς ψυχῆς τὰς ἐνεργείας σκοπεῖν, ὅτι καὶ τῶν ἡμετέρων ψυχῶν αἱ νοήσεις, κἂν εἰς τοὺς ἄλλους προέλθωσιν, ἀλλ᾽ οὖν ἐν τοῖς γεννήσασι μένουσιν (Sallust. De diis 4; p. 4, line 31 to p. 6, line 2 in Nock ed.). This, then, is the meaning of the Kronos myth in this mode, but the myth does little to show what such myths might otherwise be like. I am indebted here to Martha Malamud, who clarified the passage for me in the context of a seminar I offered at Cornell in 1984.

scendent divine and the lowest level with the deceptive perceptions within the realm of the senses, with the other two, like the hypostases νοῦς and ψυχή, lying between these extremes. His association of the various classes of myth with different groups of users makes it clear that the mixed category is viewed as the highest, uniting all the rest (with the probable exception of the lowest): "The theological myths are appropriate to philosophers, the ones relating to the nature of the universe and to souls to poets, and the mixed myths fit the mysteries, since every initiation endeavors to establish for us relationships both with the universe and with the gods."[166]

The discussion of myths in general closes with another explanation of a myth of the mixed type and its imitation in the festival of Attis. Several elements of this analysis recall Numenius and Porphyry. The nymph of the myth, like those of the cave, presides over γένεσις.[167] The participants in the festival at one point drink milk as an emblem of their rebirth.[168] The sequence of the festival, imitating the sequence of the myth, is a projection in time and space of an eternal truth.[169]

In practice, the myths of the poets seem to be treated as mixed myths of the type Sallustius associates with the mysteries, and it is unclear why he considered myths relating truths on the level of the soul and the structure of the universe particularly suitable for poetry. He seems on the one hand to have in mind the physical allegories of the Stoics, and on the other to want to define the position of poetry and to locate it just *below* the mysteries and philosophy in the hierarchy of the users of myth. The most striking fact in all of his discussion, however, is the restricted role given myth in the communication of truth, and, within that, the even smaller role reserved for the poets.

---

166. πρέπουσι δὲ τῶν μύθων οἱ μὲν θεολογικοὶ φιλοσόφοις, οἱ δὲ φυσικοὶ καὶ ψυχικοὶ ποιηταῖς, οἱ δὲ μικτοὶ τελεταῖς, ἐπειδὴ καὶ πᾶσα τελετὴ πρὸς τὸν κόσμον ἡμᾶς καὶ πρὸς τοὺς θεοὺς συνάπτειν ἐθέλει (Sallust. *De diis* 4; p. 6, lines 23–26 in Nock ed.).

167. αἱ δὲ νύμφαι γενέσεως ἔφοροι (Sallust. *De diis* 4; p. 8, lines 10–11 in Nock ed.).

168. Sallust. *De diis* 4; p. 8, line 24 in Nock ed. Cf. Porph. *De ant.* 28.

169. See ch. 5B below for the same ideas developed by Proclus.

IV

The Interaction of
Allegorical Interpretation
and Deliberate Allegory

The emergence of allegorical writing on a large scale and the mystical allegorical interpretation of non-epic literature are both developments rooted in the period of the authors we have been discussing. Neither of these developments is well understood, and if neither has found its historian, it is doubtless because the evidence is sparse, difficult to interpret, and often difficult to date. My comments will be limited to a sampling of texts providing evidence that the tradition of allegorical reading we have been examining was, in fact, crucially important in generating patterns of thought about literature and responses to literature that were soon translated beyond the limited sphere of Homer interpretation.[1]

The fourth century was, of course, the period of the final confrontation between paganism and Christianity in the Greco-Roman world. Both Neoplatonism and the allegorical interpretation of cultural and religious traditions characterized the positions of either side in this conflict.

The allegorical tradition in Christianity traced its roots to the parables and their interpretations in the Gospels themselves. Christian interpreters, with the model of Philo before them, tried to understand the Hebrew scriptures in ways that reduced the tension between the two ele-

1. The examples of deliberate allegory discussed here are those closest to the concerns of the larger study, but the list might have been extended. Perhaps the most important omission is political allegory, represented at the end of the fourth century by Synesius's *Egyptian Tale*, where the Osiris myth is retold as an allegory of events in Constantinople in the year 400. Here the procedure is very close to that of the roman à clef, with the Osiris of the story apparently representing the exiled Praetorian Prefect Aurelian, and so forth. I am indebted to Alan Cameron for calling this work and this entire category of late antique allegory to my attention.

ments of the "Judeo-Christian Tradition" (itself, as Harold Bloom rightly insists, a fabrication resting upon the violent appropriation of those scriptures by the Christian interpretive community). Interest in the spiritual meaning of Homer was undoubtedly largely confined to the pagan community, but we have already noted the important exception of the second-century Gnostics, and Homeric motifs are not infrequently to be found in Christian contexts in the period.[2] The demands made on their respective bodies of "theological" literature by the various groups show considerable similarities.

It is not surprising, then, that it was from this milieu that deliberately allegorical literature took its start.[3] Neither is it surprising, in view of the rising influence of Christianity, that the spread of deliberate allegory in epic and of allegorical interpretation in non-epic genres occurred largely in contexts that were Christian or at least influenced by Christianity.

The figure usually taken to stand at the head of the tradition of allegorical epic is Prudentius (348–after 405), whose *Psychomachia* elaborates

2. On the Gnostics, see ch. 1D above. Beyond Carcopino, mentioned there, see also Kurt Rudolph, *Gnosis*, pp. 93 and 107. Among the Christian examples is a grave of the fifth (?) century in Syracuse (Museo archaeologico di Siracusa no. 14,439) where the deceased, one Nassiana, is compared to Penelope in her fidelity to her husband. This inscription is no doubt typical of a large class. H. Leclercq (Corbet et Leclercq, *Dictionnaire d'archéologie chrétienne et de liturgie* s.v. Homère, vol. 6, cols. 2739–42) lists two other examples of Christian grave inscriptions with Homeric content.

3. Here again we run up against the problem of the precise meaning of the term "allegory" in antiquity. Allegory in the rhetorical sense of irony or sarcasm (cf. Ps.-Plut. *De vit. Hom.* 70) is, of course, present in Homer. Heraclitus cites as examples of early allegory relevant to Homer fragments of Archilochus (fr. 54 Bergk) and Alcaeus (frs. 18, 19, Bergk) that ostensibly describe storms at sea but supposedly refer in fact to war and political events. He adds Anacreon fr. 75 Bergk, where the poet ostensibly addresses a colt. The true addressee, he asserts, is an arrogant woman (Heraclit. *Quaest. hom.* 5). In all these cases, we may assume that Heraclitus is correct about the intention of the poets, but we would speak of metaphor here, rather than allegory. The images cited are brief and largely self-contained and do not seem to belong to the category of elaborated, extended metaphorical expression we call allegory. What is new in the fourth century is a kind of literature built upon the deliberate elaboration of a structure of meaning similar to that the Neoplatonists found in Homer—a story intended to be understood on one or more levels beyond the superficial. It is significant that in Christian circles a developed theory of the structure of meaning of texts existed at this time. Origen had already applied a triadic model by which serious texts were viewed as having "superficial," "moral," and "allegorical" or "anagogical" levels of meaning. See ch. 6E below.

on the theme of Christian conversion by means of the extended metaphor of a series of heroic battles between virtues and vices for the possession of the soul. The warriors bear the names of the moral qualities
they represent—Patientia and Ira, Luxuria and Sobrietas—and provide
the major precedent for the personification allegory of medieval and Renaissance allegorical epic.[4] The practice of introducing into an epic narrative figures whose names indicate that they represent abstract qualities, but whose actions are otherwise comparable to those of heroes or
gods, is as old as Homer,[5] and is an epic commonplace richly exploited
by Virgil and Ovid. In the earlier epic tradition, however, this allegory is
one figure among many. For Prudentius, it is central and dominates the
entire fiction.

Clearly this sort of allegory is not at all what we have been tracing in
the history of the interpretation of Homer.[6] The structure of meaning is
entirely different. The key to its interpretation is provided immediately.
The "secondary" level of meaning is obtrusive and takes on greater importance than the action itself, which has lost all claim even to a coherent "surface" meaning. This action merely embellishes the abstract
statement and gives it a colorful, concrete dramatization. In spite of these
differences, however, Prudentius and the Homer of the interpretive tradition come together on the level of the commonplace that the literary
artifact has meaning of more than one sort—that the story told is projected onto a plane beyond the one apparent at the surface. Prudentius
had not only an allegorized Homer to look back to but, far more immediately, an allegorized Virgil. However much his deliberate allegory owes
to the interpretive tradition of Philo, Clement, and Origen, the trappings of heroic warfare suggest that allegorized pagan epic was also an
important force in determining the nature of his poem.[7]

The Christian tradition of allegorical interpretation is an explicit element in the motivation behind Prudentius's epic. In the 68-line preface to
the *Psychomachia*, Prudentius paraphrases Genesis 14–15 and 18, the

---

4. See Macklin Smith, *Prudentius' Psychomachia*, pp. 109–14 on the development of personification allegory and the role of Prudentius.

5. For a catalogue of characteristic Greek examples of personification allegory, see M. Lavarenne in the Budé Prudentius, vol. 3, pp. 14–15.

6. I am unable to agree with Pfeiffer (*History of Classical Scholarship*, p. 5) that
the Homeric personification allegory of the Prayers in *Il.* 9.502 in any way anticipates or provides a base for the allegorists who detected hidden meanings in the
Iliad and *Odyssey*.

7. On the sources of Prudentius's allegory, see Reinhard Herzog, *Die allegorische Dichtkunst des Prudentius*, pp. 2–4.

story of Abraham's military victory over the invaders of the cities of the plain, his restoration of Lot's freedom, and Sarah's belated pregnancy. This is presented as a text—more properly, a myth—for interpretation, and in the exegesis that follows, the preface takes on the quality of a sermon.

This two-part preface imparts to the poem as a whole a triadic structure consisting of text, traditional allegorical interpretation, and finally (the *Psychomachia* proper) the paraphrase and heroic expansion of the allegory. The biblical text, we are told, prefigures the course our lives must follow. Lot imprisoned—doubly so, one might imagine, because of his normal place of residence—is the part of ourselves that is prey to the passions, and we must gather all our forces to set that part free. The 318 servants of Abraham armed to deliver Lot represent Christ,[8] whose aid is essential. Christ is also represented in the figure of Melchisedek,[9] who offers nourishment to the victorious warriors. Sarah's belated pregnancy is the direct result of the intervention of Christ, representing the trinity, and the offspring are the thoughts and acts worthy of a Christian.[10] The 915 dactylic hexameters of the *Psychomachia* proper represent the projection onto yet another plane of this interpretive sermon in 68 iambic trimeters, carefully separated from the rest of the poem by its different form and intention. The traditional epic invocation, directed to Christ but full of Virgilian echoes, comes not at the very beginning of the poem, but immediately after the preface.

The sermonlike quality of the preface is a substantial indication that allegorical literature—deliberately allegorical composition developed at some length—is the outgrowth of a tradition of interpretation impinging on a tradition of creative literature. It is clear that this interpretive tradition in its Christian manifestation had a place of respect in the intellectual and spiritual life of the community that it appears to have lost at this period in the pagan community. Indeed, the fact that we have only bits and pieces of interpretive literature from pagan antiquity, whereas the Christian tradition of textual exegesis is far better represented, is also an indication that the elaboration of the meaning of a text was never, in pagan tradition, held in the respect it had in the Christian context. The

8. As Lavarenne explains in his edition *ad loc.* (vol. 3, p. 48, n. 6), the number 318, written ΤΙΗ´ in Greek, was a natural numerological symbol for Christ, the tau representing the cross and the iota and eta the first letters of ΙΗΣΟΥΣ.

9. Here again Lavarenne supplies the key. The association of Christ and Melchisedek is traceable to *Hebrews* 7 (Prudentius [Budé], vol. 3, p. 50, n. 3).

10. Cf. Lavarenne in Prudentius (Budé) vol. 3, p. 48, n. 3.

loss of so much of pagan literature and the absence of a clearly defined body of pagan scriptures provide only partial explanations for this phenomenon. There is no doubt that, in educational contexts, Homer was expounded and explained endlessly, yet this process remained, at best, the mental exercise praised by Sallustius. It only rarely reached the level of seriousness that would have been necessary for its results to be recorded and preserved.

The *Psychomachia* provides a model that may well prove relevant to other literary forms far removed from it. The author begins with a text claimed as allegorical—though the claim is without the slightest support in any imaginable intentions of its human creators and rests exclusively on the positing of a transcendent (divine) intention manifested in the Pentateuch—and proceeds to an abstract exegesis of that text, demonstrating that on a secondary level, it communicates a mystical truth of wide application. He then elaborates a new allegory, this time quite deliberate and explicit, built on a structure of meaning analogous to that claimed for the original text and projecting the abstract truth he has distilled from that text onto another plane, expressing it in terms of new metaphors, of a new allegorical screen.

In a far more subtle manner—and yet one to which the pattern followed explicitly by Prudentius is quite relevant—this process seems to have been at work in the popular literature of late antiquity. It is clear, at any rate, from an interpretive fragment that the Greek romances were interpreted and expounded allegorically in a manner quite close to that of the interpretation of Homer discussed here.[11] It is impossible to date with certainty the fragment or its author, "Philip the Philosopher," and nothing is known of the latter beyond the text in question.[12] The novel it

11. Τῆς Χαρικλείας ἑρμήνευμα τῆς σώφρονος ἐκ φωνῆς Φιλίππου τοῦ φιλο-σόφου published from a twelfth- or thirteenth-century manuscript of Heliodorus's *Ethiopica* by R. Hercher in 1886. See "Works Cited: Ancient Authors" under "Philip the Philosopher" and the complete translation in Appendix 1.

12. Cf. Erwin Rohde, *Die griechische Roman und seine Vorläufer*, p. 353, n. 1. W. A. Oldfather attempted to demonstrate that the Philip of the piece must be Philip of Opus, Plato's student, and that the essay is thus a piece of blatantly anachronistic pseudepigraphy by a late writer, "der eigene Ansichten unter einem berühmten Philosophen-namen bekannt machen wollte" (Oldfather, "Lokrika," p. 457). Karl Praechter (*Die Philosophie des Altertums*, p. 647) emphasized its affinities with Alexandrian Neoplatonism as distinct from that of Iamblichus and that of Proclus. Aristides Colonna's observation that Theophanes the Keramite (tenth–eleventh centuries) used a similar pseudonym (see his edition of Heliodorus, pp. 365–66) does not prove either that Theophanes was the author or that the work is as late as the tenth century.

explains, Heliodorus's *Ethiopica* (or *Theagenes and Chariclea*), dates from the third or possibly the fourth century.[13] The interpretive text reflects the intellectual world of pagan Neoplatonism with a considerable admixture of Christian learning, and although it could well have been written as early as the late fifth century,[14] there is some reason to suspect that it may be an archaizing Byzantine composition. Beyond this, as a possible example of deliberate allegory, we have the *Hero and Leander* of Musaeus, belonging to the late fifth or early sixth century, which Thomas Gelzer has argued to be a Christian Neoplatonist allegory.[15] A brief examination of these two works will help throw some light on the impact on creative literature of the tradition of allegorical interpretation.

The *Ethiopica* is probably the latest of the surviving romances and as such builds on a long history of narrative prose rooted in the Hellenistic period and on a correspondingly long and complex history of the evolving demands made upon literature in late antiquity.[16] Though its content is pervasively religious and the erotic complexities of the narrative are interwoven with scenes involving cults of various descriptions, both conventional and bizarrely exotic, there is no reason to believe either that the novel is committed to any particular religious or philosophical tradition or that it is an example of deliberate allegory.[17] There is no doubt that many of the ideas expressed belong to Neoplatonism, but they are expressed directly, explicitly, and in abstract terms, not in terms of deliberate allegory.[18] The mixture of religiosity with erotic intrigue, of

13. On the problem of dating Heliodorus, see R. M. Rattenbury in Heliodorus, *Ethiopica* (Budé), vol. 1, pp. vii–xv, who prefers a third-century date to the traditional fourth-century one, but gives a valuable summary of the other arguments. For a more recent account, largely in harmony with Rattenbury's, see Ben E. Perry, *The Ancient Romances*, p. 349, n. 13, and p. 350, n. 15.

14. See Leonardo Tarán, *Academica: Philip of Opus and the Pseudo-Platonic Epinomis*, p. 115, n. 510, for a summary of arguments regarding the dating of the fragment, providing a basis for this *terminus post quem*.

15. See his recent Loeb edition of Musaeus, pp. 316–22.

16. For the most recent discussion of the *Ethiopica* in the context of ancient prose fiction, see Arthur Heisermann, *The Novel Before the Novel*, pp. 186–202.

17. This is likewise Heisermann's judgment, though he gives serious consideration to the close relation between romance and allegory. See Heisermann, *The Novel Before the Novel*, esp. pp. 173 and 193. He in fact concludes that Heliodorus's romance is far less structured by its informing ideas, and thus farther removed from allegory, than the earlier romance of Longus (p. 200, cf. pp. 130–45). See also Gerald N. Sandy, "Characterization and Philosophical Decor in Heliodorus' *Ethiopica*."

18. On specifically Neopythagorean content, see E. Feuillatre, *Etudes sur les Ethiopiques d'Héliodore*, pp. 128–32, with references (where the dependence of

an aura of profundity with sensuous exoticism, is a striking characteristic of the *Ethiopica*, and it is no doubt this quality that explains much of the novel's popularity both with its contemporary audience and with subsequent ones. These elements do not, however, indicate a complex structure of meaning in the work as a whole. All belong to a richly articulated surface, which sometimes seems to hint at a further or allegorical level of meaning. Such a level, however, fails to materialize.

This complex and suggestive surface, involving the deliberate reworking and elevation of material and themes derived from epic and particularly from the *Odyssey*, explicitly incorporates the tradition of the allegorical interpretation of Homer. In general, Heliodorus is more interested in the interpretation of dreams than of literary texts,[19] and the one passage in which Homer is explicated is significantly introduced in the context of what appears to be a dream-interpretation. The vision in question seems quite straightforward: leading the hero and heroine, Apollo and Artemis have come at night to Calasiris, the protector of the protagonists, at Delphi to tell him to take the young couple with him to Egypt and thence wherever the gods lead. The interpretive effort is an unusual one. Homer is invoked in support of Calasiris's claim that this nocturnal vision was *not* a "dream" (ὄναρ) properly speaking, but rather a waking vision (ὕπαρ).[20]

How does he know this? Because he knows the secret contained in Oilean Ajax's lines, when the latter has just recognized Poseidon, disguised as Calchas:

> I easily recognized the tracks behind his feet
> as he moved away, for the gods are easy to recognize.

Heliodorus on Philostratus, asserted by Erwin Rohde, is denied). A striking example of a specifically Neoplatonic idea occurs in the passage that particularly occupies Philip the Philosopher's attention. Calasiris is describing the meeting of Theagenes and Chariclea. The encounter is clothed in ritual. The moment is underlined by Theagenes' accepting the torch to light the sacrifice from Chariclea. Calasiris interrupts to observe that at that moment those who looked on "were given faith that the soul is a holy thing" (Heliod. *Eth.* 3.5.4). The relationship of this passage to Philip's exegesis is discussed below. For the text, see n. 32 below.

19. Aside from the present example, Heliod. *Eth.* 3.11.5–12.3, see 2.16.1–6.

20. Heliod. *Eth.* 3.12.1. Cf. on ὕπαρ and ὄναρ Rattenbury and Lumb's note to their Budé edition of Heliodorus, vol. 1, p. 114, n. 2. It would be somewhat less surprising to find Calasiris claiming to have seen a ὥραμα or straightforwardly predictive dream, in contrast to an ἐνύπνιον or non-predictive dream.

Ἴχνια γὰρ μετόπισθε ποδῶν ἠδὲ κνημάων
ῥεῖ᾽ ἔγνων ἀπιόντος, ἀρίγνωτοι δὲ θεοί περ.

(Il. 13.71–72)

What is significant in the passage of Heliodorus is not so much the interpretation given the lines, which is banal in itself,[21] but the insistence on their complex structure of meaning.

Homer is said to "hint at" (ὁ σοφὸς Ὅμηρος αἰνίττεται) a means of identifying real visions of gods, but few readers penetrate his "riddle" (οἱ πολλοὶ δὲ τὸ αἴνιγμα παρατρέχουσιν). Calasiris's interlocutor's rather testy reply is that in this case he, too, is one of the unenlightened; he has, of course, known the passage from his youth and is therefore acquainted with "the superficial meaning" (τὴν μὲν ἐπιπολῆς διάνοιαν) because he understands "the language" (τὴν λέξιν), but he remains ignorant of "the theology dispersed in the verses" (τὴν δὲ ἐγκατεσπαρμένην αὐτοῖς θεολογίαν, Heliod. Eth. 3.12.3). The clear distinction between levels of meaning, the one explicitly belonging merely to the "surface" (ἐπιπολή) of the language, and the other a theological meaning dispersed beneath the surface in the very texture of the poem, reflects a familiar model.

No doubt as an emblem of their education and culture, Heliodorus postulates a thorough knowledge of Homer in his characters, and he assumes this in his audience as well.[22] He likewise assumes that the structure of meaning requires exegesis. There is no doubt an implicit hint, as well, that the reader might want to pry beyond the "superficial meaning" of the present narrative, to explore the deeper reaches of its meaning.[23]

21. The gods are said to advance without moving their legs, comparable to the Egyptian statues of striding gods whose legs are bound together by the solid stone. The interpretation depends on taking the adverb ῥεῖ(α) with ἀπιόντος rather than the more obvious ἔγνων and is thus questionable on linguistic grounds, but the Homeric line can certainly be read as Calasiris would have it (cf. Leaf's note ad loc.).

22. Chariclea's citation from the Iliad at Heliod. Eth. 4.7.4 is probably intended to evoke the context of the lines and thus presumes a very considerable familiarity with Homer on the part of the reader.

23. Heliodorus's other specific references to Homer and to the heroes of the Iliad and Odyssey offer some tempting hints but no substantial demonstration of the author's understanding of the structure of meaning of the poems. The present passage goes on to elaborate a claim that Homer was an Egyptian (Heliod. Eth. 3.13.3–15.1; cf. 2.34.1), based on a particularly imaginative version of the poet's life. There are several decorative references to and citations of Homer scattered through the novel (e.g., 3.4.1; 4.3.1; and a rhetorical attack on Homer,

No recent critic has been convinced that the romance of Theagenes and Chariclea is allegorical, but the ancient interpretive fragment mentioned above is elaborate and emphatic in its claims for the hidden meanings stored away in the vicissitudes of the protagonists.[24] The intention of the interpretive piece is very difficult to define. It verges at times on parody, and the fact that it is incomplete makes it particularly difficult to form a solid judgment. Moreover, since it is the technique of the novel itself to play with the possibility of further levels of meaning, the interpretive essay—an allegorical exegesis attached to the text to reinforce one of its salient qualities and to define an appropriate mode of reading by shaping the reader's expectations—is exceptionally well suited to it.[25] Philip's exegesis represents a serious (if at the same time light and playful) attempt to enlist the techniques of defensive allegorical interpretation to enhance the prestige of the book and to render it acceptable to (Platonist) Christian audiences.[26]

There is a superficial resemblance between the author's attitude toward Heliodorus's romance and Julian's attitude toward myth. Philip considers erotic romances food for younger minds than his own. The more striking difference between the two attitudes is seen in Julian's scorn for the pre-philosophical youth of the spirit, replaced in Philip by a tender, even loving, tolerance, verging on nostalgia. Philip's original image— "the milk that nourished our infant education" ($οἷόν \ τι \ γάλα \ τῆς \ νηπιώδους \ . . . \ παιδεύσεως$)—is left behind when he goes on to argue that the romances belong to young men and to those in their prime, *not* to infants or to old men, who know nothing of love. Nevertheless, it is clear from

---

4.4.3) and numerous references to Achilles occur at the end of book 2 and the beginning of book 3, where the myth lying behind the ceremony at Delphi is elaborated. In a curious passage (5.22.1–5) Odysseus comes to Calasiris in a dream to rebuke him for failing to take the trouble to stop off in Ithaca to pay his respects to the hero. This might well be a reference to the cult maintained in the cave in Polis Bay, which in turn connects it with the content of Porphyry's essay on the cave of the nymphs. Cf. ch. 3, n. 123, above.

24. See the complete translation in Appendix 1 below. Among modern critics, J. Geffcken (quoted by Sandy, "Characterization and Philosophical Decor in Heliodorus' *Ethiopica*," p. 164) called the novel "a work of Neoplatonist propaganda." See Sandy's comments as well (*loc. cit.*).

25. Cf. Ernest Fortin's analysis of Basil's method of predisposing the Christian reader to find Christian truth in pagan literature, discussed in ch. 6C below.

26. On the relationship between Heliodorus's novel and the Christian Middle Ages, see Heinrich Dörrie, "Die griechischen Romane und das Christentum," pp. 275–76.

the start that Philip considers Heliodorus's romance a propaedeutic of philosophy, and in spite of his age he undertakes at his friends' behest to defend Chariclea against her detractors. In the frame-story that introduces the defensive speech, Philip makes explicit reference to the *Phaedrus*, and it is to that dialogue more than any other that the author has gone for his model in this composition.[27] The structure and Platonic echoes in any case make it abundantly clear that the author is imitating Plato,[28] and the content of the discussion—love as a metaphor for events in the life of the soul—frequently echoes that of the *Phaedrus*.

As he opens his speech to Heliodorus's detractors, Philip employs an image that, like the oblique reference to Odysseus in the oracle on the fate of Plotinus's soul,[29] makes it clear that the interpretive tradition had so transformed the meaning of certain Homeric episodes that they had become available as images charged with inherent spiritual meaning. The book is compared to Circe's potion in that it turns base men into pigs but initiates philosophers into higher realities. The *Odyssey*, allegorically interpreted, has become the source of an image to express the complex structure of meaning of the novel. The model—like that of the meaning of Homer expressed by Calasiris in the romance itself—is exceptionally clear. The meaning of Heliodorus's romance is on two levels: one, admittedly dangerous, is the level reached by those who read it "profanely" ($\beta\epsilon\beta\dot{\eta}\lambda\omega\varsigma$), but another, elevated and revelatory, is reserved for philosophers. This is precisely the position taken by Proclus in his defense of Homer against Socrates' critique. It contains a curious contradiction in that Proclus, for his part, is logically forced to admit Socrates' charge that Homer is unfit for the education of the young—they are unable to see beyond the surface meaning, which is viewed as harmful—whereas Philip takes refuge in the considerably higher, and perhaps unrealistic,

27. August Brinkmann ("Beiträge zur Kritik und Erklärung des Dialogs Axiochos," pp. 442–43) demonstrated that the opening of the piece is virtually copied from the opening of the pseudo-Platonic *Axiochus*. Nevertheless, there is also a resemblance to that of the *Republic* (see Praechter, *Philosophie des Altertums*, p. 646) and that of the *Phaedrus* itself is likewise relevant. Both our piece and the *Phaedrus* begin outside (or at the gates) of the cities in question. Phaedrus and Socrates, it is true, proceed further out of Athens along the Ilissus and sit down under a tree, but Philip and his friends are in fact truer to Socrates' opinion (Plato *Phdr.* 230d) that the natural world has little to offer the lover of learning. They immediately return inside the walls to engage in discussion of the romance.

28. Cf. Praechter, *Philosophie des Altertums*, pp. 646–47, for a list of the "Platonreminiszenzen" and other philosophical echoes in the piece.

29. See ch. 3B above.

demand that the young men to whom this sort of literature is directed must themselves learn to interpret it philosophically.

Philip's focus, then, is upon the impact of the *Ethiopica* on its reader, and his first task is to demonstrate that the story is sound on the moral plane, that it is a "teacher of ethics."[30] The novel is shown to contain illustrations of the four cardinal virtues, and a series of episodes is paraphrased to indicate that Heliodorus depicts the punishment of vice in such a way as to deter wrongdoers. This series of claims for the value of the ethical examples contained in the romance is summed up in an exhortation: "Even when you are treated unjustly, be content with the anomalies of chance and bear them nobly, suffering with Theagenes and Chariclea, so that your end may be rich and prosperous."[31]

At the end of this eulogy of the romance as a primer of ethics, Philip abruptly indicates that the "philosophical approach" to the text is only half-exhausted. The image he uses is unavoidably humorous and plays with the ambiguous relationship of the erotic and the spiritual in the novel itself. The exegesis, he tells us, has now removed Chariclea's magnificent robe (placed around her to protect her from her detractors), but she still wears her chiton, which must also be stripped away in order that her beauty may radiate forth without obstacle.

The ensuing explication of the story in terms of symbols and secondary meanings is witty and extravagant in the extreme, yet it takes its lead from the language of Heliodorus as well as from the methodology of the allegorical interpreters of early poetry (which itself intrudes into the text of the novel). Philip isolates the scene of the first meeting of Chariclea and Theagenes and explains it—and by extension the rest of the novel— as an allegory of the soul's return to its source in mind (νοῦς) and to knowledge of its true nature. In doing so, however, he has merely taken the hint dropped by Calasiris, the narrator of the scene in the *Ethiopica*:

> [As Theagenes took the torch from Chariclea] . . . we were given faith, dear Cnemon, that the soul is a holy thing and that both it and its impulses come from above. They no sooner saw each other than they were in love with each other, as if at first encounter the soul had

---

30. παιδαγωγικὴ γὰρ ἡ βίβλος καὶ ἠθικῆς φιλοσοφίας διδάσκαλος (383.30–31). References are to page and line of Hercher's edition of Philip.

31. ἀλλὰ καὶ ἀδικούμενος στέργε καὶ φέρε γενναίως τὰ τῆς τύχης ἀνώμαλα, μετὰ Θεαγένους καὶ Χαρικλείας κακοπαθῶν, ὅπως ἔχῃς τὸ τέλος πολύολβον (385.19–22).

recognized that which resembled it and rushed immediately toward that which duly belonged to it.[32]

Calasiris's observation intensifies the atmosphere of religiosity already present in the scene and evokes at some distance the Platonic discussion of love in the *Phaedrus* and *Symposium*, in order to suggest the beauty and intensity of the encounter.

Nevertheless, it is only a short step from this observation to Philip's claim that Chariclea is a symbol ($\sigma\acute{\nu}\mu\beta o\lambda o\nu$) of the soul (inseparable from the mind that organizes it). From this point on, Philip needs only his own Neoplatonic model of the life of the soul and a little help from supposed etymology in order to elaborate the allegory. Chariclea in the novel was born in Ethiopia (= darkness, the invisible) and emerges into the light (= Greece), only to return whence she came. She was raised by Charicles (= the practical life) to serve Artemis (=bravery and self-restraint). As she unyoked the bullocks (= transcended the material dyad) in front of the temple at Delphi, and ceremonially passed the torch (= desire) to Theagenes (= $\nu o\hat{\nu}s$), he took it up, filling her with the love of the highest wisdom and simultaneously opening up to her the possibility of learning her own true inheritance (= her affinity with the higher hypostases). Calasiris (= the teacher who advances the soul to initiation) then takes the couple in hand, steers them past the treachery of Trachinus (= the "rough"—$\tau\rho\alpha\chi\acute{\nu}s$—rebellion of the passions) and through Egypt (= ignorance).[33] They must still overcome Arsace (= the pleasures of the flesh, $\tau\hat{\eta}s$ $\sigma\alpha\rho\kappa\acute{o}s$) and her pimp Cybele (= the senses) with the help of a ruby (= the fear of god).[34] Again, the interpretation is summed up in an exhortation: "Here let the strong will be made yet tougher! Let it be cast into the fiery furnace of temptation!"[35] The soul will thus reach her own country to be tested by fire.

The fragment breaks off at this point while describing the couple's ex-

---

32. Cf. n. 18 above. ὅτε, φίλε Κνήμων, καὶ ὅτι θεῖον ἡ ψυχὴ καὶ συγγενὲς ἄνωθεν τοῖς ἔργοις ἐπιστούμεθα· ὁμοῦ τε γὰρ ἀλλήλους ἑώρων οἱ νέοι καὶ ἤρων, ὥσπερ τῆς ψυχῆς ἐκ πρώτης ἐντεύξεως τὸ ὅμοιον ἐπιγνούσης καὶ πρὸς τὸ κατ' ἀξίαν οἰκεῖον προσδραμούσης (3.5.4).

33. Cf. the scorn for the lowest, physical allegory as appropriate to the Egyptians in Sallustius, *De diis* 4; p. 6, lines 1–10 in Nock ed., and Nock's observations on pp. xlvii–xlix.

34. On this last etymology, see the translation in Appendix 1.

35. ἐνταῦθα τὸ ἀνδρεῖον λῆμα στομούσθω μᾶλλον καὶ τῇ καμίνῳ τῶν πειρασμῶν ἐμβληθήτω (387.23–24).

periences in Ethiopia. It is difficult to say how much is missing, though the analysis has brought us to the events of the eighth book of the ten that make up the novel, and may well be nearly complete.

In its thought and diction, the interpretive essay is dependent primarily upon the Neoplatonic tradition and specifically on Plotinus.[36] The conception of the relationship of soul, mind, and body comes from that tradition, along with terms like ὑπόστασις (385.31) and such images as that of the teacher leading the unaffected soul through the waves of life and helping it to escape the sea (387.10–16). The passage in which Philip explicates the αἴνιγμα of the scene before the temple (386.26–387.4) has close affinities with passages in *Enneads* 5.1, where Plotinus laments the soul's forgetfulness of its true family and describes its relationship to the higher hypostases.

At the same time, however, in this context with all the trappings of pagan Neoplatonism, there are words, phrases, and ideas that unavoidably belong to the Christian tradition. To say that the fates of some of the characters of the romance represent the "fulfillment" of a Hesiodic ethical statement constitutes a use of the verb πληρόω that is abundantly attested in the New Testament but rare, or perhaps absent, in pagan literature.[37] Likewise, ἐπίγνωσις (386.31) and συνομιλεῖν (387.18) are words with Christian affinities, and the concept of "fear of god" as a protective force (387.25–27) is not a part of pagan tradition.[38] What proves beyond a shadow of a doubt that Philip had read the New Testament with some care, however, is the phrase "The fire shall try every man's work of what sort it is,"[39] which is a direct but unacknowledged citation from 1 Corinthians (3.13).[40] Likewise, the "mystical song" (μυστικὸν ᾆσμα, 383.10) containing the verse "Therefore do the virgins love thee" is the Song of Solomon.[41]

36. Cf. Praechter (see n. 28 above).

37. ὁράτω . . . τὸ τοῦ Ἡσιόδου πληρούμενον ὃς κακὸν ἄλλῳ τεύχων ἑῷ κακὸν ἥπατι τεύχει (385.12–13).

38. The usual New Testament expression is φόβος θεοῦ, not ὁ εἰς θεὸν φόβος, but the idea clearly comes out of Judaism.

39. ἑκάστου γὰρ τὸ ἔργον ὁποῖόν ἐστι τὸ πῦρ δοκιμάσει (388.6–7).

40. This citation seems to have been noted first by Oldfather ("Lokrika," p. 458) and is likewise mentioned by Praechter (*Philosophie des Altertums*, p. 647). The Christian learning of the author seems to be conclusively demonstrated, though Praechter emphasized the conspicuous pagan elements in the text that show, as he claimed, that "andererseits das Heidentum noch nicht überwunden war."

41. Song of Sol. 1.3.

Our interpretive text, then, is a document that is neither explicitly pagan nor explicitly Christian, but demonstrates a close acquaintance with and a broad tolerance of both traditions. This ambiguity is quite appropriate to the author of the romance itself, Heliodorus, of whom we are told that later in life he became a Christian bishop.[42] Both the novel and the observations of Philip reflect an intellectual world in which pagan Neoplatonism and Neoplatonic Christianity complemented rather than opposed one another. It is particularly appropriate that the interpretive fragment shows the clear influence of Christianity because it probably belongs to a period when pagan Neoplatonism's practical concern with textual exegesis was a thing of the past. Philip's manner and approach to his subject draw equally on the pagan tradition of defensive allegory and on the tradition of Christian homily. His defense at several points becomes an exhortation, a sermon from a text. What is unique, of course, is the choice of text, and we have seen that the specific qualities of Heliodorus's romance may have suggested the choice. It complements the *Ethiopica* in a way that would be far less appropriate with regard to any other surviving romance.

The *Ethiopica* is, then, a romance that hints at mystical allegory, elevates epic themes, and fills them with a content both adapted to contemporary taste and quite foreign to the works that were the original sources of those themes. It is not a systematic allegory, but no doubt it was possible early in its history to read it as one. The tradition of the mystical allegorical reading of Homer is perceptible in the work itself, influencing its approach to its material and its aspirations. That same tradition pervades the critical fragment.

There is no single work from pagan antiquity that can unequivocally be demonstrated to illustrate the last phase of the interaction of interpretation and literature that our model predicts. That is, there is no single work that expresses in a fully allegorical mode the central concepts of pagan Neoplatonism. In his 1975 Loeb edition of Musaeus's *Hero and Leander*, however, Thomas Gelzer has argued persuasively that Musaeus's poem is such a work, with the important difference that it seems to come from a Christian context. There is little point in attempting to examine the problem in detail here, particularly in view of the fact that Gelzer promises a book on the subject.[43] It will be sufficient for our pur-

42. Cf. Rattenbury's remarks in his edition of Heliodorus, vol. 1, pp. vii–xv. Dörrie, ("Die griechischen Romane," pp. 275–76) goes somewhat further in his analysis.
43. See Gelzer in his Musaeus (Loeb), p. 371 and n. A.

poses to review some of the major points of Gelzer's preliminary statement of his position on the matter.[44]

It should be mentioned first that there is no explicitly Christian content in Musaeus's poem and that the assertion that its author was a Christian is based on internal evidence the significance of which has been
questioned.[45] His knowledge both of the literature of pagan Neoplatonism and of the Gospels and other Christian literature is, however, unquestionable. The poem taps the tradition of the school of Nonnus, a
hexameter poet of the late fifth century to whom are attributed both
pagan mythological epic (the *Dionysiaca*) and a hexameter paraphrase of
the Gospel of John. Much of its language is distantly imitated from Homer, and the most important models lying behind Musaeus's presentation of the tragic love affair of his protagonists are found in the *Odyssey*
and in Plato's *Phaedrus*.[46] Homer and Plato are naturally the two authors
toward whom the interpretive efforts of the later Neoplatonists were primarily directed, and, as Gelzer has seen, it is by way of Proclus and Hermias that Musaeus understands Homer and Plato.[47]

Gelzer introduces some evidence that the work was read as a Neoplatonic allegory by contemporary readers,[48] but the force of his analysis
is not that the poem was *read* allegorically, which would not be surprising in its time, but rather that it was created as a systematic Christian
Neoplatonic allegory.

The first question one must ask in such a situation is how we can perceive the existence of a second level of meaning beyond the first, in the
absence of such obtrusive indicators as those used by Prudentius. Gelzer's initial criteria are disappointingly close to those of the ancient commentators who claimed that an unacceptable or incoherent superficial
meaning indicated a deeper truth lying behind that surface. Structural
weaknesses, specifically the "logical schematism of the arrangement, the
disproportion of the parts, the total lack of vividness . . . and the frequent repetitions and variations of the same motifs" are, according to
Gelzer, "probably to be explained as technical requirements for the con-
veyance of a 'higher' meaning which Musaeus concealed allegorically beneath the surface of the love-story he narrated."[49] This in itself would be

44. Ibid., pp. 291–343, esp. pp. 316–22.
45. Ibid., p. 299 and n. B.
46. Ibid., pp. 310–11.
47. Ibid., pp. 318–19.
48. Specifically, by Procopius of Gaza: Gelzer in Musaeus (Loeb), p. 301.
49. Ibid., p. 316.

unconvincing were it not for the fact that Gelzer produces an impressive list of specifically Neoplatonic terms that Musaeus sprinkled through the poem, which do indeed seem an invitation to the reader to see in the broad outline of the action of the poem an imitation of the progress of the soul from its original abode beyond the physical universe, through the sea of matter, and back to its true home.[50] Gelzer's paraphrase, in which he restores the allegorical meaning by means of a series of analogies from Plato, the Neoplatonists, and the Christian tradition,[51] is convincing, and it seems quite possible that what modern scholarship has done here is to reconstitute and define a structure of meaning that would have been quite clear to contemporary readers, but has become opaque for modern readers because of the very different demands we are accustomed to make on literature.

Attractive as they are, however, Gelzer's conclusions will have to be judged on the basis of the more complete presentation he promises. As they stand, they bring us disturbingly close to that peculiar fallacy of the ancient interpretive tradition, the conviction that a contradictory or otherwise puzzling surface implies an allegorical meaning lying beyond. Moreover, they bring us back to Socrates' ultimate frustration with interpretation: we cannot ask Musaeus. The force of modern critical opinion is certainly against reading *Hero and Leander* as an allegory, and Gelzer's claims have left many readers skeptical.[52] If conclusive internal evidence is lacking, one would want *comparanda*. If these in turn are not to be found, a definitive conclusion seems a remote goal. One can, however, say that the time was right for such deliberate allegory, that the visual arts had exploited it for centuries, and that a pervasive interpretive tradition, known to Musaeus, had accustomed readers to make upon literature—at least upon certain literature—the sort of demands *Hero and Leander* seems to invite.

One thing that is clear is that *Hero and Leander* is not an allegory of the stamp of the *Psychomachia*. Aside from other obvious differences, the "secondary" level of meaning is not obtrusive; it does not dominate the surface meaning. Still, given the date of the poem and its cultural context, we must consider it probable that for Musaeus's audience, the fate of their souls was an issue of immediate and burning importance, one that entered into their perceptions concerning the world around them and

50. Ibid., pp. 319–20.
51. Ibid., pp. 320–22.
52. See the comments of Georges Nachtergale in his review of Gelzer's *Musaeus* in *L'Antiquité classique* 45 (1976), pp. 252–54.

especially into their perceptions regarding works of art. The degree to which such concerns permeated everyday life in the cities of the late Empire appears vividly in a famous passage of Gregory of Nyssa, where he parodies the intense, but aimless, theological speculation of his contemporaries,

> makeshift theological dogmatists . . . who philosophize pompously on incomprehensible subjects. . . . If you ask about your change, the answer is a lecture on the Begotten and the Unbegotten; if you ask the price of a loaf of bread, you get, "The Father is greater and the Son beneath him." If you ask, "Is the bath ready," the attendant demonstrates that the Son is uncreated.[53]

Whether or not Musaeus's poem was an allegory may thus be a question that would have to be settled by an interrogation, not of Musaeus, but of his audience. There are precedents in late antiquity for a popular literature playing with and hinting at secondary meanings of a theological or theosophical nature. That much is clear from what has been said of Heliodorus. It may not be unreasonable to view an allegorical *Hero and Leander* as a logical development, in this sense, from the later romances. Moreover, the second meaning *was* present, at least for Procopius of Gaza.[54] A cultural environment in which doctrinal debates were major issues may well have been prepared to see spiritual doctrines in works of literature: from that point it is a minor step to producing writers to respond to those demands by creating works contrived to be susceptible to such interpretation.

If Gelzer's reading is correct, we have in *Hero and Leander* the last term of our equation. The popular literature of late antiquity does indeed appear to develop the possibility of genuine allegory under the influence of a pervasive tradition of allegorical interpretation. This tradition was pagan in its origins, and the branch destined to bear such fruit as Museaus's poem had initially been concerned with extracting and elaborating theological truths in the *Iliad* and *Odyssey*, along with the works of the other "theologians." Porphyry, late in the third century, was the last

---

53. αὐτοσχέδιοί τινες τῆς θεολογίας δογματισταί . . . [οἳ] σεμνῶς ἡμῖν περὶ τῶν ἀλήπτων φιλοσοφοῦσιν. . . . ἐὰν περὶ τῶν ὀβολῶν ἐρωτήσῃς, ὁ δέ σοι περὶ γεννητοῦ καὶ ἀγεννήτου ἐφιλοσόφησε· κἂν περὶ τιμήματος ἄρτου πύθοιο, μείζων ὁ Πατήρ, ἀποκρίνεται, καὶ ὁ Υἱὸς ὑποχείριος. εἰ δέ, τὸ λουτρὸν ἐπιτήδειόν ἐστιν, εἴποις, ὁ δὲ ἐξ οὐκ ὄντων τὸν Υἱὸν εἶναι διωρίσατο (*Or. de deitate filii et spiritus sancti*, PG 46, col. 557b–c). The passage is cited by A. A. Vasiliev, *Histoire de l'empire byzantine*, vol. 1, pp. 100–101.

54. See n. 48 above.

important pagan spokesman for this tradition before its absorption into the increasingly Christianized intellectual world of the fourth century. Somewhat later, however, the radical demands made on literary texts by this tradition of exegesis were influential in producing a narrative literature still profoundly influenced by Homeric models but thoroughly imbued with Platonism and—perhaps—deliberately incorporating a secondary level of meaning complementing and completing the superficial meaning.

V

Proclus

A. INTRODUCTION

Proclus (ca. 410–85) stands near the end of the ancient Neoplatonic tradition and on the threshold of the Middle Ages. He was head of the Athenian school that traced its ancestry to Plato's Academy—hence the title Diadochos, or Successor, often attached to his name. In 529, less than fifty years after his death, his own successors abandoned Athens when Justinian closed the pagan philosophical schools, and although they subsequently returned, they were able to carry on their work only as private individuals. Neither his immediate predecessors nor those who followed after him in Athens and in Alexandria left a comparable body of work to provide information on later Neoplatonism, and it is to Proclus that one must turn for the basic concepts of the later phase of the tradition. This is not the place to attempt a summary of the complexities of his thought, but a brief statement of a few of the principles governing the metaphysics of the later Neoplatonists may be useful.[1]

Plotinus had developed a model of reality based on three hypostases: the One, mind, and soul. All three are available to the microcosmic human entity, living normally on the fragmented level of sense at the lower extremity of soul (ψυχή), but able to draw itself upward to the level of mind (νοῦς), and even to union with the One (τὸ ἕν). Plotinus's system

---

1. For the most recent general studies on Proclus, see Laurence J. Rosán, *The Philosophy of Proclus*, and Werner Beierwaltes, *Proklos: Grundzüge seiner Metaphysik*, and for a brief summary the article "Proclus" by Rosán in *The Encyclopedia of Philosophy*, ed. P. Edwards. An overview situating Proclus in his historical and philosophical context may be found in ch. 5 of R. T. Wallis, *Neoplatonism*.

and, in particular, his discussion of the "One"—which, properly speaking, has no qualities, since no predicate can be attached to it—left numerous open questions for the later tradition.

Whereas Plotinus had only an ambiguous respect for traditional religion, Platonists after his time increasingly extolled the virtues of ritual and theurgy. The higher hypostases became less and less accessible. The One was divided into a true One, beyond existence, and an existing One, which, by joining with the generative principle of the dyad, produced the rest of reality. The hypostases were subdivided and the distinctions among them became unclear.

By what has been called the "principle of continuity," later Neoplatonists emphasized the unbroken flow of reality from the One beyond being to the fragmented level of our own experience in this world. A further general rule, the "principle of plenitude,"[2] emphasized the fullness of creation: each level of each divine procession was occupied by an ever-increasing number of spiritual entities—gods, angels, demons, and souls. For Proclus, the resulting model of reality is diamond-shaped.[3] At the highest level, of course, is the One, followed by the monad and the dyad, then by a large number of "henads," sometimes associated with the Olympian pantheon. These in turn are the sources of various "processions" of lesser spiritual entities, down to the extremely complex and cluttered level of "appearances." From this level, near the midpoint in the life of the soul, there is a progressive simplification until the unified, dead, essentially nonexistent level of matter is reached.

Individual human beings are embodied, fragmented souls, attended by providential guardian δαίμονες and ultimately belonging to the procession of some Olympian. This last relationship also contributed to the later Neoplatonists' concern with astrology—the henads found expression in the heavens as well. Proclus himself belonged to the procession of Mercury, as his biographer (who also provides us with his complete natal chart) informs us.[4]

The three Plotinian hypostases have been substantially modified in Proclus's thought by the introduction of plurality into the realm of being. However, the Plotinian model is more familiar and provides us with a useful point of reference for discussing the later systems. The basic triadic structure is in any case retained, though the distinctions are blurred

2. See Wallis, *Neoplatonism*, p. 131, on both principles.
3. See Rosán, "Proclus," p. 481.
4. Marinus *Vit. Pr.* 28 and 35.

and the rich demonology and angelology of the later Neoplatonists give their systems a decidedly medieval flavor.

Proclus is of importance to the present study because he is at once the most complete, the most systematic, and the most carefully studied of the Neoplatonic allegorizers of Homer.[5] His work is a bizarre mixture of sensitivity, cogent analysis, and a third element that has tended to obscure the first two and to bar his contributions both to literary theory and to the interpretation of Homer from serious consideration: namely, an extraordinary willingness to depart extravagantly from the most obvious meaning of the text and to apply to Homer's words interpretations that satisfy his own demands but jar our expectations. Most of his work regarding Homer is contained in the sixth discourse of the first book of his commentary on the *Republic*, and that text is the focus of the present discussion. The context itself is indicative of the fact that Proclus's consideration of Homer—in striking contrast to Porphyry's—is an academic exercise in the pejorative sense of the term. It is the work not of a popularizer but of a scholar who, for the sake of the coherence of the tradition to which he seems himself belonging, must reconcile two major figures from the past.

B. LANGUAGE AS A SYSTEM OF MEANING

As we have already seen, interpretations of literary texts of the sort we are accustomed to call "allegorical" in the context of antiquity depend on certain preconceptions about the nature of the text as a system of meaning, and these, in turn, depend upon a broader philosophical perspective that comprehends the representative value of language itself. All of the thinkers considered here located themselves in a tradition that could be traced back to Platonic idealism. In any such philosophical tradition, the function of language will be viewed as a complex one.

5. See Ansgar Josef Friedl, *Die Homer-Interpretationen des Neuplatonikers Proklos*, James A. Coulter, *The Literary Microcosm*, and most recently Anne D. R. Sheppard, *Studies on the 5th and 6th Essays of Proclus' Commentary on the Republic*. The last work appeared after the completion of my doctoral dissertation and has rendered much of the material examined in this chapter far more accessible and clarified many obscure aspects of Proclus's contribution to the Neoplatonists' reading of Homer. As revised for publication, this study owes many corrections and insights to Sheppard's book. Especially helpful is her elucidation of the close dependence, in many instances, of the metaphysical allegories of Syrianus and Proclus on Stoic physical allegories (e.g., *Studies*, pp. 56, 81).

Without attempting to analyze in detail the complex and often playful ironies of the *Cratylus*—and at the risk of importing into what has
been called an early dialogue concepts more appropriate to Plato's mature thought and to that of his successors[6]—we may say that there Socrates attacks the recurring problem of the relationship of the human, along
with other mortal things, to the absolute, those objects of intellection
that lie outside the world of the senses and do not change or cease to
exist, and that he does so by focusing on language as a human activity
that must incessantly confront that paradox.

The word is a tool and like any tool it derives its form from its function.[7] The function here is "naming" (ὀνομάζειν), and, broadly speaking, the word must somehow represent what it names.[8] Language as we
know it is found to be, at best, an imperfect tool, not susceptible of definitive analysis (*Crat.* 425a–c). Yet the fact that language is capable of
representing things, notions, and qualities one after another already indicates that the relationship in which a linguistic sign stands to the reality it represents is both variable and complex. It is significant that in this
dialogue we find what David Ross has described as "the first appearance
in Plato of the argument from the existence of knowledge to the existence of unchangeable, non-sensible objects."[9]

Even here, then, we have at least a foreshadowing of the idea that language is a human activity relating on the one hand to the flux and characteristic fragmentation of experience in this world and on the other
hand to a reality that transcends that flux and knows no change. In the
Republic it becomes specific that the application of a single name to a
group of particulars is *the* indicator by which we determine that a single
form (εἶδος) lies behind that group (*Rep.* 596a). The world of forms is
thus "co-extensive with language."[10]

We have already examined the λόγος doctrine of Plotinus in assessing his attitudes toward language and human utterance.[11] Working both
from Plato and from Plotinus, Proclus characteristically generates a system of greater complexity by repeatedly dividing and subdividing the

6. See Paul Shorey, *The Unity of Plato's Thought*, pp. 54–56 and 75, and David
Ross, *Plato's Theory of Ideas*, pp. 4–5, for summaries of the problems relating to
the dating of the *Cratylus*.

7. Cf. I. M. Crombie, *An Explanation of Plato's Doctrines*, vol. 1, pp. 475–86.

8. The idea that words imitate what they describe is likewise found in the
Timaeus (29b).

9. Ross, *Plato's Theory of Ideas*, pp. 20–21.

10. J. E. Raven, *Plato's Thought in the Making*, p. 186 (and cf. p. 24).

11. See ch. 3A above.

traditional categories. His understanding of the nature and function of language is based upon an extensive elaboration of the function of language as mediator between the world of sense experience and the higher realities.[12]

Language is peculiarly human in that it exists uniquely on the level of soul (ψυχή). In the second hypostasis, the νοῦς, it is no longer required and no longer has functions that make it readily identifiable as language in our sense; yet that is precisely where it acquires its power, since the ability of the gods to create by naming underlies the human use of language, in the relationship of archetype to sensible copy.[13] Proclus himself accepts the idea, which he attributes to Cratylus and to Socrates, that there is a natural relationship between things and their names.[14] The linguistic sign, then, is in no sense arbitrary: Proclus's distance from twentieth-century thought on the nature and function of language is indicated by this denial of one of the most fundamental tenets of modern linguistics. His faith in etymology is no different from that of the earlier interpreters, but it is characteristic of him that he provides an explicit intellectual framework for that belief, whereas the others do not.

Proclus is extremely careful not to make the mistake of believing that we can proceed from the phenomenon of language directly to an understanding of the structure and nature of reality. The information language gives us concerning reality is distorted, and the most characteristic form that this distortion takes is fragmentation. The process of fragmentation is, of course, typical of relationships encountered repeatedly in Proclus's ontology as we proceed from the unified, ineffable, and transcendent One on the far side of reality, through beings that are increasingly "more

12. In the following analysis, I have followed the perceptive discussion of the question in Jean Trouillard, "L'Activité onomastique selon Proclos."

13. Trouillard has formulated the two apparently conflicting concepts central to Proclus's understanding of language referring to the *Cratylus* commentary, 71, p. 33.12–13, as follows: "1) Le langage au sens strict n'appartient qu'aux âmes rationnelles et discursives. 2) Pourtant il a son fondement dans la puissance unifiante et génératrice de la divinité" ("L'Activité onomastique selon Proclos," p. 239).

14. Cf. Proclus *In Crat.* 17, pp. 7–8: ὁ δὲ Κράτυλος . . . ἴδιόν φησιν ἑκάστου πράγματος εἶναι τὸ ὄνομα ὡς οἰκείως τεθὲν ὑπὸ τῶν πρώτως θεμένων ἐντέχνως καὶ ἐπιστημόνως (*In Crat.* 17:8.1–4). ὁ δὲ Σωκράτης . . . λέγει φύσει εἶναι τὰ ὀνόματα, ὡς διανοίας μὲν ἐπιστήμονος ἔκγονα καὶ οὐχὶ ὀρέξεως φυσικῆς, ἀλλὰ ψυχῆς φανταζομένης, οἰκείως δὲ τοῖς πράγμασι τεθέντα ἐξ ἀρχῆς κατὰ τὸ δυνατόν (8.7–11). κατὰ μὲν γὰρ τὸ εἶδος ἔοικε [sc. τὰ ὀνόματα] τοῖς πράγμασι, κατὰ δὲ τὴν ὕλην διαφέρει ἀλλήλων (8.13–14). Cf. Phillip DeLacy, "Stoic Views of Poetry," pp. 256–57.

partial" (μερικώτεροι), down to the "diversity" (ποικιλία) of existence in
this world, in contact with matter which stands just beyond the limits of
reality at the lower end of the scale. Hence the fragmented image must
not be assumed to provide an adequate or easily decipherable representation of the realities concerned. As Jean Trouillard formulates the problem: "La diversité de nos notions n'implique pas la diversité de leurs ob-
jets . . . le mode figuratif de nos représentations ne doit pas être attribué
à l'être représenté."[15]

On the contrary, just as there are various modes of perception that
correspond to the successive modes of being, extending from the total,
unified perception exercised by a god down to the passivity of our sense-
impressions in this world, so there are different levels of language that
correspond to these modes of perception—a hierarchy of systems of
meaning, of kinds of utterances—that extend from a creative, divine
"language" (not, presumably, recognizable as such by us) down to the
"language" that exists on the final fragmented level of the senses.[16]

In a passage of the *Timaeus* commentary to which Trouillard refers,[17]
but which he does not discuss in detail, a model of the perceptive and
expressive functions of the soul is elaborated that does a great deal to
explain the preconceptions behind Proclus's allegories. (The entire passage has been translated as Appendix 2.) It is an extraordinarily vivid
presentation of the hierarchy of faculties that Proclus understood to make
up the soul. Proclus's conception of the perceptive faculties was probably
not uniform throughout his long productive life, and the model offered in
this passage should not be regarded as the only possible one.[18] Nevertheless, it is an important key for our purposes.

The hierarchy here described may be conceived (in terms of the Plotinian model of reality) as lying between the second hypostasis (νοῦς) and
the world of matter. The important point for our purposes is that each

15. Trouillard, "L'Activité onomastique selon Proclos," p. 240. Trouillard at
this point in his analysis is preparing to examine *In Tim.* 1.352.11–19, a passage
on the diverse levels on which a single (unchanging) entity can be experienced.
The passage is paraphrased very closely at *In Rep.* 1.111.16–27, where Proclus is
attempting to defend Homer's mythic attribution of change, and specifically of
metamorphoses, to the gods. In the latter passage he develops an analogy to
theurgic practice.

16. Cf. Trouillard, "L'Activité onomastique selon Proclos," p. 241.

17. Proclus *In Tim.* 1.341.25–343.15. Cf. Trouillard, "L'Activité onomastique
selon Proclos," p. 241.

18. Cf. Henry J. Blumenthal, "Plutarch's Exposition of the *De anima* and the
Psychology of Proclus," p. 145 and passim.

level of experience is a mode of consciousness, of perception, and has its own λόγος (which one is tempted here to translate as "mode of discourse") attached to it. There exist, then, a perception and account of reality on the level of the senses, followed successively by perceptions and accounts on the levels of imagination,[19] opinion, and ἐπιστήμη, or systematic wisdom, which are followed in turn by the normally inaccessible perception and account on the level of νοῦς.

The λόγοι above the level of ἐπιστήμη would not constitute language in the usual sense of the term. Those of the gods (located in the realm of νοῦς) are the creative emanations that structure our universe, associated particularly with the demiurgic Hephaestus, whose physical λόγοι organize his creation.[20] We are concerned at this point, though, only with the successive strata of language recognizable as such.

The overall pattern is suggestive of the problem of "metalanguages" in logic, though in the latter situation no hierarchy of modes of perception is postulated. Put very simply, a series of statements (a language we shall call A) may at one or more points contain inadequacies in the form of contradictions or gaps that make it impossible to deduce from it the sorts of conclusions sought. In this case a "metalanguage," B, capable of testing the truth or falsehood of the statements in A, is imposed in order to resolve difficulties existing within A, but which A is incapable of resolving by itself.

This seems to be the sort of thing Proclus has in mind when he talks about the λόγοι that correspond to the various faculties of the soul. Each, viewed from its own level, has a certain coherence normally adequate to perception on that level. That coherence will never be perfect, however, and the ultimate contradictions and inadequacies of the λόγος corresponding to experience on the level of imagining, for instance, will never be resolved within that sphere—the metalanguage of opinion will be required to separate truth from falsehood and to build a new and more coherent account of reality, which will in turn be succeeded by others.

None of these accounts, then, has any ultimate truth value. Each mode of discourse implies its own metalanguage, in that it is incapable of resolving its own internal contradictions. If we extrapolate, according to the same principles, through the second hypostasis to the upper limits of reality, we encounter an ultimate silence.[21]

19. On the imagination as mediator within the soul in Proclus, see the important study by Trouillard, "Le Merveilleux dans la vie et pensée de Proclos," esp. pp. 447–52.
20. See p. 228 below.

Proclus speaks in the *Timaeus* commentary of a λόγος of the νοῦς that refutes all human λόγοι, but it is an important difference between the pagan and Christian modes of exegesis that the former regards all texts, and indeed all discourse, as ultimately unreliable (in spite of the fact that such material as the *Chaldaean Oracles* is sometimes treated as direct divine utterance). Direct expression on the part of a god in human language is finally an impossibility, though perhaps as early as Xenocrates demonology had developed to the point where "divine" utterance could be understood to mean the use by a lowly providential δαίμων of human speech in order to express in fragmented form for our discursive perceptions truths emanating from a higher plane.[22] Likewise, as we shall see, the highest form of poetry comes close to communicating experience on this level.

The implications of this model for the reading of literature are far-reaching. Extending the metaphor, any discourse may be regarded as a language whose very existence implies that of a metalanguage beyond it, and the process of elucidation of meaning might take the form of attempting to generate that metalanguage and so resolve the inner shortcomings of the text under consideration. In fact, however, this is an inversion of the conceptual model of Proclus and the other Neoplatonic commentators. Each *lower* language is actually the "interpreter" (ἑρμηνεύς) of the higher one, in that it renders it comprehensible at a lower level, at the expense of its (opaque, inaccessible) coherence.[23] Proclus would not presume to place his own discourse *above* that of Plato or of Homer—on the contrary, his role is conceived with the greatest humility.

The relationship becomes clearer if we consider the larger development. Proclus believed that Homer and Plato were each in touch with the highest truth. This is perhaps the most important point, that the ultimate structure of reality beyond all the inadequate accounts is static and

21. In a different context within the discussion of Trouillard's paper, Werner Beierwaltes made the point with moving simplicity: "Das Eine spricht nicht." (Trouillard, "L'Activité onomastique selon Proclos" [discussion], p. 254.) The paradox of the inadequacy of language in Proclus's system is one aspect of the larger problem of the status of truth in Neoplatonism. Strictly speaking, there *is* no absolute truth in Plotinian Neoplatonism, since the absolute lies beyond the sphere of knowledge, and all that is known is already fragmented. Cf. Trouillard, "Le Néoplatonisme," p. 895.

22. Augustine uses a Platonizing model to explain how God expresses himself in human speech, but he insists that it *is* finally the voice of God that reaches us *through* the angels (*Civ. Dei* 10.15). The passage is discussed in ch. 6D below.

23. See ch. 3A, with n. 25, above on similar ideas in Plotinus (*Enn.* 1.2).

eternal. Homer's account of that truth is inspired—it is the product of divine μανία—and its value is therefore enormous, though its expression is correspondingly obscure. Plato came later to the same truth, often in fact starting from Homer's account of it,[24] and demonstrated it more systematically. In other words, Plato elaborated a commentary on the Homeric discourse that pointed back *beyond* that discourse to the meta-language capable of resolving its internal confusions, and, though further removed from the initial inspiration, gave a more useful account of reality. Plato of course did not always start from Homer, nor is it clear that his own account is always secondary to (or inferior to) Homer's. Proclus is not concerned to rank them.[25] At an even greater remove, Proclus conceives his own undertaking as analogous to Plato's, and to the extent that he humbly constructs an explicatory discourse around the Homeric myths, he most frequently takes Plato's more accessible account as his guide. If the text appears to violate known truths believed to be represented in it, then the failure must lie in the inadequacies of the fragmented account itself, and the text is easily twisted and even ignored in favor of a synthetic effort to go beyond it and demonstrate the correspondences between myth and reality.

This model, based on the analogy of Proclus's description of the modes of perception and discourse in the soul, need not be applied rigorously to Neoplatonic exegesis—indeed, if it were, it would doubtless prove to contain numerous flaws. Nevertheless, the pattern is a revealing one, not only for the understanding of Proclus's analysis of Homer, but with regard to much of the literature of Neoplatonism after Plotinus, for one of the most striking and characteristic aspects of that literature is its frequent recourse to the form of commentary.[26] The practice of indirect expression in the guise of explication of an existing text is a part of Neoplatonism from the time of Porphyry and is responsible in part for the scholastic and medieval flavor of that tradition.[27]

The salient characteristic of the image of reality projected by lan-

---

24. See *In Rep.* 1.154–59 and 163–72.

25. Sheppard (*Studies*, p. 194, n. 91) corrects Coulter's claim (*Literary Microcosm*, p. 109) that Proclus places Plato himself no higher than "the middle rank of poets." The problem, as she shows, grows out of the lack of clarity of Proclus's account of didactic poetry in relation to myth.

26. Cf. Dalsgaard Larsen, "Jamblique dans la philosophie antique tardive," p. 5.

27. See ch. 2B, with n. 64, above.

guage as we know it is, then, fragmentation. In speaking of reality (that is, of what Proclus understands as reality: the suprasensory world characterized by permanence), language must inevitably do violence to the truth by presenting sequentially what is in fact simultaneous. A sentence could not possibly be a true representation of a fact concerning the divine, for the obvious reason that the sentence has no existence outside the sublunary world characterized by change and by time, whereas the divine transcends both.

This limitation of language (and, consequently, of myth) is one that attracts attention again and again in Neoplatonic thought. Plotinus mentions the problem,[28] and it is summed up succinctly by Sallustius when he says with reference to mythic statements and their meaning, "These things never happened: they exist eternally. Mind sees all things simultaneously, but words express first some, then others."[29] At a distance of nearly a millennium, when Dante in the *Paradiso* confronts the problem of expressing in language things outside the universe of change and time, his frequent protestations of the inadequacy of language to the task are reminiscent of the Neoplatonic formulation.[30] On the verge of the final vision, when Dante observes,

> Omai sarà piú corta mia favella
> pur a quel ch'io ricordo, che d'un fante
> che bagni ancor la lingua alla mammella,
> *(Par. 33.106–8)*

Proclus's model of a hierarchy of languages and modes of perception is called to mind. Dante is saying, in effect, that his poem has now reached the point where his account, his language, can bear no more resemblance even to what his memory can retain of the experience of that

28. See ch. 3A, with n. 31, above.

29. ταῦτα δὲ ἐγένετο μὲν οὐδέποτε, ἔστι δ᾽ ἀεί, καὶ ὁ μὲν νοῦς ἅμα πάντα ὁρᾷ, ὁ δὲ λόγος τὰ μὲν πρῶτα τὰ δὲ δεύτερα λέγει (Sallust. *De diis* 4; p. 8, lines 14–16 in Nock ed.).

30. E.g., *Par.* 4.40–42, 31.136–37, and, in addition to the passage quoted below, 33.121–23. Much of the imagery of the later portions of the *Paradiso* makes it explicit that the major problem involved in the communication of the experience of ultimate reality in language is one of translating the absolute and eternal into a medium characterized by process and change. See, for example, the Argo comparison of *Par.* 33.94–96. A detailed examination of Dante's ideas about language in the light of the thought of the Neoplatonists would be quite interesting. See, for example, Francis Fergusson's comments (*Dante*, p. 64) on the "double nature" of language as described in the *De vulgari eloquentia*.

highest, suprasensory reality than a babbling infant's pseudolanguage bears to reality as normally experienced.

The problem of the mythoplasts' distortion of reality through expression in time is mentioned repeatedly in Proclus's defense of Homer. Just after we have been told that apparitions of gods in various forms to different people imply no change in the gods themselves, but must be understood to mean only that different observers or "receivers" (ὑποδοχαί), according to their capacities, experience different images of them,[31] Proclus goes on to say,

> This, then, is one mode in which poetry presents polymorphic transformations of that which knows no change, but there is also a second mode in which the divine itself, because of its multiple powers and because it is filled with forms of all sorts, extends diverse visions to those who observe it. Here, in effect, the poem is showing the diversity of the powers and again says that that which contains all these powers itself changes into many forms, projecting first one then another, though in fact the being in question is always acting according to all its powers, but because of the multiplicity of the powers it encompasses it is constantly changing for the discursive perceptions of souls.[32]

The example that follows immediately is the interpretation of the story of Proteus (Od. 4.351–582), but the same principle finds numerous other applications in defending Homer against the Socratic accusation (Rep. 2.380d–381e) that Homer's myths attribute change to what by its very nature cannot possibly change.[33]

The general principle is again enunciated with regard to the episode of the deception of Zeus, which, as one might expect, poses serious problems for Proclus.[34] Since in that passage there is mention of several sexual encounters between Zeus and Hera, separated in space and time, and of a change in Zeus's state of consciousness from waking to sleep,

31. Proclus In Rep. 1.112; cf. n. 15 above.

32. ἕνα μὲν οὖν τρόπον εἰρημένον ἡ ποίησις τῶν ἀμεταβλήτων μεταβολὰς παραδίδωσιν. ἕτερον δὲ ὅταν καὶ αὐτὸ τὸ θεῖον πολυδύναμον ὑπάρχον καὶ πλῆρες παντοίων εἰδῶν ποικίλα προτείνῃ θεάματα τοῖς εἰς αὐτὸ βλέπουσι. τότε γὰρ αὖ τὴν ἐξαλλαγὴν τῶν δυνάμεων ἐνδεικνυμένη μεταβάλλειν αὐτό φησι τὸ πάσας ἔχον ἐν ἑαυτῷ τὰς δυνάμεις ταύτας εἰς πολλὰς μορφάς, ἄλλοτε ἄλλην προβαλλόμενον, ἀεὶ μὲν κατὰ πάσας ἐνεργοῦν, ταῖς δὲ μεταβατικαῖς νοήσεσι τῶν ψυχῶν ἀλλοῖον ἀεὶ διὰ τὸ πλῆθος τῶν περιεχομένων φανταζόμενον (In Rep. 1.112.13–22).

33. Cf. In Rep. 1.109–14.

34. See pp. 208–15 below.

Proclus indicates that, here again, the poets have adapted eternal truths to the needs of language and storytelling by representing events that are in fact simultaneous *as if* they succeeded one another: "For these things that exist simultaneously with one another the mythoplasts have separated, disguising the truth."[35]

The image of ultimate reality that may be constructed using the tool of language, then, invariably fragments that reality by introducing process, which properly has no place there. But, Proclus tells us, the image is not to be rejected utterly on that account. Any given sphere of human discourse, whether the poems of Homer, the dialogues of Plato, or the *Elements* of Euclid, has its limitations, which cannot be resolved internally. Each implies a previous, more coherent discourse, a metalanguage still more remote from us. And each requires the elaboration of an ancillary discourse of commentary for its meaning to unfold in a completely satisfactory way.

With regard to the Homeric poems, as we shall see, Proclus will conclude that the metalanguage of what he calls a "secret doctrine"[36] is essential to their complete understanding, and that, if they are *not* understood "according to the secret doctrine" (κατὰ τὴν ἀπόρρητον θεωρίαν) but rather "according to the apparent sense" (κατὰ τὸ φαινόμενον),[37] then they do indeed have the potential, which Socrates feared, of imparting a pernicious and inaccurate model of reality.

---

35. καὶ γὰρ συννπάρχοντα ἀλλήλοις οἱ μυθοπλάσται τὴν ἀλήθειαν ἐπικρυπτόμενοι χωρίζουσιν (*In Rep.* 1.140.4–6).

36. The status of the "secret doctrine" and its relationship to the text of Homer are somewhat more complex than I have indicated here. The doctrine is, in a sense, contained within the text itself, or at least implied in it, but since it is literally "secret" or "unspoken" (ἀπόρρητον) it is not to be deduced from an initial encounter with the poetry of Homer, which would presumably be confined to the "apparent sense" (τὸ φαινόμενον). The "secret doctrine" is, then, potentially within the text, but must in practice be articulated *outside*, by someone with the experience and insight to explain the text "according to" it, and only then can it come to occupy its appropriate place in the experience of the polysemous text. The word θεωρία is also problematical here, and is used in a sense common in the Church Fathers (Lampe, s.v. θεωρία, D.1 and 2): rather than a fixed and unchanging "doctrine," it seems to refer to a mystical and privileged "contemplation" or mode of seeing. Cf. Tate, "On the History of Allegorism," and his observation with reference to Julian (p. 111) that "one difficulty in using the myths as authoritative support for paganism was that their correct interpretation could not be discovered or understood by anyone who was not already a Neoplatonist."

37. *In Rep.* 1.140.11–13.

C. MYTHS OR TEXTS?

What has been outlined above amounts to a general theory of interpretation that might be applied to virtually any system of meaning, any discourse. With reference to Proclus, it is important, though, for us to ask the question that has been posed in various forms with regard to the other "critics" examined thus far: Was Proclus in his writings ever concerned with works of literature as such, or was he an interpreter primarily of myth, a religious thinker and a mystic for whom the text as such had little importance? The extravagance of some of his interpretations might lead one to suspect that the text would, for him, constitute little more than a means to an end beside which it faded into insignificance.

When we take a broad view of Proclus's activities and opinions, however, we find that there is a certain amount of conflicting evidence. His biographer and student Marinus provides us with a fascinating picture of the man, organizing his treatment not around the simple chronology of his master's life, but rather around a pyramid of "excellences" or "virtues" (ἀρεταί) in which his master stood out among other men,[38] along with the various divine interventions that steered Proclus along his destined path. We learn from Marinus that Proclus began his studies in Lycia and initially concerned himself with grammar. He went from there to Alexandria, where he studied under a sophist named Leonas and a grammarian named Orion, and "as a young man seemed to take pleasure in rhetoric above all else."[39] Fortune intervened and led him back to his birthplace, Constantinople, where the patron goddess took him in hand and turned him in the direction of philosophy. After a further sojourn in Alexandria, he went to Athens, where he arrived still aged under twenty. There is no available information that would permit us to date Proclus's abandonment of his grammatical and rhetorical studies with precision,[40] but it is striking that, like Porphyry two centuries earlier, he had moved on from an early interest in language and style that, to judge by his biographer's emphasis, must have gone beyond mere compliance with the demands of the traditional course of study, to a more mature pursuit of philosophy. The fact that Porphyry had made the

---

38. Marinus Vit. Pr. 3.
39. μάλιστα δὲ ἐδόκει νέος ὢν χαίρειν τότε ῥητορικῇ (Marinus Vit. Pr. 8).
40. Cf. Rudolph Beutler, "Proklos," col. 187.

shift at roughly thirty,[41] whereas Proclus focused his attention on philosophy at perhaps eighteen, is, of course, significant, but does not destroy the parallel.

Whatever may have been the nature of Proclus's early bookish pursuits, they were clearly less serious and less extensive than those of Porphyry. He retained, however, a profound and cautious respect for the power of language and literature over men's minds, as the anecdote with which Marinus closes his biography suggests. Marinus is making the point that, among his own works, Proclus placed the commentary on the *Timaeus* before the others:

> And he was in the habit of saying, "If I were master, the only ones of all the ancient books I would have people read would be the *Chaldaean Oracles* and the *Timaeus*, and I would do away with all the others for the men of our time, because they harm some of those who approach them casually and without due examination."[42]

This revealing statement is a reminder of Proclus's proximity to certain patterns of thought that we may consider characteristic of the Christian Middle Ages, but at the same time it is sobering to realize that this attitude as he expresses it no doubt sprang from long and serious meditation on the critique of literature and society in Plato's *Republic*.

Little more can be gleaned from Marinus on Proclus's attitudes toward literature, but late in life the philosopher wrote hymns, of which seven survive.[43] In these he uses Homeric style to celebrate the sun, the gods collectively, the Muses, Aphrodite, "Lycian Aphrodite," and "Athena Polymetis." This last title (εἰς Ἀθηνᾶν Πολύμητιν) is interesting in that it addresses Athena under an epithet Homer applies most frequently and conspicuously to Odysseus, her protégé (though the application to Athena herself is anticipated in a single occurrence of the epithet in the Homeric *Hymn to Athena*, and this can be taken to be Proclus's source for the work in question).[44] For Proclus Odysseus represents a

---

41. See Bidez, *Vie de Porphyre*, p. 58.

42. εἰώθει δὲ πολλάκις καὶ τοῦτο λέγειν. ὅτι Κύριος εἰ ἦν, μόνα ἂν τῶν ἀρχαίων βιβλίων ἐποίουν φέρεσθαι τὰ Λόγια καὶ τὸν Τίμαιον, τὰ δὲ ἄλλα ἠφάνιζον ἐκ τῶν νῦν ἀνθρώπων, διὰ τὸ καὶ βλάπτεσθαι ἐνίους τῶν εἰκῆ καὶ ἀβασανίστως ἐντυγχανόντων αὐτοῖς (*Vit. Pr.* 38).

43. Cf. Beutler, "Proklos," col. 207. Texts of the complete hymns can be found in Victor Cousin's 1864 edition of the *Opera inedita* of Proclus, pp. 1314–23, but a recent edition by Ernest Vogt does them more justice.

44. Hom. *Hymn* 28.2.

soul participating in the divine "procession" stemming from Athena, and so the transferred epithet further emphasizes the continuity and integration of the entire procession, from its unified source in the realm of νοῦς to the fragmented level of everyday experience. In any case, Proclus's hymns are abundant evidence of his intimate knowledge of Homer and of the hexameter tradition, which he imitates skillfully. It is even tempting to believe that an echo of such worldly non-epic poetry as Sappho's great hymn to Aphrodite can be heard in the cadence of the fifth line of Proclus's hymn to Athena Polymetis.[45] Several fragments of autobiographical mystical poetry from Proclus's hand, quoted by Marinus,[46] and two epigrams further indicate that his poetic activity may have been considerable and varied.[47] In the fragments as well, the language is Homeric, but the content suggests that Parmenides may have been closer than Homer to the poet's mind. That Proclus knew Callimachus is demonstrated by three citations in the *Republic* commentary (1.4,125,150), where a fragment of Solon likewise occurs (*In Rep.* 2.172). No other non-epic poetry is quoted in the commentary on the *Republic*.

If we leave aside for the moment the major defense of Homer, we have a certain amount of evidence concerning Proclus's activities as a commentator and "critic" of non-philosophical literature. Among the fifty works by (or attributed to) Proclus that Rudolf Beutler lists are two general works on Homer entitled *Notes on the Whole of Homer* (Ὑπομνήματα εἰς ὅλον τὸν Ὅμηρον) and *On the Gods in Homer* (Περὶ τῶν παρ' Ὁμήρῳ θεῶν),[48] but these titles have no authority beyond the *Suda*, where both are attributed to Proclus's master Syrianus as well as to Proclus himself. Aside from the philosophical literature that occupied him during most of his productive life, Proclus wrote essays or commentary on Hesiod's *Works and Days* and on several works in the mystical hexameter tradi-

---

45.

κέκλυθι, δέχνυσο δ' ὕμνον ἐύφρονι, πότνια, θυμῷ
                          Proclus Hymn 7.5

Cf. Sappho 1.4 (Bergk). πότνια does not occur in the fifth foot as an independent term of address in the Homeric corpus, nor is it followed by a form of θυμός.

46. Marinus *Vit. Pr.* 28.

47. On the epigrams of Proclus, see the exhaustive and important study by Gelzer, "Die Epigramme des Neuplatonikers Proklos," where they are discussed in the light of Proclus's conception of literature and of allegory.

48. On these titles and the relationship of the works to those of Proclus's master Syrianus, see Beutler, "Proklos," col. 205, and Friedl, *Homer-Interpretationen des Neuplatonikers Proklos*, p. 51.

tions: the *Hymns* of Orpheus and the *Chaldaean Oracles*.[49] When one finds Homer (and for that matter Hesiod) in this company, it is tempting to believe that Proclus made no sharp distinctions among the hexameter poets, and there is every reason to believe that he felt that Orpheus, Homer, Hesiod, and the *Oracles* all tapped a single tradition of wisdom that was also represented in different form in Pythagoras and Plato.[50]

The *Chrestomathy* (Χρηστομάθεια γραμματική) that comes down to us under Proclus's name by way of a summary in the *Bibliotheca* of Photius, would, if it is properly attributed, be evidence of quite extensive literary studies and of a high esteem for traditional literature extending at least to the epic cycle. The sequence and contents of the poems that recounted the Panhellenic traditions of the heroic age—that vast panorama of epics of which our *Iliad* and *Odyssey* are the major survivors— would be virtually unknown today if we did not have the summaries that Photius and others derive from this Proclus. Modern scholars have questioned the attribution of the *Chrestomathy* to Proclus the Neoplatonist, but the *Suda* confirms that it was accepted in the Byzantine period, and we have no compelling reason to reject it.[51] Photius furthermore attri-

---

49. A title not mentioned by Beutler, but attributed to Proclus by J. E. Wenrich, *De auctorum graecorum versionibus et commentariis Syriacis Arabicis Armeniacis Persicisque*, might be added here: "A Commentary on the Carmina Aurea of Pythagoras." See Rosán, *Philosophy of Proclus*, p. 223, n. 7, and his comment that the work in question might be one by Proclus's contemporary Hierocles of Alexandria.

50. Note the title Περὶ συμφωνίας 'Ορφέως, Πυθαγόρου, Πλάτωνος πρὸς τὰ Λόγια, which the *Suda* again attributes both to Proclus and to Syrianus. Cf. Beutler, "Proklos," col. 206.

51. Cf. Beutler, "Proklos," cols. 207–8 and Friedl, *Homer-Interpretationen des Neuplatonikers Proklos*, pp. 53–55. Friedl believed, with Schmidt and others, that internal evidence demonstrated convincingly that Proclus the Neoplatonist was *not* the author of the *Chrestomathy*. Nevertheless, there is no compelling evidence that this work is not simply an example of an otherwise unattested side of Proclus's literary interests. Furthermore, at least one of Friedl's demonstrations is based on a misunderstanding. He claims (pp. 52–53) that for Proclus it was historical fact that Homer was blind, whereas in fact Proclus at *In Rep.* 1.174.7–13 interprets Homer's blindness as symbolic—an attitude not inconsistent with that of the author of the *Chrestomathy* (cf. Homer [OCT], vol. 5, p. 101, lines 3–5). G. L. Huxley (*Greek Epic Poetry from Eumelos to Panyassis*, pp. 123–24) alludes briefly to the problem and considers it still unresolved. Albin Lesky (*Geschichte der griechischen Literatur* [2nd ed.] p. 100, n. 1) points to Martin Sicherl's demonstration of the extreme weakness of the positive external evidence for the attribution of the *Chrestomathy* to the Neoplatonist (*Gnomon* 28 [1956], pp. 210–18). I

butes to Proclus the opinion that the hexameter was first invented for prophecy (hanging his argument by an exceptionally weak etymological thread),[52] and this adds support to the presumptive evidence that Proclus associated theurgical powers with the very form of epic diction. That he was primarily concerned with the content of literary works and their truth value to the exclusion of stylistic criticism is clear when he expresses casual disdain for "troubling over style."[53]

The Pythagoreans' use of passages from Homer for incantations was familiar to Proclus, and as Boyancé points out, he would appear to have used Pythagorean musical purification with a double force, both medical and spiritual.[54] The fact that he echoes a verse from the passage in which Athena opens Diomedes' eyes (*Il.* 5.127) in one of his hymns,[55] and that he turns this into a dynamic and personal prayer, provides us with a vivid illustration of Proclus's attribution of supernatural power to Homer's words.[56]

The internal evidence from the defense of Homer in the commentary on the *Republic* does not convince the reader that Proclus is paying the texts he discusses the kind of meticulous attention that characterizes Porphyry's description of the cave of the nymphs. Occasionally, an argument is based on careful attention to the interpretation of a single word,

---

can add only that the marked contrast between the sober paraphrases of the *Chrestomathy* and the allegorizing of epic in the commentaries of Proclus has been an obstacle to the attribution, and that my own work has convinced me that such contrasts are widespread in the writings of Platonists concerned with literature. I can see no reason why the *Chrestomathy* should not be attributed to Proclus the Successor.

52. καὶ ὅτι τὸ ἔπος πρῶτον μὲν ἐφεῦρε Φημονόη ἡ Ἀπόλλωνος προφῆτις, ἐξαμέτροις χρησμοῖς χρησαμένη· καὶ ἐπειδὴ τοῖς χρησμοῖς τὰ πράγματα εἵπετο καὶ σύμφονα ἦν, ἔπος τὸ ἐκ μέτρων κληθῆναι (Phot. *Bibl.* cod. 239, incl. in Homer [OCT], vol. 5, p. 96, lines 21–24).

53. τὴν περὶ τὴν λέξιν πολυπραγμοσύνην ἄλλοις ἀφέντες (*In Rep.* 1.164.8).

54. See ch. 1D above and Boyancé, *Le Culte des Muses chez les philosophes grecs*, pp. 121–31.

55.

κλῦτε, σαωτῆρες μεγάλοι, ζαθέων δ' ἀπὸ βίβλων
νεύσατ' ἐμοὶ φάος ἁγνὸν ἀποσκεδάσαντες ὀμίχλην,
ὄφρα κεν εὖ γνοίην θεὸν ἄμβροτον ἠδὲ καὶ ἄνδρα·
Hymn 4.5–7 (ὕμνος κοινός)

This sort of use of Homeric lines is amply anticipated in the oracular literature. See in particular the oracle quoted at length in Porph. *Vit. Plot.* 22.

56. Cf. Boyancé, *Culte des Muses*, pp. 127–28.

but all too often when this does happen, we find that Proclus's interpretation of the word or expression in question is not easily supported.[57]

The general picture that emerges from this evidence concerning Proclus as a student of literature is revealing but somewhat disappointing. He knew the Homeric diction well enough to mimic it and to be a competent hexameter poet, but he sometimes demonstrates surprising insensitivity to the meanings of words or expressions in his interpretations. He appears to have had considerable knowledge of grammar, rhetoric, and literature, and to have been quite sensitive to the power and complexity of literature itself, as well as of the experience of a literary text. Nevertheless, there are obstacles to classifying him as a literary critic, even in the sense in which the term applies to Porphyry, because he would appear never in his mature life to have taken an interest in literature beyond its capacity to illuminate the transcendent realities on which his attention was fixed. An amazingly prolific annotator, he was, when he examined works we place in the category of literature, concerned primarily with seeing *through* the texts on which he worked. In spite of his occasional close attention to the wording of a given passage, one must conclude that his own use for literature is summed up in the verses of the hymn mentioned above:

> Hear me, great saviors, and from the most sacred books
> grant me holy illumination, scattering the mist,
> so that I may clearly recognize immortal gods and men.[58]

57. See Proclus *In Rep.* 1.115, where Zeus is acquitted of the charge of having deceived Agamemnon by sending the dream of *Il.* 2 on the basis that Zeus specifically told Agamemnon to attack "with the whole army" (πανσυδίη interpreted as equivalent to πανστρατιᾷ—an interpretation compatible with the use of the word in later authors, but not accepted for the Homeric passage by modern lexicographers). Agamemnon made the mistake of going ahead and attacking with only part of the army (i.e., without Achilles) and so lost, but was himself responsible for the loss. *In Rep.* 1.165 on Διὸς ἔνδον at *Il.* 20.13 insists on a literal interpretation of Homer's phrase, which helps to support Proclus's own theological notions, but does some violence to the apparent meaning of the text. Finally, at *In Rep.* 1.104, Proclus seems unaccountably to take ἀντίθεος at *Il.* 4.88, applied to Pandarus, to have an adversative meaning similar to the sense "contrary to God," offered by LSJ citing only Philo. We would expect a reader with Proclus's familiarity with Homer to realize that this very general and frequently employed epithet, which is used for various kings, heroes, and nations, and even for Penelope, can hardly have had such a force. On this last example, cf. Festugière's note *ad loc.* in his translation of the commentary (vol. 1, p. 121, n. 1).

58. See n. 55 above.

D. THE MAJOR EXEGESIS OF HOMER
IN THE COMMENTARY ON THE *REPUBLIC*

Proclus's Motives

In the anecdote from Marinus quoted above, Proclus indicates that, if the choice were his, the *Iliad* and *Odyssey* would disappear from the face of the earth along with all the other books of antiquity, excepting only the *Chaldaean Oracles* and the *Timaeus*. Why, then, did he devote over a hundred pages to the defense and explication of an author for whom he had so little use? The answer is clear from a careful look at the anecdote itself. Proclus is, indeed, dividing the literature of antiquity into two classes, but the criteria he applies are very close in spirit to those Socrates used in the *Republic*: he would retain the *useful*, and reject the potentially dangerous.

Implied but not stated in Proclus's discussion of the relationship of literature both to society and to truth is another twofold division, no doubt close to what Heinrich Dörrie perceived in Plotinus's attitude toward literature.[59] Plotinus, Dörrie argued, made a sharp division between literature in which he was convinced some eternally valid truth, however veiled or distorted, must lie, and the other category, including all of tragedy and comedy, and presumably virtually all lyric poetry, for which no such claim could be made. Proclus seems to have divided up the works of the ancients in a similar manner, and though poetry from the second category appears with some frequency in Plotinus, Proclus seems largely indifferent to it, in spite of occasional echoes.[60]

Proclus's definition of the first category of literature may appear naive to us, and his classification of Homer with the *Chaldaean Oracles* (which, Dodds argued, Plotinus ignored, "recognizing them for the theosophical rubbish that they are")[61] may even seem hopelessly misguided. Nevertheless, it is hardly surprising that for Proclus the antiquity of a work should be an indication of its credibility, and Marinus's anecdote makes it clear that Proclus considered the *Chaldaean Oracles* to be ancient. The antiquity of the Orphic hymns, which he would also have placed in this category, was unquestioned, and they were widely believed to predate Homer. The myth, after all, makes Orpheus an Argonaut, and the voy-

---

59. Heinrich Dörrie in the discussion of Cilento's paper "Mito e poesia nelle *Enneadi* di Plotino," p. 316.
60. Cilento, "Mito e poesia," pp. 297–305. See also n. 45 above.
61. Dodds, "Numenius and Ammonius," p. 11.

age of the Argo took place a generation before the Trojan War. The special status Proclus gives the *Timaeus* among the dialogues of Plato no doubt stems from a belief on his part that it also tapped an older tradition, though he may have selected it because he perceived no irony or dramatization of false positions in it.[62] Whatever their status in terms of the criterion of usefulness, it is clear that all the dialogues of Plato would be included with Homer in the category of works able to give an inkling of the truth.

For Proclus, this class of poets and writers constituted the "theologians" (θεολόγοι). The expression is used in the headings of the second and third chapters of the sixth part of his commentary on the *Republic* (the section dealing with the defense of Homer), and it is clear that Homer is included. In the context, one might even say that he is viewed as preeminent among the θεολόγοι. The use of the term is not entirely consistent within the discourse, and at *In Rep.* 1.126.21, the θεολόγοι are clearly the explicators and not the creators of myth.[63] However, in all other instances in the essay the term refers to the class of poets with special access to the divine. Homer is often said to speak "by divine inspiration" (ἐνθέως, *In Rep.* 1.112.2, etc.) and simply called "divine" (θεῖος, *In Rep.* 1.117.6; 123.4, etc.) and even the "best and most divine of poets" (Ὁμήρῳ τῷ ἀρίστῳ καὶ θειοτάτῳ τῶν ποιητῶν, *In Rep.* 1.158.9, quoting Plato's *Ion* 530b).[64] The expression ὁ ποιητής, however, does not belong exclusively to Homer, as its use at *In Rep.* 1.126.1 to refer to Callimachus demonstrates.[65]

62. Cf. Proclus *In Rep.* 1.159–64. The choice was, of course, not original. In the Neoplatonic tradition generally the *Timaeus* was viewed as Plato's crowning achievement. See Wallis, *Neoplatonism*, pp. 18–19.

63. Cf. Festugière's note *ad loc.* (vol. 1, p. 146, n. 3) in his translation of the commentary. It is striking that these two groups—the mythoplasts and the interpreters—are drawn so closely together in Proclus's treatment of them. Both may be called θεολόγοι; both may also be described as "inspired."

64. The expression ἡ ἔνθεος ποίησις at *In Rep.* 1.120.6 is also striking. For an index of comparable phrases in the *Timaeus* commentary (including a reference to ἡ παλαιὰ θεολογία παρ᾽ Ὁμήρῳ) see Diehl's edition, vol. 3, p. 364.

65. There is a certain irony in this in view of the fact that the *Chrestomathy* is one of the few ancient sources that actually comment on the fact that Homer had usurped the term ὁ ποιητής to refer exclusively to himself. Nevertheless, this inconsistency should not be taken as serious evidence against Proclus the Neoplatonist being the author of the *Chrestomathy*. Cf. A. M. Harmon, "The Poet κατ᾽ ἐξοχήν," esp. pp. 45–46, on the history of the term and Proclus's comments. This quote from Callimachus and another at *In Rep.* 1.150.14–15 are among the rare examples of lyric poetry quoted in the essay. Most of the other lyric quotations and references come from Plato. Cf. *In Rep.* 1.186–87.

Proclus makes it clear from the start of his discussion of Homer that it is, for him, an article of faith, consecrated by tradition, that Homer is to be numbered among "those who are knowledgeable . . . in teachings about the classes of the divine and those things that exist eternally."[66] In order to defend that traditional evaluation, Proclus proposes to answer systematically the accusations raised against Homer by Socrates in the *Republic*. At the beginning of his discussion, which constitutes an extensive independent essay within the commentary and may well have existed as a separate work,[67] he briefly considers the possible consequences of the Socratic attack on Homer.[68] If, on the one hand, Socrates proves to have been correct in his accusations, then it will be impossible to respect the tradition of numbering Homer among the wise or, more important, among the sources of wisdom. Plato seems to be saying that Homer is unacceptable, and moreover that the *whole* of the traditional wisdom of the past, cloaked in the obscurities of myth and poetry, is to be rejected. This amounted to a cultural revolution of enormous implications, and one that was extremely discomforting to heirs of the Greek tradition who were intensely concerned with demonstrating the coherence and validity of that tradition.[69]

Proclus is initially upset, then, at the prospect of losing Homer. But there is another side to the question. Socrates' attack may prove to be *unfounded*. Then what would happen to Plato's prestige and credibility? It is possible, to a considerable extent, to separate Socrates from Plato, and Proclus is prepared to do this, but on the other hand he claims that one may take the opinions expressed in the dialogues by "Parmenides, Socrates, Timaeus, or another of those who are divine in this way,"[70] to

66. ἐν τοῖς ἐπιστήμοσιν . . . τῆς περὶ τῶν θείων γενῶν καὶ τῶν ἀεὶ ὄντων διδασκαλίας (*In Rep.* 1.70.10–12).

67. Cf. Festugière in the preface to his translation of the commentary, vol. 1, p. 7. This commentary differs from Proclus's other commentaries in its organization into separate essays, departing from the usual line-by-line elucidation of the text. Sheppard (*Studies*, pp. 15–38) offers a detailed discussion of the relationship of the two sections of the commentary concerned with poetry to each other and to the work as a whole.

68. *In Rep.* 1.70–71.

69. Cf. Phillip DeLacy, "Plato and the Intellectual Life of the Second Century A.D.," passim, and particularly p. 10 on Aelius Aristides and Plato: "[Aristides] does not want to reject Plato, but only Plato's rejection of the Greek heritage. This predicament, I suggest, would face us too if we really took Plato seriously."

70. ἀλλ᾽ ὅταν Παρμενίδης ἢ Σωκράτης ἢ Τίμαιος ἢ ἄλλος τις τῶν οὕτω θείων φθέγγεται, τότε τῶν Πλάτωνος ἀκούειν ἡγούμεθα δογμάτων (*In Rep.* 1.110.15–17).

be the opinions of Plato himself. There were evident contradictions in Plato's attitude toward Homer: in the *Phaedo* he is a "divine poet" (θεῖος ποιητής, *Phaed*. 95a), and in the *Republic* he is "third in line from the truth" (τρίτος ἀπὸ τῆς ἀληθείας, *Rep*. 10.579e), and the two observations seemed to make diametrically opposed statements on the credibility of Homer as a source of wisdom concerning divine things. If the *Republic*'s claim that Homer is unreliable is false, Proclus asks, how can we say that Plato has acted "wisely and in accordance with irrefutable wisdom" (κατὰ νοῦν . . . καὶ τὴν ἀνέλεγκτον γνῶσιν, *In Rep*. 1.70)? Clearly, this is what Proclus expects of Plato, that the wisdom he imparts be of the highest order, and that his demonstrations be irrefutable. Furthermore, the problem is not confined to Homer, for Plato's teachings on poetics in general contain the same fundamental contradiction, claiming at one moment that poetry is "possession by the Muses and divine madness and that poets are divine, whereas at another time he calls them fabricators of images and fantasies, and far removed from the truth."[71]

Neither possibility—the loss of Homer or the loss of Plato—is one Proclus could easily accept. His characteristic solution will be to search beyond the apparent contradictions in Plato's text and to try to resolve them, demonstrating that his praise and his blame of Homer are both part of a larger "irrefutable" plan, and at the same time showing that both Plato and Homer contemplated the same transcendent truths and that their writings, properly interpreted, can be shown to have handed down the same teachings about those truths. Broadly speaking, Proclus approaches the problem as if it were one of apparent conflict between two philosophers, and his concern with this question is in some ways similar to the concern of Neoplatonists as early as Porphyry with the resolution of apparent conflicts between Plato and Aristotle.

Conceptual Framework

Proclus's motives, then, are complex—he must save both Homer *and* Plato from any loss of prestige or credibility—but at the same time these motives place him securely in that group of allegorizers whose primary motive for their interpretive efforts is defensive. Indeed, the starting point of Heraclitus, "Homer was totally impious unless he was in some

---

71. καὶ τὴν ποιητικὴν αὐτὴν τότε μὲν ἐκ Μουσῶν κατοκωχήν τε καὶ μανίαν τιθέμενος καὶ θεῖον τὸ ποιητικὸν γένος ἀποκαλῶν, τότε δὲ εἰδωλοποιὸν καὶ φαντ- αστικὸν καὶ πολλοστὸν ἀπὸ τῆς ἀληθοῦς γνώσεως ἀποφαίνων δόξειεν ἄν (*In Rep*. 1.70.28–71.1).

respect allegorizing,"[72] is close in spirit to Proclus's undertaking, though the two otherwise have little in common. Proclus's discussion of the matter is far richer and more complex than that of Heraclitus, and basically defensive though its allegory is, it also, by implication, brings the prestige of Homeric precedent to late Neoplatonic demonology and angelology.

There are two basic lines of argument open to those who would defend Homer against Socrates: it is possible to claim either that Socrates failed to realize *what* Homer means, or that he failed to understand *how* Homer means. A defense falling into the first category might be exclusively concerned with the elucidation of meaning, whether by allegorical or by other means; a defense of the second sort will focus its attention rather on the impact of the work of art, the reader's or listener's experience of it, its structure of meaning, and, finally, its ability to influence the reader's life and that of his community. Ultimately, any argument defending Homer against Socrates must return to these moral criteria, for they are the ones Socrates emphasized in his condemnation of Homer. No single surviving defense of Homer falls exclusively in one category or the other, but Heraclitus's work lies primarily in the first.

The second approach would appear to have been taken by Aristotle. Plato had claimed (*Rep.* 10.606a–b) that the natural desire to weep and lament over our own misfortunes is reinforced by the poets, who show the heroes doing so, and so this natural but undesirable impulse becomes irresistibly strong when we ourselves are confronted by difficulties. Proclus himself provides evidence[73] that Aristotle responded to Plato on this very point, indicating that the catharsis doctrine of Aristotle was directed specifically against this claim on Plato's part that poetry, by exciting the emotions, harms the spectator.[74]

Proclus does not take Aristotle's side against Plato, but he does question Socrates' understanding of the nature, impact, and meaning of Homer's poetry. That portion of the argument centered around moral issues (the question of whether Homer portrays the heroes as greedy and the impact of such description on the audience, for example) will not occupy us here, because no important efforts of interpretation are involved: one passage, understood in the most obvious sense (κατὰ τὸ φαινόμενον), is simply played off against another until the weight of evidence mustered by Proclus tips the scale in Homer's favor. Further, Proclus argues in a

---

72. πάντα γὰρ ἠσέβησεν, εἰ μηδὲν ἠλληγόρησεν (*Quaest. hom.* 1.1).

73. *In Rep.* 1.49.13.

74. Cf. Stefan Weinstock, "Die platonische Homerkritik und seine Nachwirkung," p. 130.

cogent and convincing way that Socrates' attack on the poets was motivated by specific historical circumstances, and hence that the goals and intentions of Plato (and of Socrates) must be taken into account in evaluating it.[75] Finally, in a manner distantly reminiscent of Plutarch,[76] he argues that there are many passages demonstrating Plato's respect for the greatness and even the divinity of Homer, which may be taken to outweigh the evidence of the aberrant critique in the *Republic*. The theories of interpretation lying behind Proclus's defense of Homer have recently been explored in two important studies,[77] and a brief summary of Proclus's key concepts will be sufficient for the present analysis.

Proclus insists from the start of his discussion of Homer that a myth (and we may include much of what we call literature in this category— certainly, at any rate, the *Iliad* and *Odyssey*) is far more complex than a casual hearing or reading would indicate. The surface or, in the case of a narrative poem, the apparent sense of the story ($\tau\grave{o}$ $\phi\alpha\iota\nu\acute{o}\mu\epsilon\nu o\nu$) is repeatedly called a "screen" ($\pi\alpha\rho\alpha\pi\acute{\epsilon}\tau\alpha\sigma\mu\alpha$),[78] serving simultaneously to reveal one kind of information and to conceal another.

Though this observation has not gone unnoticed,[79] the problem of the implications of Proclus's metaphor when actually applied to the experience of a work of art seems to have been largely ignored. Proclus is telling his reader that what one encounters in a work of art is a complex surface, combining a more or less coherent imitation of reality as we experience it in our everyday lives with certain cryptic signals referring to a further level of meaning that lies beyond that surface and is not immediately apparent. We might be inclined to say that this is the essential condition of all allegory: the work of art presents a surface like that of the *roman à clef*, and only the reader armed with the key, the table of equivalents, will be able to sort out the entire meaning of the work. Allegory,

75. *In Rep.* 1.202–3.
76. Cf. Plut. *De aud. po.* 20d–e: ὅσα δ᾽ εἴρηται μὲν ἀτόπως εὐθὺς δ᾽ οὐ λέλυται, ταῦτα δεῖ τοῖς ἀλλαχόθι πρὸς τοὐναντίον εἰρημένοις ὑπ᾽ αὐτῶν ἀντυαναιρεῖν.
77. Coulter, *Literary Microcosm*, and Sheppard, *Studies*. The emphasis of Coulter's important study is on theory rather than practice, and on the advances in literary theory that can be securely attributed to the later Neoplatonists. Sheppard's more recent work offers a few corrections of Coulter, but in general her more detailed examination of the two central essays of Proclus complements the earlier work.
78. *In Rep.* 1.44.14, 66.7, 73.15, 74.19, 159.15; 2.248.27.
79. See, for example, Festugière's comment in his translation of the commentary, vol. 1, p. 89, n. 3.

understood in this way, easily becomes an esthetic exercise of little interest. The procedures of the mode are all too simple and monotonous—or, more damning yet, too subjective and arbitrary. The point that needs to be made, however, is that this understanding of allegory is relevant neither to Proclus's discussion of the complex, screenlike surface of the Homeric poems nor to the actual experience of most genuinely allegorical works of art.

One modern critic who has attempted, though not in a classical context, to return to the concept of allegory and to understand its meaning in terms of the audience's experience of the work of art is Jean-Claude Margolin. He emphasizes the element of mystery involved in the experience of allegorical art, the enigmatic surface that appears constantly to be referring to something beyond itself. He argues, in fact, that the ability to match up each element in the allegorical work with its referent (as in the example of the *roman à clef*) may be a hindrance to the full experience of "ce plaisir délicat de l'allégorisme, fait de dépaysement, de goût de l'inconnu, du sentiment de participer plus ou moins à la création, de l'incitation à la rêverie."[80]

It is important to realize that it is qualities such as these that Proclus is insisting upon in his systematic discussion of the *Iliad* and *Odyssey*. This surface, which is a παραπέτασμα, simultaneously revealing and masking its truths, is an invitation to participation in the creation of the meaning of the work—the challenge of an esthetic experience that goes far beyond the passive mode of perception of the senses, and involves us actively as spectators and participants in the articulation of meaning. However far this may be from our own ideas regarding Homeric style,[81] we are dealing here with qualities essential to the esthetic experience for many thinkers of the Middle Ages.[82] The demands Proclus made upon

80. Jean-Claude Margolin, "Aspects du surréalisme au xviᵉ siècle," p. 520. Cf. also Gay Clifford, *The Transformations of Allegory*, pp. 36–53, for a discussion of "the reader as participant" in allegorical literature.

81. For most modern critics, the *Iliad* and *Odyssey* have seemed to lie at the far extreme of esthetic experience from what Margolin describes in discussing Renaissance allegory and what Proclus, I believe, saw in the poems. See Erich Auerbach, *Mimesis*, ch. 1, for a compelling and antithetically opposed analysis of Homeric style.

82. Dante's letter to Can Grande on the polysemous structure of the poetic statement is the canonical medieval statement on the matter, but perhaps more instructive is the experience of major works of medieval or early Renaissance allegorical visual art, such as the famous unicorn tapestries of the Cloisters or those of the Musée de Cluny.

the text of Homer were symptomatic of the revolution in taste characterizing the transition from ancient to medieval. Proclus's insistence on the *absence* of the very qualities of clarity, directness, and explicitness Erich Auerbach appreciated in Homer (and which we are inclined to think Pericles' contemporaries might have appreciated as well) is evidence not of his insensitivity to literature but rather of his desire to communicate the greatness of Homer in contemporary terms. That insistence is most obviously motivated by the desire to make Homer appear to be saying something quite different from what he might superficially appear to mean, but I suggest that it had another side as well: the Homeric poems required a commentator able to demonstrate their enduring greatness not only on the level of philosophical insight, but also on the level of esthetics. Proclus is attempting to bridge not only the gap between the philosophical or theological demands of the archaic period and those of the fifth century after Christ, but also the gap between archaic or classical demands on art and those of his own time.[83] That allegory (whether taken to mean simple irony or sarcasm or more complex structures of meaning) and the stylistic ideal of clarity were at odds with one another is an idea expressed repeatedly in ancient writings on rhetoric.[84] An anonymous author, possibly to be identified as the Stoic Cornutus,[85] includes ἀλληγορία in a list of modes of expression that contribute to "lack of clarity" (τὸ ἀσαφές), and the same attitude can be found in the *De elocutione*'s fascinating discussion of the use of "allegories" in the mysteries: "Therefore the mysteries are spoken in allegories as well, for the sake of shock and fear, as if from darkness and night. For allegory is like darkness and night."[86]

83. Proclus feels the need to find an authoritative statement to back up his claims regarding the mysterious quality of Homer's poetry, but can do no better than a quotation from the (pseudo-) Platonic *Second Alcibiades*: ἔστιν τε γὰρ φύσει ποιητικὴ ἡ σύμπασα αἰνιγματώδης καὶ οὐ τοῦ προστυχόντος ἀνδρὸς γνωρίσαι (Plato *Alc.* 2 147b; *In Rep.* 1.186).

84. Cf. Richard Hahn, *Die Allegorie in der antiken Rhetorik*, pp. 29–31, who provides the examples I have incorporated into the text.

85. Hahn, *Allegorie*, p. 29 and n. 31, gives the arguments regarding the identification of the author. The text is in *Rhetores Graeci* I, pars ii, pp. 352–98.

86. διὸ καὶ τὰ μυστήρια ἐν ἀλληγορίαις λέγεται πρὸς ἔκπληξιν καὶ φρίκην, ὥσπερ ἐν σκότῳ καὶ νυκτί. ἔοικεν δὲ ἡ ἀλληγορία τῷ σκότῳ καὶ τῇ νυκτί (Demetr. *De eloc.* 101, cited by Hahn, *Allegorie*, p. 30). See the edition of W. Rhys Roberts for the text (p. 118) and for an excellent discussion of the meaning of ἀλληγορία in "Demetrius" with valuable *comparanda*. Though attributed to Demetrius of Phaleron (fourth century B.C.), the *De elocutione* is actually a text of the first century after Christ (cf. Roberts's edition, pp. 49–64).

This fundamental ambiguity of the literary artifact, its polysemous structure, constitutes its major point of resemblance to the world it mirrors, itself conceived of as a screen simultaneously representing and hiding a truth that is eternal, whereas all things in the world as we know it are transitory. Sallustius, again, puts the matter concisely in a passage with which Proclus could easily have agreed: "The cosmos as well may be described as a myth, for bodies and things are manifest in it, but souls and minds lie hidden."[87]

For those who took Plato's critique of mimetic art in book 10 of the *Republic* seriously,[88] the imitative function of the artist was severely discredited. Aristotle,[89] and the author of the essay *On the Sublime*[90] were, of course, able to use the term μίμησις fruitfully and suggestively, but in Proclus's vocabulary it is reserved (along with the complex μίμημα, μιμητής, μιμεῖσθαι) for art of an inferior, though not necessarily utterly contemptible, type. The association of the complex of words with the genre of the mime, which was very popular from the Hellenistic period through Proclus's time, but is generally treated with contempt by our surviving sources, may also have been a factor in discrediting "mimetic" art in late antiquity. Proclus indicates that all mimesis relates exclusively to appearances (τὰ φαινόμενα) and not to true things (τὰ ἀληθῆ).[91] It is confined to the fragmented experience of this world and has no reference to the transcendent, unified experience of the other.

Proclus divides poetry (ἡ ποιητική) into three major divisions, each corresponding to a level of the soul.[92] The model of the "lives" (ζωαί) or "conditions" (ἕξεις) of the soul that Proclus offers here is somewhat dif-

---

87. ἔξεστι γὰρ καὶ τὸν κόσμον μῦθον εἰπεῖν, σωμάτων μὲν καὶ χρημάτων ἐν αὐτῷ φαινομένων, ψυχῶν δὲ καὶ νῶν κρυπτομένων (*De diis* 3; p. 4, lines 9–11 in Nock ed.). Cf. Hermias *In Phdr.* 192.9–11: ὅλον γὰρ τὸ περὶ ἡμᾶς φαινόμενον σῶμα καὶ περιαγόμενον καὶ ὁ πᾶς διάκοσμος ὁ φαινόμενος μύθῳ ἔοικεν. For Proclus on the mythoplasts as imitators of nature, see *In Rep.* 1.77.9–28.

88. Plato *Rep.* 10.600e, 603a–608b. Cf. Plato *Soph.* 265b.

89. Arist. *Poet.* 1.1447a, etc. In fact, Aristotle makes it quite clear that the business of the epic poet is to be a μιμητής and to avoid passing into the first person, at which point one ceases to imitate in the dramatic sense: οὐ γάρ ἐστι κατὰ ταῦτα μιμητής (*Poet.* 24.1460a). Homer is his example of an epic poet who fully understood and acted upon this principle.

90. Ps.-Long. *De sublim.* 22.

91. *In Rep.* 1.162–63.

92. *In Rep.* 1.177–99.

ferent from the model of the perceptive faculties in the *Timaeus* commentary, discussed above. The three "lives" differ from the levels of experience (and discourse) of the *Timaeus* model in that Proclus is concerned here with the relationship of soul to the other hypostases, and not with its internal complexities and the intricacies of everyday perception. The conception of the three hypostases behind this exposition is, in fact, more suggestive of the Plotinian model[93] than of the more complex one Proclus developed. The three "lives" seem to be (a) virtual communion, if not with the One, then with those gods that are the immediate effects of the One,[94] (b) experience on the level of νοῦς, and (c) experience on the level of soul (comprehending the further subdivisions discussed in the *Timaeus* commentary).

The highest and most perfect "life" of the soul is on the level of the gods: the soul utterly abandons its own identity, transcends its individual νοῦς and attaches "its light to the transcendent light and the most unified element of its own being and life to the One beyond all being and life."[95] Poetry that corresponds to this condition is characterized by the absolute fusion of subject and object. It is divine madness (μανία), which is a greater thing even than reasonableness (σωφροσύνη) and fills the soul with symmetry.

Throughout this description of the varieties of poetry, the emphasis is clearly on the quality of experience *of the poet*. The artifact produced is secondary: the art is conceived as a performance art that communicates the poet's quality of experience directly to the audience and makes them participants in it. Proclus demonstrates the presence of all of his three kinds of poetry in the *Iliad* and *Odyssey*, claiming that each of a series of bards mentioned in the poems represents a given level of poetry and citing passages of Homer to illustrate each type.

The examples of the first type are rather surprising. They include two of the most superficially offensive passages, the song of Ares and Aphrodite (presented in the *Odyssey* [8.266–366] as the song of the Phaeacian bard Demodocus, whom, according to Proclus, Homer created as a self-portrait and as a symbol of the highest, inspired poetry),[96] and the

93. Cf. Plot. *Enn.* 5.1, and for a synthetic description see Wallis, *Neoplatonism*, pp. 47–61.

94. Cf. Rosán, *Philosophy of Proclus*, p. 131.

95. συνάψασα . . . τῷ ἐκεῖ φωτὶ τὸ ἑαυτῆς φῶς, τῷ ὑπὲρ οὐσίαν πᾶσαν καὶ ζωὴν ἑνὶ τὸ ἑνοειδέστατον τῆς οἰκείας οὐσίας τε καὶ ζωῆς (*In Rep.* 1.177.20–23).

96. *In Rep.* 1.193.26–194.11.

episode of the deception of Zeus (*Il.* 14.153–351).[97] In these passages, Proclus exclaims, "I would say that he is clearly in a state of inspiration, and that he composed these myths through being possessed by the Muses."[98] The significant point is that the passages are taken to represent a reality far removed from their apparent meaning. The *lack* of resemblance between the action described—the fiction—and the truth behind its "screen" is accepted as a criterion of value. These passages represent no mere mimetic art; they far transcend imitation and communicate their truths not by making images (εἰκόνες) or imitations (μιμήματα) of them, but by making *symbols* (σύμβολα or συνθήματα). Perhaps the most striking and original point in Proclus's poetics is this: "Symbols are not imitations of that which they symbolize."[99] On the contrary, symbols may be just the opposite of that which they symbolize. That which is disgraceful may stand for that which is good, that which is contrary to nature (τὸ παρὰ φύσιν) for that which is natural (τὸ κατὰ φύσιν), and so forth. This highest level of art—the one Proclus claims is most characteristic of the *Iliad* and *Odyssey*[100]—is not mimetic at all. Its mode of representation of reality is far more complex than simple imitation, or representation by resemblance.[101] Anne Sheppard quite rightly emphasizes the intimate connection between the σύμβολα of Proclus's critical vocabulary and the σύμβολα of theurgy, which Proclus took very seriously.[102] Proclus's symbols are related to their referents on higher levels of reality in a relationship conceived of as a real and necessary part of the

97. The fact that these episodes provided subject matter for comic-erotic pantomimes may have contributed to Proclus's feeling that they needed emphatic defense. Cf. Ernst Wüst, "Pantomimus," col. 848, who indicates references by both Lucian and, significantly, Augustine to mimes of Ares and Aphrodite.

98. τότε δὴ φαίην ἂν αὐτὸν ἐνθουσιάζειν σαφῶς καὶ διὰ τὴν ἐκ τῶν Μουσῶν κατοκωχὴν τὰ τοιαῦτα διατιθέναι μυθολογήματα (*In Rep.* 1.193).

99. τὰ γὰρ σύμβολα, τούτων ὧν ἐστι σύμβολα, μιμήματα οὐκ ἔστιν (*In Rep.* 1.198.15–16). Contrast the Stoic position by which, according to DeLacy ("Stoic Views of Poetry," pp. 257, 262), symbolic or allegorical representation is consistently classified as mimetic. Even here, Proclus makes no claim to originality, attributing a distinction between εἰκόνες and σύμβολα to the Pythagoreans in the *Timaeus* commentary (*In Tim.* 1.29; cf. *Theol. Plat.* 1.4). I am indebted to John Dillon for these references.

100. *In Rep.* 1.195.13–196.13.

101. *In Rep.* 1.198.18–24.

102. See Sheppard, *Studies*, pp. 146–51. She explores the double tradition behind this vocabulary in Proclus, stemming first from its use in the philosophical tradition (where it had already become a dead metaphor in Chrysippus) and secondly from theurgy itself, now taken seriously and practiced as an adjunct to philosophy.

structure of that reality: they participate in the chain of emanation from those higher ranks of beings.

The second "life" of the soul is the one that Plotinian Neoplatonism would associate with the level of νοῦς, the second, intermediate hypostasis.[103] It is characterized by the soul's turning within itself, departing from "the inspired life" (τῆς ἐνθέου . . . ζωῆς) of the highest level and setting νοῦς and wisdom (ἐπιστήμη) as the first principles of its activity. Again on this level there is a fusion, this time of "knower and known" (τό τε νοοῦν καὶ τὸ νοούμενον), and the soul "reproduces the image of the noetic essence, drawing together into one the nature of the noetic objects."[104] The poetry that belongs to this level of the soul's experience likewise knows "the essence of the things that truly exist"[105] and loves to contemplate good and beautiful actions and words. It is a large category of poetry, "full of advice and the best counsel and packed with intelligent moderation: it offers participation in prudence and the other virtues to those so inclined by nature."[106] Proclus clearly has in mind what we might call didactic poetry, though (as Sheppard argues) his concept of didactic or instructional poetry is something of an anomaly.[107] Phemius in Ithaca (Od. 1.33–34) symbolizes this sort of poetry, and among the examples in Homer are the description of the relationship between Heracles' soul and its "image" (in the nekyia, Od. 11.601–26) and unspecified passages where Homer describes "the various natures of the parts of the soul," or "the arrangement of the elements of the universe (earth, water, mist, aither, heaven)."[108] This poetry as well (though to judge by Proclus's description alone it would seem to form a relatively minor part of the Homeric corpus) is free from all taint of imitation, for its procedures are not mimetic; rather it "uses systematic wisdom to reveal to us the very order of things."[109]

---

103. In Rep. 1.177.23–178.2.

104. ἀπεικονίζεται δὲ τὴν νοερὰν οὐσίαν ἐν ἑνὶ τὴν τῶν νοητῶν φύσιν περιλαβοῦσα (In Rep. 1.177.29–178.2).

105. τὴν οὐσίαν τῶν ὄντων (In Rep. 1.179.6).

106. νουθεσίας καὶ συμβουλῶν ἀρίστων πλήρη καὶ νοερᾶς εὐμετρίας ἀνάμεστα φρονήσεώς τε καὶ ἄλλης ἀρετῆς προτείνοντα τὴν μετουσίαν τοῖς εὖ πεφυκόσιν, ἀνάμνησίν τε παρεχόμενα τῶν τῆς ψυχῆς περιόδων καὶ τῶν ἀιδίων ἐν αὐταῖς λόγων καὶ τῶν ποικίλων δυνάμεων (In Rep. 1.179.10–15).

107. Sheppard, Studies, pp. 182–87.

108. τὰς διαφόρους ὑποστάσεις τῶν μορίων τῆς ψυχῆς . . . τὴν τάξιν τῶν ἐν τῷ παντὶ στοιχείων, γῆς ὕδατος ἀέρος αἰθέρος οὐρανοῦ (In Rep. 1.193.4–8).

109. ἐπιστήμῃ χρώμενος αὐτὴν ἡμῖν ἐκφαίνει τὴν τάξιν τῶν πραγμάτων (In Rep. 1.198.21–22).

The lowest "life" of the soul, the third, is dominated by the lowest "powers" (δυνάμεις) and "makes use of imaginings and irrational sense-perceptions." [110] To this sphere, one assumes, belong our everyday experience and our participation in the material universe. The poetry corresponding to this condition of the soul is mimetic poetry, "mingled with opinions and imaginings." [111] It has the properties of amplifying the emotions to huge proportions, of shocking the audience and manipulating the dispositions of their souls, and of projecting a false image of reality. "It is a shadow painting of things that are, and not a clear perception." [112] Its goal is modifying the consciousness of the audience, and it appeals to the emotions. It is further subdivided into a category described as "image making" or accurately mimetic poetry (εἰκαστικόν), which, though it creates only imitations (μιμήματα), at least strives toward precision in its imitation of its objects, and produces copies in every way like their models, and a contrasting mode described as "illusionistic" poetry (φαν-ταστικόν), which cultivates the *appearance* of reality but abandons the goal of exact reproduction of the model. Proclus refers here to a passage in the *Sophist* (235d–236a) where the contrast is developed in terms of sculpture.[113] Plato is relating the esthetic to the moral with the peculiar insistence that is one of his most irreconcilable attitudes from the standpoint of modern thought. Proclus, too, believes intensely in the interrelatedness of the esthetic and the moral, and he builds on Plato's distinction between sculpture that reproduces the exact proportions of the model and that which, for example, enlarges the head to make it *appear* to be of natural size when viewed from far below. This latter procedure is analogous to that of the "illusionistic" sort of poetry, which utterly abandons "right opinion" (ὀρθὴ δόξα) and projects a false and deceptive image of its subject matter.[114] A bard mentioned quite casually in the *Odyssey* (3.267–68) is produced to symbolize the accurately mimetic mode, and Proclus offers as examples of this sort of art passages in the Homeric poems where Homer "imitates the heroes fighting, or taking counsel or

---

110. φαντασίαις τε καὶ αἰσθήσεσιν ἀλόγοις προσχρωμένην (*In Rep.* 1.178.4–5).

111. ἡ δόξαις καὶ φαντασίαις συμμιγμένη (*In Rep.* 1.179.16). The entire description occupies lines 15–32. Note that the discussion has again returned to that "life" of the soul where the *Timaeus* model is relevant and the modes of perception discussed here correspond to those introduced there. See pp. 167–70 above and Appendix 2.

112. σκιαγραφία τις οὖσα τῶν ὄντων (*In Rep.* 1.179.25–26).

113. *In Rep.* 1.189.

114. *In Rep.* 1.189.5–190.2.

talking, according to their various characters, some reasonably, some bravely, some ambitiously."[115]

Given this description of the accurately mimetic element in Homer, it is difficult to understand how Proclus can go on to claim that it is not this mode, but rather the inspired one, that is most characteristic of Homer.[116] One is inclined, on the one hand, to wonder just how extensive Proclus's direct experience of Homer was. Did he, in fact, have the kind of perspective on the relative importance of the various sorts of poetry contained in the *Iliad* and *Odyssey* that can only come from direct reading of the poems from beginning to end? The question is not easily answered. As early as the second century after Christ, Homer was read in the schools in the form of a fairly standard set of selections, and few authors of the time show evidence of a direct knowledge of either poem in its entirety.[117] To pick an example closer to Proclus, Macrobius, a generation earlier, quotes Homer abundantly in the *Saturnalia*, but the evidence is quite convincing that he had never read the *Iliad* or *Odyssey*.[118] However, neither the rhetoricians of the second sophistic nor Macrobius were scholars in the sense that Proclus was. His ability to quote obscure passages that would not have appeared in the anthologies and his knowledge of detail seem evidence at least of access to a complete text.[119] Per-

115. ὅταν τοὺς ἥρωας πολεμοῦντας ἢ βουλευομένους ἢ λέγοντας κατὰ τὰ εἴδη τῆς ζωῆς, τοὺς μὲν ὡς ἔμφρονας, τοὺς δὲ ὡς φιλοτίμους, τῆς εἰκαστικῆς ἂν εἴποιμι τὸ τοιοῦτον ἔργον ὑπάρχειν (*In Rep.* 1.198.28–193.3).

116. *In Rep.* 1.195.13–196.13.

117. Kindstrand, *Homer in der zweiten Sophistik*, pp. 1–110, examines the evidence for direct experience of Homer on the part of Dio Chrysostom, Aelius Aristides, and Maximus of Tyre.

118. See Flamant, *Macrobe et le néoplatonisme latin*, pp. 300–304. Macrobius is discussed in ch. 6D below.

119. The exhaustive *Index auctorum* prepared for Festugière's translation of the *Republic* commentary indicates quotations or references involving thirty-seven of the forty-eight books of Homer, the vast majority of them in the section of the commentary devoted to the defense of Homer. Many of these come directly from the *Republic* or from other dialogues of Plato, however, and so tell us little about Proclus's independent knowledge of the poems. In order to give a somewhat more general picture of Proclus's use of Homer, the references to the books of the *Iliad* and *Odyssey* in four of the major works of Proclus are presented graphically in Appendix 3. Various factors bias the sample—most obviously the importance of Plato as intermediate source in three of the four works—but outside the *Republic* commentary most references are independent, and collectively they indicate a general knowledge of Homer, with marked preference for the *Iliad* over the *Odyssey* and for certain sections over others, with only six books receiving no use at all, quite possibly by chance.

haps we should give him the benefit of the doubt and assume that he viewed the "inspired" poetry of Homer as the most important and characteristic element not because his perspective was warped by an uneven experience of the text but because he was basing his observations on the quality he perceived in Homer and not on a line count.

Proclus observes repeatedly that this first class of mimetic poetry, which respects the true proportions of the model, is harmless and may serve as a vehicle for discourse of higher sorts. Plato himself, after all, is a mimetic writer, a creator of dialogues in which characters are seen interacting and presenting their opinions and ideas.[120] When Proclus discusses the differences between Homer and Plato, he presents Homer as "inspired" and "ecstatic," an author who offers a direct revelation and is in contact with absolute truth.[121] Plato is seen as coming later to the same information and treating it differently, "establishing it solidly by the irrefutable methods of systematic thought."[122] The matter is the same, then, and both treatments rely heavily on mimesis, but one comes from an ecstatic visionary and the other from a systematic philosopher whose demonstrations can be expected to be rigorous. The model is reflected in the discussion of Plato's development of ideas adapted from Homer (In Rep. 1.171–72).

There is a last subcategory in Proclus's classification of the kinds of poetry: the "illusionistic" (φανταστικόν) class of mimetic poetry, which will effectively become the scapegoat for all the other sorts. Again, a casually mentioned singer is brought forth as exemplifying this lowly mode.[123] Examples are predictably difficult to find in the works of Homer, but Proclus concedes that Odyssey 3.1, where the sun is said to rise out of a pond,[124] is poetry of this sort. The offense against ὀρθὴ δόξα

120. In Rep. 1.163–64.

121. ἐνθουσιάζων and ἀναβακχευόμενος (In Rep. 1.159.1). The latter term is perhaps more suggestive of the epic practice of Proclus's contemporary Nonnus (Dion. 1.11–44) than of that of Homer.

122. ταῖς ἀνελέγκτοις τῆς ἐπιστήμης μεθόδοις κατεδήσατο (In Rep. 1.159.3–4).

123. Thamyris, at Il. 2.595 (in the catalog of ships).

124. The scholiast on Il. 8.485, where the sun is said to "fall into Ocean" when setting, uses language reminiscent of Proclus: οὐκ ἀληθῆ οὖν δηλοῖ ἔμπτωσιν τοῦ ἡλίου ἀλλὰ φαντασίαν δίδωσιν, ὡς ἐπὶ τὸν Ὠκεανὸν ἔρχεται ἐπὶ τὴν δύσιν ἐλθών (Schol. in Il., ed. Erbse, vol. 2, p. 379). A further analogy—perhaps a source—for the observation is to be found in the anonymous commentary on the Parmenides published by Kroll (cf. Pierre-Henry Hadot, "Fragments d'un commentaire de Porphyre sur le Parménide"), where the error of everyday speech

seems to come from the fact that the sun does not really come up out of the pond (as we all know) but only *appears* to, while Homer says it actually does.[125]

Here again, there is a peculiar mixture of insight and apparent obtuseness. Proclus's description of inspired poetry is quite beautiful, and his development of the Platonic concept that there is a divine μανία in poets that surpasses σωφροσύνη and puts them in touch with the highest reality is decidedly an anticipation of the Romantic conception of the imagination.[126] Yet when he reaches "illusionistic" mimetic poetry, his observations descend to the trivial. He appears, from our perspective, to be splitting hairs. This disproportion may be viewed, however, as a function of Proclus's larger goals, which are neither unsympathetic nor trivial. He is attempting to evolve a concept of poetry free of the stigma of mimesis, a poetry that springs from, and somehow communicates, the highest level of human experience. In this context, the "lower" sort of poetry, which makes no such claims, is treated somewhat less satisfactorily, but we can hardly hold this against Proclus.

Along with the makers of myths, the poets, Proclus gives some attention to the interpreters, and it should be stressed that the two categories are quite close in his mind. We have seen that the word θεολόγος can be applied to interpreters, though it more often applies to the mythic poets themselves. An interpreter's activities can likewise merit the description "very inspired,"[127] often applied to poets of the first class.

In contrast, one of Proclus's prime examples of one who failed to understand the structure of meaning in myth is Stesichorus. The context of his observation is the discussion of a passage in the *Phaedrus* (243a) where Socrates seems to be saying that Stesichorus was superior to Homer.[128] Stesichorus, Socrates claims, found the remedy for his blindness,

---

in speaking of the "rising" and "setting" of the sun is brought into the discussion of the One in relationship to other things: ὥσπερ οὖν εἰ περὶ δύσεων ἡλίου ζητοῖμεν, λέγοι δέ τις μὴ εἶναι ἡλίου δύσιν, εἴπερ ἡ δύσις σκοτισμός ἐστιν φωτὸς καὶ νυκτὸς ἐπαγωγή, ἥλιος δὲ οὐδέποτε σκοτίζεται οὐδὲ νύκτα ὁρᾷ, ἀλλ' οἱ ἐπὶ γῆς ἐμπεσόντες εἰς τὸ σκίασμα, λέγοι ἂν ὀρθῶς πάθημα λέγων τῶν ἐπὶ γῆς τὴν δύσιν· ὥσπερ οὐδ' ἀνατολὴ λέγοιτ' ἂν ἡλίου, etc. (W. Kroll, "Ein neuplatonischer *Parmenides*-commentar in einem Turiner Palimpsest," p. 604 [fol. 94ʳ, 13–21]).

125. *In Rep.* 1.192.21–28.

126. Trouillard explores these foreshadowings (see n. 19 above).

127. ἐνθεαστικώτατα (*In Rep.* 1.133).

128. *In Rep.* 1.173–77.

"being an accomplished artist," or "inspired by the Muses" (ἅτε μουσι-κὸς ὤν). In the *Palinode* he retracted his slander of Helen and thus regained his sight. Homer was ignorant of the necessary ritual and remained blind.

On the contrary, Proclus replies, Homer was never guilty in the first place, and therefore never needed purification. Stesichorus's actual mistake was that he failed to understand the nature of myth: he took the story of Helen to be a true story like any other[129] and wrote the offending poem "in that mode" (κατὰ τοῦτον . . . τὸν τρόπον). Homer, on the other hand, acted "according to another and more perfect condition of the soul."[130] He did not confuse μῦθος and λόγος. The implication is that his account, properly interpreted, is no offense against gods or demigods. Furthermore, Proclus takes Homer's blindness to be an image, a symbol dreamed up "by those who tell stories about such things,"[131] to communicate the truth of Homer's transcendence of the senses and his suprasensory "vision." The ancient lives of the poets, then, are myth structures like their poems. Proclus would seem to be among the first to point this out.

Proclus goes on to maintain that Socrates, like Stesichorus, is deceived as regards the way in which myths represent the truth. In saying that Homer shared Stesichorus's guilt and his punishment, Socrates is making use only of the superficial meaning of the story,[132] whereas in fact, Proclus argues, that surface is only a "screen," behind which another, very different, truth lies awaiting its exegete.

There is a danger, then, in making use of myths: one must understand the way they mean in order to use them properly. Early in the essay, Proclus has spoken of those who make the mistake of seeing blasphemies in the traditional stories.[133] Their mistake is that just mentioned: they go only to the surface and are deceived by it (through their own fault, of course, since ignorance of the law—here, the structures of meaning of myth—is no excuse).

129. ὡς λόγον ὄντα [i.e., *not* a μῦθος] καὶ γεγονότων μόνον πραγμάτων ἀφήγησιν (*In Rep.* 1.173.27–28).

130. κατ᾽ ἄλλην οἶμαι καὶ τελεωτέραν τῆς ψυχῆς ἕξιν (*In Rep.* 1.174.4–5).

131. ὑπὸ τῶν τὰ τοιαῦτα διαμυθολεγεῖν εἰωθότων (*In Rep.* 1.174.9–10). Given this observation, it is difficult to understand how Friedl could claim that Proclus "nimmt die Blindheit Homers als historisch" (*Homer-Interpretationen des Neuplatonikers Proklos*, p. 53; cf. n. 51 above), in contrast to the author of the *Chrestomathy*.

132. τῷ φαινομένῳ χρώμενος (*In Rep.* 1.176.14).

133. *In Rep.* 1.74–76.

Myths may further be divided according to the users for whom they are intended. Some may be considered properly "educational" (παιδευ-τικοί) and appropriate for the young, whereas others are "more divinely inspired" (ἐνθεαστικώτεροι) and appropriate, therefore, only for those who are ready for instruction into higher realms of experience.[134] The first group is later called "more philosophical" (φιλοσοφώτεροι) and the second characterized as "appropriate to hieratic custom" (τοῖς ἱερατικοῖς θεσμοῖς προσήκοντες) and therefore reserved for the initiate.[135] The myths of Plato, designed with a specifically educational aim in view, be-long to the first group, but those of Homer are decidedly better placed in the second.

Proclus has, in fact, already answered an important charge in the So-cratic indictment by pleading guilty on Homer's behalf. The myths of the *Iliad* and *Odyssey* are not appropriate for children—Socrates is right. Pro-clus goes no further, but he might have added that nearly a thousand years of Greek educational thought and practice were on trial as well. Greek educators, he would say, however, must take the blame them-selves: their use of the Homeric poems is in fact another misuse, and the responsibility is theirs, not Homer's.

E. THE MEANING OF THE *ILIAD* AND *ODYSSEY*

There is an extraordinary continuity in the Neoplatonic exegesis of Ho-mer. The same myths would seem to have been explained again and again in essentially the same manner, over a period of centuries.[136] Por-phyry reminds us often that the interpretations he is presenting are not his own, but those of Numenius and Cronius, a century before his time. Proclus likewise refers frequently to his master Syrianus (diadochos from 432 to 437 or perhaps later)[137] as the source of the doctrines he is

134. *In Rep.* 1.76–77.
135. *In Rep.* 1.79.5–18.
136. See Friedl, *Homer-Interpretationen des Neuplatonikers Proklos*, pp. 59–65, for an excellent discussion of the problem of sources in Neoplatonic allegory from the perspective of Proclus.
137. On the problem of Syrianus's dates, see Karl Praechter, "Syrianos," cols. 1728–29. Praechter's date of 450 for his death is rather arbitrary, and with Shep-pard (*Studies*, p. 38) I am convinced by the arguments for 437 put forward by Saffrey and Westerink (Proclus, *Théologie platonicienne* [Budé], vol. 1, pp. xv–xvii). On the dependence of Proclus's discussion of Homer on Syrianus, see Sheppard, *Studies*, ch. 2. Her analysis of Proclus's sources is far more meticulous

using in his defense of Homer, though at some points he does give us what is explicitly his own analysis.[138] Olympiodorus makes no distinction in his commentary on the *Phaedo* between the teachings of Proclus and those of Syrianus,[139] and in general it is possible to distinguish a very large element in Proclus's thought that goes back to that of his master. Proclus mentions a work of Syrianus's entitled "Solutions to Homeric Questions,"[140] which must have been a major source for the interpretations found in his own defense of Homer.

A. J. Friedl distinguished two separate strata of sources in Proclus's essay: Syrianus for the specifically Neoplatonic material and another collection of allegories from various sources.[141] The latter may have been the *Homeric Questions* of Porphyry, of which we have only the first book intact. Interpretations of this class are often preserved by the scholiasts as well. Proclus's major accomplishment in this context would seem to lie in his presentation of the theoretical analysis of the meaning of myth discussed above. His interpretations themselves are largely received ones, and his own contribution on this level is difficult to assess, though the sheer bulk of material he passes down to us makes him the most important of our ancient sources and the one that comes closest to presenting a comprehensive account of the Homeric epics as the Neoplatonists read them. Only Eustathius preserves a greater bulk of exegetical material on Homer in a single work.

In an attempt to reconstruct as much as possible of this comprehensive picture, I have ignored the structure of Proclus's essay (which is organized around his responses to the various Socratic criticisms) and rearranged the major interpretations in the sequence of the events and

---

than that of Friedl and shows us in detail how Proclus "is fitting Syrianus' comments on Homer, from a variety of sources, into a framework of his own" (*Studies*, p. 85). She attributes a substantial individual contribution to Syrianus in the development of Neoplatonist metaphysical allegory (*Studies*, pp. 48, 79), though since we know very little of the nature of Syrianus's sources, it would perhaps be more judicious to grant him priority over Proclus without passing judgment on his own originality.

138. *In Rep.* 1.116.24–117.21 on Agamemnon's dream.

139. Proclus had a contemporary and fellow student under Syrianus by this name, with whom he studied Aristotle (Mar. *Vit. Pr.* 9), but Wallis (*Neoplatonism*, p. 140, n. 1) cautions against identifying this Olympiodorus with the Alexandrian Neoplatonist.

140. ἐν ταῖς λύσεσιν . . . τῶν Ὁμηρικῶν προβλημάτων (*In Rep.* 1.95.30–31).

141. Friedl, *Homer-Interpretationen des Neuplatonikers Proklos*, pp. 63–65, 69.

references within the poems themselves.[142] Many of Proclus's minor references, involving little or no interpretation on his part, have not been mentioned.

There are, of course, abundant references to Homer in the other works of Proclus as well, and occasionally interpretations cited below have been drawn from those sources to supplement the comprehensive picture offered in the *Republic* commentary. A sampling of the citations of Homer in the other works, however, indicates that the heart of what Proclus had to say about Homer is here, and the other works have relatively little to add.[143]

The Iliad

It is almost casually, in the second part of the essay,[144] that Proclus mentions his understanding of the meaning of the *Iliad* story in the broadest sense and offers an interpretation of the myth of the Trojan War. He is specific on the point that this reading is his own, or at least that it is the one to which he subscribes. The passage occurs in the context of a discussion of the secondary myth of Homer's blindness and the motives of the mythoplasts in that particular fabrication. He concludes:

> The myths want to indicate, I believe, through Helen, the whole of that beauty that has to do with the sphere in which things come to be and pass away and that is the product of the demiurge. It is over this beauty that eternal war rages among souls, until the more intellectual

142. The risk in this procedure is the equation of Proclus's undertaking with those of commentators such as Heraclitus, who treat the Homeric material sequentially, as it occurs in the epics. Nevertheless Proclus's essay does aspire to present a comprehensive analysis of the Homeric poems, although the emphasis and presentation are determined by the pattern of the Socratic charges.

143. Taking the *Timaeus* commentary as an example (chosen because it is exceptionally well indexed in Festugière's translation), of seventy-two allusions or quotes listed by Festugière, the vast majority are without interest from our point of view, and eleven involve lines interpreted allegorically in precisely, or nearly precisely, the way they are treated in the *Republic* commentary. Ten passages seem to offer some slight extension of the material in the *Republic* commentary, but none is surprising or would change our impression of how Proclus understood the poems. All of these complementary passages, moreover, echo the patterns of interpretations found in the *Republic* commentary. To give an example, Athena's garments symbolize (a) her transcendent activity—the peplos of *Il.* 5.734, and (b) her providential activity—the chiton of *Il.* 8.385 (*In Tim.* 1.167).

144. *In Rep.* 1.175–76.

are victorious over the less rational forms of life and return hence to the place from which they came.[145]

Helen, then, is worldly beauty, the fragmented, imperfect copy of the form of the beautiful inhabiting the material world. The implication is that it is this beauty that entices souls (i.e., the Greeks) to leave their true home and to enter into a mode of existence for which war provides the most apt metaphor. Once they have "overcome the barbarous flood,"[146] in the tenth year (representing the millennial cycle of souls of the myth of Er), they return to their own realm. A similar conception of the Troy tale's allegorical meaning is implied in Plotinus (*Enn.* 1.6.8.16–21).[147] As a myth of the descent of souls into matter, this interpretation is distantly reminiscent of a passage in the *Hermetica* where the "archetypal man" is described breaking through the superstructure of the cosmos, seeing the beauty of the material world (in this case his own image reflected in it), falling in love with that beauty, and thus being committed to existence in the flesh.[148] The entire allegory of the Troy tale, in a form related to that found in Proclus, is elaborated in terms of etymologies (Ἴλιον from ὕλη, etc.) by Hermias (*In Phdr.* 77–79), and Sheppard argues convincingly that we can trace the larger exposition to Syrianus as well.[149]

This, says Proclus, is the level of truth that Homer loved to contemplate, and it is in this sense that the mythoplasts called him "blind"; his characteristic vision was turned toward the suprasensory, not toward the objects of this world.

The interpretation itself appears to belong to the same stratum of Neoplatonic allegory as the comprehensive frame allegory formulated in Porphyry's explanation of the cave of the nymphs. The ambiguous relationship of soul (life, consciousness) to matter (the body) is, for this tradition, the compelling mystery of the world of our everyday experience. Any text that is obscure and is assumed to have some claim to represent a transcendent truth may, sooner or later, be found to be an expression of some fact concerning that relationship. This is a major focus of Pro-

---

145. ἅπαν γὰρ οἶμαι τὸ περὶ τὴν γένεσιν κάλλος ἐκ τῆς δημιουργίας ὑποστὰν διὰ τῆς Ἑλένης οἱ μῦθοι σημαίνειν ἐθέλουσιν, περὶ ὃ καὶ τῶν ψυχῶν πόλεμος τὸν ἀεὶ χρόνον συγκεκρότηται μέχρις ἂν αἱ νοερώτεροι τῶν ἀλογωτέρων εἰδῶν τῆς ζωῆς κρατήσασθαι περιαχθῶσιν ἐντεῦθεν εἰς ἐκεῖνον τὸν τόπον, ἀφ' οὗ τὴν ἀρχὴν ὡρμήθησαν (*In Rep.* 1.175.15–21).

146. κρατεῖν μὲν τοῦ βαρβαρικοῦ κλύδωνος (*In Rep.* 1.175.28).

147. See ch. 3, with n. 78, above.

148. *Corpus Hermeticum* 1 (= *Poimandres*) 14.

149. Sheppard, *Studies*, pp. 66–67.

clus's mythoplasts' attention, though naturally they never express themselves directly on the subject.

In defense of Proclus and his tradition, it should be said that, however far the relationship of soul to body may have been from the minds of
Homeric bards, his observation is no more absurd than Claude Lévi-
Strauss's perception that a vast number of myths and folktales are concerned with the dichotomy between nature and culture. Proclus also
resembles the structuralists in his emphasis on the broad patterns of
myths and his use of paraphrases in preference to specific texts. Viewed
in entire isolation from the historical circumstances that gave rise to the
myths—viewed, that is, in the test-tube environment of structural analysis—a large number of stories do, in fact, fall into the pattern that an
earlier generation of structuralists characterized by the formula "separation—initiation—return." The Neoplatonic tradition of exegesis recognized that pattern and went one step further, identifying it with what it
took to be a true account of the nature of reality and viewing the stories
as copies imitating that archetype. Perhaps the best way of describing the
phenomenon before us is to say that Proclus has successfully analyzed a
mythic structure and related it to a genuine pattern observable in a variety of instances, but from our perspective his accomplishment loses
credibility when he immediately erects yet another mythic structure,
taken as an account of "things as they are," around his explanation.[150]

In speaking of the story of Troy as a whole, Proclus is dealing not
with a literary text but with a myth that was never entirely contained in
any one text (unless we take the epic cycle as a continuous work—and
here we return to the shadowy Proclus of the *Chrestomathy*, who is responsible for the summaries that preserve the cycle as a single story for
us). Proclus never examines extended passages from the text of the *Iliad*
or the *Odyssey*. He prefers to refer, more or less explicitly, to specific
statements or lines in the poems, rarely citing more than two verses together, or to speak more generally about whole episodes such as the
battle of the gods in books 20–22 or the song of Ares and Aphrodite.
The majority of the passages in the *Iliad* that attract his attention fall in
the opening and closing books. There are no references to books 6–7, 10,
or 12–13.[151] Books 1–2 receive the same exaggerated attention from Proclus that J. F. Kindstrand observed in his examination of the use of Homer by the rhetors of the second sophistic, and it is quite probable that

150. Sheppard likewise compares Proclus to the structuralists (*Studies*, p. 161).
151. See Appendix 3.

this pattern does reflect the emphasis these parts of the poem received in the schools.[152] Since Proclus is primarily answering Socrates' accusations, however, and thus is concerned almost exclusively with the passages Socrates singles out for criticism, any conclusions drawn from the distribution of his quotations and references within the *Iliad* and *Odyssey* must be viewed with caution.

The judgment of Paris is not properly speaking a Homeric myth. The Proclus of the *Chrestomathy* indicates that it was narrated in the *Cypria*,[153] and the single reference in the *Iliad* (24.29–30) has been treated with suspicion since Aristarchus. Proclus apparently considers the story Homeric, however, and in the title of the seventh section of the first part of the discourse[154] attributes it to ὁ ποιητής, which in the immediate context can be taken to refer to Homer. Proclus's understanding of the meaning of the story is that it "hints at" (αἰνίττεται) the choice among lives of different sorts, the regal (Hera), the philosophical (apparently Athena), and the erotic (Aphrodite). An important source for this is to be found in two passages of the *Phaedrus*, but the passages from Plato are not very well suited to the explanation of the myth, and Proclus must twist them considerably in the attempt to make them appear so.[155] In fact, the episode of the myth of Er, where Plato insists that souls choose their lives and are therefore responsible for the choices they make,[156] seems a more important model in Proclus's mind here, though the association of various "lives" with gods who preside over them is borrowed from the *Phaedrus* passage. Whatever the source of his ideas, Proclus here elaborates a moral allegory so familiar in its basic claims that few of us would deny its relevance to the myth in question. Since there is conveniently no text to interpret, there is no danger of contradiction on that level. The vocabulary used to describe the structure of meaning of the myth is interesting: Proclus speaks of the myths as "transferring" (μεταφέροντες) specific kinds of lives to the gods themselves in order to describe Paris's choice.[157] The term from which our "metaphor" is derived is Aristotelian and is

152. See Kindstrand, *Homer in der zweiten Sophistik*, p. 103.

153. Homer (OCT), vol. 5, p. 102.

154. *In Rep.* 1.108.1.

155. Plato *Phdr.* 252e–f, 265b. Proclus himself refers us to the *Phaedrus*. Festugière *ad loc.* in his translation (vol. 1, p. 126, n. 2) notes the distortion of the Platonic passages.

156. Plato *Rep.* 10.617d–18b.

157. *In Rep.* 1.108.15–17.

not commonly used by Proclus to describe the ways in which discourse functions.[158]

Among the passages in book 1 of the *Iliad* to which Proclus makes reference, the first three are relatively unimportant. Several lines are quoted and used to argue for or against charges of greed and lack of σω-φροσύνη on the part of Achilles.[159] The apparition of Athena to Achilles is mentioned as an example of an attempt on the part of the mythoplasts to portray a "formless" apparition of an authentic goddess.[160]

Three elements from the first book do, however, receive interesting explanations. Zeus's visit to the Ethiopians (*Il.* 1.423–25) is given as an example of a passage that anyone with any sort of experience of "this sort of doctrine" (τῆς τοιᾶσδε θεωρίας) could decipher.[161] The greatest of the gods on his way from the realm of intelligible entities to a feast is clearly returning "to his own first principles" (πρὸς τὰς οἰκείας ἀρχάς), and he will renew himself "from those transcendent and uniform good things" (ἀπ᾽ ἐκείνων . . . τῶν ἐξῃρημένων καὶ ἑνοειδῶν ἀγαθῶν). There he will find the Ethiopians "glowing with divine light" (οἱ τῷ θείῳ φωτὶ καταλαμπόμενοι) and primal Ocean "flowing from noetic springs" (ὁ τῆς νοητῆς πηγῆς ἀπορρέων), and he and the gods dependent on him will receive their sustenance there.

This passage has been given *in extenso* because it provides a ready model typical of many of Proclus's minor exegeses. A myth is often explained by superimposing on it an abstract statement within which it takes on the role of imagery. Here Proclus paraphrases Homer's (or Thetis's) description, inserting the "hidden meaning" as a running commentary on the fiction. The demonstration is by no means "irrefutable," but if a few givens are accepted—that the gods exist in the realm of νοῦς, that every realm of existence springs from, is sustained by, and contemplates a higher, simpler realm—then it is, in fact, clear that the king of the gods cannot be conceived descending into the material world for sustenance (in spite of the fact that this is patently what Homer intends us to believe). Removed from the quite necessary logic of the original compo-

158. See Arist. *Rhet.* 3.13.1405b.
159. *Il.* 1.167–68 at *In Rep.* 1.145.1–2.
160. *In Rep.* 1.114. These references are mentioned here to provide an indication of the range of Proclus's use of such passages, but in general no attention will be paid to references of this sort in the present discussion. On the last, cf. ch. 3, n. 44, above.
161. *In Rep.* 1.166.28–167.9.

sition, the elements of the imagery lend themselves rather well to Proclus's rearrangement—with the possible exception of the paradoxical Ethiopians. There is nevertheless little doubt that, if pressed, Proclus could find convincing equivalents for them in his cluttered celestial realms.

The fall of Hephaestus, cast out of Heaven by Zeus (*Il.* 1.590–94), is discussed early in the essay,[162] along with the non-Homeric myths of the imprisonment of Kronos[163] and the castration of Ouranos, all taken as preeminent examples of offensive myths that, by the very fact that they attribute indecent actions to the gods, invite interpretation not as mimetic representations of reality but as symbolic ones. As we have seen, symbolic representations of reality characteristically proceed by the use of opposites, and here Proclus elaborates on that principle and draws up what amounts to a table of equivalents for the actions described, contrasting the meaning of "bondage" (δεσμός), "being hurled" (ῥῖψις), and "mutilation" (τομαί), on the one hand "among us" and then "among the gods."[164]

In our world, ῥῖψις means "violent movement caused by someone else," an explanation that might presumably be placed in the category of those κατὰ τὸ φαινόμενον. On the higher level, however, it "indicates generative emanation and free and unrestrained attendance on all things, not separated from its own first principle but proceeding from this in an orderly manner through all things."[165] To judge by this example, the opposites involved in the complex system of meaning of symbolic utterance are what we might call subjective elements. There is a shared objective, structural element that bonds the meaning of ῥῖψις "here" and its meaning "there." What we must overcome in order to perceive the link are our associations of (apparent) good and evil with this and the other terms, along with other aspects relevant to our own fragmented perceptions only. The concept "being hurled" is for us a negative, ugly one, implying

162. *In Rep.* 1.82–83.

163. Hera does in fact mention the underground imprisonment of Kronos at *Il.* 14.203–4, quoted by Proclus (*In Rep.* 1.93.16–17), though in another context. The canonical source is Hes. *Theog.* 717–35.

164. παρ' ἡμῖν, a realm likewise evoked by the terms "here" (ἐνταῦθα) and "in the context of fragmented and material things" (ἐν τοῖς . . . μεριστοῖς καὶ ἐνύλοις). The other pole, παρὰ τοῖς θεοῖς, is similarly "there" (ἐκεῖ) and "in the context of first-working causes" (ἐν τοῖς πρωτουργοῖς αἰτίαις).

165. τὴν γόνιμον ἐνδείκνυται πρόοδον καὶ τὴν ἄφετον ἐπὶ πάντα παρουσίαν καὶ εὔλυτον, οὐκ ἀφισταμένη τῆς οἰκείας ἀρχῆς, ἀλλ' ἀπ' ἐκείνης διὰ πάντων ἐν τάξει προϊοῦσαν (*In Rep.* 1.82.25–29).

violence and separation. But "there" there is no violence; there is no separation. If we remove these "impossible" associations from the concept, then, and examine what remains, effectively subtracting process and time as well (further "subjective" elements, with no reality or meaning in the sphere in question), we are left with a description of creative emanation by which the first principle streams forth continually to create the world.

The other examples discussed in the passage bear out this description of Proclus's understanding of the double meanings of the symbolic building-blocks of myth. When we are dealing with isolated words (ῥῖψις, τομαί, etc.), as here, we are again brought very close to a problem in Plato's own model of language, already mentioned. If the existence of a single term for a group of particulars implies that an εἶδος lies behind that group, how are we to conceive the εἴδη of groups whose very definition would appear to involve process or fragmentation, elements said to be absent from the realm of ideas? Proclus's analyses of the violent vocabulary of theological myth constitute attempts to resolve this problem and to show how these words can have referents beyond the sublunary realm.

In another context, late in the essay, Proclus again has occasion to speak of Hephaestus and his role as demiurge.[166] There are no apparent contradictions with the present passage, and one is inclined to believe that Proclus had firmly in mind a comprehensive doctrine regarding the mythology of Hephaestus. He is described as "lame in both legs" (ἀμφιγυήεις, Il. 1.607) because, as Timaeus had said, the created world is "legless."[167] Just as the same name can be applied to various levels in the procession of a given divinity,[168] so the name "Hephaestus" can extend even to the last expression of the demiurgical procession, the created world itself. Plato's explanation of the term "legless" is transferred to the Homeric myth: "that which is moved by the motion generated around intellect and thought had no need of feet."[169]

Here, as in many of Proclus's observations, the formulations of the "reliable" speakers in the Platonic dialogues, and especially those of Timaeus, are presented as the interpretive discourse that resolves and

166. *In Rep.* 1.126–27.
167. *In Rep.* 1.126.25–127.1. Cf. Plato *Tim.* 34a (where the universe is described as ἀσκελές).
168. *In Rep.* 1.94.147.
169. τῷ γὰρ τὴν περὶ νοῦν καὶ φρόνησιν κινουμένῳ κίνησιν οὐδὲν ἔδει ποδῶν (*In Rep.* 1.126.27–28).

"irrefutably demonstrates" the inner coherence of the inspired, but superficially chaotic, Homeric utterance. The fit is not always a perfect one, as the present example indicates, and one often has the impression that the Homeric poems are, for Proclus, a perverse and problematical sort of scripture, their language not quite in harmony with the myths they contain. Proclus appears to conceive his first task to be the elaboration of the structural principles and meanings of the myths. A secondary task, where feasible, is the explication of Homer's actual language, sometimes with the help of the more orderly presentation of what Proclus believes to be the same insights in the Platonic dialogues.

The gods' reaction to the limping Hephaestus, their "undying laughter" ($\check{\alpha}\sigma\beta\epsilon\sigma\tau\sigma\varsigma\ \gamma\acute{\epsilon}\lambda\omega\varsigma$, Il. 1.599), is emblematic of their participation, as providential beings, in the created world. This level of their being, the lowest, in contact with the world of our immediate experience, is summed up in the Timaeus's description of the encosmic gods—that is, those implicated in the cosmos—as "young." [170] Concern with this world is said to be "the play of the gods" ($\pi\alpha\iota\delta\iota\grave{\alpha}\ \tau\hat{\omega}\nu\ \theta\epsilon\hat{\omega}\nu$). Hence their laughter. This bizarre and rather beautiful interpretation of the scene recalls the continuing problem within Neoplatonism of relating the utterly detached highest reality to this world of our immediate experience: that the One should remain one and that divine providence should nevertheless exist in the world constituted an endlessly fascinating paradox. Still, the conception Proclus has articulated of the Iliad scene may perhaps suggest to a modern reader a poetic text with more affinities to Yeats than to Homer.

The only passage in book 2 that receives close attention is the dream sent by Zeus to Agamemnon (Il. 2.1–34).[171] The problem as stated is clearly a moral one: Zeus appears to deceive Agamemnon by sending the "baneful dream" with its false promise of success, and yet the divine is "incapable of deception" ($\mathring{\alpha}\psi\epsilon\upsilon\delta\acute{\epsilon}\varsigma$). To resolve this dilemma and free Homer of the charge of lying about the divine, Proclus offers first the rather unsatisfying solution of "most of the exegetes" ($o\mathring{\iota}\ \pi o\lambda\lambda o\mathring{\iota}\ \tau\hat{\omega}\nu\ \mathring{\epsilon}\xi\eta$-$\gamma\eta\tau\hat{\omega}\nu$),[172] and then that of his master Syrianus, followed by his own supplemental comments. This discussion provides an excellent illustration of the separate levels of exegesis that feed into Proclus's reading of Homer, but in this instance the passage is read $\kappa\alpha\tau\grave{\alpha}\ \tau\grave{o}\ \phi\alpha\iota\nu\acute{o}\mu\epsilon\nu\sigma\nu$, and the

170. $\tau o\hat{\iota}\varsigma\ \nu\acute{\epsilon}o\iota\varsigma\ \pi\alpha\rho\acute{\epsilon}\delta\omega\kappa\epsilon\nu\ \theta\epsilon o\hat{\iota}\varsigma\ \sigma\acute{\omega}\mu\alpha\tau\alpha\ \pi\lambda\acute{\alpha}\tau\tau\epsilon\iota\nu\ \theta\nu\eta\tau\acute{\alpha}$ (Plato Tim. 42d).
171. Proclus In Rep. 1.115–17. Cf. Sheppard, Studies, pp. 58–62.
172. For the first argument, centering on the word $\pi\alpha\nu\sigma\upsilon\delta\acute{\iota}\eta$, see n. 57 above.

assignment of responsibility is accomplished both by Proclus and by his master with devious logic, but without departing from the apparent meaning of the text, so that their arguments need not detain us at this point.

The mention at *Il.* 2.813–14 of a landmark on the Trojan plain with two names, one used by gods and the other by men, is explained along with similar double names by a compressed paraphrase of Plato's discussion of these pairs in the *Cratylus* (391c–393b).[173] Again, Plato points to the metalanguage capable of bringing order out of the chaos of the Homeric statement. Proclus scarcely does justice to the *Cratylus* arguments in this discussion and is indifferent to the irony that most modern readers have detected throughout the dialogue.[174]

The action taken by Athena in influencing Pandarus to shoot Menelaus and so ensure the resumption of hostilities (*Il.* 4.86–103) is the subject of a discussion close in spirit and method to that dealing with the deceitful dream of book 2.[175] The divine cannot be guilty either of deception or of bringing evils upon men, and Proclus's reasoning allows him to believe that neither charge is valid here. The passage is occasionally reminiscent of Gorgias's *Encomium of Helen* in its inversion of the most obvious values of an epic myth, but the project of freeing Athena from responsibility for Pandarus's action seems, if anything, yet farther from Homer's intentions than freeing Helen of responsibility for the war.[176]

The final section of this analysis is interesting in that it refers to Plotinus[177] to explain the paradox that Athena, whose special province is "thought" (φρόνησις) should be a cause, in whatever sense, of "mindless folly" (ἄνοια) in Pandarus. The passage referred to is from the essay bearing the title *Are the Stars Causes?* (*Enn.* 2.3). Plotinus is speaking of the necessary debasement of the pure qualities radiating from above, first when they leave their appropriate places and secondly when they become mixed with matter and with one another. He does, in fact, say that "that which flows from νοῦς becomes deviousness" (καὶ νοῦ ἀπόρροια πανουργία, *Enn.* 2.3.11.8–9), but Proclus expands this observation on the debasement of astral influences and makes it appear that the pro-

173. Cf. *Il.* 14.291 and 20.74. The discussion takes place at *In Rep.* 1.169–70.

174. Cf. Shorey, *Unity of Plato's Thought*, p. 75, for a typical reaction.

175. *In Rep.* 1.101–6.

176. Gorgias, at least, could point to Priam's assertion of Helen's innocence (*Il.* 3.164), a passage that might itself have troubled Proclus, in that the guilt is transferred to the gods. He does not mention it.

177. *Enn.* 2.3.11.

cessions of the divine tend to produce effects in the material world that are diametrically opposed to their true natures. If expanded (though Proclus does not choose to do so) this observation might provide a model to reinforce his doctrine of symbolism-by-opposites, and even as it stands it is a partial indication of his reasons for believing that truths about the divine expressed in this world may take the form of obscenities and apparent breaches of morality.

There is a gap of nearly ten books before the next passage that Proclus explains—the deception of Zeus (*Il.* 14.153–351). A casual reference to the gulf of Tartarus in Zeus's threats to the other gods at *Il.* 8.14 finds its way into the discussion of the geography of Hades,[178] and several citations from the embassy in book 9 enter the discussion of Achilles' alleged greed.[179] The gap is easily explained, of course, by the structure imposed on Proclus by the specific Socratic charges to be answered.

The deception of Zeus on the other hand receives exhaustive treatment.[180] It is specifically mentioned by Socrates (*Rep.* 3.390b–c), along with the song of Ares and Aphrodite, as an example of a myth utterly "inappropriate" (οὐ[κ] . . . ἐπιτήδειον) to the young, and was apparently the subject of an extensive discussion by Syrianus.[181] Proclus informs us that he will follow his master closely, excerpting the appropriate parts of his discussion of the passage.[182] It is striking that Syrianus is said to have interpreted the myth "in a very inspired manner" (ἐνθεαστικώτατα).

It is rather surprising that Proclus virtually ignores the aspect of the passage that gave it its ancient title: if he felt that Zeus was "deceived" in this passage,[183] he gives little indication of it, though the possibility of

178. *In Rep.* 1.169.

179. *In Rep.* 1.143–46.

180. *In Rep.* 1.132–40. See Sheppard, *Studies*, pp. 62–74, with references (p. 62, n. 59).

181. Cf. Proclus *In Rep.* 1.133.5–7. This seems to have been a separate essay. For the meaning of προηγουμένην πραγματείαν, see Sheppard, *Studies*, p. 44, n. 19.

182. *In Rep.* 1.133.5–10.

183. Here again Proclus's emphasis seems to be dictated by that of Socrates. The word ἀπάτη occurs only at *In Rep.* 1.133.13 (twice), in the list of subjects treated. When Proclus actually reaches the promised discussion (*In Rep.* 1.137.2–139.19), the word is never repeated, and we are given only an elaborate explanation of Hera's adornments, with never the slightest mention of her motives. Unless Proclus feels that the allegorical explanation of the elements of Hera's clothing and makeup has obviated the necessity of discussing her motives, which are quite explicit and moreover crucial to the entire development of the *Iliad*, then he must be ignoring the matter deliberately.

Homer's attributing deviousness to the gods is one he finds quite upset-
ting elsewhere.[184]

One is constantly reminded by instances such as this of Proclus's
enormous distance from the text itself. Here, for instance, he is repeating the ideas expressed perhaps 30 years earlier by Syrianus in response
to a critique written some 800 years before that, dealing in turn with a
text whose origins went back at least another 300 years. It would be a
mistake to expect of him a fresh, vital, and complete response based on
personal experience of whole passages. He has inherited from a long
tradition of exegetical scholarship the habit of conceiving the interpretation of Homer in terms of response not to texts but to specific "questions." The titles of critical works containing the words ζητήματα or
προβλήματα, including Syrianus's own,[185] set the tone. Bearing this in
mind, it is somewhat less surprising that the total experience of the *Iliad*
is something Proclus mentions only casually.

The treatment of the present passage is fragmented into five separate
problems,[186] the first of which is the meaning of the divine copulation.
Here, as in several other passages of the essay, a strong Pythagorean element is apparent in the thought that comes to Proclus by way of Syrianus, specifically an impulse to analyze and explain phenomena in terms
of polarities and columns of opposites.[187] It is this polarity, which is fundamental to the structure of the universe, that Proclus takes to lie behind
the mythoplasts' motives in talking about copulation and mating among
gods.[188]

184. It does not take a terribly sensitive reading of the passage to perceive
that he *is* deceived. Even if one missed the tone entirely, the epithet δολοφρο-
νέουσα, used no less than three times for Hera in the passage (*Il.* 14.197, 300,
329), would provide the key. Cf. *In Rep.* 1.115–17 on the deceitful dream of *Il.* 2,
discussed above.

185. See n. 140 above.

186. Proclus *In Rep.* 1.133.10–15.

187. On the Pythagorean συστοιχίαι, see G. S. Kirk and J. E. Raven, *The Presocratic Philosophers*, pp. 236–42. The passage on the two jars of Zeus (*In Rep.*
1.96.16–17) has the most characteristically "Pythagorean" language.

188. Neoplatonic allegory is not invariably puritanical. This essay itself sometimes responds to the passages it paraphrases in an intensely sensual manner.
Moreover, Hermias (*In Phdr.*, 54.28–31) discusses Odysseus's relations with Calypso and Circe (and even Athena) in terms of man's successive encounters with,
and participation in, various divine powers in the course of his life. There is a
world of difference between sex as a metaphor for communion with a higher
power—the literature of Christian mysticism is rich in examples— and sex as a
metaphor for the creative act of the monad and dyad.

In discussing this particular copulation myth, he begins with two principles, "finite" (πέρας) and "infinite"(ἄπειρον), which are clearly in some sense Pythagorean, but which Proclus cites as Platonic and Socratic on the evidence of *Philebus* 23c.[189] The Olympians are not the primary gods in Proclus's pantheon—space is left previous to them, in more perfect realms, for the earlier generations of gods. Nonetheless, for Proclus, as for Homer, the Olympians are the highest divinities that have any manifest relationship to our own lives. In Proclus's ontology, they occupy the level of νοῦς and are sometimes collectively called "demiurges," although, properly speaking, Hephaestus is the demiurge and the other Olympians participate in his creation only to the extent that they are providential deities concerned with the fate of souls in this world.

Each level of divinity (or of reality) reproduces those above it,[190] and so (in a system of meaning that approaches the complexity of a hall of mirrors) the story of the copulation of Zeus and Hera *represents* in a fragmented, mythic form an event on the level of νοῦς, which in turn reflects fundamental facts about reality that come yet closer to first principles. Zeus is (or represents) the primal, self-sufficient, finite monad, resembling the "noetic finitude" (τὸ πέρας τὸ νοητόν): he therefore generates reality "in the order of the monad" (ἐν μονάδος τάξει). Hera is (or represents) the generative dyad, infinite (and therefore *less* perfect than Zeus) but containing in herself the generative principle of plurality, without which the perfection of the One would be sterile and nothing could exist but it alone. Even the mention of their first sexual adventures, when their parents were not looking (*Il.* 14.295–96), is turned humorlessly into a further level of meaning.[191] There are two "different" copulations in-

189. Both here and in the later discussion of the theomachy of books 20–21, Sheppard (*Studies*, pp. 53, 65) shows Syrianus to be responsible for Proclus's emphasis on these principles.

190. Cf. Wallis, *Neoplatonism*, p. 137.

191. At *In Rep.* 1.34.11, the reference to τὴν πρωτίστην σύζευξιν Διὸς καὶ Ἥρας seems to be a reference to *Il.* 14.295: οἶον ὅτε πρῶτόν περ ἐμισγέσθην φιλότητι. At any rate, there are two separate pairs of sexual encounters discussed: (1) the *first* and the *present* one, and (2) the *potential* encosmic encounter, to which Hera invites Zeus, but which is not actually accomplished, and the *actual* transcendent copulation on Mount Ida. At this point in Proclus's discussion (*In Rep.* 1.135.9–13), only the meaning of the latter pair is developed. He returns to the discussion of the first pair at *In Rep.* 1.139. The entire analysis is somewhat reminiscent of Chrysippus's similarly humorless physical allegory of a painting on Samos depicting a scene of fellatio involving Zeus and Hera (and to a lesser extent of the rather prissy moral outrage of Origen the Christian in reporting it).

volved here—the one that is actually narrated and the one existing only potentially in Hera's invitation to return home to the bed Hephaestus has made for them. Since time and space do not exist among the gods, they must, in fact, be the same and simultaneous, and yet they are somehow distinct. They emerge respectively as the transcendent and encosmic creative acts, in reality simultaneous but separated by the mythoplasts in their characteristic way.

The second problem that Proclus discusses regarding this episode is that of Zeus's going to sleep[192]—the goal of the whole exercise, after all, in Hera's mind. The attribution of two successive states of consciousness to Zeus is not acceptable to Proclus, and the question is again resolved by the claim that both states are simultaneous, Zeus's sleep (somewhat in the manner of Homer's blindness) indicating his transcendence and self-sufficient existence in the realm of νοῦς, his waking his providential concern for events in this world. The two states are somewhat awkwardly identified respectively with the transcendent copulation and the encosmic one.[193]

A suggestive analogy for this interpretation is found in Philo's references to the "rest" of Jahweh on the seventh day (Gen. 2.2).[194] Like Proclus confronting the Homeric account of Zeus's sleep, Philo is dissatisfied with the apparent meaning. Insisting on the voice of the active (and therefore causative) verb κατέπαυσεν in his Septuagint text (represented in the King James version by "rested"), he goes on to claim that "God never stops [παύεται] creating, but as it is the property of fire to burn and of snow to be cold, so it is the property of God to create."[195] Here

Both attitudes seem equally removed from what one guesses to have been the intentions of the artist and the responses of the audiences for whom the works in question were created. Chrysippus's explanation of the painting claimed that Hera represents matter receiving the σπερματικοὶ λόγοι from god, and provides an interesting Stoic precedent for the Neoplatonic allegory of the deception of Zeus. See Chrysippus frs. 1071–74 (Stoic. vet. frag. vol. 2, p. 314). The interpretation is cited by Franz Cumont, Recherches sur le symbolisme funéraire des romains, p. 20, n. 2.

192. In Rep. 1.135.17–136.14.

193. In Rep. 1.136.8–9. Festugière in his translation ad loc. notes the resemblance of the passage to the very beautiful fr. 2 of Numenius. An analogy certainly exists, but fr. 12, where the god's attention to the cosmos is equated with the creative act and contrasted with the withering away accompanying his withdrawal, seems an even clearer parallel.

194. Philo Leg. alleg. 1.2.5–3.1; 1.6.16; 1.7.18.

195. παύεται γὰρ οὐδέποτε ποιῶν ὁ θεός, ἀλλ᾽ ὥσπερ ἴδιον τὸ καίειν πυρὸς καὶ χιόνος τὸ ψύχειν, οὕτως καὶ θεοῦ τὸ ποιεῖν (Philo Leg. alleg. 1.3.1).

again a sequence of states in the mythic account is found to represent
what are in fact two *modes* of creation. The mythic account, Philo tells us,
is distinguishing between the creation of "mortal things" (θνητά), accomplished before the seventh day, and the subsequent creation of transcendent realities: "God stops fashioning the mortal classes when he begins to create those that are divine and fit the number seven." [196] Though
Philo does not insist upon the simultaneity of the modes of creation and
the mythic distortion that introduces time into the eternal, he does consider it "foolish" (εὔηθες) to think the world was created in six days, "or
any other period of time" (ἢ καθόλου χρόνῳ), because time is a function
of the existence of the world (the sequence of days and nights) and therefore the world must have existed before time could exist. [197]

Philo's exegesis of the Old Testament may have been known to pagan
Platonists as early as Numenius, and it seems quite likely that by the
time of Porphyry, who declared open war on the Christians and studied
his enemy with care, [198] this monument of exegesis had been carefully
examined and its lessons learned, however distasteful their content.
Nevertheless, there is no certainty that Philo's exegesis influenced Porphyry's, [199] and the similarities between the passages of Philo and Proclus
mentioned here may well be the products merely of the common heritage of allegorical interpretation extending back far before Philo's time.

The first two interpretations relating to the episode of the deception
of Zeus are in many ways the most interesting. The third is another etymological fantasy with a certain charm, but little power to convince. The
scene of the copulation, Mount Ida (Ἴδη) is identified with the realm of
ideas (ὁ τῶν ἰδεῶν τόπος) and contrasted with the bedroom made by
Hephaestus (which Hera proposes as an alternative to the less socially
acceptable proposition of her consort, which, she squawks, "would
be shocking" [νεμεσσητὸν δέ κεν εἴη]). The bedroom is taken to be
the physical universe, hence the location of the encosmic copulation, to
which the representative of the generative dyad (Hera) invites the representative of the finite monad (Zeus). The final choice of the realm of
ideas as the scene of the encounter is an expression of the overriding

196. τὰ θνητὰ γένη παύεται πλάττων ὁ θεός, ὅταν ἄρχηται ποιεῖν τὰ θεῖα καὶ
ἑβδομάδος φύσει οἰκεῖα (Philo *Leg. alleg.* 1.6.16).
197. Philo *Leg. alleg.* 1.2.2. Philo's discussion of the relationship of time to the
creation of the world recalls Plato's in the *Timaeus* 37c–39e.
198. Cf. Bidez, *Vie de Porphyre*, pp. 65–79, and esp. pp. 73–74.
199. See Pépin, "Porphyre, exégète d'Homère," and esp. the discussion of
his paper, p. 270.

truth that (however many copulations, real or potential, there may be) the union is best expressed as transcendent, for the monad is more perfect, hence dominant, and draws the dyad up to it. In spite of the fact that the moral slur on the gods implied in the "deception" of Zeus by Hera is virtually ignored, Proclus makes it explicit that this open-air copulation does *not* decrease Zeus's dignity, because of its "true meaning" hinted at through the toponym Ἴδη.

The fourth question,[200] involving the adornments of Hera, and at least by implication the deception itself, is not in any meaningful sense resolved. We are told that Hera, through her adornment of herself, is assuming the role of her mother Rhea, for, as mentioned above, this particular copulation mimics on the level of the demiurgic Olympians the "previous" event at a further remove from our sublunary world. The symbolism of the clothing is said to be complex, and Proclus draws on the *Chaldaean Oracles* and the *Orphica* to provide keys for its interpretation.[201] Briefly stated, the elements are these: (1) her hair, with the help of an oracle,[202] is identified with Rhea's hair; (2) the fringed girdle (*Il.* 14.181) represents a similar object "there,"[203] the tassles symbolizing the great number of souls dependent on this particular divine procession; (3) her earrings and sandals (*Il.* 14.182) "are images of" (ἀπεικονίζεται)[204] the fragmented powers radiating down from her, the highest and lowest having their sources at her extremities; (4) ambrosia and oil (*Il.* 14.171–72) are symbolic of her "pure powers" (τῶν ἀχράντων . . . τῆς θεοῦ δυνάμεων), or, more specifically, the ambrosia symbolizes transcendent purity, and the oil, strength (by association with athletics). The discussion of the κέστος (*Il.* 14.214)[205] and the assistance of Aphrodite are likewise made to contribute to the identification of Hera with Rhea. The

200. Proclus *In Rep.* 1.137.2–139.19.
201. *In Rep.* 1.137.21–22 and 138.14–15, respectively.
202. On the fragment, cf. Festugière's note *ad loc.* in his translation (p. 156, n. 4) and Des Places's more recent comment in his Budé edition of the *Chaldaean Oracles* (fr. 55, n. 1, pp. 133–34).
203. The use of the term ἐκεῖ is a reminder of the symbolic hierarchies. Just as statements in this world (ἐνταῦθα) signify things there (ἐκεῖ) in the true realities, so from the perspective of the demiurgic Olympians, ἐκεῖ is at yet another remove, with Kronos and Rhea, the more remote "intelligible gods."
204. The rather surprising verb points to the third mode of representation in Proclus, allied to the symbolic, which is not mimetic but still is based on εἰκόνες that represent παραδείγματα. This sort of representation is discussed in the following pages.
205. *In Rep.* 1.138.31–139.19.

attributes of this εἰκών of the goddess are analyzed in a manner reminiscent of Porphyry's work on statues.

The fifth question announced at the beginning of the discussion, that of the special power of the "exceptional" love Zeus is said to feel for Hera at this moment, is quickly dismissed. The discussion returns to the first sexual encounters of Zeus and Hera, obliquely mentioned earlier, which were, we are told, inferior to this one in that now, rather than acting without their parents' knowledge, they are in fact drawn up to them and identified with them.[206] The analysis closes on general reflections concerning myth's procedure of fragmenting the simultaneous and eternal, and with the assertion that all of the passage just considered was written "in the theological mode." [207] This presumably means that it belongs (as already stated) to the first class of poetry. The support of Socrates for this assertion is claimed by virtue of the derivation of Hera's name from "lovely" (ἐρατή) in the Cratylus (404b). Proclus, with a characteristic attention to specifics at the expense of the larger context, takes the etymologies with deadly seriousness.

Proclus asserts finally that "according to the secret doctrine" (κατὰ τὴν ἀπόρρητον θεωρίαν), no accusations are to be made against Homer arising from his treatment of the deception of Zeus. This is, presumably, a reference to the exegetical process just demonstrated in action, and it will be worthwhile to stop for a moment and examine its actual procedures, having established some of its basic theoretical principles.

If inspired poetry is symbolic and not mimetic, we would expect its symbols to indicate that to which they refer, not by resemblance, but by some more subtle form of reference. This class of representation, these "symbols," clearly include etymological hints (Ἴδη/εἴδη; Ἥρα/ἐρατή), and there are several instances of symbolism by "opposites" (Zeus's sleep = transcendent awareness; "disgraceful" open-air copulation = a transcendentally pure creative act). Some elements of the interpretation, however, are not even presented as symbols,[208] and it is quite clear that the neat categories and models Proclus has built in his introduction are not reflected in practice in this exegesis κατὰ τὴν ἀπόρρητον θεωρίαν. The problem is largely resolved by Sheppard, who makes it clear that there is a further mode of "theological" representation, through εἰκόνες, though this non-mimetic mode is not clearly defined in the theoretical

---

206. Cf. n. 191 above.

207. κατὰ τὸν θεολογικὸν τρόπον (In Rep. 1.140.6).

208. Cf. ἀπεικονίζεται at In Rep. 1.138.1, noted above. This must surely refer to an εἰκών, rather than to a σύμβολον.

section of the essay.[209] In practice, the highest poetry may proceed by pure σύμβολα, commonly antithetical to their referents, or it may proceed by employing εἰκόνες to refer to transcendent παραδείγματα.[210] Here, then, what appears to be a "symbolic" utterance is found to contain images, and a clear distinction is not maintained among the various kinds of meaning.[211] Proclus's elegant systematization of literary phenomena sacrifices something of its purity when applied to actual texts— as indeed it should. His interpetive *practice* is largely determined by tradition and may be as chaotic and varied as that of his predecessors.

Books 15 through 19 receive only incidental references and quotations. Some of these are striking because Proclus builds his defense on the principle of literary realism.[212] If souls are depicted groaning as they abandon strong young bodies, Proclus is able to stand back from Socrates' claim that this will have a deleterious effect on the bravery of the young guardians (*Rep.* 3.386c–387a) and to claim that the description is acceptable simply because such things do, in fact, happen. It may be true that, in the ideal state Plato projects, such descriptions could be harmful, but in view of more immediate goals and ideals, this accurately mimetic (εἰκαστικόν) poetry is acceptable.[213] Realism likewise justifies the Homeric description of the exaggerated mourning of Achilles and Priam[214]— *they* were no philosophers, and acted as one would expect heroes, men of action, to act in such circumstances. The principle of justification by realism is extended even to the defense of Achilles' mutilation of Hector's corpse, where Proclus calls on a "traditional" explanation, citing a

209. Sheppard, *Studies*, p. 197.

210. E.g., Hera uses oil; athletes use oil; therefore, Hera's oil is emblematic of her strength. Ambrosia = transcendent purity. Numerous tassles of the fringe = numerous dependent souls.

211. Moreover, Coulter's attempt to associate Proclus's interpretation of "symbolic" poetry with symbolism in the modern sense and that of "eiconic" poetry with allegory, criticized by Anne Raphael (Sheppard) (*Classical Review*, n.s., 28 [1978]: 173–74, and *Studies*, p. 197, n. 97) does, as she claims, prove to have little bearing on Proclus's practice.

212. An example, discussed below, is found in the passage on the wailing of souls on their way to Hades (*In Rep.* 1.118.9–10; 121.10–23) where the apparent reference is to the groaning of Patroclus's soul (*Il.* 16.857).

213. Cf. *In Rep.* 1.162.5–163.9.

214. The symbolism of Thetis's tears (*Il.* 18.84) and Zeus's lament for Sarpedon (*Il.* 16.433–38) on the other hand, attributing πάθη τοῖς ἀπαθέσιν (*In Rep.* 1.123.22–23), is interpreted differently. Theurgic analogies are evoked, including wailing in the mysteries and initiations. The tears and lamentations become the symbols of specific acts of divine providence (*In Rep.* 1.124.1–126.4).

Thessalian custom.[215] Achilles, then, was simply doing what might be expected of him and is depicted acting "according to the rule appropriate to him."[216] The description is defended as accurate, and therefore justifiable, historical (and cultural) realism.

The main focus of Proclus's attention in the later books of the *Iliad* is the battle of the gods in books 20 and 21. Socrates had listed the "theomachies" of Homer (θεομαχίαι, *Rep.* 2.378d) among the passages unacceptable "with or without secondary meanings."[217] Proclus clearly understands the reference to be to these books and to the part of the poem that bore the ancient title θεῶν μάχη.[218] Socrates and Proclus would agree that these myths are lies: the gods are correctly described by Homer in numerous passages as living eternally at ease on Olympus, which is to say, beyond our changeable sphere.[219] Strife has no place in that existence. Socrates might also agree that there are hidden meanings behind the screen of the apparent meaning of Homer's description, but for his purposes in the *Republic* those hidden meanings might as well not be there, since the young cannot distinguish them. Here again, Proclus makes no attempt to counter Socrates' central point. He merely argues that, for those capable of understanding them, these hidden meanings contain important insights.

Proclus's approach to this problem is characteristic. He does not go directly to the text, but rather begins by asking himself just what known properties of the gods the mythoplasts could be aiming at in attributing strife to them. He concludes that there are two possible referents (or, to use his expression, the image could be used according to two "modes," or τρόποι), one of which fits the Homeric theomachies better than the other.

The first goes back to the Pythagorean model of the universe brought into the discussion of the deception of Zeus. The interpretation is dependent on the idea that, at the level immediately below the One, all realities

215. εἴρηται μὲν οὖν καὶ ὑπὸ τῶν παλαιῶν ὡς Θετταλικόν τι τοιοῦτον ἔθος ἦν (*In Rep.* 1.150.10–11). This idea is reflected in somewhat different form in the scholia. Its earliest traceable source seems to be the *Homeric Questions* of Aristotle.

216. κατὰ τὸ προσῆκον αὐτῷ μέτρον (*In Rep.* 1.151.16).

217. For the text, see Preface, n. 4, above. Cf. Proclus *In Rep.* 1.87.4–15.

218. That is, he sees here a reference not to the myths of warfare among the gods quite apart from mankind (developed in Hesiod's *Theogony*), but to books 20 and 21. The stories in Hesiod are the ones usually now designated by the term "theomachy."

219. Cf. *Od.* 6.42–46.

are generated by a pair of principles called respectively the unifying monad and the generative dyad. The fundamental schism dividing all reality is traced from this level down through the phenomena experienced by the soul. The mythoplasts observed this and "hint at it"[220] in the theomachies, representing at once the oneness of the gods (in that they are all called gods) and their division into two separate classes (since they are seen fighting with one another). Certain unspecified traditional accounts of battles of the gods are said to have this sort of meaning.

Homer, on the other hand, depicts the gods at war with quite another truth in view, specifically the progressive fragmentation of the divine influences, which are unified at their source but become increasingly more divided as they proceed down to the level of angelic and demonic ranks in touch with the material universe and filled with strife.[221] Proclus is more interested at this point in Homer's support for his own elaborate angelology and demonology than in his support (demonstrated elsewhere in any case) for Pythagorean dualism.

This fragmentation at our end of the scale of being is also related to the providential role of the lower gods—the angels and the demons. Proclus emphasizes the fact that, in the *Iliad*, Zeus does not enter the fighting.[222] "The monad remains solidly fixed in itself"[223] whereas the gods proceeding from the monad enter into the strife of the material world to watch over the fate of souls. Not all the gods do so: some, Proclus claims, remain "within Zeus,"[224] which is to say, detached from the material world, transcendent. This is an interesting claim (hardly supported by the apparent meaning of the text of book 20) in that it seems to rest upon an implicit interpretation of sequential events (Zeus's summoning the gods to him and then sending them out to fight) as simultaneous. Proclus has used this principle elsewhere, but when he has done so, he has generally made it explicit. Here, on the other hand, he seems simply to assume that, when Homer says about the gods, "They did *A* and then

220. τί . . . θαυμαστόν, εἰ οἱ μυθοπλάσται . . . αἰνίσσοιντο . . . ; (*In Rep.* 1.89.3–6).

221. *In Rep.* 1.89.10–24.

222. Contrast the theomachy of Hesiod (*Theog.* 617–885) where Zeus's role is active and decisive. Presumably this is an indication that Proclus's first theomachy interpretation applies in the case of Hesiod, and not the second. Proclus in fact says as much (*In Rep.* 1.93.13–24), citing the casual Homeric reference to the imprisonment of Kronos (*Il.* 14.203).

223. ἐκείνης [sc. τῆς μονάδος, line 16] ἐν ἑαυτῇ σταθερῶς ἱδρυμένης (*In Rep.* 1.90.19).

224. Διὸς ἔνδον, *Il.* 20.13, cited by Proclus *In Rep.* 1.90.25.

they did B," he actually means that "A and B are simultaneously existing permanent conditions."

A peculiar aspect of Proclus's accommodation of his elaborate demonology to the "ancient theology" becomes central to the interpretation of the theomachy at this point.[225] The Olympians are taken to be henads, unified transcendent beings immediately below the level of the primal monad and the generative dyad. When we refer to Athena or Hephaestus, then, we refer to a transcendent being. But the gods' names themselves are polysemous.[226] They refer not only to the henad at the source of each procession, but also to all the members of that procession, down to the level of the demons immediately in touch with the fate of souls on earth:

> For each chain bears the name of its monad and the partial spirits enjoy having the same names as their wholes. Thus there are many Apollos and Poseidons and Hephaestuses of all sorts, some of them separated from the universe, some distributed through the heavens; some preside over the elements in their totality; some have been assigned authority over specific elements.[227]

This constitutes yet another inversion of the structures of meaning we have been led to expect: when Homer says "Apollo," a name most obviously having its referent in a higher reality and designating an entity commanding respect and awe, he may not mean *that* Apollo, but rather a lower Apollo, an angelic or demonic entity in touch with the fate of souls. The higher may stand for the lower. Proclus's emphasis is on the continuity of the chains or processions of the divine. Once time and conflict are removed, the paradoxical attribution of strife to the gods be-

---

225. *In Rep.* 1.90.22–92.27.

226. Proclus asserts the principle that a given linguistic sign may have different referents on different levels of reality. Cf. Trouillard, "L'Activité onomastique selon Proclos," pp. 241–42. The idea of countering accusations of impiety in the poets' attribution of various actions to the gods with the claim that the gods' names sometimes indicate entities other than their divine persons goes back to the time of Plutarch (*De aud. po.* 23a–24c) and Apuleius, and is rooted far earlier in the thought of Xenocrates in the fourth century B.C. (Sheppard, *Studies*, p. 54 with n. 40). Cf. DeLacy, "Stoic Views of Poetry," p. 258 and n. 58, where Cic. *De nat. deor.* 2.60 is also mentioned, though in that passage the concept is treated neither as defensive nor as pedagogic.

227. ἑκάστη γὰρ σειρὰ τὴν τῆς μονάδος φέρεται προσηγορίαν καὶ τὰ μερικὰ πνεύματα τοῖς ὅλοις τὴν αὐτὴν ἐπωνυμίαν δέχεσθαι φιλεῖ. διὸ καὶ Ἀπόλλωνες καὶ Ποσειδῶνες καὶ Ἥφαιστοι πολλοί τε καὶ παντοδαποί, καὶ οἳ μὲν αὐτῶν χωριστοὶ τοῦ παντός εἰσιν, οἳ δὲ τῶν ὅλων προεστήκασιν στοιχείων, οἳ δὲ περὶ ἕκαστον κατενείμαντο τὴν ἐπιστασίαν (*In Rep.* 1.92.2–9).

comes a description of one of the enduring wonders of Proclus's spiritual world: the gods are transcendent (hence their Olympian names), and yet they are concerned with the fate of beings in this world (hence the description of them at war).[228]

Each pair of warring gods is interpreted separately, and each conflict is seen to represent some fundamental truth about reality.[229] The idea was a time-honored one, and Proclus no doubt had numerous possible interpretations of the pairs to choose among.[230] His selection ranges from adapted Stoic physical allegory to more characteristically mystical interpretations. The interpretation of Hephaestus and Xanthus as the contributors, respectively, of heat-and-dryness and cold-and-wetness, viewed as a fundamental tension maintaining the physical body, is quite close to the scholiast's more laconic physical interpretation: "Water against fire" ($\tau\grave{o}$ $\ddot{v}\delta\omega\rho$ $\dot{a}\nu\theta\acute{\iota}\sigma\tau\alpha\tau\alpha\iota$ $\tau\hat{\omega}$ $\pi\upsilon\rho\acute{\iota}$).[231] At the other extreme, the interpretation of the unopposed presence of Aphrodite as representing "love" ($\phi\iota\lambda\acute{\iota}\alpha$), present here because "all oppositions must end in mutual harmony,"[232] goes beyond the fragmentary interpretations of the scholiasts and emphasizes an element insignificant in the text itself but that, in Proclus's contemplation of the total myth above and beyond the text, provides a redeeming coherence, a reminder of the unified, static reality lying behind the mythoplasts' turbulent $\pi o\iota\kappa\iota\lambda\acute{\iota}\alpha$.

Later, in discussing Plato's debts to Homer, Proclus returns to Zeus's speech to the gods (Il. 20.20–30) to make the claim that this was Plato's source for the speech of the demiurge to the gods in Timaeus 41a–d.[233] Thus the theomachy becomes Homer's true account of creation—more perfect, one might infer, than the account in Genesis, because the surface fiction is further removed from the reality it represents. This subtle truth is contained in the myth's representation of Zeus's gathering of the gods through Themis (Il. 20.4–6) and his subsequent injunction to them

228. In Rep. 1.94.25–28.
229. In Rep. 1.94.28–95.26.
230. Cf. the exegetic scholia on the passage (Il. 20.67–74), which suggest that, for example, the Apollo-Poseidon opposition refers to the antithesis disease (= the plague god) vs. health (= the god who purifies through his sea breezes) and that Artemis is the moon eclipsed by Hera (= $\dot{a}\acute{\eta}\rho$ by the usual etymology)—Schol. in Il., ed. Erbse, vol. 5, pp. 15–16. Cf. also Heraclit. Quaest. hom. 54–58, and see Buffière, Mythes d'Homère, pp. 549–53 and Sheppard, Studies, pp. 49–58.
231. The scholiast on Il. 20.73–74. Schol. in Il., ed. Erbse, vol. 5, p. 18.
232. $\pi\acute{a}\sigma\alpha\varsigma$ $\dot{a}\nu\acute{a}\gamma\kappa\eta$ $\tau\grave{a}\varsigma$ $\dot{\epsilon}\nu\alpha\nu\tau\iota\acute{\omega}\sigma\epsilon\iota\varsigma$ $\epsilon\dot{\iota}\varsigma$ $\tau\grave{\eta}\nu$ $\pi\rho\grave{o}\varsigma$ $\dot{a}\lambda\lambda\acute{\eta}\lambda\alpha\varsigma$ $\dot{o}\mu o\lambda o\gamma\acute{\iota}\alpha\nu$ $\tau\epsilon\lambda\epsilon\upsilon$-$\tau\hat{a}\nu$ (In Rep. 1.95.21–22).
233. In Rep. 1.165.13–166.11.

to go into the fighting (*Il.* 20.23–25), which represent, respectively, the transcendent monad (1) drawing all of the gods up to himself in isolated transcendence beyond the natural world, and (2) his (simultaneous) providential projection of the gods into the world. Providence is identified with the act of creation. This discussion throws some light on the observation, much earlier, that not all of the gods go into the fighting.[234] Homer does not, in fact, describe any gods as remaining with Zeus on the lookout on Mount Ida, but Proclus, either from misreading or from a tacit act of interpretation, claims that some do. This means, we learn here, that effectively all both remain transcendent with Zeus *and* enter the universe to exercise creative providence.

In the discussion of the final books, Proclus's demonology and the principle that the name belonging to the henad serves as well for the δαίμονες in its procession is applied several times. It serves most significantly to protect Achilles from the charge of disrespect for the gods when he chases and insults Apollo.[235] The "Apollo" that disguised himself as Agenor and led Achilles astray, Proclus argues, was clearly not the henad but a lowly δαίμων watching over Hector, and in view of this fact Achilles' language was not blasphemous. Furthermore, the principle of continuity comes into play here. The very greatest of the heroes are contiguous in the chain of being with the very lowest of the δαίμονες and there is no clear line of demarcation of powers. Therefore, if Achilles defeats a god (Xanthus), Homer is revealing that "the very first from the last classes are somehow equal to the very last from the first classes, especially when they are moved and protected by the gods themselves."[236]

The portion of the *Iliad* that follows the last day of fighting receives many quotations and references in Proclus's discussion, but few touch on points that have not already been raised. The magnificent image of the two pithoi on the doorstep of Zeus (*Il.* 24.527–33) is the last passage singled out for special comment.[237] It appears to attribute evil to the gods, something Socrates had absolutely forbidden in the myths to be used for the instruction of the guardians.[238]

Proclus's defense turns on the meaning of the words "good" and "bad," and his procedure is reminiscent of the techniques of satire,

234. *In Rep.* 1.90.25.
235. *Il.* 22.7–20. *In Rep.* 1.146.17–148.24.
236. ἐνδεικνυμένη τοῖς τῶν τοιούτων ἐπαΐειν δυναμένοις ὅτι καὶ τὰ πρώτιστα τῶν τελευταίων ἐξισοῦταί πως τοῖς ἐσχάτοις τῶν πρώτων, καὶ διαφερόντως ὅταν ὑπ' αὐτῶν κινῆται καὶ φρουρῆται τῶν θεῶν (*In Rep.* 1.149.7–10).
237. *In Rep.* 1.98–100.
238. Plato *Rep.* 2.379c–d.

undercutting preconceptions and accepted evaluations. There is a fundamental dualism in Proclus's world-view that is difficult to reconcile with Socrates's view of providence and his belief in human responsibility, yet Proclus sets out to reconcile these positions by arguing that Zeus's pithoi contain only *apparent* goods and evils, only those things dependent on fate, those externals that can be turned to good or to evil, depending on the condition of the soul to which they are attached. Once again we catch a distant echo of the myth of Er. This fate (εἱμαρμένη) is indeed in the hands of divine providence, but it does not in any real sense bring evil upon men.

In formulating this problem, Proclus reveals both his weakness and his strength as an interpretive critic, viewed from a modern perspective. He asks why Homer has chosen the image of the pithoi.[239] It might, on the one hand, be because of the resemblance of the word πίθος to the verb πείθω (persuade), which Timaeus uses to talk about the way in which νοῦς influences necessity to turn most things toward the good.[240] This etymological argument is quaint at best. But the other alternative emphasizes the physical quality of the image and strongly suggests that Proclus had entered imaginatively into it to assess its real impact: "or he might have been showing their vastness, their capacity to contain the whole enormous variety and complexity of human events."[241]

The Odyssey

No comprehensive view of the meaning of the *Odyssey* or its associated myths is offered in Proclus's essay beyond the very broad interpretation of the Troy tale mentioned above, but since that general overview includes the story of the return of the Greek heroes, of which the *Odyssey* is, so to speak, the last chapter, we may take it to give an indication of Proclus's thoughts on the matter.

The Greeks represent souls lured into the warlike state of this exis-

239. *In Rep.* 1.99.9–14.

240. Plato *Tim.* 48a, cited by Proclus *In Rep.* 1.99.10–12. It is perhaps misleading to belittle this etymological fantasy without mentioning that later Platonism placed great emphasis on this passage of the *Timaeus* and on "persuasion" and "necessity" as constituents of reality. Calcidius (*In Tim.* 199 = Numenius fr. 52) says Numenius is said to have equated "matter and necessity": "*eamque silvam et necessitatem cognominat; ex qua et deo mundi machinam constituisse* deo persuadente, necessitate obsecundante." Calcidius had just made the point that for the Pythagoreans, including Numenius, evil is an inherent quality of matter.

241. εἴτε καὶ τὸ χωρητικὸν αὐτῶν καὶ περιληπτικὸν τῶν παντοδαπῶν καὶ ποικίλων ἀποτελεσμάτων ἐνδεικνύμενος (*In Rep.* 1.99.12–13).

tence, from which the "more intellectual" return successfully to the higher reality that is their true home. If one extends the image, Odysseus might represent a soul so drawn to, and fascinated by, this world that its return is exceptionally difficult. This interpretation does communicate some of the charm and uniqueness of Odysseus, but we can hardly attribute it to Proclus.

The *Odyssey* is far less interesting and suggestive to Proclus than the *Iliad*,[242] though he indicates his awareness of the tradition of allegorical interpretation of the poem. Moreover, he shies away from an allegorical interpretation in his defense of Odysseus against the charge of lack of moderation and of a generally positive disposition toward the pleasures of the flesh:

> Now, with regard to the blame laid upon Odysseus, let it be said that, first of all, those who refer the wanderings of Odysseus to secondary, allegorical meanings and place the Phaeacians and the "good cheer" among them beyond the sphere of mortal nature, prefer to interpret these things more symbolically. Thus "banquet," "feasting," and "harmonious song" will be said, as far as they are concerned, in another sense and not the one recognized by most men. It should be emphasized, however, that those who interpret the poem literally are also able to answer such accusations.[243]

Proclus goes on to build a conservative argument based on careful attention to the text and on the demonstration that Odysseus praises "good cheer" (εὐφροσύνη), not "pleasure" (ἡδονή). It is the latter that Socrates (together with virtually the entire Greek philosophical tradition with the exception of the Epicureans) condemned as a goal in life, and that has the associations of indulgence in the appetites of the flesh.

242. See the data in Appendix 3, which indicate only the presence or absence of references in four works by Proclus to the various books of the *Iliad* and *Odyssey* and give no information on quantity of references to a given book. A rough calculation of the use of the two poems in the *Republic* and *Timaeus* commentaries alone indicates 130 references to the *Iliad* as against only 73 to the *Odyssey*, or nearly 80 percent more for the *Iliad*. In the *Timaeus* commentary, where fewer citations are dependent on Plato, the imbalance is even greater, with more than twice as many references to the *Iliad* (51:23).

243. πρὸς δὲ αὖ τὴν κατὰ τῶν Ὀδυσσέως λόγων ἐπιτίμησιν λεγέσθω μὲν καί, ὅτι τὰ τοιαῦτα συμβολικώτερον ἀφερμηνεύειν δέδοκται τοῖς τὴν καλουμένην πλάνην ἐπ᾽ ἄλλας ὑπονοίας μεθιστᾶσι καὶ τοὺς Φαίακας καὶ τὴν παρ᾽ αὐτοῖς εὐδαιμονίαν ἀνωτέρω τῆς θνητῆς φύσεως τάττειν ἀξιοῦσιν. καὶ γὰρ ἡ δαὶς παρ᾽ ἐκείνοις καὶ ἡ θοίνη καὶ ἡ ἐναρμόνιος ᾠδὴ τρόπον ἕτερον ῥηθήσεται καὶ οὐ τὸν τοῖς πολλοῖς συνεγνωσμένον. λεγέσθω δὲ αὖ, ὅτι καὶ τοῖς τὸ φαινόμενον τῆς ποιήσεως μεταθέουσιν ἔξεστιν ἀπαντᾶν πρὸς τοὺς τοιούτους λόγους (*In Rep.* 1.131.5–14).

The *Odyssey* seems to present Proclus with a quite different critical problem from the *Iliad*. That the two poems belong to very different modes of storytelling is a cliché of modern criticism, but it would be interesting to have the testimony of ancient critics on their similarities and differences.[244] For Proclus, after all, the two poems are decidedly the work of a single man, however distorted his biography may have become at the hands of secondary mythoplasts.

There are no positive signs of a perception on Proclus's part of the differences between the poems, beyond his general inclination to avoid the apparently prevalent allegorical mode of interpreting the *Odyssey*. There is nevertheless at least a possibility that there is an indication here of a general pattern of attitude toward the two poems against which Proclus is reacting.

It seems intuitively clear to most modern readers that the *Iliad* is to be read as mythically distorted history (i.e., as saga), and that the *Odyssey*, focusing as it does on the adventures of a single hero, has a structure of meaning that is quite deliberately manipulated, in a manner considerably closer to the modern novel, to make a generalized statement about the life of the individual. If we look at Chapman's Homer—taking it as a document in the recent history of the interpretation of Homer—it is clear that the two Homeric epics entered the English Renaissance tradition as a heroic saga and an allegory of man's conquest of himself respectively.[245]

The two poems invite quite different kinds of critical analysis and the approaches taken in late antiquity would appear to have been different as well. Although Proclus is generally reluctant to react against tradition and to approach a problem in an innovative way, he appears in his attitude toward the two poems to be doing just that. Both, for him, are inspired utterances. They contain comparable structures of meaning, of great complexity. However, to judge by the pattern of Proclus's argument, the *Iliad* would appear to have been read most commonly as history or as physical allegory: Proclus (adhering, it is true, to an alternative tradition, and hardly breaking trail on his own) in most instances insists

244. Cf. Buffière's note in his edition of Heraclitus's *Homeric Allegories*, p. 66, n. 2, referring to Arist. *Poet.* 24.1459b: "Les anciens considéraient l'*Iliade* comme plus 'pathétique,' l'*Odyssée* plus 'éthique.'" The Aristotelian passage becomes clearer if we follow Else's translation (p. 63) and read παθητικόν as "fatal." The passage reads, καὶ γὰρ τῶν ποιημάτων ἑκάτερον συνέστηκεν ἡ μὲν Ἰλιὰς ἁπλοῦν καὶ παθητικόν, ἡ δὲ Ὀδύσσεια πεπλεγμένον (ἀναγνώρισις γὰρ διόλου) καὶ ἠθική (Arist. *Poet.* 24.1459b.13–15). The indication even in Aristotle, however, that the *Odyssey* must be interpreted as having a generalized moral content, is unavoidable. See also Ps.-Plut. *De vit. Hom.* 4.

245. Cf. Lord, *Homeric Renaissance*, p. 43.

upon interpretations connecting that fiction to a reality that is anything but historical or physical. The *Odyssey*, on the other hand, would appear traditionally to have been read as allegory, most often moral allegory, but Proclus, fully aware of this tradition and quite willing to use it when it suits his purposes, responds in this important instance by insisting that, even in a literal reading, the *Odyssey* and its hero are defensible.

The alternative approaches to Homer, literal and "allegorical" interpretation, based respectively on views of the literary artifact as a simple system of meaning and as a polysemous structure, are at least as old as Plato. Nowhere before Proclus, though, do we see the two interact in such a way that conclusions may be drawn about their relative importance and uses. If we were to judge by the relative levels of attention to the two poems in the *Homeric Allegories* of Heraclitus, we would have to conclude that the efforts of the physical and moral allegorists were concentrated on the *Iliad*, but what we are seeing there is probably no more than a reflection of the traditional assessment of the *Iliad* as the superior poem. Proclus seems to give an indication (though by no means a proof) that our modern understanding of the differences between the two poems was anticipated in late antiquity by a general tendency to read the *Iliad* κατὰ τὸ φαινόμενον and the *Odyssey* as a polysemous structure—a tendency against which Proclus reacts on both counts in his defence of Homer, though he does so in his characteristically gentle way. There is, further, the implication that, given the choice between an acceptable interpretation κατὰ τὸ φαινόμενον and an unnecessary allegory, Proclus will choose the former: looking through the screen of the fictive surface is required only when the surface itself does not yield a satisfactory meaning.[246]

An overall allegory of the *Odyssey* comparable to that expressed by Heraclitus[247] is implied but not developed in a passage of the prologue to Proclus's commentary on the *Elements* of Euclid.[248] He is discussing the relationship of geometry to the various levels of perception and ap-

246. Servius in his Virgil commentaries also reacts against superfluous allegorical interpretation. Cf. Hahn, *Allegorie in der antiken Rhetorik*, pp. 78–80. The idea is expressed as early as Plutarch (*De aud. po.*): see Daniel Babut, *Plutarque et le Stoïcisme*, p. 376.

247. Heraclit. *Quaest. hom.* 70. For Heraclitus, the *Odyssey* is a coherent moral allegory.

248. Proclus *In Euc.* 55.18–23. See n. 251 below for the text. The passage is cited by Werner Beierwaltes, "Das Problem der Erkenntnis bei Proklos," p. 161, n. 2, along with the following *comparanda*, discussed below: Proclus *In Parm.* 1025a.29–37; Herm. *In Phdr.* 214.19–24; Porph. *De ant.* 34 (= Numenius fr. 33).

prehension of the soul.[249] The geometrical figures conjured up in the mind (only one step removed from those actually drawn for purposes of demonstration) are used as tools by the understanding (διάνοια), which is too weak to comprehend all the λόγοι it contains and so lays them out on its doorstep, so to speak, on the level of "imagination" (φαντασία).[250] This envisioning, then, is "a path to their true noetic essence" (ὁδὸς μὲν εἰς τὴν διανοητικὴν . . . οὐσίαν), but the goal would never be reached if the understanding did not first do an about-face and turn back inside itself:

> Then it would see the essential, non-spatial, unfragmented λόγοι that are its true substance. And this very action of the understanding would be the highest goal of the discipline of geometry, truly performing the task of Hermes' gift, liberating the understanding from a Calypso and leading it upward to a more perfect and more noetic knowledge, freeing it from the partial perceptions of imagining.[251]

Here, Odysseus seems (at least for the duration of the casual illustrative image) to be the understanding (διάνοια); his true goal is union with the νοῦς, and he contains noetic λόγοι, but in order to understand them, he must descend into φαντασία and fabricate mental images of them. The final union, though, can be reached only through his turning back within himself, armed with the experience gained by envisioning these figures, to contemplate the noetic realities that lie behind them. This is accomplished only through the intervention of grace in the form of Hermes commanding φαντασία (= Calypso) to release him.[252]

In the *Parmenides* commentary he again develops the general meaning of the figure of Odysseus:

249. Proclus *In Euc.* 54–55.

250. On the φαντασία as a repository of λόγοι of mental acts, cf. Plot. *Enn.* 3.3.30.

251. τότ᾽ ἂν διαφερόντως τοὺς λόγους τοὺς γεωμετρικοὺς ἴδοι τοὺς ἀμερίστους, τοὺς ἀδιαστάτους, τοὺς οὐσιώδεις ὧν ἐστι πλήρωμα. καὶ ἡ ἐνέργεια αὐτῆς αὕτη τέλος ἂν εἴη τὸ ἄριστον τῆς περὶ γεωμετρίαν σπουδῆς καὶ ὄντως τῆς Ἑρμαϊκῆς δόσεως ἔργον, ἀπό τινος Καλυψοῦς ἀναγούσης αὐτὴν εἰς τελειοτέραν καὶ νοερωτέραν γνῶσιν καὶ ἀπολυούσης τῶν ἐν φαντασίᾳ μορφωτικῶν ἐπιβολῶν (Proclus *In Euc.* 55.16–23).

252. The word "gift" (δόσις) hints that Proclus may be conflating the Calypso and Circe stories in his mind—the moly would be a gift in a more obvious sense than the intervention with Calypso, and Circe is in many ways a better metaphor for the φαντασία. The two stories are easily confused, and Plotinus (*Enn.* 1.6.8.18) mentions them both together, apparently attaching the same meaning to each.

Many are the wanderings and circlings of the soul: one among imaginings, one in opinions and one before these in understanding. But
only the life according to νοῦς has stability and this is the mystical
harbor of the soul to which, on the one hand, the poem leads Odysseus through the great wandering of his life, and to which we too
shall draw ourselves up, if we would reach salvation.[253]

As Porphyry suggests in the essay on the cave of the nymphs (34), the
stable "mystical harbor" of the soul is indicated in the *Odyssey* myth
by the central, but decidedly problematical, prediction of Tiresias that
Odysseus will finally travel inland to a place where the sea is unknown
(*Od.* 11.119–34). It is clear, in any case, that in the present passage,
Odysseus represents the soul (and not the understanding), and the goal
to which the poem "leads" him is still union with the νοῦς, far from the
chaos of life as we know it. A passage in Hermias[254] indicates that this
was a current interpretation. It may have originated in the first or second
century after Christ, found expression in the interpretations of Numenius and his circle, and been passed on to Proclus through Porphyry and
others. By way of Macrobius it enters the medieval Latin tradition.[255]

Though Proclus does not in any way deny the validity of such an interpretation of the *Odyssey* in his defense of Homer in the *Republic* commentary, he does not make any extensive use of it either. Only two passages, the Proteus episode (*Od.* 4.351–592) and the song of Ares and
Aphrodite (*Od.* 8.266–366) are interpreted allegorically,[256] though about
a dozen other passages are brought up in various contexts.[257]

The interpretation of the Proteus episode has already been mentioned, but the subsequent discussion of Proclus's demonology should
make its significance clearer at this point. Like the myths of the the-

253. πολλαὶ οὖν αἱ πλάναι καὶ αἱ δινεύσεις τῆς ψυχῆς· ἄλλη γὰρ ἡ ἐν ταῖς
φαντασίαις, ἄλλη δὲ πρὸ τούτων ἡ ἐν δόξαις, ἄλλη ἡ ἐν αὐτῇ τῇ διανοίᾳ· μόνη δὲ
ἡ κατὰ νοῦν ζωὴ τὸ ἀπλανὲς ἔχει, καὶ οὗτος ὁ μυστικὸς ὅρμος τῆς ψυχῆς, εἰς ὃν
καὶ ἡ ποίησις ἄγει τὸν Ὀδυσσέα μετὰ τὴν πολλὴν πλάνην τῆς ζωῆς, καὶ ἡμεῖς,
ἐὰν ἄρα σώζεσθαι θέλωμεν, μᾶλλον ἑαυτοὺς ἀνάξομεν (*In Parm.* 1025a.29–37).
254. See n. 248 above for the reference.
255. Macrob. *In somn. Scip.* 1.12.2–3. Cf. Flamant, *Macrobe et le néoplatonisme
latin*, appendix 9.
256. Heraclitus (*Quaest. hom.* 64–67 and 69) gives interpretations of both. The
Proteus episode is viewed as an account of creation (65), and in this Heraclitus
approaches the cosmic universality of Proclus's interpretations, but there is
otherwise little similarity.
257. E.g., Demodocus, Phemius, and Clytemnestra's nameless bard (*Od.*
3.267–68) are claimed to be symbols of different modes of poetry, as discussed
above.

omachy, this one is interpreted as presenting the lower phases of a divine procession, elaborated in space and time in the manner of the mythoplasts. An angelic νοῦς in the procession of Poseidon, Proteus "contains in himself the forms of all things in this world."[258] Among the higher (disembodied) demonic souls placed immediately below him in the procession is Eidothea, who contemplates these forms through him. Her relationship to the numerous other "rational and eternal" souls in the procession is not entirely clear, but they are below her, represented by the mythoplasts as the seals. The clue in the "screen" of the fiction that points to their immortality is the fact that Proteus counts them: the number of things that come to be and pass away is infinite and cannot be calculated.[259] When Proteus is perceived by a fragmented soul unable to grasp these forms simultaneously, he appears to pass from one to another, though in fact he simultaneously contains all of them. Though Proclus does not expand upon it, Eidothea's talk with Menelaus, her role as mediator between his fragmented, embodied soul and the angelic νοῦς, is clearly taken to depend upon her intermediate status in the procession. As a soul she participates in Menelaus's mode of perception and so is able to instruct him on what he will experience and how to respond (Od. 4.383–93), but as a soul of the highest order, contiguous with νοῦς, she is also capable of grasping the whole of Proteus's identity, and therefore of communicating it to Menelaus on a theoretical level.

This Odyssey passage is rejected by Socrates only in the most general terms, and without any discussion. It is striking, then, that only a generation before Proclus's commentary was written, it had been taken up by Augustine (Civ. Dei 10.10), who quotes its Virgilian adaptation (Georg. 4.411) and goes on to observe that such transformations and deceptions come exclusively from Satan, not from the true God. Thus the issue of the immutability of the divine had a currency in Proclus's time that makes of his explanation of the Proteus episode something more than an exercise in the reconciliation of ancient texts.

The other important Odyssey exegesis is that of Demodocus's song of Ares and Aphrodite, and this forms an exceptionally complete and structured interpretive essay.[260] Proclus begins, not with the text, but with the gods, and with the fundamental principles that they and their processions represent. Ares is the separator of the opposites in the uni-

258. ἔχων καὶ περιέχων ἐν ἑαυτῷ τὰ εἴδη πάντα τῶν γενητῶν (In Rep. 1.112.28–29).

259. In Rep. 1.113.7–8.

260. In Rep. 1.141.1–143.16.

verse: thanks to him, the cosmos is perfect and the forms are maintained separate from one another and filling it. One is reminded of Empedocles' "strife" (brought, as it were, into balance with φιλία so that the oscillation is brought under control and periodic catastrophes are averted). Hephaestus, as we have seen, is the demiurge, projecting the physical λόγοι into matter and establishing the order of the material world.

The union of Ares and Aphrodite creates "harmony and order for the opposites";[261] that of Hephaestus and Aphrodite creates in this world beauty and radiance "to make the world the most beautiful of all visible things."[262] The hypercosmic nuptial embrace and the encosmic adultery are, in fact, simultaneous and eternal, but the mythoplasts have distorted the account according to the familiar pattern. If the cuckolded husband observes the encosmic goings-on from his hypercosmic perch and binds the couple together, the truth behind the screen is that this world has need both of the power of separation (Ares) and of that of combination (Aphrodite),[263] and if he subsequently breaks the chains (at the urging of Poseidon, whose preeminent role it is to preside over the cycle of coming to be and passing away), it is because a static union of the two would bring the process to a standstill—Hephaestus's act simultaneously destroys the physical universe and (since eternal destruction and eternal coming to be are the life of that universe) creates it anew.

Having sketched out the model lying behind the fiction, Proclus establishes first that the teaching is in line with that of Plato, on the basis that the Timaeus uses the image of "chains" for the demiurgic λόγοι (Tim. 43a). The connection is not, in fact, obvious from a reading of the Timaeus passage and one must admit that this is another instance where Proclus's intense need to refer a concept to a higher authority has led him to distort the apparent meaning of the text.[264] After establishing to his satisfaction that Homer is in harmony with Plato, he proceeds to the second goal of establishing that Homer is in harmony with "the nature of

261. ἵνα τοῖς ἐναντίοις ἁρμονίαν ἐμποιήσῃ καὶ τάξιν (In Rep. 1.141.17–18).

262. ἵνα τοῖς αἰσθητοῖς δημιουργήμασιν κάλλος ἐναπεργάσηται καὶ ἀγλαΐαν, ὅση καὶ τόνδε τὸν κόσμον κάλλιστον ἀποτελέσαι τῶν ὁρωμένων ἠδύνατο (In Rep. 1.141.20–21).

263. Again, the Empedoclean model is visible behind this account of the maintenance of the world-order.

264. Cf. E. R. Dodds's comments in the introduction to his edition of Proclus's Elements of Theology (p. xi), on Proclus's "constant appeals to authority— now to Plato now to 'Orpheus' or to the Chaldaean Oracles—which irritate the reader of the major works and confuse him by their ingenuity of misinterpretation."

things."²⁶⁵ The bonds of the physical universe are breakable, and it is not, according to Proclus, a breach of realism for Hephaestus to smash them after creating them.

When he has made these two points, the ones essential to his defense of the passage, he recapitulates its true meaning, reintroducing the elements of the Homeric myth as imagery to enrich the abstract statement:

> The universal demiurge, in bringing the cosmos to be out of opposing elements, and through proportion working attraction into it, seemed to be uniting the actions of Hephaestus, Ares, and Aphrodite into one: in producing the opposition of the elements, he was creating according to the Ares in him; in contriving attraction, he was acting by the power of Aphrodite; and in bonding together the Arean and the Aphrodisian, he had taken the craft of Hephaestus as his model. For he is all things and acts with all the gods.²⁶⁶

The formulation echoes many others, in a tradition at least as old as the tragedians, of attempting to distill from the polytheism of the myths a unified concept of the divine.

Throughout the discussion, the distance from the language as well as from the tone of the Homeric passage has been very great. There is not a single citation of the passage under discussion—one feels that the words of Homer would only get in the way. More important, the whole emotional texture of the Homeric passage is lost, the rage and bitter frustration of Hephaestus, the comic impatience of Ares to jump into the trap, and the laughter of the gods. In a sense it is unfair to demand that Proclus respond to these elements of the passage; they have nothing to do with what he is seeking in the myths. But at the same time the fact that they have been so utterly ignored, and that Proclus's interpretation is so often at odds with them, is a serious factor in discrediting his interpretations as representations of the intentions of the poets (as he would claim them to be).

The relationship of Proclus's levels of discourse is demonstrated in its complexity in the passage quoted above. This abstract, partially demythologized, statement is the interpreter's attempt to indicate the meta-

265. κατὰ τὴν ⟨τῶν⟩ πραγμάτων . . . φύσιν (In Rep. 1.143.1).
266. καὶ ἔοικεν ὅ τε ὅλος δημιουργὸς ἐκ τῶν ἐναντίων στοιχείων τὸν κόσμον συνιστὰς καὶ δι' ἀναλογίας ἐν αὐτῷ φιλίαν ἀπεργαζόμενος συνάγειν εἰς ταὐτὸν τὰς Ἡφαίστου καὶ Ἄρεως καὶ Ἀφροδίτης ἐνεργείας, καὶ γεννῶν μὲν τὰς ἐναντιώσεις τῶν στοιχείων κατὰ τὸν ἐν ἑαυτῷ γεννᾶν Ἄρεα, φιλίαν δὲ μηχανόμενος κατὰ τῆς Ἀφροδίτης δύναμιν ἐνεργεῖν, συνδέων δὲ τοῖς Ἀρεικοῖς τὰ Ἀφροδίσια καὶ τὴν Ἡφαίστου τέχνην ἐν παραδείγματι προειληφέναι· πάντα γάρ ἐστιν αὐτὸς καὶ μετὰ πάντων ἐνεργεῖ τῶν θεῶν (In Rep. 1.143.3–11).

language of "secret doctrine" that resolves the problems inherent in the Homeric myth. Yet the myth itself, here reintroduced for the sake of clarifying its relationship to the doctrine, is superior to its exegesis. It, after all, is the inspired utterance. The interpreter, building on what Proclus took to be the technique of Plato, merely tries to establish its meaning and to demonstrate its truth, simultaneously fragmenting it and pointing beyond it to the "more unified" level of truth previous to it.

If Proclus's defense of Homer entirely ignores the colorful episodes of the middle books of the *Odyssey*, the reason is surely to be found in Socrates' indifference to them in his indictment. They were dear to the allegorists, as we have seen, and indeed their affinities with folktale and fairy tale make them particularly appropriate subjects for allegorical interpretation. However, when Proclus discusses the Sirens (the only myth in the series he treats in any detail), his approach has little to do with the simple moral allegories of the fables. The passage occurs in the commentary on the *Republic* during the discussion of the myth of Er, and it is only the necessity of explaining Plato's Sirens that leads Proclus back to those of Homer.

Proclus's demonstration proceeds systematically, building from a paraphrase of the passage in Homer. We may not simply identify the Sirens with the Muses, because there are only eight Sirens (in the myth of Er) and we have no right to meddle with the numbers (*In Rep.* 2.237.16–25). The fact that they are carried along with the rings of the model of the universe shown to Er in the other world is an indication that they are souls that stand over bodies (*In Rep.* 2.237.26–28). Returning to his understanding of the mythic distortion of reality, Proclus at this point depicts the "mythoplasts" as decidedly perverse: "If it were not a myth, it would say the rings were borne along by the Sirens, but since the mythoplasts love to turn things around, it says the Sirens are borne along by the rings." [267] That is, the Sirens are the souls, the life principles, that animate the spheres, rather than the reverse. The circular movement indicates affinities with mind, for (paraphrasing *Laws* 10.897c) "circular movement is an image of mind" [268] Their harmony indicates access to ἁρμονικοὶ λόγοι, which reside in νοῦς. The fact that each produces a single, unchanging tone is emblematic of the unified perception they direct toward τὰ ὄντα, contrasting as it does with our own fragmented perceptions,

267. καὶ εἰ μὴ μῦθος ἦν, εἶπεν ἂν ταῖς Σειρῆσιν τοὺς κύκλους συμπεριάγεσθαι· νῦν δὲ ὡς φιλοῦσιν οἱ μυθοπλάσται ποιεῖν, ἀνέστρεψε τὴν τάξιν καὶ τοῖς κύκλοις εἶπεν συμπεριφέρεσθαι τὰς Σειρῆνας (*In Rep.* 2.238.1–4).

268. νοῦ γὰρ εἰκὼν ἡ περιφορά (*In Rep.* 2.238.7).

and their unvarying harmony is related to their dance around the world-soul (*In Rep.* 2.238.9–20). This brings us finally to the relationship between these Sirens of Plato's and Homer's Sirens:

He called them "Sirens" to indicate that the harmony they impart to the rings is always bound to the material world, but he called them "celestial Sirens" in order to distinguish them from the Sirens within γένεσις, which he himself elsewhere agrees that Odysseus sailed past, as in Homer's story [*Phdr.* 259a]. These last Sirens, however, proceed from the dyad, for the poet uses the dual to refer to them as if there were two of them. These, however, proceed from the monad, for the one that presides over the circle of the One, the outermost circle, leads the rest. Thus it is entirely fitting that an appropriate quantity be spread below this dyad, and if the celestial monad is followed by seven, then the dyad that generates the universe of change must have twice seven, and often in the theologians the zones of heaven are said to be doubled in the sublunary zones. There are likewise Sirens in Hades, which he clearly mentions in the *Cratylus* [403d], saying that they will not leave Hades because they are bewitched by the wisdom of Pluto.

Thus there are three classes of Sirens by Plato's own account: the celestial ones belonging to Zeus; the ones that function in this world, belonging to Poseidon; and the chthonic ones belonging to Pluto. All three produce a physical harmony, tied to matter, for the Muses are specifically granted the noetic harmony. This is why they are said to conquer the Sirens and crown themselves with their feathers, for they draw the Sirens up into contact with them and fasten the Sirens' own unruly powers to their wisdom.[269]

269. Σειρῆνας μὲν οὖν αὐτὰς ἐκάλεσεν, ἵνα ἐνδείξηται τὴν ἁρμονίαν σωματοειδῆ πάντως οὖσαν, ἣν αὗται τοῖς κύκλοις ἐνδιδόασιν· οὐρανίας δὲ Σειρῆνας, ἵνα τῶν γενεσιουργῶν διακρίνῃ ταύτας Σειρήνων, ἃς δὴ καὶ αὐτὸς ἀλλαχοῦ συμβουλεύει κατὰ τὸν Ὁμηρικὸν ἐκεῖνον Ὀδυσσέα παραπλεῖν. ἀλλ' ἐκεῖναι μὲν ἀπὸ δυάδος ἄρχονται· λέγει γοῦν ὁ ποιητής·

φθογγὴν Σειρήνοιιν

ὡς ἂν δυεῖν οὔσαιν· αὗται δὲ ἀπὸ μονάδος· ἡ γὰρ τοῦ ἑνὸς κύκλου τοῦ ἐξωτάτου προηγεῖται τῆς ἑβδομάδος. ὥστε κἀκείνῃ τῇ δυάδι πλῆθος οἰκεῖον ὑπεστρῶσθαι πάντως εἰκός· καὶ εἰ τῇ οὐρανίᾳ μονάδι ἑβδομαδικόν, τῇ γενεσιουργῷ δυάδι πάντως δὶς ἑβδομαδικόν, οὕτω καὶ τῶν θεολόγων πολλαχοῦ τὰς οὐρανίας ζώνας διπλασιαζόντων ἐν τοῖς ὑπὸ σελήνην. εἰσὶ δὲ ἄρα τινὲς καὶ ἐν Ἅιδου Σειρῆνες, περὶ ὧν αὐτὸς εἶπεν ἐν Κρατύλῳ σαφῶς, ὡς οὐδὲ ἐκείναις ἀπολείπειν τὸν Ἅιδην φίλον, θελγομέναις ὑπὸ τῆς τοῦ Πλούτωνος σοφίας. ὥστε τριττὰ γένη κατ' αὐτὸν Σειρήνων· οὐρανία Διός, γενεσιουργὰ Ποσειδῶνος, ὑποχθόνια Πλούτωνος· κοινὸν δὲ πάντων τῶν γενῶν ἁρμονίαν ὑφιστάνειν σωματοειδῆ, τῶν Μουσῶν τὴν νοερὰν ἁρμονίαν μάλιστα δωρουμένων, διὸ καὶ κρατεῖν λέγονται τῶν Σειρήνων καὶ τοῖς πτεροῖς αὐτῶν στεφανοῦσθαι· καὶ γὰρ ἐκείνας ἀνάγουσιν ἑαυταῖς τε συνάπτουσιν, τὰς ἀναγωγοὺς αὐτῶν δυνάμεις ἐξάπτουσαι τῆς ἑαυτῶν νοήσεως

Though this text is not primarily concerned with the interpretation of Homer, it provides a valuable capsule history of the evolution of a Homeric image by way of Plato into an element in an essentially medieval model of the structure of the universe. Proclus's progression of concentric spheres, with their ever-increasing numbers of attendant souls, probably did, in fact, have a great influence on the development of medieval angelology. It seems certain that the author of the influential *Celestial Hierarchy* attributed to St. Dionysius the Areopagite and translated into Latin in the ninth century by John Scotus Eriugena, was in fact an Athenian Neoplatonist, and he may well have been a Christian student of Proclus himself.[270]

Proclus is thus a crucially important link between the spiritualized mythology of late antiquity, much of which he draws directly from Homer, with frequent reference to Plato, and the Christian mythology and iconography of the Latin West. His initial goal in the present passage is to elucidate Plato, though a point of agreement between Plato and Homer is always worthy of his notice. The synthesis he offers, as he emphasizes, draws all its data from passages in Plato himself. Examination of the Platonic passages does not increase one's confidence in Proclus's conclusions: the references to the Sirens, except for that in the myth of Er, are quite casual and have no more substance, no more reference to the subject at hand, than the references to bards in the *Odyssey* from which Proclus spins the myth of Homer's portraits of the various "levels" of poetry. Clearly, the focus of Proclus's attention lies far beyond the text, whether Homer or Plato is before him. He has convictions regarding the structure of the universe and its hierarchies of meticulously subdivided, mutually dependent entities that find illustration in virtually any authoritative text.

(*In Rep.* 2.238.21–239.14). Σειρῆνες seems here to be derived from εἴρω, "speak," and the point is thus that they make an actual, physical sound. Similar etymologies were known to Plutarch and Macrobius and may ultimately be traceable to Hesiod (*Theog.* 36–38) describing the Muses. Cf. ch. 1, n. 10, above and Pierre Boyancé, "Les Muses et l'harmonie des sphères," p. 14.

270. See Wallis, *Neoplatonism*, pp. 160–61, and ch. 6C below. This is not to join the group, scorned by Stephen Gersh (*From Iamblichus to Eriugena*, p. 10 and passim) who make Ps.-Dionysius "simply a Proclus baptized." The sources of the Dionysian corpus are complex and Gersh has made great strides in elucidating them. There is, however, no precedent for Ps.-Dionysius's interpretive efforts more obviously relevant than Proclus.

VI

The Transmission of
the Neoplatonists' Homer
to the Latin Middle Ages

A. THE PATHS OF TRANSMISSION

Up to this point, with the exception of a brief discussion of Prudentius, this study has been concerned exclusively with Greek literature and thought. In fact, much of what has been discussed has been of Italian origin, from the archaic Pythagoreanism of southern Italy to the teachings of Plotinus and Porphyry in Rome. Virtually all the material examined, however, has been Greek in language and tradition. Traces of the Platonized Homer can be found in Latin authors as early as Apuleius,[1] a contemporary of Numenius, but there is no single work in Latin that explores at length the conception of Homer we have been tracing.

The history of the mystical allegorical interpretation of Homer from Proclus to Eustathius, as well as of its place in Byzantine tradition, would require a special study of its own. Up to the present, little work has been done in this area.[2] The *Iliad* and *Odyssey* were found by the Byzantines to be Christian allegories, or at least to communicate allegorically truths compatible with Christian doctrine,[3] much as Virgil had been mustered

---

1. Cf. Apuleius *Met.* 9.13, where Homer is referred to as *priscae poeticae divinus auctor*, and the discussion of Odysseus and Athena (the latter taken as a representation of *prudentia*) at the end of *De deo Socratis* (24). Augustine mentions Apuleius as an interpreter of myth (*Civ. Dei* 9.7).

2. The most recent contributions are Agni Basilikopoulou-Ioannidou, Ἡ ἀναγέννησις τῶν γραμμάτων κατὰ τὸν ιβ´ αἰῶνα εἰς τὸ Βυζάντιον καὶ ὁ Ὅμηρος, esp. pp. 66–70, and a valuable survey in Robert Browning, "Homer in Byzantium."

3. Browning, "Homer in Byzantium," pp. 25–29.

to the Christian cause since the time of Constantine.[4] It is a premise of the present study, however, that the mystical allegorical interpretation of Homer has importance for the development not only of Byzantine culture but also, and from our perspective more significantly, for the development of Western European literature. Thus the Byzantine tradition of Christianizing Homeric allegory will interest us only in its earliest phases, those susceptible of transmission to the Latin West.

Traces of awareness of the mystical allegorical interpretation of Homer can be found in Western European literature from Dante to Blake. This study has proposed a model for the early development of allegorical literature in late antiquity that, if sound, extends the influence of this interpretive tradition far beyond those who had any knowledge of the ancient interpretive texts themselves.[5] Those influenced would include the writers of the Middle Ages and Renaissance who worked in a mode that owed its origin to the demands upon literature generated by the interpretive tradition. This, however, is a distant influence and difficult to trace.

Scholars have demonstrated links between the tradition of allegorical interpretation and the understanding of the Homeric poems in the English Renaissance under the influence of Chapman's *Odyssey*.[6] That influence was discontinuous, and one finds little trace of it during the eighteenth century,[7] but by the end of that century Thomas Taylor's translations were making available to the poets and intellectuals who were creating the Romantic movement in England not only the whole of Plato—translated into English for the first time—but a vast amount of Neoplatonic commentary, including Porphyry's essay on the cave of the

4. A Christian interpretation of *Eclogue* 4 appears in an oration of Constantine appended to Eusebius's *Life of Constantine*, along with a Greek translation of the eclogue.

5. See Preface and ch. 4 above.

6. See Lord, *Homeric Renaissance*. Lord describes the allegorical interpretation of Homer in Renaissance England as part of an "unbroken tradition extending 2,000 years back to classical times," (p. 35) and emphasizes Chapman's "'almost religious attitude'" (p. 39—the words are Donald Smalley's) toward Homer and his belief that "his highest duty as a translator [was] the revelation of Homer's concealed mysteries" (p. 40).

7. Even eighteenth-century critics "were intrigued by the fact that the tradition of antiquity, which was theirs as well, had seen Homer as a divinely inspired, omniscient poet" (K. Simonsuuri, *Homer's Original Genius*, p. 152). Nevertheless, after (and in spite of) Joshua Barnes's edition of 1711, the major eighteenth-century critics seem to have taken the sort of anti-allegorical, Enlightenment stance one might have expected with regard to the meaning of the text.

nymphs and part of Proclus's defense of Homer. The fact that Blake painted a representation of the Ithacan cave, based manifestly on Porphyry rather than Homer, suggests that the lesson was not ignored. One would like to know a great deal more about the relationship between the claims for Homer made in Porphyry's essay and Blake's conception of his own epic poetry.[8]

Such works as Georg Finsler's comprehensive history of the literary fortunes of Homer from Dante to Goethe (*Homer in der Neuzeit*) do little to trace this development, and it is clear that the *Odyssey* as read, for example, by Chapman, by Pope, by Blake, and by Joyce constitutes four quite different works of art.

It is far beyond the scope of the present study to examine all of the authors who have made use of Homer since the late Middle Ages to try to assess the level of influence of the mystical allegorical interpretive tradition upon them. In most of the cases mentioned—Chapman and Blake are the ones in point—the availability of at least some of the ancient interpretive texts we have examined can be demonstrated. The problem with regard to Dante is a far more difficult one. Dante lived in a culture ignorant of the *Iliad* and *Odyssey*. He did not know Greek, and no translation was available to him (*Convivio* 1.7). At the same time, however, he expressed his awe of Homer and elaborated on Homeric themes in the *Divina Commedia*. One source for this attitude can no doubt be found in the Latin literature available to Dante, and especially in Virgil. It is clear that though he had no direct knowledge of Homer's poetry, Dante had certain ideas about the nature of that poetry and of the goals and structure of meaning of epic poetry in general, which point to the influence of the tradition discussed in this study.

It is impossible to prove that Dante or his contemporaries supposed Homer to be the sort of poet Porphyry or Proclus thought him to be. It will be the purpose of this final chapter to indicate, however, that the conception of Homer articulated by Greek Neoplatonism was transmitted through influential authors who were read in the West at a time when Homer was not. It is generally accepted by scholars that the Plato known to the Middle Ages was a creation of the Middle Platonists and the Neo-

---

8. See Kathleen Raine, *Blake and Tradition*, esp. vol. 1, pp. 69–98. Raine's explanation of the iconography of the "Arlington Court Painting" served as a basis for tracing many elements of Blake's imagery back to Porphyry. Her explanation of the painting has not been universally accepted (see Martin Butlin, *The Paintings and Drawings of William Blake* [text], pp. 549–50, contra), but both her discussion of the iconography and her demonstration of links between Thomas Taylor and Blake seem quite convincing.

platonists, and that the "essential" Plato of the dialogues had to be rediscovered, beyond the Neoplatonists' intrusions, by the eighteenth century.[9] Very much the same thing may be said to have happened to Homer. The traditional master poet, no longer read, followed the path of the traditional sage and was submerged by his earlier readers and commentators. The evidence is meager but not without substance. If anything, the absence of a text of Homer would have aided the Latin Middle Ages to take with complete seriousness the testimony of Calcidius or Macrobius on the *kind* of meaning to be found in the *Iliad* and *Odyssey*. Our task, in any case, will be limited to an examination of that evidence and to the presentation of a model for the transmission of the Neoplatonists' understanding of the *Iliad* and *Odyssey* to the Latin West. Even to accomplish this will require excursions into bodies of literature far from the major expertise of the author, and therefore greater dependence on existing scholarship. Nevertheless, whatever gaps it contains, this survey represents an attempt to document a survival that remains marginal to the concerns of most intellectual and literary histories—the survival not of a text but of a reading.

The most important of the lines of transmission through which the ideas we have been discussing reached the West was the Latin tradition that extended directly from the influential authors of late antiquity to the major thinkers of the Middle Ages. But this was not the only path; two others command our attention as well. The model of transmission we shall follow is that formulated by Raymond Klibansky in his outline of the projected *corpus platonicum medii aevi*.[10] His "three main currents," the Arabic tradition, the Byzantine tradition, and the Latin tradition all contribute, if unequally, to the transmission of the "divine Homer"—a figure who, by late antiquity, had become part of the general baggage, not simply of Platonism (since Platonism no longer had any serious rivals), but of philosophy as a whole.

B. THE ARABIC TRADITION

Greek philosophy entered the Near Eastern tradition in two major waves, the first in the sixth century (following the closing of the philosophical

9. See E. N. Tigerstedt, *The Decline and Fall of the Neoplatonic Interpretation of Plato*, esp. pp. 7–12, and, on the influence of Porphyry, Pierre Courcelle, *Les Lettres grecques en occident de Macrobe à Cassiodore*, pp. 22–35 and 397–99.

10. Klibansky, *Continuity of the Platonic Tradition*.

schools by Justinian in 529 and doctrinal disputes within the church that later in the century drove the Nestorians and Monophysites of Edessa east to Persia), and the second from the eighth century to the tenth century, when the Alexandrian schools were revived in Baghdad and the central Platonic dialogues (including the *Timaeus* and the *Republic*) were translated into Arabic.[11] In the absence of translations of the *Iliad* and *Odyssey*, readers in this tradition must have been bewildered by Socrates' attacks on the epic poets and by the wealth of literary references in the dialogues. Aristotle reached the Arabs by way of the schools of Syria and intermediate Syriac translations in the eighth century. The *Organon* came first, and was relatively easily separable from the tradition of Greek literature, but by the early tenth century the *Poetics* had been translated and used by al-Fārābī.[12]

It should be no surprise that the Arab commentators tend simply to absorb from their philosophical sources traditional judgments of Greek poets, and to pass over in silence passages that demand a direct knowledge of Greek poetry. This is exactly what Avicenna does in his commentary on the *Poetics* (ca. 1020); he echoes Aristotle's praise of Homer and declares him the model encomiastic poet, avoiding references to the specifics of Greek poetry.[13] There is a similarity between the dim and garbled perceptions of Homer we find among the Arabs and those that penetrate the Latin West—a similarity that is simultaneously surprising and sobering. There is, of course, no reason why we should expect the *Iliad* and *Odyssey* to have taken root in Visigothic Spain or Ostrogothic Italy but not in the cultural centers of the Arab world, but to find on either side the same rudimentary perceptions based on the same incomprehension of Homer's language and the same inheritance of judgments and interpretations encysted in the philosophical authors is nevertheless a reminder that for nearly a thousand years the undying fame of Homer glimmered only faintly outside of Byzantium.

At the same time, however, a very special aura attached to that fame and to the name of Homer (or Ūmīrūs), an aura that was the product of the transformation of Homer brought to completion by the Neoplatonists. His name appears in lists of sages that include Hesiod, Pythagoras, and various ill-matched heroes and gods.[14] Although the first trans-

11. Ibid., p. 14.

12. F. E. Peters, *Aristoteles Arabus*, pp. 7–23, 28–30. On al-Fārābī, see also I. M. Dahiyat, *Avicenna's Commentary on the Poetics of Aristotle*, p. 4.

13. Dahiyat, *Avicenna's Commentary on the Poetics*, p. 76, n. 2, and p. 109, n. 1.

14. Franz Rosenthal, *Das Fortleben der Antike im Islam*, p. 57.

lation of the *Iliad* into Arabic would appear to have occurred only in 1904, there is evidence from the late Middle Ages for a Syriac version of "the two books of Ūmīrūs on the ancient conquest of the city of Īlyūn" prepared in the eighth century by Theophilus of Edessa, court astrologer of the Maronite Khalif al-Mahdi.[15] It is striking that it was thus within the Syrian Christian community, with its link to the Greek tradition by way of the Greek scriptures and the Church Fathers, that a need was felt to translate Homer into a Semitic language. The Arab translators of the period (who often worked from Syriac intermediaries) knew Homer in the original, but apparently felt no need to translate him into Arabic, beyond minor elaborations of Homeric texts found quoted in Greek philosophical authors, and even these quotations of Homer are frequently garbled, and eventually tend to be replaced by lines from Arab poets.[16]

Jörg Kraemer's survey of the fate of Homer in Islam notes a number of isolated survivals that bear along with them the baggage of the interpretive tradition. The eleventh-century writer on India al-Bīrūnī cites a supposedly Homeric verse on the harmony of the spheres. Whatever the lost connection between the passage quoted and Homer, one can clearly see Pythagoreanizing interpreters at work here. Another citation from the same author seems to be lifted from a commentary on Aratus and brings along a Stoicizing gloss as the opinion of the poet, interpreting Zeus as equivalent to spirit (ar-$rūḥ$ = $\pi\nu\epsilon\hat{\upsilon}\mu\alpha$) active in matter (al-hayūlā = $\H{\upsilon}\lambda\eta$).[17]

Among the varied shreds of the Greek tradition that the Arabs attributed to Homer, the most remarkable—and the most indicative of what must seem to us a chilling insensitivity to the range and richness of Greek literature—are the "Sayings of Menander" transmitted as excerpts from Homer. These were preserved independently in Greek, but other facile moral precepts and observations equally transmitted by Arabic collections as *dicta Homeri* are untraceable beyond the Arabic and resurface (without Homer's name) in medieval books of precepts.[18] Homer the Sage was clearly at home in Islam, and although the Arabs, in ignorance of the development of non-philosophical Greek literature, naively

15. Jörg Kraemer, "Arabische Homerverse," p. 261, with discussion. I am indebted to Kraemer for the bulk of the following material on Homer's fate in Islamic tradition. It is probable that these "two books" represented a work on the scale of the first-century *Ilias latina*.

16. Kraemer, "Arabische Homerverse," pp. 264, 287.

17. Ibid., pp. 275–79.

18. Ibid., pp. 290–302. On the *sententiae Menandri*, see also Manfred Ullmann, *Die arabische Überlieferung der sogenannten Menandersentenzen*.

incorporated into their "Homeric" corpus material from other poets and genres, the broad lines of the development of the figure of the visionary, allegorical poet remain the familiar ones. The principal difference would seem to lie in the Arabic tradition's greater willingness to go to the poets for moral precepts than for metaphysical or cosmological ones, a tendency that led them to create a Homer who was primarily a purveyor of instructions on how to live and not on the fate of souls and the structure of the universe.

The Arabic tradition, then, did not constitute an important path of communication between the Byzantine tradition and the Latin West for the "divine Homer," but our brief consideration of the Arabs here has revealed instead a pattern of cultural assimilation vividly analogous to that which emerged in Western Europe. The traditions of Homer the Sage in the Arab world and in the Latin West are siblings that have followed separate paths to such an extent that their common ancestry can only rarely be perceived.[19]

Although the translation of Greek philosophical works from Arabic into Latin, along with the creation of Latin versions of Arabic pseudepigrapha, constituted an influential channel for Greek ideas reentering the West in the late Middle Ages and Renaissance, the importance of these texts for the Neoplatonists' idea of Homer would appear to have been negligible. The Greek texts that entered the Latin tradition by way of the Arabs were translated into Latin for the most part during the late twelfth and early thirteenth centuries,[20] a date too late to be of much help to us. The importance for the Latin tradition of the Arabic transmission of Plato is only now receiving intensive study, and until the Plato Arabus project progresses further, it would be premature to predict what might be found in these texts to illuminate our inquiry. There are already tantalizing hints. Klibansky mentions the (unpublished) preface to al-Fārābī's paraphrase of the *Laws*, containing a discussion of "the theory of a discrepancy between the literal and the real meaning,"[21] and this raises the possibility that the Neoplatonists' theories of interpretation may in fact have gained some currency in the Latin West by way of the Arabs.

19. Kraemer, for example, traces both the Latin *Scholia Sangermanensia* on Aratus and those that are the source for al-Bīrūnī's citation of Homer back to a Greek commentary of the third century after Christ by one "Achilleus" ("Arabische Homerverse," p. 275).

20. Klibansky, *Continuity of the Platonic Tradition*, pp. 14–18, esp. 17, and 53–54.

21. Ibid., p. 16.

Moreover Averroes (in the twelfth century)[22] expresses a conviction that allegorical interpretation of theological narratives is necessary, though the work in question (*Fasl al-maqāl,* "The Decisive Treatise") was not translated into Latin along with his commentaries on Aristotle. Whatever hidden influence may lie here, it remains true that in the latter part of the twelfth century, the Latin West already knew about texts that were "screens" (παραπετάσματα in Proclus; *integumenta* or *involucra* in the interpretive vocabulary of the School of Chartres)[23] for hidden meanings. Whatever contributing elements may be found coming from the Arabs are unlikely to constitute more than a superfetation.

Mention should be made in this context, however, of the influence of two twelfth-century translations from the Arabic that swelled the Aristotelian corpus, the *Liber de pomo* and the *Liber de causis.* Both are pseudepigrapha of Arabic origin, the former a dialogue depicting Aristotle's last moments (and clearly an imitation of the *Phaedo*), the latter (also titled *De expositione bonitatis purae*) a discourse on causality and the structure of the universe, derived from Proclus.[24] Both of these works were probably known to Dante and will be mentioned later in that context, and neither mentions Homer or interpretation as such. Their importance here relates to the position of Aristotle in late medieval philosophy. If Aristotle is the "maestro di color che sanno" for Dante, that opinion (which comes to him through Aquinas) is at least in part inherited from the Arabs, who treated Aristotle somewhat in the same way they treated Homer. That is, Aristotle was taken as a model sage, the Greek philosopher par excellence, and much that was in fact non-Aristotelian (including material from Plotinus, Porphyry, and Proclus) was attributed to him.[25] In this form, and so attributed, it entered the Latin West, either in the late Middle Ages with the two books in question, or during the Renaissance with the *Theologia Aristotelis,* a compendium of Plotinian Neoplatonism. As Richard Walzer emphasizes, "The essential identity of Plato's and Aristotle's thought" was an idea "common to all the Muslim philosophers" and derived ultimately from the Neoplatonists' synthesis of Plato and

22. See Peter Dronke, *Fabula,* pp. 19–20, n. 3, to whom I owe this reference.

23. Winthrop Wetherbee, *Platonism and Poetry in the Twelfth Century,* pp. 38–49.

24. For the texts and translations, see "Works Cited: Ancient Authors" under Ps.-Aristotle.

25. Cf. Kraemer, "Arabische Homerverse," pp. 301–2 for the comparison of the Arabs' use of the two names.

Aristotle initiated by Porphyry,[26] but this situation was made considerably more complex by the naive attribution of a variety of extraneous texts and ideas to Aristotle himself.

If the Arabs can give us little of substance to add to our understanding of the transmission of the Neoplatonists' visionary Homer, they nevertheless set the stage for a period in which Aristotle could be imagined describing the contents of his *Metaphysics* as follows: "Blessed is the soul that is not infected with the corrupt works of this world and perceives its creator; this is the soul that returns to its home in great ecstasy."[27] This Aristotle also expounds a stratified model of the universe extending from the first cause beyond all speech by way of *intelligentia* and *anima* down to the level of *sensus* and the physical world (*Liber de causis*, ch. 11). The disguise was not impenetrable; Aquinas saw through it and realized that the *Liber de causis* was mistakenly attributed to Aristotle, and Dante himself may have done so as well. But for those of their respective contemporaries who did not, central ideas of pagan Neoplatonism constituted the consummation of "Aristotelian" philosophy, and the model of reality the Neoplatonists had found in Homer (and indeed wherever else they chose to look) could easily be attributed to Aristotle as well.

C. THE GREEK EAST

Thus far, the Greek pagan tradition of mystical allegorical interpretation of Homer has been traced as far as Proclus, late in the fifth century. Long before Proclus's time, however, the issue of the relationship of the epics to Christian *paideia* (to use Werner Jaeger's term) had commanded attention. It should be no surprise that Christians taught Homer to Christians in the schools of the fourth-century empire, nor should it be surprising that in doing so they made claims regarding the meaning of the text that were offensive to men such as Julian. It is impossible to generalize satisfactorily concerning the receptiveness of Christian intellectuals to Homer in this period. A wide range of attitudes toward pagan literature can

26. Richard Walzer, *Greek into Arabic*, p. 240.

27. "*Beata est anima, que non est infecta prauis operibus huius mundi et intellexit creatorem suum, et ipsa est, que revertitur in locum suum in deliciis magnis*" (*Liber de pomo*, 370–72).

be documented, ranging from general hostility or indifference, by way of the liberal, but reserved, receptiveness of Basil of Cappadocia,[28] to the eclectic allegorizing of Clement of Alexandria.

In his *Griechische Mythen in christlicher Deutung*, Hugo Rahner has brought together a substantial body of material on the assimilation of Homer to Christian thought. Perhaps the most striking revelation emerging from his historical survey is the early date at which an authoritative Homer is to be found in Christian sources. The claim that Homer had read Moses and the Prophets goes back at least to the contemporaries of Numenius, and the dependence of Homer on scripture is also asserted by Clement.[29]

Clement and Origen have already been discussed in their proper context, that of Middle Platonism. At this point it will be useful to look briefly at some of the Greek Christian thinkers who followed them, from the contemporaries of Porphyry to those of Proclus. The logic of this presentation, and of isolating this tradition of thought from its pagan counterpart, becomes clear as we proceed. By the fourth century, there was a manifest alienation of the two intellectual communities. Certainly the later Athenian Neoplatonists had Christian students, but little of their interaction is visible in the surviving literature, which documents a radical dichotomy of concerns and interests.

A century after Clement, an attitude closely comparable to his own may be found in the writings of Methodius of Olympus (d. 311).[30] Here again are the marks of the assimilation of an authoritative Homer and a fabricated connection between his poetry and the Hebrew scriptures; and here again Plato must stand as an authority alongside Homer (evoking the specter of the difficulties raised by Socrates in the *Republic*).[31] And

28. On Basil's essay on the Christian use of the Greek classics, see most recently the perceptive essay by Ernest L. Fortin, "Christianity and Hellenism in Basil the Great's Address *ad adulescentes*." I share with Fortin (p. 193 and n. 35) the sense that Hugo Rahner's chapter "Der heilige Homer" in his *Griechische Mythen in christlicher Deutung* gives a rather one-sidedly bright view of the early Church Fathers' attitudes toward Homer (see, for example, p. 284). I owe to Fortin as well the reference to V. Buchheit's article "Homer bei Methodios von Olympos," which, even if it does not develop the "critical evaluation of Rahner's thesis" Fortin claims (p. 35), nevertheless does document with care and a sense of balance the complexities of one early Christian writer's attitude toward Homer.

29. Rahner, *Griechische Mythen*, p. 243, n. 7. See Clem. *Strom.* 5.4.24.1 = GCS 2.340.25–28.

30. See Buchheit, "Homer bei Methodios von Olympos."

31. Ibid., p. 35.

yet the Homeric poems serve Methodius most strikingly as sources of warnings: the Christian will *not* desire to hear the Sirens' song in bondage, but to hear the voice of God in freedom. Such images and myths are ingeniously manipulated; the Hellenic myth "becomes a Christian one," with little retained of its pagan source beyond the prestige and power of Homer and his language.[32]

Hugo Rahner's survey of the "divine Homer" in early Christian thought contains many more examples of this sort of assimilation, but perhaps the most striking point is the extent to which the Homeric source of assimilated myth and imagery recedes into the background. Clement aside, the early Church Fathers rarely praise Homer directly, though they exploit his poetry freely. One striking exception is Basil (d. 379), whose famous address *On the Value of Greek Literature* constitutes the central evidence for the manner in which Homer was assimilated into Greek Christian education, not in Alexandria with its rich and sophisticated literary and philosophical tradition, but in remote and pious Cappadocia. Basil echoes Socrates' criticisms of Homeric myth (*Ad adules.* 4.15–28), incorporating the Christian monotheistic theme already heard in Clement. Yet he reports with approval the opinion that "the whole of Homer's poetry is praise of virtue" (*Ad adules.* 5.25–28), and it is primarily from the ethical point of view that he advocates the reading of Homer.

Ernest Fortin has recently offered an insightful analysis of Basil's methods and goals in this essay, and he is surely correct in pointing to Basil's duplicity.[33] The ostensible argument, as Fortin shows, is a red herring. Basil insists that the crucial issue in the use of pagan authors is selection of appropriate passages, but this is impractical and falls before Socrates' original attack. The young are unable to distinguish good from bad and the pagan texts would therefore have to be rejected entirely in order to protect the young from their pernicious passages and meanings. What Basil *does* accomplish here is subtly to create a predisposition in his readers to find just the sort of ethical message in pagan literature that has a place in Christian education as he understands it. "The risk involved in any contact with a pagan writer was neutralized by the superimposition of a Christian image which not only valorized certain elements at the expense of others but created the illusion of a greater kinship than actually existed between the poet's thought and the teaching of the Bible,"[34] For-

32. Ibid., pp. 20–23.
33. See n. 28 above.
34. Fortin, "Christianity and Hellenism," p. 195.

tin writes. The observation rings true and bespeaks a sensitivity to the relationship of reader and text common to both the ancient Neoplatonists and modern hermeneutics.[35]

This brief survey should not be cut short without mention of the thinker who is both the most important bridge between pagan Neoplatonism and Byzantine Christian thought and an equally important link between East and West—the author of the Dionysian corpus. The writings attributed to Dionysius the Areopagite, the patron saint of the Greek church, converted by Paul (Acts 17.34), have been variously dated from the time of Paul to the sixth century.[36] Since 1900, increased understanding of the dependence of the corpus on Syrianus and Proclus has led scholars to date it to the fifth or sixth century.[37] With regard to the interpretation of "theological" texts, the author not only uses the vocabulary of Proclus conspicuously and extensively—a fact noted by recent scholars[38]—but even appears to adapt specific interpretations derived from Syrianus by way of Proclus.

There is no mention of Homer, indeed no mention or citation of a single pagan author or reference to a mythological figure, in the entire corpus.[39] All but a handful of citations are from the scriptures, and even these are not numerous, given the bulk of the corpus. The visionary Homer will thus not be found here, but the hermeneutical principles lying behind that figure nevertheless have an important place.

Most of the surviving works attributed to Dionysius are concerned with negative theology and metaphysics, and this is sufficient to account for the author's relatively sparse use of texts in support of his arguments.[40] Our evidence for the author's concern with the meaning of texts

35. On prejudice and reading in modern hermeneutic philosophy, see Gadamer's discussion of Heidegger on the "fore-structure of understanding" (*Truth and Method*, pp. 235–40). Heidegger's and Gadamer's ideas on the subject provide a background against which the power of a technique such as Fortin ascribes to Basil may be understood. The passage is discussed below in the afterword.

36. The principal conjectures are helpfully presented in tabular form by Ronald F. Hathaway, *Hierarchy and the Definition of Order in the Letters of Pseudo-Dionysius*, pp. 31–35.

37. For a short summary of the Dionysian adaptation of the late pagan Neoplatonist model of reality to Christian thought, see I. P. Sheldon-Williams in CHLGEMP, pp. 457–72. Stephen Gersh (*From Iamblichus to Eriugena*) has recently made substantial advances in our understanding of the complex origins of Dionysius's thought.

38. Hathaway, *Hierarchy and the Definition of Order*, p. 109.

39. See Albert van den Daele, *Indices Pseudo-Dionysiani*, pp. 149–54.

40. For a brief summary of lost and surviving works, see J. D. Jones's introduction to *The Divine Names and Mystical Theology*, pp. 16–19.

comes principally from two sources, the fascinating Ninth Letter and *The Divine Names*. In the former, he refers to a work called *Symbolic Theology*, which he indicates contained his exegeses of many obscure symbols from "the Oracles" (τὰ λόγια, his consistent designation for the scriptures), beyond those related in the Ninth Letter itself. There is no reason, beyond this dubious claim, to assume that such a work ever existed,[41] but if it did it must have contained a great deal that would be of interest to us, and quite possibly a great deal of interpretive material closely dependent on Proclus and his tradition.

Dionysius carries over from late Athenian Neoplatonism the concept of multiple modes of representation of the divine. In *The Celestial Hierarchies* he builds on a concept of the symbol that echoes Proclus. Symbols (such as celestial eagles and wheels) do not imitate what they represent. They represent "through the *dissimilar*" (διὰ τὰ ἀνόμοια) and not "through the similar" (διὰ τὰ ὅμοια).[42] This is the normal mode of theological discourse, "to hide beneath secret and holy riddles, inaccessible to the masses, the sacred and hidden truth concerning the hypercosmic noetic entities."[43] The scriptures themselves constitute adaptations to our limited perceptions: "The divine discourse [θεολογία] has quite simply employed poetic divine fictions to designate the shapeless noetic entities, in consideration of what we may call the νοῦς in *us*, and in order to provide an appropriate and connatural uplifting for that νοῦς, has shaped the anagogical scriptures specifically for it."[44] By way of John Scotus Eriugena's translations of the Dionysian corpus, the term *symbolum* (σύμβολον) subsequently took on a central role in Western medieval thought.[45]

For the author of the corpus, the Hebrew Bible constitutes an authoritative theological source nearly as remote and problematical as the poems of Homer were for Proclus. His response to this problem closely parallels the approach of the pagan Athenian Neoplatonists. Like Proclus, the au-

41. Hathaway, *Hierarchy and the Definition of Order*, p. 151, n. 3.

42. *Hier. cel.* 2.3. Similar distinctions are sketched out in *Epistle* 8 and in *The Divine Names* (1.6). See Maurice de Gandillac's note on *Hier. cel.* 2.3 (*Sources chrétiennes*, no. 58, p. 77, n. 3).

43. τὸ δι᾽ ἀπορρήτων καὶ ἱερῶν αἰνιγμάτων ἀποκρύπτεσθαι καὶ ἄβατον τοῖς πολλοῖς τιθέναι τὴν ἱερὰν καὶ κρυφίαν τῶν ὑπερκοσμίων νόων ἀλήθειαν (*Hier. cel.* 2.2 [140a–b]).

44. καὶ γὰρ ἀτεχνῶς ἡ θεολογία ταῖς ποιητικαῖς ἱεροπλαστίαις ἐπὶ τῶν ἀσχηματίστων νόων ἐχρήσατο τὸν καθ᾽ ἡμᾶς ὡς εἴρηται νοῦν ἀνασκεψαμένη καὶ τῆς οἰκείας αὐτῷ καὶ συμφυοῦς ἀναγωγῆς προνοήσασα καὶ πρὸς αὐτὸν ἀναπλάσασα τὰς ἀναγωγικὰς ἱερογραφίας (*Hier. cel.* 2.2 [137a–b]).

45. Dronke, *Fabula*, p. 44.

thor lives in a world of παραπετάσματα, simultaneously masking and (to the initiate) revealing the divine,[46] and the most striking and disorienting of the mythic attributes of the divine are explicitly the most valuable, because they stimulate the search for truth.[47]

Ps.-Dionysius's list of shocking attributes of God from the Hebrew Bible is indeed rather surprising even to our jaded perceptions. "The Oracles" tell us, according to our author, that God gets drunk, sleeps, wakes up with hangovers, and is subject to malicious rage (though not necessarily in that order).[48] The passages in question, many of them in Psalms, are duly singled out for us either by Maximus the Confessor in his scholia to the *Letters* or by more recent editors, and the information is assembled in Ronald Hathaway's recent edition, though in many instances other equally appropriate passages could be found.

Since there is nothing Homeric here, a single example will suffice, one that clearly seems to echo Proclus. Like Philo before them, both Proclus and the author of the Dionysian corpus are greatly disturbed by claims of alterations of the state of consciousness of the divinity. Sleep or cessation of consciousness creates obvious problems. We have seen how Proclus explained away Zeus's slumber after his intercourse with Hera. Sleep was said to be appropriate "to the symbolism" of the Homeric myth because "the waking state indicates the providence of the gods projecting into the cosmos and the sleep, that life that transcends all lower things."[49] The passage to which "Dionysius" refers in this context is (at least according to the nineteenth-century editor John Parker) Ps. 44 (43).23:

Bestir thyself, Lord; why dost thou sleep?
Awake, do not reject us forever.

Or in the Septuagint:

ἐξεγέρθητι· ἵνα τί ὑπνοῖς, κύριε;
ἀνάστηθι καὶ μὴ ἀπώσῃ εἰς τέλος.[50]

46. *Hier. cel.* 121b, *Hier. eccl.* 476b, *Nom. div.* 592b, *Ep.* 8.1098a, *Ep.* 9.1108b.
47. *Hier. cel.* 141a–144c, and esp. 141a–b. Compare Proclus *In Rep.* 1.85.16–86.10. See Hathaway, *Hierarchy and the Definition of Order*, p. 109 and n. 86.
48. *Ep.* 9.1105b.
49. τῆς μὲν ἐγρηγόρσεως τὴν εἰς τὸν κόσμον πρόνοιαν τῶν θεῶν δηλούσης, τοῦ δὲ ὕπνου τὴν χωριστὴν ἀπάντων τῶν καταδεεστέρων ζωήν (*In Rep.* 1.135.19–21).
50. Equally appropriate would be Parker's candidate for the verse on God's hangover, Ps. 78 (77).65.

Seen in context, the claim is less shocking, the anthropomorphism easily understood in terms of the conventions of the poetry of Psalms. Ps.-Dionysius, however, approaches the passage in the spirit—very nearly in the words—of Proclus on the sleep of Zeus: "We say, the divine sleep is the transcendence of God and his freedom from participation on the part of the objects of his providence, his awakening his attention to his providence for those in need of teaching or salvation."[51] "Transcendence" (τὸ ἐξῃρημένον), a characteristically Neoplatonic term central to the explanation of God's sleep here, likewise occurs in the corresponding passage in Proclus, just beyond the lines quoted.[52] This is by no means the only Dionysian interpretation that echoes Proclus. Anne Sheppard notes that in *The Celestial Hierarchies* (15.9), Ps.-Dionysius interprets the rejoicing of the angels (Luke 15.10) much the way Proclus explains the laughter of the providential gods.[53]

The Dionysian corpus was translated into Latin during the ninth century, first by Hilduin and then again a generation later by John Scotus Eriugena. The impact of this infusion of the final form of pagan Neoplatonism into Western medieval thought was very great. Although Eriugena's writings were condemned in part in his own time and his *De divisione naturae*, or *Periphyseon*, heavily influenced by Proclus, was burned on the order of Honorius III in 1225, the influence of the Dionysian corpus remained strong, surfacing most conspicuously in the Platonism of the School of Chartres.[54]

The final expression of the Athenian Platonists thus came to the West in Christian guise. It did not bring the divine Homer with it—indeed the total absence of references to pagan authors in the Dionysian corpus is striking and puzzling, so much so that one might suspect that the author is here deliberately suppressing all reference to paganism, for whatever reason.[55] But it did bring with it the hermeneutics, and even some of the

51. [καὶ ὅταν] φῶμεν, θεῖον ὕπνον εἶναι τὸ ἐξῃρημένον τοῦ θεοῦ καὶ ἀκοινώτητον ἀπὸ τῶν προνοουμένων· ἐγρήγορσιν δὲ, τὴν εἰς τὸ προνοεῖν αὐτοῦ τῶν παιδείας ἢ σωτηρίας δεομένων προσοχήν, [ἐπ᾽ ἄλλα θεολογικὰ σύμβολα μετελεύσῃ] (Ps.-Dion. *Ep.* 9.1113a–b).

52. Proclus *In Rep.* 1.135.27.

53. Sheppard, *Studies*, p. 82, n. 98.

54. On the enduring impact of Eriugena's own works after 1225, cf. Jean Jolivet ("La Philosophie médiévale en occident," p. 1259), who considers the condemnation to put an end to his direct influence, but contrast the position of Sheldon-Williams (CHLGEMP, p. 533), who insists on the continuing influence of the condemned books. Dronke notes that Abelard, accused of following Eriugena, never mentions his name: "clearly it was unsafe to do so" (*Fabula*, p. 60).

55. Cf. Hathaway, *Hierarchy and the Definition of Order*, pp. xiii, xvii, for the

interpretations, of Proclus and the idea of texts (and the world) as παρα-πετάσματα whose mysterious symbols reveal truth only to the elect.

We may take note of one last phenomenon in the Byzantine East, a link to the Christianizing allegorical commentaries of the later Byzantine scholars of the eleventh and twelfth centuries. In his *Fragmente griechischer Theosophien*, Hartmut Erbse published a short text ultimately dependent on the "Tübingen Theosophy" (which itself belongs to the last quarter of the fifth century) entitled *The Narrative of a Philosopher Concerning the Seven Greek Philosophers on the Providence Above*,[56] in which an oracular text, elsewhere attributed to the Sibyl, is put in the mouth of Homer. The seven philosophers (Plutarch, "Ares," ὁ Δῶν ὁ τρισμέγιστος, "Cleomedes," Plato, Aristotle, and Homer) sit down with Diogenes, who expresses concern for the fate of the Greeks and what the "higher providence" has in store for them when the end comes (ἐν ἐσχάτοις καιροῖς). Christian prophecies are placed in the mouth of each "philosopher," concluding with Homer:

> Last of all, Homer said, "At last shall come to us the Lord of the celestial sphere of the world, and he shall appear as flesh without imperfection. And he will take on flesh out of a Jewish virgin, and they shall call him "Forgiveness" and "Exultation." And he shall be crucified by the faithless race of Jews. And blessed shall be those who hear him—and woe to those who do not hear."[57]

As we see, the incorporation of Homer into a Christian context has a sordid side. That Homer should foretell the coming of Christ is a predictable (if absurd) consequence of the patterns of thought we have been tracing, but to find Homer here the spokesman of an antisemitism elabo-

---

suggestion that the Dionysian corpus might represent a deliberate masquerade—a Christianization (or more properly a depaganization) of the teachings of the Athenian Platonists accomplished near 529, when the future of this philosophical tradition could be seen to depend on dissociating it from the pagan ideology so central to its development down through the great synthesis of Proclus. The complete elimination of *all* references to pagan thinkers and poets from this corpus, which otherwise shares so much with the works of Proclus, might be considered another piece of circumstantial evidence pointing toward such a genesis for the Dionysian corpus.

56. Hartmut Erbse, ed., *Fragmente griechischer Theosophien*, pp. 220–22.

57. τέλος δὲ πάντων Ὅμηρος εἶπεν· ἥξει πρὸς ἡμᾶς ὀψὲ γῆς ἄναξ πόλου καὶ σὰρξ φανεῖται δίχα τινὸς σφάλματος· καὶ λαμβάνει σάρκα ἀπὸ Ἐβραΐδος παρθένου· καὶ καλέσουσιν αὐτὸν ἄφεσιν καὶ ἀγαλλίασιν· καὶ σταυρωθήσεται ἀπὸ ἀπίστου γένους τῶν Ἐβραίων. καὶ μακάριοι οἱ ἀκούοντες αὐτοῦ. οὐαὶ δέ, οἱ μὴ ἀκούοντες (*Frag. gr. theos.*, pp. 221–22).

rated out of Johannine themes is nevertheless chilling. It may in fact communicate even to readers such as ourselves some sense of Julian's rage at the abuses of Christian interpretation and Christian assimilation of the Greek tradition as authority for a repellent ideology.

D. THE LATIN TRADITION

The loss of Greek in Italy was gradual. The language was naturally limited, even during the period of its greatest currency during the late Republic and early Empire, to the well-educated, and hence to the relatively affluent, and the radical changes in the social and economic order during the fourth century greatly depleted the potential audience for Greek literature in the West.

The Latin authors of greatest importance for the development of Platonism in late antiquity were Cornelius Labeo (mid third century), Calcidius, Marius Victorinus, and Vettius Agorius Praetextatus (probably all fourth century), Macrobius (whose commentary on Scipio's dream dates from about 430),[58] Favonius Eulogius and Martianus Capella (also fifth century), and finally Boethius (d. 524 or 525).[59] With these should be included St. Augustine of Hippo (d. 430), whose debts to Neoplatonism were very great.

None of these authors is explicitly concerned with expounding the meaning of the *Iliad* and *Odyssey*. Few of them had extensive direct personal knowledge of the text of Homer, and their references to Homer are sparse and largely at second hand. This in itself does not lessen their value as testimony to the transmission of the conception of the meaning of the poems we have been exploring. The process we see at work in these authors is one that was to influence the understanding of Homer throughout the Middle Ages. The text became progressively less accessible, and the meagre remains of the Greek philosophical tradition through which it filtered shaped conceptions of the sort of poet Homer was.

Of the earliest of the thinkers listed, Cornelius Labeo, there is little to

58. This is the recent dating of Alan Cameron, "The Date and Identity of Macrobius," somewhat reluctantly accepted by Jacques Flamant, *Macrobe et le néoplatonisme latin à la fin du iv* siècle, p. 140, over the earlier date (ca. 400) accepted by, for example, Karl Praechter, *Die Philosophie des Altertums*, pp. 651–52.

59. The basis for this list is the treatment of Latin Neoplatonism in Praechter, *Philosophie des Altertums*, pp. 647–55.

say.[60] He was apparently contemporary with Porphyry, to whom Wissowa compared him for his antiquarian interests.[61] His work survives only in references and citations in such authors as Arnobius, Macrobius, Augustine, Servius, and John Lydus. The references in Lydus's *De mensibus* are characteristic. He is cited as a source for a list of thirty names for Aphrodite (*De mens.* 1.21) and for accounts of various calendar customs (*De mens.* 3.10) including etymological explanations of month names (*De mens.* 3.1.25). Many of the subjects that interested him, including the problem of good and bad *numina*, that of whether intermediate beings should be called δαίμονες or ἄγγελοι, and an apparent desire to find a place for the God of the Old Testament in the Olympian system,[62] suggest that, like Porphyry, he may have been tapping a milieu such as that of the second-century Pythagoreans Numenius and Cronius. We cannot say with certainty whether he wrote of Homer, but in view of his other interests the probability that he did seems quite high. Although we cannot demonstrate it, the possibility remains that he may have passed on some elements of the allegorized Homer.

Calcidius offers us something rather more substantial to work on, with nine references to Homer and two to Hesiod.[63] Although Calcidius

60. Along with the articles in P-W ("Cornelius [168] Labeo," P-W 4 [1901]:1351–55) and Real. Ant. Chr. ("Cornelius Labeo," vol. 3, cols. 429–37), the basic source on Cornelius Labeo remained W. Kahl, "Cornelius Labeo," until the recent appearance of a comprehensive study by Paolo Mastandrea, *Un Neoplatonico latino, Cornelio Labeone* (cf. on allegorical interpretation, pp. 181–82).

61. P-W 4 (1901):1352.

62. See Macrob. *Sat.* 1.18.21–22.

63. This total is calculated on the basis of a concordance of the *index nominum* and *index locorum* of Waszink's edition with the *index auctorum* of Wrobel (see "Works Cited: Ancient Authors" under Calcidius). Since some of the references and citations are clustered, it would perhaps be more accurate to say that of the 355 sections of Calcidius's commentary, 11 either (a) mention Homer, (b) cite the *Iliad* or *Odyssey*, or (c) both refer to Homer and quote him. The Hesiodic references (Calc. *In Tim.* 123, 134) need not concern us. They relate, respectively, to the status of earth (*terra*) in the created universe and to demonology. Hesiod is credited with the assertion that there are 30,000 δαίμονες. Likewise, one of the references to Homer (Calc. *In Tim.* 254) is by way of the *Crito* (44b), and the ultimate Homeric source is incidental (though the fact that the divine nocturnal apparition to Socrates quotes Homer had doubtless a richer meaning for Calcidius and his readers than it had for Plato and his contemporaries). Finally, the reference to Thetis's prophecy to Achilles (*Il.* 18.95–96, Calc. *In Tim.* 154) to support the Platonic denial of divine responsibility and assertion of the importance of human choice (*Rep.* 617c), though it does use Homeric myth as a basis on which to illustrate a truth regarding the relations between the human and the divine, stops short of asserting the theological authority of the epics.

almost certainly wrote after the time of Porphyry, he shows little influence from Plotinian Neoplatonism.[64] Rather, his sources are to be sought among the Middle Platonists and, beyond them, in the Platonizing Stoic Posidonius.[65] More important than his sources, however, is his influence, which was perhaps greater than that of any other Latin Platonist. His version of the *Timaeus* was the only dialogue of Plato's known in Latin translation until the *Phaedo* and *Meno* were added to the list during the twelfth century,[66] and the commentary attached to that translation no doubt profoundly influenced the understanding of the meaning of Plato and of his relationship to the rest of Greek culture that was transmitted to the Latin West. His *Timaeus* may have been read by Augustine, though it appears probable that the latter used the now only partially preserved Ciceronian translation.[67]

In his commentary on the *Timaeus*, Calcidius turns not infrequently to Homer for support for his assertions. These references do not tell us anything about his understanding of the meaning of the passages in question, but they do make it clear that he considered Homer to be both a touchstone to test the validity of statements about reality and an authoritative theologian. Some of these references and citations recall the method of the Ps.-Plutarch essay on the life and poetry of Homer. In support of the claim that the faculty of vision is superior to that of hearing, Calcidius quotes several Homeric lines (*Il.* 3.217 and 12.466) demonstrating that the poet uses descriptions of the eyes to communicate truths regarding the *mens atque animus* of the individual.[68] The Platonic tripartite division of the soul, asserted as a Homeric doctrine by Ps.-Plutarch,[69] likewise appears in Calcidius and is illustrated by one of the Homeric passages also used in the same context by the author of "The Life and Poetry of Homer."[70] For Ps.-Plutarch, Odysseus addressing his heart and counseling patience during the period of his humiliation in his own palace represents the victory of the rational part of his soul (τὸ λογικόν) over the passionate part (τὸ θυμικόν, or simply ὁ θυμός), and in Calcidius these lines illustrate the victory of *ratio* over *iracundia*.[71] Equally striking

64. Wallis, *Neoplatonism*, p. 166.

65. Praechter, *Philosophie des Altertums*, p. 649.

66. Klibansky, *Continuity of the Platonic Tradition*, pp. 22–29, and esp. p. 27, and Wallis, *Neoplatonism*, p. 166.

67. Courcelle, *Les Lettres grecques en occident*, p. 157.

68. Calc. *In Tim.* 266.

69. Ps.-Plut. *De vit. Hom.* 129–31.

70. *Od.* 20.18; see Calc. *In Tim.* 183 and Ps.-Plut. *De vit. Hom.* 129.

71. The contrasting citation, illustrating the victory of *iracundia* over *ratio*, is

as a demonstration of the connection between Calcidius and the Ps.-Plutarch essay is the claim that Homer shared the doctrine of Thales that the first principle was water:

> And Homer is seen to be of the same opinion when he calls Oceanus and Tethys the parents of γένεσις and when he makes the oath of the gods to be water, which he calls "Styx," attributing this reverence to the ancients and considering nothing more revered than that which is sworn by.[72]

This similarity, however, may simply reflect the ultimate dependence of both passages on Aristotle[73] or some other commentator.[74] A very similar point is made, though ironically, in the *Theaetetus*, where Socrates claims that the verses on Oceanus and Tethys (*Il.* 14.201, 302) were Homer's way of saying "that all things are born of streaming and movement."[75] Socrates is probably parodying Theaetetus's teachers here, and seems to be supporting Heraclitus rather than Thales by the Homeric reference, but it remains likely that Calcidius had in mind what he doubtless took for a Platonic/Socratic confirmation that the lines were to be read as a cosmological allegory. This likelihood is strengthened by his use of another allegory from the *Theaetetus* (*In Tim.* 328, echoing *Theaet.* 149c), this time based in etymology. In this passage, Calcidius explicitly cites the *Theaetetus* in claiming Homeric authority for the concept of the "wax in the soul" (κῆρ/κηρός), the central metaphor developed in Socrates' account of perception in that dialogue.

Likewise, in the discussion of the concentric spheres of the universe (Plato *Tim.* 36b–d), the rather puzzling assertion that the outer sphere, that of the fixed stars, is rotated "on the side on the right" (κατὰ πλευρὰν ἐπὶ δεξιὰ περιήγαγεν, Plato *Tim.* 36c6) is explained by reference to *Il.* 12.239,

---

from Euripides' *Medea*. It is difficult to say whether this is an indication that Homer is here classed with less obviously "theological" literature such as fifth-century drama, or that Euripides, in Calcidius's mind, is a potential source of truth as well.

72. *Inque eadem sententia Homerus esse invenitur, cum Oceanum et Tethyn dicat parentes esse geniturae, cumque iusiurandum deorum constituat aquam, quam quidem ipse adpellat Stygem, antiquitati tribuens reuerentiam et iureiurando nihil constituens reuerentius* (Calc. *In Tim.* 280). Cf. Ps.-Plut. *De vit. Hom.* 93 and scholia *ad loc.*

73. Arist. *Metaph.* A 983b. See Buffière, *Mythes d'Homère*, p. 87.

74. Cf. Buffière in his edition of Heraclitus's *Homeric Allegories*, p. 26, n. 8 (p. 101) for a list of sources for this commonplace.

75. πάντα . . . ἔκγονα ῥοῆς τε καὶ κινήσεως (Plato *Theaet.* 152e).

dexter ad eoum volitans solemque diemque

[. . . ἐπὶ δεξί' ἴωσι πρὸς ἠῶ τ' ἠέλιόν τε],

which is apparently intended to give Homeric authority to the identification of the east with the right and the source of the apparent movement of the "fixed stars" (*In Tim.* 93).[76]

Thus Calcidius carries on the eclectic tradition, represented in Ps.-Plutarch, in Heraclitus, and elsewhere, that saw in Homer a traditional source of wisdom anticipating later philosophical developments. Like Numenius, however, Calcidius includes astrology among the important sources of wisdom and finds in Homer allegorical structures masking information about the stars.

Calcidius finds in the *Timaeus* the doctrine that, although stars do not produce events in this world, they do foretell them.[77] The doctrine is likewise shown to be Homeric because the "seer Homer" (*vates Homerus*) indicates it in his description of the Dog Star:

iste quidem clarus sed tristia fata minatur.

[λαμπρότατος μὲν ὅ γ' ἐστί, κακὸν δέ τε σῆμα τέτυκται.]
(*Il.* 22.30)

The comparative material, including the observation that the Egyptians call the same star Sothis, suggests a possible Numenian source,[78] though there is no confirmation of this in the text and Calcidius does not hesitate elsewhere to cite Numenius by name.[79] Thus far the astrological wisdom attributed to Homer seems reasonable enough, and it would be difficult to deny that Homer does include some sort of astrology among the modes of divination. The distance between the sort of statements actually present and those Calcidius finds in Homer comes out, however, in the subsequent chapter of the commentary. There we are told that the Egyptians had a star—a god, naturally enough, because here the context is the dis-

76. On this passage and its interpretation, see Taylor's note *ad loc.* (*Commentary on Plato's Timaeus*, pp. 150–52).

77. Calc. *In Tim.* 125. Note the textual problem at *Tim.* 40d1 that permits this conclusion by Calcidius. The manuscript tradition is divided on whether the stars send signs of things to come "to those unable to calculate [their movements]" (τοῖς οὐ δυναμένοις λογίζεσθαι, so Burnet) or simply τοῖς δυναμένοις λογίζεσθαι with no negative particle, as translated by Calcidius: *qui de his rebus ratiocinari possunt.*

78. Cf. Numenius fr. 31 = Porph. *De ant.* 21–24.

79. E.g., Calc. *In Tim.* 295–99.

cussion of the stars of the *Timaeus* that are explicitly gods (Plato *Tim.* 40d)—named Ach, that appeared only in certain years and portended great sickness and death:

> Homer, moreover, who was an Egyptian (since he is said to have been Theban and so from the noblest city of the Egyptians) secretly designated this very star when, in the opening of the *Iliad*, he attributed the sickness and destruction not only of the heroes but of all the animals and cattle necessary for war to the "wrath of *Ach*illes," whose father was Peleus, but whose mother was a sea-goddess. Starting from this beginning, he fashioned the rest by poetic license.[80]

The scholia and commentators introduce astrological allegories,[81] but the present one is exceptionally farfetched, as well as far-reaching in its implications. The class of literature in which Calcidius places this strange allegorical epic is illustrated by an immediate parallel, the ostensible purpose of which is to show that the exceptional rising of a star can portend extraordinary good as well as extraordinary evil. We are told that "another holier and more venerable story" (*alia sanctior et venerabilior historia*) made a star the precursor of the descent of God to redeem mankind and led the Magi to him (*In Tim.* 126).[82]

Another reference, bearing not upon a passage in the epics but simply on the cliché "Homer is a divine poet," is particularly interesting, though it does not attribute any special knowledge or surprising intentions to the poet. Calcidius is arguing against those thinkers who follow Heraclitus and deny the reality of the past and future (*In Tim.* 106). The past, he claims, exists "in that the mind perceives that it happened" (*ut intellegatur fuisse*), just as we say "Homer *is* a divine poet" (*ut cum Homerum esse dicimus divinum poetam*). The example is an ingenious one and the slightly unusual but easily understood use of the present infinitive makes the point extremely well. Any statement about Homer clearly refers to the very remote past. Still, by virtue of received tradition (both

---

80. *Homerus denique, qui idem fuerit Aegyptius, siquidem Thebanus fertur, quae ciuitas est apud Aegyptum nobilissima, ad ipsum latenter exequitur in Iliadis exordio, cum dicit propter iram Achillis, cuius pater Peleus, mater vero maritima fuerit dea, morbum atque interitum non modo clarorum virorum, sed aliorum quoque animalium et pecorum bello necessariorum extitisse. Quo quidem sumpto exordio cetera poëtica licentia finxit* (Calc. *In Tim.* 126).

81. See Buffière, *Mythes d'Homère*, pp. 593–94, for a selection of astrological commentaries.

82. This reference to the New Testament is unique in Calcidius's commentary, but it is nevertheless probable that the author was a Christian. See, on this subject, Waszink in the preface to his edition, pp. xi–xii.

oral and written) the cliché retains its truth and thus testifies to the reality of the past as something more substantial than the unknowable "downstream" of Heraclitus's famous image. As far as the cliché itself is concerned, Calcidius may be assumed to understand it as his other references to Homer suggest: Homer is "divine" in constituting an authoritative source of information about the human and the divine, and this information is regularly cloaked in allegory requiring explanation.

The final Calcidian reference to Homer is in many ways the most interesting because it makes explicit both the context in which Calcidius placed Homer and the tradition of interpretation that fed into the *Timaeus* commentary:

> If the world is made of matter, then surely it was made of some previously existing evil substance. For this reason Numenius praises Heraclitus of Ephesus for rebuking Homer, since the latter desired the destruction and end of the evil that afflicts life, not realizing that what would please him would be the destruction of the world, because it would entail the destruction of matter, which is the source of evil.[83]

The exact reference in Homer could be any of several.[84] The impulse to expel evil from the world is, in any case, a commonplace, and Homer represents only a conspicuous and monumental statement of frustration and bitterness at the distance between what we can imagine our existence might be and what it is. Homer's assertion, however, as reflected in Calcidius's borrowed reference, takes on the force of a philosophical statement, subject to refutation. It furthermore demonstrates that Calcidius's Homer—and beyond that, Numenius's Homer—was authoritative but not infallible.

The Numenian source is explicit here, and much of the chapter in question, "On Matter" (*In Tim.* 248–355), is paraphrased from Numenius. There is a distinct possibility, moreover, that there is an intermediate source to be found for much of this material in Porphyry, either in the now fragmentary *Timaeus* commentary or in the lost treatise "On Matter" (Περὶ ὕλης).[85] There is, as already mentioned, little trace of Plo-

83. *Quod si mundus ex silua, certe factus est de existente olim natura maligna. proptereaque Numenius laudat Heraclitum reprehendentem Homerum, qui optauerit interitum ac uastitatem malis vitae, quod non intellegeret mundum sibi delere placere, siquidem silua, quae malorum fons est, exterminaretur* (Calc. *In Tim.* 297).

84. Cf. J. C. M. van Winden, *Chalcidius on Matter*, p. 113 and n. 1 and Des Places in his edition of Numenius (on fr. 52), p. 97, n. 9.

85. Van Winden, *Chalcidius on Matter*, p. 247.

tinian Neoplatonism in Calcidius, but Porphyry was deeply influenced by Numenius and commonly went directly to him, circumventing Plotinus, in commenting on a text. Although Calcidius's dependence on Porphyry remains conjectural and is by no means universally recognized,[86] it nevertheless raises the possibility that we have in Calcidius yet another example of the chain of transmission running from Numenius to Porphyry to the Latin Middle Ages, comparable to that which transmitted the cave of the nymphs allegory to Macrobius and beyond.[87]

The next figures of interest to us—Marius Victorinus, Augustine, Vettius Agorius Praetextatus, and Macrobius—are all associated with the pagan revival of the late fourth century and the Christian reaction against that revival.[88] We may look first at the contributions of the two Christians.

Marius Victorinus is remembered primarily as a Christian theologian and his intense interest in pagan philosophy predates the period of the revival, properly speaking, which may be taken to belong to the period between midcentury and 394. He was converted to Christianity in extreme old age between 353 and 357.[89] We may pass him by with only brief mention because there is little evidence that he was important in the developments under consideration. His major importance lies in his Latin translations of Greek philosophers and particularly in his influence on Augustine.[90] He translated Porphyry's *Introduction to the Categories of Aristotle* and certain "Platonic books" read by Augustine, variously said to have been selections from the *Enneads* or possibly Porphyry's *De regressu animae*.[91] His influence extends beyond Augustine to Boethius, Cassiodorus, and Isidore, and through all of these to the Latin Middle Ages.

86. Dillon (*Middle Platonists*, p. 403) insists that "none of the alleged dependences on Porphyry . . . involve any compelling verbal or doctrinal similarity."

87. See Appendix 4.

88. See Herbert Bloch, "The Pagan Revival in the West at the End of the Fourth Century." Even accepting the very attractive suggestion of Alan Cameron ("Date and Identity of Macrobius," pp. 37–38), that Macrobius is glorifying the generation of Symmachus at a distance of half a century, the *Saturnalia* still issued, however indirectly, from that milieu and attempts to represent its values. On the milieu in general, see the recent comprehensive study by J. Wytzes, *Der letzte Kampf des Heidentums in Rom*.

89. Cf. KP s.v. Marius Victorinus and Markus in CHLGEMP, pp. 331–40.

90. See August. *Conf.* 8.2. On Victorinus's use of Porphyry and Numenius, see Mary T. Clark, "The Neoplatonism of Marius Victorinus the Christian."

91. For a summary of the scholarly debate on the identification of the *libri Platonicorum* translated by Victorinus, see J. J. O'Meara, "Augustine and Neoplatonism," pp. 91–101.

His surviving works, however, which are either rhetorical or theological, indicate no concern with the meaning of early poetry. We must nevertheless consider it probable that he provided the bridge by which Porphyrian Neoplatonic allegory of myth and ritual reached Augustine.

Although St. Augustine was unable to read Greek with ease and depended almost entirely on Latin sources,[92] his enormous influence during the Latin Middle Ages justifies some comments on his references to Homer. The influence of Plotinus and Porphyry on Augustine by way of the translations of Marius Victorinus was substantial.[93] His ideas on interpretation, however, clearly owe more to Christian tradition than to the pagan Neoplatonists, and he normally addresses himself only to biblical texts.[94] In one curious passage, however, he applies an allegorical interpretation to a passage from a pagan author. In discussing the claim in the Hermetic dialogue *Asclepius* (24) that Egypt was to become "full of tombs and dead men," Augustine claims that the voice here is not that of the author (Hermes Trismegistus), but rather that "the agony of the demons was speaking through him" (*sed dolor daemonum per eum loquebatur*), anticipating the power of the relics and tombs of the Christian martyrs to exorcise them. Thus a pagan work, the fruit of the perverse inspiration of the *daemones*, takes on a complex structure of meaning that must be understood in terms of the motives of the dictating voices, and the *Asclepius* joins the Hebrew scriptures as a prefiguration of the triumph of Christianity (*Civ. Dei* 8.26). The Virgil of *Eclogue* 4 belongs in the same company,[95] though as we shall see, the *Aeneid* is fatally flawed.

Augustine's theory of signs, the scope of which is wide enough to include language, seems to represent a genuine innovation, though it grows out of earlier Stoic thought, with perhaps some admixture of Plotinus.[96] We find in Augustine a developed concept of the relationship of language to truth closely comparable to the one expounded a genera-

92. "Nothing suggests that he ever read profane Greek authors, not even Plato, except in Latin translation." Harald Hagendahl, *Augustine and the Latin Classics*, p. 445. See, however, p. 586 of the same work on Augustine's school Greek.

93. See Markus in CHLGEMP, pp. 339–40. Augustine uses Plotinus to explicate the Sermon on the Mount (*Civ. Dei* 10.14).

94. On the Old Testament as an allegorical representation of Christ and his Church to come, see *Civ. Dei* 16.2, and 13.21. On methodology of exegesis and on the deliberate obscurity of the scriptures, see *Civ. Dei* 11.19.

95. See Hagendahl, *Augustine and the Latin Classics*, pp. 440–47. On Virgil's speaking *poetice* of Christ, see *Civ. Dei* 10.26.

96. See R. A. Markus, "Augustine on Signs," pp. 64–65.

tion later in Proclus, and here the analogy of divine apparition to linguistic sign is explicitly developed. God, though invisible in his true
being (*secundum quod est*) makes himself visible—that is, he projects into
the world an image of himself suited to the capacities of those who see
him (*secundum quod poterant ferre cernentes*).

> It should not disturb us that although God is invisible he is often said
> to have appeared in visible form to our ancestors. For just as the
> sound that renders audible a thought formulated in the silence of
> mind is something other than that thought itself, in the same way the
> shape by which God, who is by nature invisible, was made visible
> was something other than God himself. And yet he was seen in that
> bodily shape just as the thought was heard in the sound of the voice.[97]

This model of apparition corresponds to the first of the three modes
of poetic representation of the divine discussed by Proclus.[98] In this
mode, Proclus explains, apparent change attributed to the divine by the
mythoplasts constitutes the adaptation to the capacities of the "receivers"
(ὑποδοχαί) of the eternal essences existing beyond the sphere of coming-
to-be and passing-away. Manifestations of the divine must be adapted to
the capacities of the "participating beings," and thoughts in much the
same way must endure fragmentation in time, which is absent from their
true medium, in order to be communicated in language to our fragmented consciousness. Our senses encounter something other than the
divine, than the thought—and yet the divine and the thought are in fact
experienced in that something else.

This equation (God : God's manifestation :: thought : speech) is further
developed by Augustine into a theory of divine expression that resolves
the fundamental difficulty inherent in the idea of scripture as the word of
God, and does so in a manner that again anticipates the similar discussion in Proclus.[99] Intermediaries are invoked in the form of angels, and
although the process is not spelled out in detail, it is clear that the immediate communications from God to the highest angels are accomplished
telepathically and non-discursively (*non temporaliter sed, ut ita dicam,*

97. *Nec movere debet quod, cum sit invisibilis, saepe visibiliter patribus apparuisse
memoratur. Sicut enim sonus quo auditur sententia in silentio intelligentiae constituta
non est hoc quod ipsa, ita et species qua visus est Deus in natura invisibili constitutus non
erat quod ipse. Verum tamen ipse in eadem specie corporali videbatur, sicut illa sententia
ipsa in sono vocis auditur* (*Civ. Dei* 10.13). Cf. Proclus on the divine: ἀμετάβλητον
καθ᾽ αὑτὸ καὶ μονίμως ἱδρυμένον, ἄλλοτε δὲ ἀλλοῖον διὰ τὴν αὐτῶν ἀσθένειαν
τοῖς μετέχουσι φανταζόμενον (*In Rep.* 1.111.25–27).

98. *In Rep.* 1.111. See n. 97 above.

99. See ch. 5B above.

aeternaliter) and these communications are simultaneous and eternal (*nec incipit loqui nec desinit*). Through his intermediaries, however, God actually expresses himself syllable by syllable, each with its tiny duration, in the words of human speech (*syllabatim per transitorias temporum morulas humanae linguae vocibus*).[100]

We are on familiar ground, then, when we examine Augustine's basic conception of language and the nature of the linguistic sign, and the privileged status of the scriptures is established along familiar lines. But Augustine, of course, benefitted from a clearly defined canon of scripture beyond which he had no need to look in search of truth. Even if *Eclogue* 4 has some affinity with the prophetic literature of the Jews, its privilege does not extend to the other works of Virgil. Augustine's condemnation of the *Aeneid* constitutes his only developed discussion of the meaning of an epic poem and serves to bring into focus an important aspect of his criticism of the pagan tradition. The *Aeneid*, for Augustine, is vitiated by the ultimate submission of the hero to the power of the *daemones* the pagans mistook for the divine itself. Bits of etymological fantasy penetrate into his language at this point and betray the underlying interpretive literature on Virgil that formed Augustine's conception of the meaning of the poem. Aeneas, we are told, may be envisaged as a type of the Christian hero—a martyr before the fact—in his *attempt* to combat the "powers of the air," the *daemones* or *aeriae potestates* (*Civ. Dei* 10.21). What is meant is his battle with Hera (etymologized into ἀήρ) and her attendants. Virgil's failure, in Augustine's mind, is his final counsel of submission to these corrupt powers, delivered through the seer Helenus to Aeneas (*Aen.* 3.438–39). A Christian Aeneas would have persevered to victory over the *daemones*, until Juno was forced to say *vincor ab Aenea* (which she *does* say at *Aen.* 7.310, but that defeat is short-lived). The potentially liberating myth of the *Aeneid* is corrupted by the defeatism common to pagan demonology in general, and Virgil glimpsed the truth that might have freed him from bondage to the evil *daemones*, but (like Porphyry) was unable to realize that vision and liberate himself.

There is no direct evidence for Augustine's understanding of the meaning of the Greek epics, though he had read at least selections from Homer in the original Greek in his youth.[101] His only direct paraphrase of Homer is in connection with the interpretation of Virgil.[102] Nevertheless,

100. *Civ. Dei* 10.15.

101. August. *Conf.* 1.14 (23). Cf. Henri-Irénée Marrou, *Saint Augustin et la fin de la culture antique*, p. 28 and n. 1.

102. August. *Civ. Dei* 3.2. Cf. Marrou, *Saint Augustin*, p. 33, n. 4.

Augustine was aware of Stoicizing allegorical interpretation of the myths and absorbed some of the Neoplatonic allegory of Homer from Plotinus.[103] He ridicules Stoic attempts to save the myths by explaining the gods as representations of the elements,[104] and when he mentions Homer it is primarily to dismiss his lies.[105]

He is aware, by way of Varro, of a *mythicon genus theologiae*, but he discusses it only to reject it (*Civ. Dei* 6.5). It is the theology "mainly used by the poets," and Varro's own description of it is, for Augustine, a sufficient condemnation: "Thus in this theology all things are ascribed to the gods that may befall not merely a man, but the most contemptible of men."[106] Augustine's position, then, recalls that of Xenophanes and is close to that of Socrates in the *Republic*. In echoing with approval Socrates' rejection of Homer (*Civ. Dei* 2.14), Augustine was not alone in the early Church. The same sentiments were expressed by Origen (*Contra Cels.* 1.36) and by Augustine's younger contemporary Theodoret.[107]

Augustine indicates that he knows that the Platonists, and specifically Apuleius, tried to salvage some of the stories by claiming that they referred not to gods but to demons.[108] He does not specifically reject this notion, but his ultimate goal in the passage in question is the demonstration that Christ is the only mediator between the divine and the human (*Civ. Dei* 9.15). The Homeric passage evoked in this context is that where Athena restrains Achilles (*Il.* 1.199–200), and Apuleius is represented as

103. See August. *Civ. Dei* 7.16 and Green's note *ad loc.* in the Loeb edition, vol. 2, p. 432, n. 1. The connections between Augustine's view of allegory in the Scriptures and the pagans' ideas about allegory are explored by Jean Pépin in "Saint Augustin et la fonction protreptique de l'allégorie," pp. 267–85.

104. August. *Civ. Dei* 4.10.

105. Cf. August. *Civ. Dei* 15.9 and 4.26 and 30, where Augustine introduces a Stoic denunciation of Homeric anthropomorphism for which his own source is Cicero. In a blanket denunciation of the "poets also called theologians" (*poetae, qui etiam theologi dicerentur*), Homer is surprisingly absent from the list, which includes only Orpheus, Musaeus, and Linus (*Civ. Dei* 18.14). The subsequent list of their impious fables, however, includes the fall of Troy (*Civ. Dei* 18.16). There is an echo of this denunciation in Aquinas *Met. Arist. Exp.* 1.4.82–83.

106. *Denique in hoc omnia diis adtribuuntur quae non modo in hominem, sed etiam in contemptissimum hominem cadere possunt* (*Civ. Dei* 6.5). Cf. *Civ. Dei* 8.5, where Varro's allegorizing of repellent rituals is likewise rejected, on the grounds that it is *wrong: quia nec ipsa illis ritibus significatur quae ipse* [sec. Varro] *insinuare conatur*.

107. Theodoret *Serm.* 2 (*De principio*), cited *ad loc.* in Migne, PG 11 (Origen 1), col. 1083, n. 26.

108. August. *Civ. Dei* 9.7.

asserting that this would have been the act not of the divinity herself, but of some *daemon*.[109]

It is clear that Porphyry, for whom he retained great respect, was Augustine's source for at least some aspects of the Neoplatonic exegesis of myth and ritual. He offers Porphyry's explanation of the castration of Attis, and, though he approves neither of the myth nor of the interpretation, he does not allow Porphyry to bear the brunt of his scorn.[110]

Augustine never refers to pagan attempts to elevate the *Iliad* and *Odyssey* to the level of scripture, but he appears to be aware of such treatment of the early poetic tradition and to consider it both dangerous and contemptible. This attitude comes out in a passage in which he is citing with approval the Stoic belief in a fate that has its source in the will of Zeus (*Civ. Dei* 5.8). A Latin version of a Homeric passage is cited in support of the opinion, but Augustine is quick to add that it is the ideas of his proximal Stoic source that are of interest to him and that he is quoting Homer only because the Stoics did so in this context, "not that a poet's opinion would have any authority in this matter."[111]

It is hardly surprising that Augustine should have so little use for Homer. What is striking in his sparse references to Homer is his knowledge and understanding of the philosophical interpretive tradition in isolation from the text of the poems, of which his knowledge must have been minimal. He nonetheless displays and passes on, albeit with contempt, an understanding of the way that text was *read*, both by Stoics and by Platonists. These traditions of interpretation had, for him, largely obscured and replaced a text in which he had little interest.

Returning to the pagan revival itself and to the Roman senatorial establishment that held off the eventual repression of the pagan cults for

109. The passage as a whole provides an interesting precedent for one of Proclus's defensive-allegorical procedures. He was to present the same idea in far more schematic form in his discussion of the theomachy of *Il.* 20 and 21 and that passage has affinities with Augustine's discussion of Apuleius's method (*Civ. Dei* 9.7).

110. August. *Civ. Dei* 7.26. See Green's note *ad loc.* in the Loeb edition, vol. 2, p. 466, n. 1.

111. *nec in hac quaestione auctoritatem haberet poetica sententia* (*Civ. Dei* 5.8). This scorn for the elevation of poetry to a position of authority is also heard in the earlier *De magistro* (28): *Non enim horum* [sc., *poetarum*] *auctoritati subiecti sumus in talibus rebus*. Here the subject is the relationship of the knowledge of signs to the knowledge of the things signified, and a line of Persius has entered the discussion.

decades both before and after the brief rule of Julian the Apostate, we may consider the contributions of Vettius Agorius Praetextatus and Macrobius, as well as the less direct contribution of the Virgilian commentator Servius.

The first of these figures was primarily a man of action. He was at the center of the senatorial pagan resistance, a group whose lack of reading and culture is ridiculed by Ammianus Marcellinus.[112] Whatever the reading habits of these aristocrats as a group, however, we owe to them the transmission of much that might otherwise have been lost from classical culture, and they and their successors after the military and political disaster of 394[113] demonstrably read, annotated, and copied the classics in the hope that at least in this way the traditions might survive.[114]

Praetextatus is agreed to have been an intellectual as well as a political leader for this group,[115] and he was active as a translator of Aristotle and of other Greek authors. John Lydus mentions a work where Praetextatus apparently spoke of "Ianos" as a force presiding over the "two bears" (the Big and Little Dippers) and directing divine souls to the lunar paradise.[116] W. Ensslin[117] asserts that this work will have been "im Geiste der Theologie des Iamblichos," but the true spirit of the observation may well be Numenian and have reached Praetextatus by way of Porphyry.[118] Iamblichus and his followers were clearly the major influence on Julian and so on the pagan revival in the East, but Porphyry almost certainly had more currency in Platonist circles in the West, even during Julian's reign.

Virtually nothing survives of Praetextatus's writings, perhaps in part because of the quite understandable hostility of the Christian tradition. He emerges as a personality and an intellectual presence, however, in

---

112. Cf. Bloch, "The Pagan Revival," pp. 206–7.

113. Bloch, "The Pagan Revival," p. 201. In 394, the two-year reign of the pagan Eugenius, raised to power in the West by the *magister militum* Arbogast, was ended when Theodosius came to the support of Valentinian II.

114. Bloch, "The Pagan Revival," pp. 213–16.

115. Bloch, "The Pagan Revival," passim; cf. Ensslin in P-W ("Praetextatus [1]"): "Auch wurde ihm, der noch des Griechischen mächtig war, Beschäftigung mit per Philosophie und der alten Literatur durch Übersetzungen und Emendieren zur Stützung des Götterglaubens nach gerühmt" (col. 1579).

116. John Lydus *De mens.* 4.2.

117. Ensslin, "Praetextatus," col. 1579.

118. Another possibility is that Lydus is referring to Praetextatus's long speech in the first book of the *Saturnalia*, where he discusses the name Ianus at length, though without offering the bit of lore in question (Macrob. *Sat.* 1.9).

the major literary accomplishment of the pagan revival, Macrobius's *Saturnalia*, composed about 430, nearly half a century after Praetextatus's death, but set in the 380s.[119] This work is an imitation of an imitation—an indication of the complexity and the conservatism of the tradition that produced it.[120] Macrobius presents us with a dialogue in imitation of the *De re publica* of Cicero, itself based on Platonic models and most obviously on the *Republic*.[121]

Stating as his goal the presentation of his learning in useful form for the education of his son (to whom the work is addressed), Macrobius evokes a manifestly fictional conversation involving many of the leaders of the pagan senatorial resistance of an earlier generation. The speakers have decided to devote the period of the Saturnalia to conversations about philosophical and religious traditions. Praetextatus is the most important among them in the surviving portions of the treatise, along with Symmachus, who in 384 succeeded him as leader of the group and later debated with St. Ambrose. Other contributors include Nichomachus Flavianus, Rufinus, and Caecina Albinus, who were, like the preceding, important figures in pagan senatorial society, as well as a philosopher named Eustathius and a rhetor named Eusebius, both Greeks and otherwise unknown. Among the less important contributors appear several stock figures, a Cynic named Horus and an uninvited boor named Evangelus, as well as the famous Virgilian commentator Servius. The last is presented as much younger than most of the company, however, and never speaks unless spoken to.[122] Much of the work as we have it is dedicated to the glorification of Virgil and, as a recent historian has put it, to the elevation of the *Aeneid* to the status of a "pagan Bible."[123] In the process, frequent reference is, of course, made to Homer. We may examine these references in two groups, first isolating the use made of Homer by

119. The dialogue contains some deliberate anachronisms, justified by reference to the example of Plato (Macrob. *Sat.* 1.5). On the identity of its author, see Cameron, "Date and Identity of Macrobius," as well as Flamant, *Macrobe*, pp. 91–141. Cameron argues compellingly (p. 29) that the dramatic date of the dialogue may be set at Dec. 17–19, 384.

120. On Macrobius and his sources, see Courcelle, *Les lettres grecques en occident*, ch. 1.

121. Cf. Bloch, "The Pagan Revival," pp. 208–9.

122. On all of the participants and the society they represent, see Flamant, *Macrobe*, pp. 25–87.

123. So Bloch, "The Pagan Revival," p. 210. The expression is perhaps too strong. See Cameron, "Date and Identity of Macrobius," p. 36, on Macrobius's goals.

Macrobius's Praetextatus,[124] then considering in more general terms the idea of Homer's poetry contained in the *Saturnalia*.

Praetextatus dominates the opening book of the *Saturnalia*, previous to the extended discussion of Virgil (books 3–6) and two sections (books 2, 7) devoted to less structured chatter on subjects ranging from the favorite anecdotes of Cicero (*Sat.* 2.3) to the question of the relative antiquity of the chicken and the egg (*Sat.* 7.16). He emerges as the highest authority on religious matters in the gathering and as a source of virtually unimpeachable information on the proprieties of religious law and custom. With only brief interruptions, he holds forth from the seventh to the twenty-third chapter of book 1, covering first the origins of the Saturnalia (ch. 7), then various religious and calendar questions (chs. 8–16), and concluding with an extensive exposition of solar theology, recalling Julian's hymn to the sun (chs. 16–23).[125] The special appropriateness of this discourse, coming from the mouth of the *pontifex solis*, has been noticed,[126] and this seems a strong argument against those who have wished to see in Macrobius's portrait of Praetextatus a reflection of the religious thought of a later generation.[127]

If Praetextatus's goals are similar to Julian's, his use of Homer likewise recalls that of the emperor, without the latter's explicit reservations regarding myth and poetry. He knows a variant of the Κρόνος/χρόνος allegory in which Zeus's father devouring his children becomes an image of time as the producer and destroyer of all things (*Sat.* 1.7.10).[128] Homer is evoked as an expert on the character of Mars (*Sat.* 1.12.9) and in support of the supposed ancient custom of counting the days of the month retrograde, this last by a dubious interpretation of *Od.* 14.162 (*Sat.* 1.16.42). Virgil is also cited as an authoritative source and at one point called *Homerus vester Mantuanus* (*Sat.* 1.16.43). Homer is likewise referred to by the simple, unexplained epithet *poeta*, translating the Hellenistic ὁ ποιητής.[129]

124. On Macrobius's portrait of Praetextatus, see Flamant, *Macrobe*, pp. 33–36. It is Flamant's belief that the theology attributed to Praetextatus in the *Saturnalia* belongs to Macrobius himself and to the 420s, rather than to Praetextatus and the 380s (see pp. 36, 662–80).

125. See Flamant, *Macrobe*, p. 659 and n. 43, on the correspondences.

126. Bloch, "The Pagan Revival," pp. 209–10.

127. See n. 124 above.

128. The derivation of the name Κρόνος from χρόνος is as old as Pherecydes (sixth century B.C.) and is repeated in Porphyry's *Homeric Questions*. Cf. Pfeiffer, *History of Classical Scholarship*, p. 12.

129. E.g., Macrob. *Sat.* 1.17.38.

It is primarily as a theological authority to help him associate various deities with the sun that Macrobius's Praetextatus makes use of Homer, just as Julian had done before him.[130] Though he uses none of the same passages—a good argument for the complete independence of the two pieces—the procedure is essentially the same. To pick a single example, "Mars" is shown to be, for Homer, a name for one effect of the sun, by virtue of the line

He raged like Mars waving his spear, or like destructive fire.

μαίνετο δ᾽ ὡς ὅτ᾽ Ἄρης ἐγχέσπαλος ἢ ὀλοὸν πῦρ

(Il. 15.605)

This is the last of a series of assertions justifying the conclusion that "the effect of the sun bringing about warmth in souls and heat in the blood is called Mars."[131]

The problem of the identification of Zeus with the sun—the high point and climax of Praetextatus's speech—reposes on an extended discussion of Thetis's lines to Achilles,

For yesterday Zeus went off to the Ocean to feast
among the beautiful Ethiopians and all the gods followed.
He will come back to Olympus on the twelfth day.

Ζεὺς γὰρ ἐς Ὠκεανὸν μετ᾽ ἀμύμονας Αἰθιοπῆας
χθιζὸς ἔβη κατὰ δαῖτα, θεοὶ δ᾽ ἅμα πάντες ἕποντο·
δωδεκάτῃ δέ τοι αὖτις ἐλεύσεται Οὔλυμπόνδε.

(Il. 1.423–25)

Praetextatus's cited sources for his analysis are all Stoics. Cornificius supplies the information that "Zeus" here means "sun," because the exhalations of the ocean nourish the sun.[132] Cornificius's testimony is supplemented by the testimony of Posidonius and Cleanthes that it is for this reason that the sun remains in the "burning zone," through which Ocean flows, since heat is universally agreed to be nourished by moisture.

The passage is examined phrase by phrase in a manner not characteristic of Macrobius but familiar from Porphyry's essay on the cave of the nymphs. The "gods" that follow Zeus to his feast are the stars, and this

130. See Macrob. Sat. 1.17.11, 21, 38, 44; 1.19.6, 9; 1.20.5; 1.22.4; and 1.23.1, 9.

131. In summa pronuntiandum est effectum solis, de quo fervor animorum, de quo calor sanguinis excitatur, Martem vocari (Sat. 1.19.6).

132. Jovis appellatione solem intelligi Cornificius scribit cui unda Oceani velut dapes ministrat (Sat. 1.23.2). Porphyry mentions this doctrine of Stoic physics in the cave essay.

is supported by the familiar etymology of θεοί from θέειν ("run"), with which is juxtaposed a derivation from θεωρεῖσθαι ("to be contemplated") (*Sat.* 1.23.3). The isolated adjective "twelfth" (δωδεκάτη) is said to refer not to the twelfth *day* (sc., ἡμέρᾳ) but rather to the twelfth *hour* (sc., ὥρᾳ), which returns a star that has set to the opposite horizon (*Sat.* 1.23.4). This requires of course that we ignore the amount of time required by the *Iliad* narrative—quite explicit at *Il.* 1.493–94—but we are clearly dealing with an interpretive tradition accustomed to viewing passages and individual phrases as isolated, oracular utterances independent of any context.

The analysis of the Homeric passage is immediately supported by means of a substantial citation from the *Phaedrus* (246e). The fit between the Homeric and Platonic passages is exceptionally good, and the "explanation" of the use of the number twelve by the juxtaposition of the two passages is rather subtle. The further cumulative material, drawn from Euripides among many more exotic sources (*Sat.* 1.23.8), need not concern us. The probability is that the cited Stoic sources are not the proximal ones tapped by Macrobius, though his own source cannot be identified with certainty.[133] The most recent theory of the source of most of the material seems particularly plausible in view of the light the present study throws on the history of the interpretation of the passage. Jacques Flamant[134] points to a series of Porphyrian sources, specifically the Περὶ ἀγαλμάτων, the Περὶ θείων ὀνομάτων, and a treatise on the sun. He emphasizes the idea that the Porphyry who influences Macrobius is the Porphyry of the "philological period,"[135] but we have seen that this distinction may well be an artificial one. Suffice it to say that the theological Homer of Praetextatus's discourse in book 1 of the *Saturnalia*, for all his Stoic affinities, may well be dependent, once again, on a Porphyrian source.

Looking now at the references to Homer elsewhere in the *Saturnalia*, and leaving behind both the fictionalized and the historical Praetextatus, it becomes clear that the various speakers in Macrobius's dialogue represent a spectrum of attitudes toward the poets. Praetextatus himself was, of course, a native Roman, and the vast bulk of his discussion of religious law and tradition refers to Roman sources. His scholarship and his knowledge of Greek allow him to reach beyond that tradition at will, but

133. See Flamant, *Macrobe*, pp. 655–68.
134. Ibid., pp. 667–68. He is following F. Altheim—see pp. 657–61 with notes for the sources.
135. Flamant, *Macrobe*, p. 668.

he rarely feels the need. His most frequent antiquarian authority is "your Mantuan Homer."

The two Greeks portrayed in the dialogue, Eustathius and Eusebius, have an appropriately differing view of the tradition. The devil's advocate, the intruder Evangelus, is a Roman prig with a strong anti-Greek prejudice reminiscent of the *personae* of Juvenal's *Satires*.[136] The thrust of his first offensive remark at the end of Praetextatus's speech is nevertheless extremely revealing. He objects specifically to Praetextatus's frequent use of Virgil as evidence and support for his theological exposition:

> Am I supposed to believe that when [Virgil] says "Liber" and "alma Ceres" for "sun" and "moon," he hasn't simply done this in imitation of some earlier poet and repeated what he has heard without knowing why it was said? Unless, of course, like the Greeks, who exaggerate enormously the importance of everything Greek, we also want to claim that *our* poets are philosophers.[137]

He goes on to observe that Cicero, for all his rhetorical skill, is least elegant when talking about the gods, a further proof that style and poetic effectiveness have no connection with theological authority. The point was made by Augustine as well,[138] and from our perspective seems perfectly sound. It is immediately clear in the dialogue, however, that Evangelus's remark is considered not only inept (and doubtless offensive to the Greeks present) but wrong. The feeling of the assembly is that early poetry—Virgil, for his demonstrable scholarship, included—is philosophically and theologically authoritative. Two prevalent attitudes emerge from this polarization: first, it was possible, at the end of the fourth century, to view the elevation of early poetry to a position of theological and philosophical authority as a contemptible and characteristically Greek form of exaggeration, and second, this position was not shared by the Platonizing pagan senatorial class in Rome, who were disposed to treat Virgil as well as early Greek poetry in the manner in which the Greek Platonists treated Homer.

Symmachus's reply to Evangelus evokes the Socratic critique of Homer. He asks whether in fact the verses of Virgil are fit for the education

136. The idea that Evangelus's name might be an indication that he is a Christian is examined and rejected, I think rightly, by Flamant (*Macrobe*, pp. 74–75).

137. *An ego credam quod ille, cum diceret* Liber et alma Ceres pro sole ac luna, *non hoc in alterius poetae imitationem posuit, ita dici audiens, cur tamen diceretur ignorans? Nisi forte, ut Graeci omnia sua in immensum tollunt, nos quoque etiam poetas nostros volumus philosophari* (*Sat.* 1.24.3–4).

138. See n. 111 above.

of the young (*Sat.* 1.24.5). Evangelus's reply is negative—when we were children, he says, *sine judicio mirabamur*, but Virgil was wise to will his flawed poem to the flames (*Sat.* 1.24.6–7). Symmachus then tries without success to make Evangelus admit Virgil's rhetorical power (*Sat.* 1.24.8–9). Finally, after emphasizing the breadth of Virgil's wisdom, he laments the fact that the critics habitually limit themselves to examining Virgil's language and consider the vast *content* of his poetry forbidden ground (*Sat.* 1.24.10–12). He then sets the tone of the discussion to follow:

> [Unlike such critics,] since we have no business acting in a crude manner, let us not allow the secret places of the sacred poem to remain shut up, but by exploring the access to its arcane meanings let us offer its newly opened sanctuary to be celebrated by the adoration of the wise.[139]

The task is divided up among the participants. Eusebius (the Greek rhetor) will expound Virgil's oratory, and each person present will examine Virgil in the light of his own specialty. Praetextatus will "show Virgil to be our high priest."[140] Flavianus will expound his mastery of augury, Eustathius (the Greek philosopher) will demonstrate the poet's knowledge of astrology and philosophy as well as his use of Greek material, the Albinii will explore his use of Latin sources, and Servius will be available for help with obscure points (*Sat.* 1.24.14–20).

We are not concerned here with the interpretation of Virgil, but the project that forms the core of the *Saturnalia* has been sketched out to emphasize the dependence of the interpretation of Virgil—at least for this milieu—on the developments in the interpretation of Homer that concern us. It is quite significant that Evangelus's judgment is borne out at least to the extent that the task of the exposition of the "philosophy" of Virgil is conferred on a Greek. His speech, which for our purposes would have been the most interesting part of the discussion of Virgil, is sadly lost in a lacuna at the beginning of book 3. In book 4, also fragmentary, Eusebius illustrates various rhetorical tropes from Virgil in exactly the manner applied by Ps.-Plutarch to Homer. When it is agreed that Virgil is an orator and superior even to Cicero as a rhetorical educator (*Sat.* 5.1), Eustathius takes over again to complete the second part of his task and to demonstrate Virgil's borrowings from the Greek tradition.

---

139. *Sed nos, quos crassa Minerva dedecet, non patiamur abstrusa esse adyta sacri poematis, sed, arcanorum sensuum investigato aditu, doctorum cultu celebranda praebeamus reclusa penetralia* (*Sat.* 1.24.13).

140. *promitto fore ut Virgilius noster pontifex maximus asseratur* (*Sat.* 1.24.16).

Since he is a Greek and more familiar with Homer than with Virgil, Eustathius begins by requesting a copy of Virgil to stimulate his memory. He opens at random, announces that the port of Ithaca has been turned into the city of Dido, reads *Aeneid* 1.159–69, and then cites from memory the passage on the description of the cave of the nymphs in the *Odyssey*, the subject of Porphyry's essay. It is difficult to say what significance can be attached to this choice, since there is no explicit reference to Porphyry and no interpretation of the passage is offered. In view of Macrobius's demonstrable knowledge of some of the works of Porphyry, however, it is tempting to believe that the passage had a special "theological" significance for him. The commentary on the dream of Scipio, probably written a few years later than the *Saturnalia*,[141] shows a full knowledge of Numenius's ideas on the passage, obtained in all probability by way of Porphyry.

Eustathius's performance goes on at great length, proceeding first to explore the *Aeneid* from beginning to end for borrowed passages, then to look for passages in which Virgil outdid his model, those where they are equal, and those where Homer was beyond him. Eustathius's true allegiance comes out at this point in his assertion that Virgil wanted to imitate Homer in everything, "but with his human forces he was unable everywhere to match that divinity."[142] This should not be taken much more seriously than the references by other speakers to Virgil the "high priest."[143] It does, however, testify to an attitude that saw in Homer the theologian the predecessor and master of Virgil, in an age when the latter had eclipsed the former in the West.

There is little more in the *Saturnalia* that evokes the Homer of late Platonic tradition. The contribution of Servius to the discussion is limited to the explanation of uniquely Virgilian figures and vocabulary (e.g., *Sat.* 6.6–9). The allegorical portion of Servius's own surviving commentary on Virgil, dating from the early fifth century, has been examined by J. W. Jones, who emphasizes that the substantial element of allegorical exegesis in the Servian commentary differs from that found in some of the medieval commentators in its lack of "a single system or plan."[144] In other

141. See Flamant, *Macrobe*, p. 140.

142. *nec tamen humanis viribus illam divinitatem ubique poterat aequare* (*Sat.* 5.13.33).

143. Aside from the instance already cited, cf. *divinus ille vates* at *Sat.* 7.10.2, where the context is quite trivial and the epithet casual.

144. J. W. Jones, "Allegorical Interpretation in Servius," p. 224. This element is indeed small enough that Emile Thomas (*Essai sur Servius et son commentaire sur Virgile*, p. 245) was able to ignore it and to paint Servius as the defender of "les

words, it is allegory of the piecemeal, eclectic type we have been examining, dealing not with the global meaning of the work, but more often with specific elements within that work, and characterized by methodological diversity. The universe of book 6 of the *Aeneid* predictably requires cosmological explanation,[145] and various moral allegories are expounded, some of them explicitly Pythagorean. Again, this tells us little about the fate of the understanding of Homer, but the fortunes of the two poets were to a considerable degree intertwined. Like the *Saturnalia*, Servius's commentary on Virgil enjoyed a large public in the Middle Ages.[146] Not surprisingly, Homer is evoked or quoted very frequently, and these references serve to perpetuate his image as Virgil's antecedent and master,[147] the greater sage behind the magus that Virgil was to become for the Middle Ages.[148]

The importance of Macrobius for the transmission of the conception of Homer under discussion is far more obvious in the *Commentary on Scipio's Dream* than in the *Saturnalia*.[149] Here, piecemeal allegory abounds. Macrobius's version of the Numenian cave allegory, already mentioned,[150] constitutes the most significant evidence of Macrobius as the vehicle of a "Pythagorean" reading of Homer. It is through him that this allegory reached, among others, Albertus Magnus, the master of Aquinas.[151] Other references to Homer include the association of Menelaus's imprecation to the Greeks, "May you all become earth and water," with the doctrine of the φυσικοί that the line of demarcation between earth and water

---

droits de la raison et du bon sens" against the allegorists, but his opinion merely reflects an understandable and widespread prejudice against the mode of interpretation under consideration here.

145. Jones, "Allegorical Interpretation in Servius," pp. 220–21.

146. Cf. Thomas, *Essai sur Servius*, pp. 303–50 for the medieval manuscript tradition.

147. For references, see J. F. Mountfort and J. T. Schultz, *Index Rerum et Nominum in Scholiis Servii et Aelii Donati Tractatorum*, pp. 79–80.

148. The basic source on this development remains Domenico Comparetti, *Virgilio nel medio evo* (1870).

149. The basic modern study of the commentary is Karl Mras, *Macrobius' Kommentar zu Ciceros Somnium*. He emphasizes Macrobius's use of Porphyry and his acceptance of the concept that the teachings of Homer and Plato are identical (p. 55). The commentary itself uses the dream of Scipio at the end of the *De re publica* of Cicero (in the position of the myth of Er in Plato's *Republic*) as a pretext for the elaboration of Neoplatonic ideas.

150. See above, pp. 71–72.

151. Aquinas *Sum. theol.* 2.12. q. 72. m. 4, art. 3. See Stahl's annotated translation of the commentary, p. 133, n. 18, and p. 134, n. 3.

is called *necessitas* (*In somn. Scip.* 1.6.37) and a reference to Homer as an authority on the credibility of dreams (*In somn. Scip.* 1.3.14). Macrobius defends Zeus's conduct in sending the deceitful dream to Agamemnon using exactly the same arguments put forward by Proclus in the same context. Perhaps the common source used by Macrobius and Proclus on this point,[152] Porphyry is explicitly the source of a passage commenting on the gates of horn and ivory (*Od.* 19.562–67), which cannot itself be described as allegorical but is built upon the commonplace that "all truth lies concealed" (*latet . . . omne verum*).[153] The interpretation of Thetis's description of Zeus's journey to feast with the Ethiopians is repeated from the *Saturnalia* and attributed simply to *physici* and not specifically to the Stoics. The allegorical understanding of the Homeric lines is attributed to the *physici* along with the associated conception of the relationship of fire and water. In this context Homer is described as "the fount and origin of all inventions concerning the divine" (*divinarum omnium inventionum fons et origo*) and said to have "delivered this truth to the understanding of the wise beneath a cloud of poetic fiction" (*sub poetici nube figmenti verum sapientibus intellegi dedit*) (*In somn. Scip.* 2.10.11).

Many of these interpretations from the commentary are physical and moral rather than mystical allegories, but aside from the association of Homer with Pythagorean doctrines on the fate of souls, this work is also an important source for the specifically Neoplatonic allegory of the golden chain of Zeus (*Il.* 8.19). This passage has a rich tradition among the interpreters, which has been meticulously examined and analyzed.[154] The Neoplatonic branch, which probably goes back to Porphyry, saw in Homer's image a description of the chain of spiritual powers extending from the highest god to the material universe.[155] Macrobius's formulation depends on the triad of hypostases of Plotinian Neoplatonism and incorporates an image from Plotinus:

> Thus, since mind emanates from the highest god and soul from mind, and soul both shapes and fills with life all that follows and that single blaze illuminates everything and appears in all things, as a single face reflected in a series of mirrors, and since all things follow on one another in a continuous succession, degenerating progressively as they descend, he who looks closely will find a continuous bond, com-

152. See Stahl's annotated translation of Macrobius's commentary, p. 119, n. 3, where he summarizes the positions of earlier scholars on the problem of Macrobius's source here.

153. Macrob. *In somn. Scip.* 1.3.17–18.

154. See Pierre Lévêque, *Aurea Catena Homeri.*

155. Lévêque, *Aurea Catena Homeri*, p. 56.

posed of interlocking links and never broken, extending all the way from the highest god to the last dregs of the material universe. This, moreover, is Homer's golden chain, which he says god ordered to be hung from heaven to earth.[156]

The image enjoyed great popularity in the Middle Ages and beyond, though the Homeric source is seldom explicit.[157] The fact that Macrobius was aware of its Homeric origin and mentions it is, however, a guarantee that this was also known to some of the medieval authors to whom he transmitted it. The golden chain appears without mention of Homer in Bernard Silvestris, who may in turn have influenced Dante.[158]

In view of the probability that Macrobius's extensive citations from Homer are all at second hand, and that his direct knowledge of Homer was minimal,[159] we have here striking evidence of the pervasive influence of the interpretive tradition in isolation from the text. As early as the beginning of the fifth century in the Latin West, we must consider a certain conception of the *kind* of poet Homer was to be replacing the direct experience of the poems.

It is a peculiar coincidence that we have another commentary on Scipio's dream, perhaps two decades older than that of Macrobius.[160] It likewise uses the passage from Cicero's *De re publica* as a pretext for the elaboration of Neoplatonic ideas, and its author, Favonius Eulogius, was a Carthaginian rhetor and a student of Augustine's.[161] Karl Praechter

---

156. *Secundum haec ergo cum ex summo deo mens, ex mente anima fit, anima vero et condat et vita compleat omnia quae sequuntur, cunctaque hic unus fulgor illuminet et in universis appareat, ut in multis speculis per ordinem positis vultus unus, cumque omnia continuis successionibus se sequantur degenerantia per ordinem ad imum meandi: invenietur pressius intuenti a summo deo usque ad ultimam rerum faecem una mutuis se vinculis religans et nusquam interrupta connexio. et haec est Homeri catena aurea, quam pendere de caelo in terras deum iussisse commemorat* (*In somn. Scip.* 1.14.15). See Lévêque, *Aurea Catena Homeri*, pp. 46–47, and cf. Plotinus's comparable use of the image of the string of mirrors at *Enn.* 1.1.8.

157. The literature is summarized by Lévêque, *Aurea Catena Homeri*, pp. 57–60.

158. Bernard Silvestris, *De mundi universitate libri duo* 2.7.1, cited by Lévêque, *Aurea Catena Homeri*, p. 57, n. 3. For the possible connection between Bernard Silvestris and Dante, see David Thompson, *Dante's Epic Journeys*, p. 28. See also ch. 6E, with n. 212, below.

159. See Flamant, *Macrobe*, pp. 300–304.

160. On the date of Favonius's commentary see Van Weddington in his edition of Favonius, p. 7.

161. The evidence is from the *De cura pro mortuis gerenda* of Augustine, cited and discussed by Van Weddington in his edition of Favonius, p. 5 and n. 2.

listed him among the significant Latin Neoplatonists,[162] but the brief commentary that is his only surviving work throws little light on our problem. His sources are primarily Latin rather than Greek (as one might expect from a student of Augustine's), and his interests are numerological and musical. Without mentioning Homer, however, he does explain the "first marriage" as described by "the poets" using the same Pythagoreanizing Neoplatonic numerology applied by Proclus to the intercourse of Zeus and Hera in the episode of the deception of Zeus (*In Rep.* 1.133–35). Juno is identified with the dyad and Jupiter with the monad.[163]

The famous *De nuptiis Philologiae et Mercurii* of Martianus Capella, approximately contemporary with Macrobius, constitutes a unique document in the late history of Latin Platonism. Its trappings of myth and personification allegory make it clear that it is esthetically close to Prudentius, but as we have seen, personification allegory is only distantly related to the interpretive tradition, and the genuinely Neoplatonic contents of Martianus's book are minimal.[164]

Martianus undertook to create a digest of classical rhetoric and learning, clothing it in an allegory representing the apotheosis of Philologia and her marriage to Mercury, the god presiding over *eloquentia*. Despite his knowledge of Greek, his references to Homer and to specifically Homeric myth are extremely sparse. Homer is cited only once,[165] when the line,

A fierce man—he'd be likely to cast blame even on an innocent
   person,

δεινὸς ἀνήρ · τάχα κεν καὶ ἀναίτιον αἰτιόῳτο

(*Il.* 11.654)

is used to describe the proverbially incorruptible and severe statesman Gaius Fabricius Luscinius, who appears with Cicero among the foremost orators. It is revealing that glosses on Martianus Capella indicate that by the ninth century this isolated line of Greek had been totally garbled and could not be understood.[166]

162. Praechter, *Philosophie des Altertums*, p. 652.

163. *Primumque conubium poetae fabulosae dixerunt sororis et coniugis, quod videlicet unius generis numero coeunte copuletur; et Iunonem vocant, uni scilicet Iovi accessione alterius inhaerentem* (Favonius *Disp.* 6 [17.27–19.1]).

164. So Praechter, *Philosophie des Altertums*, p. 652.

165. Mart. *De nupt.* bk. 5 (213.11). References are to page and line of Dick's Teubner edition.

166. Dunchad *Gloss. in Mart.* p. 40 and n. 91.

The single presentation of Homer in the *De nuptiis* that casts light on the tradition under examination is his appearance in book 2, where a chorus of Muses greets Philologia and, after she has encountered the gods and demigods, she enters a clearly Pythagoreanizing paradise of intellectuals: "You saw Linus, Homer and the Mantuan seer, redeemed and singing—Orpheus and Aristoxenus resounding their beliefs—Plato and Archimedes rolling down golden spheres."[167] The situation seems to be precisely the one we encounter later in Dante. Homer's fame and his association with visionaries and philosophers had outlived any clear knowledge of the text. Significantly, the ninth-century commentator already mentioned misreads the passage and takes Linus and Homer to be the same poet.[168]

Beyond this triumphant epiphany, the references to Homeric material are few. In the classification of speeches the type *an Aiacem Ulixes occiderit* occurs (*De nupt.*, bk. 5 [236.3]), and there are linguistic and morphological comments on the names of Ajax and Agamemnon.[169] Finally, in the geographical excursus of book 6, two locations are associated with Homer, four with Ulixes, and one each with Circe, Aeolus, and Achilles. These references, slight as they are, are nevertheless indicative of important survival patterns for Homeric material. Martianus clearly has geographical sources that use the *Odyssey* and trace Odysseus's wanderings. In isolation from the text, this stratum of Homeric lore would seem to have taken refuge in the geographers and in the oral tradition in the form of founding myths.

The last link in our chain is Boethius. This ambitious scholar had planned to translate the whole of Plato and Aristotle into Latin but earned the displeasure of Theodoric the Ostrogoth and was tortured and put to death in 524 or 525. Although his translation project remained far from complete (and there was not to be a complete Latin Plato before Ficino), Boethius remains, as Praechter put it, "der Vermittler κατ᾽ ἐξοχήν zwischen Altertum und Mittelalter."[170] That he was a Christian is shown by five theological treatises that survive under his name, but the famous

167. *Linum, Homerum, Mantuanumque vatem redimitos canentesque conspiceres, Orpheum atque Aristoxenum fidibus personantes, Platonem Archimedenque sphaeras aureas devolventes* (Mart. *De nupt.* bk. 2 [p. 78.10–13]).

168. Or perhaps he took *linum* as an adjective modifying *Homerum*. See Dunchad, *Gloss. in Mart.* p. 12 (on 78.10) and n. 41.

169. Mart. *De nupt.* bk. 2 (88.4, 21; 92.10) and bk. 3 (p. 122.5).

170. Praechter, *Philosophie des Altertums*, pp. 652–55.

Consolation of Philosophy and the translations and commentaries [171] show no trace of explicit Christian content.

The position of Homer in the works on logic is negligible, as might be expected. The *Consolation*, infused as it is with classical culture viewed from the perspective of an eclectic Platonism, repeatedly associates Homer with the philosophical tradition and specifically with Neoplatonic doctrines.

The *Consolation* is a complex mixture of philosophical dialogue, Menippean satire, and personification allegory. The author, imprisoned and depressed, looks up from the self-indulgent lyrics in which he is expressing his misery and sees the figure of Philosophy before him. She drives away his Muses (comparing them to Sirens, *Cons.* 1.1 [prose] 40–41), replaces them with her own, and proceeds to offer him exhortations and consolations with the goal of reconciling him to the true nature of things.

There can be little question that Boethius had both a solid command of Greek and direct experience of the Homeric poems. There is no reason, however, to believe that this experience extended to the entire *Iliad* and *Odyssey*. When Philosophia, making the banal point that no life contains unmixed blessings, asks, "Did you not learn as a little boy that 'two jars, the one of evils, the other of good things' lie on Zeus's threshold?" [172] she throws light on Boethius's relationship to Homer. We have no reason to believe that he studied Homer beyond the excerpts that would have been the inevitable introduction to his Greek education or that he returned to Homer as an adult with more developed philosophical interests.

Boethius is clearly aware of a variety of uses of Homer. He employs him both decoratively and rhetorically to enhance the vividness of his dialogue and appeals to him as a higher authority. These appeals often involve some implicit effort of interpretation. Of all the authors considered thus far, Plotinus is perhaps the closest to Boethius in his use of Homer, in that explicit efforts at exegesis are relatively insignificant, though Homer remains constantly available as a source of citations and images charged with spiritualized meaning. These meanings may be de-

171. He left translations of Aristotle's works on logic (the *Organon*) with commentaries on the *Categories* and Περὶ ἑρμηνείας, a translation and two commentaries on Porphyry's *Introduction* to the *Categories*, and a commentary on Cicero's *Topica*.

172. *Nonne adulescentulus* δοιοὺς πίθους τὸν μὲν ἕνα κακῶν τὸν δ᾽ ἕτερον ἐάων *in Iovis limine iacere didicisti?* (*Cons.* 2.2 [prose] 40–42).

veloped in the immediate context or they may depend on the tradition of
interpretation implied in their use. Here, Homer is by no means replaced
by the interpretive tradition, but Boethius's use of the *Iliad* and *Odyssey* is
deeply affected by that tradition.

Aside from the references to the Muses, just mentioned, the opening
tableau exploits several unacknowledged but unquestionably Homeric
images and details. When Philosophy tears Boethius's attention from his
poetic lamentations and stands before him *oculis ardentibus*,[173] the mind
of a reader versed in Homer would be directed to the familiar description
of Athena when she appeared to Achilles, and "her eyes blazed terribly"
(δεινὼ δέ οἱ ὄσσε φάανθεν, *Il.* 1.200). The description of her size depends on the Homeric description of ἔρις,[174] and as she wipes away
Boethius's tears, the reference to Athena removing the mist from Diomedes' eyes is unavoidable. Philosophy wants to make Boethius capable
of recognizing her (just as Athena had wanted to make it possible for
Diomedes to perceive gods on the battlefield and distinguish them from
men), and she says, "So that he may be able to do this, let us clear his
eyes for a while from the mist of mortal things that clouds them."[175]

Two of these details have possible significance in that they borrow descriptions of Athena from the *Iliad* to describe Boethius's *Philosophia*, an
obvious correspondence. This sort of use of Homer, however, whatever
it might imply about the spiritual message of Homer to an audience that
knew Homer by heart, could mean little or nothing to most of Boethius's
readers, even in his own time. Of more interest in the present context are those passages where Homer is quoted directly or mentioned
by name.

It is significant, first of all, that it is always *Philosophia* and not Boethius who quotes or alludes to Homer. Passages from Homer are employed as educational touchstones and, as in the passage on the jars al-

173. *Cons.* 1.1 (prose) 4.
174. *Cons.* 1.1 (prose) 8–11 echoes *Il.* 4.442–43.
175.

Philosophia speaks:	Athena speaks:
Quod ut possit, paulisper lumina eius	ἀχλὺν δ' αὖ τοι ἀπ' ὀφθαλμῶν
mortalium rerum nube caligantia	ἔλον, ἥ πρὶν ἐπῆεν,
tergamus	ὄφρ' εὖ γιγνώσκῃς ἠμὲν θεὸν ἠδὲ
Cons. 1.2 (prose) 15–16.	καὶ ἄνδρα
	Il. 5.127–28.

Note also the use of this *Iliad* passage with the force of an incantation in Proclus
(see ch. 5C, with notes 55 and 56, above).

ready cited, Philosophy uses Homer primarily to help Boethius *return* from his present despair to the sound principles of philosophy imparted during his first education, which his emotion has now blocked from his mind. She makes explicit reference to Homer four times in the prose passages and once in verse and at several other points alludes to specifically Homeric myth.[176]

The first instance is very close in spirit to the non-explicit borrowings in the opening tableau, but with the important difference that Homer is cited directly in Greek. Philosophia and Boethius now take on the pose of Thetis and Achilles in the scene where the hero reluctantly and poutingly shares his grief with his mother (*Il.* 1.348–427). After the quoted line, "Tell it out; don't hide it in your mind" ('Εξαύδα, μὴ κεῦθε νόῳ, *Il.* 1.363), Boethius responds exactly as Achilles had, by asking Philosophia if her demand is really a necessary one. Here again, however, the allusion is merely decorative, and the echoed Homeric scene soon fades from consciousness without providing more than an imaginatively charged epic backdrop for the symbolic encounter.

In the following chapter, however, when Philosophia cites (with slight modification) the Homeric phrase "let there be one shepherd of the people, one king" (εἰς κοίρανος ἔστω, εἰς βασιλεύς, *Il.* 2.204–5), the context makes it clear that Homer is being evoked in a manner reminiscent of the Plotinian interpretive allusions. Philosophia has just called upon Boethius to remember his true homeland,[177] and the Homeric phrase constitutes an attempt to characterize *that* realm, in contrast to the political chaos of which Boethius is presently the victim. The "native land" evoked here is not necessarily that to which Plotinus enjoins the soul to return, but it is at the very least the focused and unified realm of mind and reason, and it is to this sort of reality that the Homeric passage is made to refer.

Considerably later in the dialogue, Philosophia cites a Homeric line in the rather surprising context of asserting the impossibility of explaining ultimate reality in human speech or of comprehending it with human

176. Philosophy quotes Homer with acknowledgement in the prose sections of Boeth. *Cons.* 1.4; 1.5; 2.2; and 4.6, as well as in the verse section of 5.2. She also alludes to Circe in the poem of 4.2 and to Agamemnon and Odysseus in that of 4.7. The infernal landscape of the Orpheus and Eurydice poem (3.12) is peopled from the *nekyia* of the *Odyssey*. A reference to Tiresias at 5.3 is not relevant here because Boethius's source is a Horatian parody of oracular utterance (Hor. *Sat.* 2.5.59) and the story in question is not Homeric.

177. Cf. Plot. *Enn.* 5.1.1.

reason. She has attempted to reconcile "chance" and "providence": "But it is a hard thing for me to tell all this like a god ['Αργαλέον δέ μοι ταῦτα θεὸν ὣς πάντ' ἀγορεύειν, *Il.* 12.176] for it is not allowed for a man either to comprehend all the devices of the workings of god within his mind or to explain them with his speech." [178] Homer thus becomes the unwilling spokesman of the negative theology. In its original context the line had referred simply to the pressures placed upon the singer by a complex battle narrative, but here it has absorbed the Plotinian understanding of the difficulty of making meaningful statements about the divine through the vehicle of articulate human speech.

In one of the most impressive of the verse passages, Philosophia quotes Homer in Greek and then mentions him by name in order to correct him and bring his statement into line with the truth. The procedure is again Plotinian:

> Honey-voiced Homer sings
> that Phoebus shining with pure light
> "sees and hears all things"
> but he cannot break through
> to the deep center of earth or sea
> with his feeble shimmer.
> The maker of this great universe
> is not so weak: no mass of earth,
> no black clouds of night
> block his view from above.
> He grasps in a single impulse of mind
> what is and was and is to be
> and you might call him the *true* sun
> since he alone sees all things. [179]

178. *Neque enim fas est homini cunctas divinae operae machinas vel ingenio comprehendere vel explicare sermone* (*Cons.* 4.6 [prose] 196–99).

179.
πάντ' ἐφορᾶν καὶ πάντ' ἐπακούειν
puro clarum lumine Phoebum
melliflui canit oris Homerus;
qui tamen intima viscera terrae
non valet aut pelagi radiorum
infirma perrumpere luce.
haud sic magni conditor orbis;
huic ex alto cuncta tuenti
nulla terrae mole resistunt,
non nox atris nubibus obstat.
quae sint, quae fuerint veniantque
uno mentis cernit in ictu;
quem, quia respicit omnia solus,
verum possis dicere solem.
    Cons. 5.2 (poem, complete).

The Homeric material, of course, goes beyond the line quoted in Greek, and the eleventh verse is a translation of τά τ᾽ ἐόντα, τά τ᾽ ἐσσόμενα πρό τ᾽ ἐόντα (*Il.* 1.70). The attributes of the highest god here are derived almost exclusively from Homeric sources, and the only correction, finally, is the clarification that the god in question is the sun only in the sense that the material sun might be taken as a representation of that higher, noetic reality. Related conceptions have come up in Plotinus, Julian, and Macrobius.

Although these are the only references and citations in the *Consolation* leading us directly to the text of Homer, Philosophia also draws upon Homeric exempla to make moral points. Circe's victims are evoked, along with Odysseus's narrow escape (*Cons.* 4.3 [poem]). The moral tag attached to the decorative fable is, however, a paradox. Circe's potions are dismissed as negligible, in that they only transform the body, but leave the mind intact. The poisons most to be feared, according to Philosophia, are those that do the opposite, attacking the mind rather than the body. This adaptation of the *Odyssey* material, though apparently original, is inseparable from the previously existing tradition that imposed moral allegory on the passage. Odysseus and Agamemnon are similarly introduced in the poem of section 4.7, and their function is again a moral one. Their heroism against a backdrop of despair is to inspire Boethius to a similar victory, and the more appropriate Heracles rapidly takes over as the dominant mythological figure of the fable.

Perhaps the most important point to be retained from Boethius's use of Homer is the persistent association of Homer with Philosophia. Just as for Macrobius (drawing upon Numenius and Porphyry) Homer was a philosopher whose doctrines were compatible with those of Plato, so for Boethius Homeric language and myth, properly understood, yield truths about the nature of man and the universe compatible with Platonism.

The authors discussed thus far were the principal philosophical and cultural sources that transmitted a knowledge of the intellectual world of Greece and Rome to the Latin West. Their influence was widespread and demonstrable, and we shall see when we turn to the later Middle Ages that this influence remained strong until the twelfth century and beyond. There is another body of literature, that of the mythographers, that had a comparable role in keeping alive the interpretive tradition, and here again the influence of the texts can be traced through the Middle Ages to the Renaissance. This large and complex literature cannot be explored in depth here, but a sample will suffice to indicate the nature of the stories and interpretations transmitted.

The mythographer Fulgentius was in all probability a contemporary of Boethius's, and is probably to be identified with a sainted bishop of Ruspe in North Africa, known also through his surviving theological writings, who died in 533.[180] Fulgentius's *Mitologiarum libri tres* constitutes a retelling and interpretive analysis of fifty mythological tales. It is interesting to contrast Fulgentius's attitude toward the stories of the pagans with that of Augustine. For Augustine, in an environment in which paganism still constituted a vital threat to Christian orthodoxy, the pagan stories were pernicious and distracting, and attempts to explain and assimilate them to Christian values appeared not only futile but undesirable. For Fulgentius, a century later, at Ruspe (less than 300 km. from Hippo Regius), the situation was radically different and the tools of etymology and allegory are freely applied to pagan stories to harness their esthetic appeal to Christian ends.

The majority of Fulgentius's expositions of myth turn on etymologies, and it must be admitted that these are among the most outrageous specimens of a class of speculation in which extravagant free association is the norm. It is to be assumed that Fulgentius's command of Greek was limited, and of course his historical perspective on the development of language was rudimentary and faulty, but these facts can hardly be held against him. He stands, after all, halfway between the time of Augustine and that of Isidore of Seville, in whose *Etymologiae* the whole of human knowledge is organized around etymologies. Fulgentius's explanations of words are seldom convincing, but in the midst of this methodological chaos, there is a single sound procedure (though even this can be misused). A considerable number of Fulgentius's etymologies for the names of mythological characters are derived from or illustrated by quotations from Homer, presented as authoritative touchstones for the meanings of Greek words.[181] This is certainly a modest and easily defensible use of Homer as authority, and it is Fulgentius's most characteristic form of appeal to him.[182]

180. This is in any case the opinion of Rudolf Helm, the modern editor of Fulgentius (in the preface of his edition, pp. iii–iv), and the reasons for denying the identification seem to stem largely from the deep-seated prejudice against the ancient allegorists, rather than from any solid historical information. See for example Otto Hiltbrunner in KP (2.628): "Gegen die Identität spricht die Torheit des Mythographen, die dem Bischof kaum zuzutrauen ist."

181. Bellerophon (3.1) is an interesting example. Fulgentius would derive the name from *bouleforunta = sapientiae consultator*, a fantasy he supports by citing *Il.* 6.162 (ἀγαθὰ φρονέοντα δαΐφρονα Βελλεροφόντην), apparently taking the formula ἀγαθὰ φρονέοντα to be an explanation of the name.

182. On Fulgentius's twenty-four citations of Homer, see Vincenzo Ciaffi, *Fulgenzio e Petronio*, pp. 54–55. Ciaffi has calculated that Fulgentius had at hand a

The stories from Homer explained in Fulgentius are not conceived of as being more authoritative than other stories. It is clear, too, that although Fulgentius retained a command of Greek unusual for his time and culture, the tales of the Greeks had reentered the oral tradition for him. He is concerned with myths, not texts, and his analyses and interpretations focus on names, first of all, and then on motifs. The predominant mode of Fulgentius's allegory is moral, but the various modes are never neatly separable. Here, for example, is his explanation of the Sirens:

THE TALE OF ULYSSES AND THE SIRENS

The Sirens' name means "attracters," for most men are attracted in various ways by the enticement of love, either by a song, or a pretty face, or a way of acting—for some are loved [lacuna] for the beauty of their faces and some for their lewd habits. Those whom Ulysses' companions pass by with their ears blocked, he himself passes bound. Ulysses' name is the Greek *olonxenos*, that is, "stranger to all," and since wisdom is a stranger to all the things of this world, it is ingeniously called "Ulysses." Thus he both hears and sees—that is, perceives and judges—the Sirens (that is, the enticements of pleasure), and yet passes by. And because they are heard, they are dead, for in the senses of the wise man every passion dies away. They are flying things because they quickly penetrate the minds of lovers, and they have chickens' feet because the passion of lust scatters all that it grasps, and finally that is why they are called "Sirens," for *sirene* [σύρειν] is in Greek "draw, attract." [183]

Since stories such as this are not directly linked to Homer by Fulgentius, these interpretive exercises are of limited value in elucidating the transmission of the divine Homer. It is nevertheless true that Fulgentius cites Homer more frequently than any other Greek author and treats him as an authoritative source (albeit primarily only for the meanings of words),

---

selection from the *Iliad* that probably included the whole of books 1 and 2 and at least the Glaucus and Diomedes episode of book 6.

183. *Fabula Ulixis et Sirenarum. Sirenae enim Grece tractoriae dicuntur; tribus enim modis amoris inlecebra trahitur, aut cantu aut uisu aut consuetudine, amantur enim quaedam . . . quaedam speciei uenustate, quaedam etiam lenante consuetudine. Quas Ulixis socii obturatis auribus transeunt, ipse uero religatus transit. Ulixes enim Grece quasi olonxenos id est omnium peregrinus dicitur; et quia sapientia ab omnibus mundi rebus peregrina est, ideo astutior Ulixes dictus est. Denique Sirenas, id est delectationum inlecebras, et audiuit et uidit id est agnouit et iudicauit, et tamen transiit. Nihilominus ideo et quia auditae sunt, mortuae sunt; in sensu enim sapientis omnis affectus emoritur; ideo uolatiles, quia amantum mentes celeriter permeant; inde gallinaceos pedes, quia libidinis affectus omnia quae habet spargit; nam denique et Sirenes dictae sunt: sirene enim Grece trahere dicitur* (Fulg. Mit. 2.8 [all]).

and that Fulgentius was read and utilized along with Servius, Macro-
bius, and Martianus Capella by the mythographers of the late Middle
Ages, starting at least with Albricus (d. ca. 1217), whose influence on
Petrarch is demonstrable.[184]

Our survey of the use of Homer by the Latin Platonists of the third to
the sixth centuries cannot claim to constitute proof that Homer was universally conceived of in the Latin Middle Ages as a visionary sage who
covertly revealed a Platonic model of reality and the fate of souls in his
poems. It does, however, indicate that authors such as Calcidius, Macrobius, and Boethius, whose influence on the medieval mind was enormous, referred to such a figure when they referred to Homer. The Homeric tales largely returned to the oral tradition during the Middle Ages
and became thoroughly dissociated from the poetry that had been their
vehicle. The name tradition associated with that poetry took on a life of
its own.

If the Homer depicted by Dante resembles the Homer of Martianus
Capella, it is because in the absence of a text, the fragmentarily transmitted portrait of the visionary bard that emerged from the philosophical tradition of late antiquity was the one that prevailed. This portrait
could be sketched only in its general outline in 1300, and much of the
detail that had enriched it a millennium earlier in the commentaries of
Porphyry and Proclus had been lost. Still, it was not as insubstantial as
the "divine" Homer of Plato—couched in ironies and deprived of authority—had been. Even in its reduced, transmitted form it implied a
structure of meaning and a philsophical content to be found in epic poetry that were the products not of a creative but of an interpretive tradition, one that had survived the text it interpreted.

E. THE LATE MIDDLE AGES AND DANTE

Our goal thus far has been to trace the paths by which the hermeneutics
of the later Neoplatonists, and more specifically their eclectic tradition of
Homeric exegesis, were transmitted to the Latin West. At this point, near
the end of our path, we have come too far from the central concerns of
the present study to attempt to do justice to the complex of ideas and
influences that shaped the Latin Middle Ages' conceptions of allegory,

184. Jean Seznec, *The Survival of the Pagan Gods*, pp. 170–74. See ch. 6E, with
n. 213, below on Dante's knowledge of the allegorical interpretation of the *Aeneid*
developed in Fulgentius's *Expositio virgilianae continentiae*.

both active and interpretive. Medieval allegory is in certain of its manifestations demonstrably an outgrowth of such authors as Prudentius, whose background in turn depended on the ancient interpretive traditions. But by the twelfth and thirteenth centuries, Dionysian Platonism, the tradition of allegorical interpretation of myth stretching back to Fulgentius, the traditions of Christian exegesis, and the ideas about meaning in literature transmitted through Macrobius, Boethius, and Martianus Capella had all interacted over such a long period that they had generated a complexity of attitudes and practice regarding text and meaning that lies beyond the scope of our inquiry. It is nevertheless important to establish that, even when Homer was little more than a name associated with such heroes as Achilles and Ulysses, the intellectuals of late medieval Europe had reason to see that dim figure, whose works they could not read, as a poet of visionary authority. We must establish as well that the interpretive tradition we have been tracing is the source—albeit remote—of the attitudes toward the poetry of Homer that enabled the poet of the *Divina Commedia* to attempt in his own powerfully original way to add yet one more masterpiece to a tradition he explicitly traced to Homer. Dante provides an appropriate terminus for this survey, because he stands just on the brink of the *return* of the text of Homer (which occurred within a generation of his death) and at the end of a period of some 900 years in which Homer had existed for the West only as fragments embedded in the literature of rhetoric and philosophy, a poetic reputation without a text.[185]

The ninth-century translations of the Dionysian corpus brought into the Latin West a tradition of exegesis, confined in its application to scriptural texts, that sprang from the milieu of Proclus. But the Latin Middle Ages already had a deep tradition of biblical exegesis stemming from a closely related ancient Platonist tradition and traceable at least as far as Origen. This exegetical method was based on the postulation of three or four levels of meaning in scripture, and its major modern historian, Henri de Lubac, takes the following thirteenth-century formulation as canonical:

Littera gesta docet, quid credas *allegoria,*
Moralis quid agas, quo tendas *anagogia.*[186]

185. On the mechanics of the return and the first perceptions of Homer in fourteenth-century Italy, see D. S. Carne-Ross, "The Means and the Moment."

186. Henri de Lubac, *Exégèse médiévale,* vol. 1, p. 23. "The letter indicates what was done, the allegory what you are to believe, / The moral sense, what you are to do, the anagogic what you are to strive for."

Several important forms of the tripartite model (consisting of historic-mystical-moral meanings and historic-moral-anagogical/allegorical meanings) can be found in Origen, who anticipates the later Neoplatonists on the "literary microcosm" by associating it with a tripartite model of human psychology that he derives from Saint Paul.[187] For de Lubac, Origen and Clement stand at the very beginning of the tradition of Christian exegesis, and his masterful history stresses their originality and independence from their predecessor Philo. Many elements of their thought concerning the meaning of scriptural texts can nevertheless be found in Philo, and the great Philo scholar H. A. Wolfson insisted that the threefold model of scriptural meaning could be traced straight to him (and that Philo's own method in turn owed much to pagan exegesis of Homer).[188] If Origen's intellectual debts remain the subject of debate, his influence is nevertheless easy to trace. Condemned in the East by Justinian in 543, his writings had already been translated into Latin during the last years of the fourth century and the early fifth, and it was in the Latin West that his influence was greatest.[189]

Although the essentials of threefold and fourfold exegesis were frequently restated and constantly applied in the West from at least the sixth century on, the reunion of a complex model of meaning in literature with the impulse to generate new works incorporating such structures does not seem to have occurred before the twelfth (with the exception of the popular personification allegory on the model of Prudentius, whose origins have already been discussed). In the time of Bernard Silvestris and Alain de Lille, many of the threads of thought about the epic tradition and about structures of meaning in literature we have been discussing came together in the School of Chartres. Here we find the decisive influence of the *Timaeus* (by way of Calcidius), of Martianus Capella, and of Boethius, infused with the Neoplatonism of Proclus imported by way of the Dionysian corpus.[190] We find as well an ancient epic poem—the *Aeneid*—as the focus of an influential commentary that taps

187. De Lubac, *Exégèse médiévale*, vol. 1, p. 198. Cf. Chadwick in CHLGEMP, p. 183.

188. Wolfson, *Philo*, vol. 1, pp. 117–33. Cf. de Lubac, *Exégèse médiévale*, vol. 1, p. 204.

189. De Lubac, *Exégèse médiévale*, vol. 1, p. 219.

190. Winthrop Wetherbee, *Platonism and Poetry in the Twelfth Century*, pp. 6–7. Ernst Robert Curtius (*European Literature in the Latin Middle Ages*, pp. 203–7) likewise emphasizes the continuity of the allegorical tradition from the Neopythagoreans to Alain de Lille, culminating in the latter's assertion of the presence of multiple meanings in his own *Anticlaudianus*.

the tradition we have been examining (Servius, Macrobius, Fulgentius, and the other mythographers). The central subject of the *Aeneid* is said to be precisely the one Porphyry found central to the *Odyssey*: "As a philosopher, [Virgil] has described the nature of human life. He proceeds as follows: within the covering [*integumentum*, i.e., the story] he describes the acts and experiences of the human soul temporarily located in a human body."[191]

This commentary was formerly attributed with confidence to Bernard Silvestris, but that attribution has since been doubted.[192] It belongs in any case to the twelfth century, and to the milieu of Bernard, and, with his name attached to it, had sufficient authority to become a school text in Italy.[193] Following Fulgentius, the commentary makes the claim that Virgil was both poet (and maker of *integumenta*) and philosopher (cryptically conveying human truths), but that the sequence of the two resultant *Aeneids* remains different. The fiction, beginning *in medias res*, follows the *ordo artificialis*, but the "philosopher's truth" lying beneath follows the *ordo naturalis* and proceeds sequentially. Thus the shipwreck of book 1 is a metaphor for birth (= Fulg. *Expos. Virg. cont.* 91.6–11), books 2 and 3 contain fables of childhood, and so forth. The cycle would seem to be complete with book 6, which takes up most of the commentator's time and energy, but he breaks off as Aeneas is about to enter Elysium, and his conclusions are lost to us.

Although his major sources knew Greek, the commentator clearly does not—the few words with which he sprinkles his text are badly garbled—and so he predictably makes little reference to Homer. His perspective on Homer is, in fact, remarkably close to Dante's. He considers Virgil the author of a poetic fiction about the Trojan War, "not following the historical truth, which Dares Phrygius described," but rather following the wishes of Augustus (p. 1). In creating his *ficmenta*, the *Latinorum poetarum maximus* followed the *Graecorum poetarum maximus* (p. 1), and it is impossible not to conclude that the "twin doctrines" (the poetic fiction and the philosophical truth) discussed at length in elucidating Virgil were present as well in the works of Homer. This, however, is the only point at which our commentator mentions Homer's name, and it is clear

191. *Scribit ergo in quantum est philosophus humane vite naturam. Modus agendi talis est: in integumento describit quid agat vel quid paciatur humanus spiritus in humano corpore temporaliter positus* ([Bernardus Silvestris], *Commentum super sex libros Eneidos Virgilii*, p. 3).

192. See the comments of J. W. Jones and E. F. Jones in their edition, pp. ix–xi.

193. Jones and Jones (n. 192 above), p. xix.

that the gap separating him from Virgil is very great, and that from Homer hopelessly greater.

The influence in the School of Chartres of Neoplatonism, and specifically of the interpretive ideas transmitted by the traditions under examination here, has been explored in a recent study by Winthrop Wetherbee. He argues for a development in the twelfth century closely analogous to the one we have found in the fifth: a wedding of ancient works (themselves with some allegorical content) and recent Platonizing allegorical commentary to produce a new kind of deliberately allegorical poetry. "In satires, didactic and cosmic 'visions', and a host of occasional lyrics, [Martianus, Boethius] and the insights of their commentators are assimilated to the uses of original creation." [194] The result is that "new kinds of literary expression become possible," [195] and the *kinds* of meaning postulated by an interpretive tradition are incorporated in new works that themselves imitate ancient models conceived in ways that would have bewildered their authors and their first public.

This pattern of influence by way of a transforming interpretive tradition may well be very widespread indeed. In the cases of antiquity and the Middle Ages, the process is very slow and in some instances recoverable. Some surviving interpretive texts allow us to examine the complete equation:

The text generates a literature of commentary that stands in greater and greater opposition to the text's apparent meaning until at last a new text emerges, able to replace both. To put it rather differently, the author conceives his relationship to a tradition as one of imitation, or at least of participation, but his own historicity (given concrete form in the traditions under discussion by the commentaries that mediate between him and the text) has transformed that text and imposed on the imitation a radically new structure of meaning.

Wetherbee is concerned principally to explore the influence of Platonizing allegorism in the poetry of Bernard Silvestris and Alain de Lille, both working in genres removed from epic as usually conceived. But he goes on to explore the influence of these poets in vernacular poetry and

194. Wetherbee, *Platonism and Poetry*, p. 126.
195. Ibid., p. 143.

in the narratives of Marie de France and Chrétien de Troyes. A passage from the prologue to the *Lais* of Marie de France calls up the familiar idea that there is a deliberately maintained distance between the poetic fictions of the ancients and their intention:

Es livres ke jadis feseient
Assez oscurement diseient . . .[196]

Her idea of their motivation in "speaking obscurely" is more original. The early poets, she claims, anticipated the subtler understanding of later readers and wrote not for their limited and boorish contemporaries but for the ideally sensitive audience they anticipated. Wetherbee finds only slight traces of Chartrian influence here, but the *Erec et Enide* of Chrétien de Troyes displays "an elaborate pattern of allusions to the 'philosophical' *Aeneid*." [197] Thus, over a century before Dante, vernacular poetry in an epic mode had begun to show the influence of a renewed interest in ancient epic seen through the eyes of an allegorizing Platonist interpretive tradition. In an intellectual world virtually without Greek, the commentators and poets of the twelfth century looked no further than Virgil. But Homer stood there beyond Virgil as his master and model, who had doubtless taught him the basic procedures of his poetry and the relationship between *integumentum* and philosophical truth. Neither poet, certainly, had been satisfied with the mere historical facts of the Trojan War. As the commentary attributed to Bernard Silvestris indicates, the twelfth century held that Dares Phrygius constituted the reliable historical source. The goals of the epic poets were far more elevated and complex.

Looking further among the Chartrians and beyond, we find the influence of Platonist exegesis in a form manifestly derivative from the Dionysiac corpus in Guillaume de Conches (himself a student of Bernard of Chartres) and in his contemporary Abelard. Peter Dronke, the most recent scholar to examine the critical theories of these thinkers, calls attention to the adoption by Richard of St.-Victor and by Guillaume de Conches and Abelard of the Dionysian term σύμβολον in the transliteration (*symbolum*) used by John Scotus Eriugena in his translation.[198] It would appear from Dronke's study of a number of still unpublished twelfth-

196. Ibid., p. 228.
197. Ibid., p. 236.
198. Dronke, *Fabula*, pp. 4, 44–47. Hilduin's earlier translation used *indicium* or *consulcio* for σύμβολον. Dronke equally emphasizes the importance of the term αἴνιγμα for these interpreters.

century interpretive texts that the distinction between σύμβολα and εἰκόνες, already complicated in Proclus by the postulation of non-mimetic εἰκόνες of eternal παραδείγματα, was further blurred in the late Middle Ages. The idea, however, of a non-mimetic, symbolic art, directing the mind toward the divine through "dissimilar" symbols, and the claim that this is the theological mode of myth, are an important part of the legacy of late Athenian Neoplatonism brought to fruition in the twelfth century.

In his glosses on Macrobius, moreover, Guillaume de Conches shows a particular interest in the Porphyrian allegory of the cave of the nymphs. As Jean Pépin has pointed out, Guillaume's language makes it clear that he had another source beyond Macrobius for Porphyry's essay.[199] The Chartrians were clearly fascinated by Neoplatonic mystical allegory and had access to sources beyond the most obvious ones surveyed above.

Dante never leaves us in doubt concerning the tradition in which he is working. Indeed, one is inclined to say that he is too clear about that tradition, and that that clarity can be misleading. The Virgil who breaks his long silence in the dark wood of the first canto of the *Inferno* will constitute Dante's liberation from error, his mentor and guide. Why Virgil? In the personification allegory that is the prevalent mode of that opening canto, Virgil is usually said to represent Reason, the highest aspiration of man short of the revelation of true religion. Though there is doubtless much truth in this reading, he represents something more as well for Dante. He stands for the poetic imagination that can (as in *Eclogue* 4) clothe itself in the language of prophecy and so reveal more than it can know.

By 1300 Virgil was seen as a poet whose fictive *integumenta* cloaked a philosophical core, and when he takes Dante by the hand to lead him as far on the spiritual journey as his own limitations permit, he is accepting Dante into the company of such poets, those who aspire to the grand challenge of epic. As the two descend together past the forbidding gates, the first sight that greets them is the school of poets, gathered around its founder, Homer. Now the equation is complete. Dante aspires to speak as Virgil's mouthpiece—that is, to give voice again to the epic tradition Virgil had taken up from Homer. I would suggest that, without the interpretive tradition that has been the subject of this study, Dante could not have conceived of his own poem as the heir of the *Aeneid* and ultimately of the mysterious and forgotten *Iliad* and *Odyssey*.[200]

199. Pépin, "La Fortune du *de antro nympharum* de Porphyre en occident," pp. 532–33.
200. This position is taken by David Thompson in *Dante's Epic Journeys*. De-

The problem of Dante's use of this tradition, and of his debts to it, can be broken down into several smaller problems. First, there is Dante's own allegory in the *Commedia*; second, there is the theoretical statement on allegory contained in the letter to Can Grande; and finally—particularly interesting from our point of view—there are the references to Homer and to Homeric stories in Dante's works. Before starting, however, it should be stated clearly that we are dealing here with intangibles. There is no proof that Dante knew the *Aeneid* commentary attributed to Bernard Silvestris.[201] There is no irrefutable proof that he knew even so widely influential an author as Macrobius, though several passages in his works would appear to echo the *Saturnalia* and the *Commentary on Scipio's Dream*.[202] By the end of the twelfth century, the influence of these Platonizing authors was pervasive, and even Aristotle, Dante's "maestro di color che sanno," could become a spokesman for Neoplatonic ideas in such pseudepigrapha as the *Liber de causis*.[203] For all the influence of Aquinas on Dante's intellectual development, it remains plausible that this popular and pervasive Platonizing tradition, inclined as it was to give a special position of authority to early epic, lies behind Dante's choice of genre and his definition of the tradition that, by his own declaration, he set out to extend.

The French Dante scholar André Pézard has suggested that the influence of the Platonic tradition on Dante was indeed very great, and that in the period 1290–92 Dante actually read not only such authors as Macrobius but the philosophers themselves. Pézard even expresses the belief that the late thirteenth century had Latin translations of Plato, Plotinus, and Porphyry, since lost.[204] We may not want to follow Pézard to the extent of postulating lost translations, but we may take seriously

---

veloping an idea he traces to H. T. Silverstein ("Dante and Virgil the Mystic"), Thompson attempts to "relate Dante's major allegorical mode to classical and medieval interpretations of epic poetry rather than to patristic Biblical exegesis" (*Dante's Epic Journeys*, p. ix; cf. pp. 4–11), and relies heavily on the commentary on the *Aeneid* attributed to Bernard Silvestris.

201. Thompson, *Dante's Epic Journeys*, p. 28 with note.

202. See Georg Rabuse, "Saturne et l'échelle de Jacob," and for a summary, his article "Macrobio" in the *Enciclopedia Dantesca* (vol. 3, pp. 757–59).

203. See ch. 6B above. Dante mentions the *Liber de causis* seven times without naming its author. He may well not have been deceived by the prevalent attribution of the work to Aristotle.

204. A. Pézard, "*La rotta gonna*," vol. 3, p. 258. Another possibility, raised by P. Renucci, is that allegorical reading of the Latin epic was introduced to Dante in Bologna, around 1304–6. See Pépin, *Dante et la tradition de l'allégorie*, p. 101, n. 1. Pépin surveys the instances of allegorized classical myth in Dante, pp. 101–18.

his exposition of the pervasive Platonist themes not only in the *Commedia* but in the earlier works as well, and also his suggestion that Dante's conversion to philosophy after the death of Beatrice *must* (given the intellectual climate of his time) have exposed the poet to Platonism. There is even considerable evidence that Dante was influenced by Porphyry's essay on the cave of the nymphs. No medieval translation is known, but a series of echoes of the essay in the *Commedia* suggests that his knowledge of it went beyond what he could have learned from Macrobius.[205] If Dante does not mention such sources by name, we must remember that the *Commedia* is in a sense an antidote to Boethius's *Consolation of Philosophy*. Dante's conversion to philosophy was short-lived, and the shaping ideology of the *Commedia* repeatedly reminds us of philosophy's inadequacy. The actual content of Dante's intellectual adventure of 1290–92— the books read and discussed—remains clothed in silence. But Pézard's proposal is a plausible one, which might explain not only scattered Platonic themes in Dante but even the eventual choice of epic as the vehicle for his most ambitious undertaking.

Dante's practice of allegory cannot be summed up simply, because it takes on multiple forms.[206] No one will deny the presence in Dante of personification allegory of a type easily traceable to Martianus Capella and to Prudentius, and far beyond them to Homer himself. We can class together here the personifications of abstractions whether named (Fortuna, Amor) or left nameless. Of the first sort there are few examples in Dante, and those are purely conventional. Dante's Fortuna has a wheel (*Inf.* 15.95), and of the eighteen instances of the noun, Vandelli's edition capitalizes six. This example is characteristic of a small class of personified abstractions, which have a role in the *Commedia* roughly comparable to that of such figures as Eris in the *Iliad*. More striking, but still not characteristic of Dante's style in general, are such figures as the three beasts of *Inferno* 1, variously interpreted as luxury, pride, and avarice, or as incontinence, violence, and fraud. This passage, along with the allegorical procession of *Purgatorio* 19, stands out as profoundly different in esthetic impact from the greater part of the poem. Here there exists little

205. Pézard points to the influence of the essay in numerous passages including *Par.* 4.52–54 and 58–60; *Par.* 30.61–69, 90, 109; *Par.* 31.7–9 and 106, and *Purg.* 25.88–108. See the comments of Pépin ("La Fortune du *de antro nympharum* de Porphyre en occident," pp. 533–36), who concludes that Dante must have had some access to the essay other than Macrobius.

206. There is a long bibliography on this subject, but the recent synthesis in Robert Hollander's *Allegory in Dante's Commedia* includes a useful survey of theories (pp. 3–14). Hollander's conclusions are discussed in n. 218 below.

doubt that the surface of the fable is meant to be seen *through*, populated as it is by purely symbolic creatures with none of the immediacy and specificity of detail that characterize the greater part of the poem. Here, indeed, Dante evokes the "plaisir délicat de l'allégorisme" [207] central to the esthetics of much medieval art, and these passages were enough to set Dante's early commentators to work finding and explicating such symbolism throughout the poem. Nevertheless, these passages do stand out as uncharacteristic of the poem as a whole—personification allegory of this sort is within the range of Dante's styles, but it is by no means a major mode of expression in the *Commedia*.

What other modes of allegory characterize the *Commedia*? Beyond this most familiar type, we encounter major problems of definition, and the most useful procedure will be to look to the poet's own statements on allegory. Given the extent of Dante's recorded statements on interpretation, the difficulty of relating those statements to his practice (at least in the *Commedia*) is an indication of the richness and freedom from system of the poem. The most obviously relevant passages are in the *Convivio*, where a fourfold model of interpretation is developed, clearly dependent on the widespread medieval tradition of Christian exegesis. Dante distinguishes the literal, allegorical,[208] moral, and anagogical[209] meanings. This model from scriptural exegesis is here applied to three of Dante's own *canzoni*. The *Convivio* was abandoned before the beginning of work on the *Commedia*, but was originally intended to explicate fourteen poems in all. The obsession with explanation—the sense that the complete work consists not simply of poems but of poems accompanied by texts that instruct the reader and mediate between him and the poem—goes back still further, to the *Vita Nuova*, where poems and prose text are separated in time by the death of Beatrice (1290) and complement each other to create a complete narrative. Aside from the explanation of a few figures that hardly seem to us to require justification (e.g., *VN* 25), the interpretive texts of the *Vita Nuova* are descriptive and unambitious. And even in the *Convivio*, where the model from scriptural exegesis is evoked and applied, the emphasis remains on the literal meaning: "siccome quello nella cui sentenza gli altri sono inchiusi" (2.1.67–68). This emphasis is borne out in the explanations themselves, and has made it

207. See ch. 5, with n. 80, above.

208. Dante characterizes the allegorical meaning as "quello che si nasconde sotto il manto di queste favole, . . . una verità ascosa sotto bella menzogna" (*Conv.* 2.1.22–25).

209. "cioè sovra senso" (*Conv.* 2.1.53).

easy for those who would underline the modernity of Dante and the methodological acceptability of his mode of reading to minimize these matters.[210] Yet the fact remains that for Dante reading was a complex act of intellectual searching. It is doubtless true that he starts with the surface and treats that surface with great respect. When he is explicating his own poems, we may even say that he "respects the intention" of the poet. But in doing so, he is constantly aware that the goal lies beyond the surface. When the "litterale sentenza" is explained, then it is time to go on to the "allegorical and true exposition."[211]

When we look at Dante on poems remote from his own time, we find him reading epic in the framework provided by earlier allegorical commentators. Thus the *Aeneid* as an allegory of the ages of man reaches him from Fulgentius (*Conv.* 4.26).[212] We will certainly agree that Dante's view of antiquity is vastly richer and more complex than that of Fulgentius, whose naiveté and absurd etymologies represent one of the most extreme and least credible manifestations of the interpretive tradition.[213] Nevertheless, it was the tradition that insisted on the polysemous quality of poetry (and particularly of epic) that shaped Dante's conception of the poetic text, and that is the source to which we must go in order to understand the *Commedia* in the context of its tradition.

The letter to Can Grande (*Ep.* 10 in Toynbee's edition), whatever doubts may have been expressed regarding its authenticity,[214] is the logical outgrowth of the *Vita Nuova* and the *Convivio*. It is the interpretive complement to the *Paradiso*, and if its implications and its authenticity could be fully accepted, it should probably appear as preface to the final section of the *Commedia*.[215] The part of the letter that concerns us (sections 7–11) opens with the claim that there is no simple meaning of the text at hand (i.e., the *Paradiso*), but rather that it is "*polysemos*," (a word Dante apparently found in the lexicon of Uguccione da Pisa, likewise the source of the

210. See, for example, R. S. Haller's comments on Dante's interpretive efforts in *Literary Criticism of Dante Alighieri*, pp. 122–23.

211. ". . . è da procedere alla esposizione allegorica e vera" (*Conv.* 2.13.1–3).

212. The commentary attributed to Bernard Silvestris is a likely intermediary. See Giorgio Padoan (s.v. "Bernardo Silvestre" in the *Enciclopedia Dantesca*, vol. 1, p. 607), who asserts that the interpretation is "quasi sicuramente" derived from the commentary, whether directly or indirectly.

213. On Fulgentius and Dante, see Ubaldo Pizzani in the *Enciclopedia Dantesca* vol. 3, p. 72 s.v. "Fulgenzio."

214. See Paget Toynbee, *Dantis Alagherii Epistolae*, p. 163.

215. *Itaque, formula consummata epistolae, ad introductionem oblati operis aliquid sub lectoris officio compendiose aggrediar* (*Ep.* 10.4).

etymologies of *comoedia* and *tragoedia* in the same passage).[216] The distinction among the levels of meaning that follows is familiar, and is based on an initial separation of the *literalis sensus,* which the text has *per literam,* and the *allegoricus sive mysticus sensus,* which it possesses *per significata per literam.* These levels are illustrated in an analysis of Psalm 114.1–2, where in fact four levels are distinguished by subdividing the *allegoricus sensus* into three. The illustration makes it clear that the "literal sense" may be taken to be equivalent to the historic and the "allegorical" (*sensu stricto*) is the typological (by which the Hebrew scriptures are taken to prefigure the Gospels). There remain the "moral sense" and the "anagogical sense," this last the heir of Neoplatonic mystical allegory that found in diverse texts the encoded message that souls temporarily trapped in bodies will escape to their true home.

After blocking out this model exegesis, Dante turns to his own poem and applies the model there as well. It, too, can be taken *literaliter,* in which case its subject is the *status animarum post mortem;* it can also be taken *allegorice,* and viewed thus its subject is "man, in that according to what he has deserved or failed to deserve in the exercise of his freedom of will he is subject to the reward or punishment of justice."[217] This constitutes a curious structural inversion. The *sensus literalis* of the *Paradiso* is similar in content to the *sensus anagogicus* of scripture, and Dante's poem read *per significata per literam* becomes a statement about *this* world, dominated by what must be considered a *sensus moralis.* Thus through the literal description of what scripture treats allegorically (in its anagogical aspect), Dante claims to have built a moral allegory, a statement to the reader centering on *quid agas.* None of this is terribly surprising or audacious, and if we read the letter to Can Grande in this way, it hardly seems to demand that we read the *Paradiso* differently than we might otherwise do. We are concerned here, though, with the background of Dante's conception of his art and the relationship of that conception to his understanding of the epic tradition. It is in this sense that the multiple levels of meaning claimed for the poem indicate a significant continuity of tradition.

It is surprising, first of all, that Dante moves so easily from scripture to his own poem. Must this not have seemed culpably pretentious to the devout apologist of faith over reason? What right had Dante to imitate (and to invert) the structure of meaning of scripture? His right, I would

216. Toynbee *ad loc.* (*Dantis Alagherii Epistolae,* p. 173, n. 2).

217. *Si vero accipiatur opus allegorice, subiectum est homo prout merendo et demerendo per arbitrii libertatem iustitiae praemiandi et puniendi obnoxius est* (*Ep.* 10.8).

suggest, lay in the genre he practiced and in the epic tradition itself, which was the one body of literature aside from the Hebrew and Greek scriptures that deserved to be designated *scriptura* or *scrittura*.[218] Only by way of the allegorists had *scriptura* come to encompass this entire body of literature, and it is thanks to the allegorists that Dante can find a place to stand in the epic tradition. His conception of the nature of the *Aeneid* may in some ways be closer to our own than to that of "Bernard Silvestris" or Fulgentius, but his conception of the scope of intention and the complexity of meaning of the epic tradition belonged securely to his own historical moment, and it was this conception that made the *Commedia* possible.

But what of the forerunner of Virgil and founder of the tradition, Homer? Dante mentions him by name only seven times, always drawing his references from later authors, usually Aristotle.[219] The association with Aristotle (whose citations Dante may have taken, more seriously than can a modern reader, as appeals to poetic authority) reminds us of the persistent association of Homer with Philosophy in the *Consolation of Philosophy*. Macrobius, for his part, must have conveyed to Dante, directly or indirectly, the notion that Homer was Virgil's model, for that is surely the conception of the epic tradition conveyed by the portrayal of the poets of the "nobile castello." And these remain the central elements of Dante's evocation of Homer—he is the "poeta sovrano," the one who soars like an eagle over the others (*Inf.* 4.88), the one whom the Muses nourished more than any other (*Purg.* 22.101), the master of Dante's master in song, and an authoritative voice quoted by the "maestro di color che sanno" (e.g., *Conv.* 4.20). But Homer was unavailable: "non si mutò di Greco in Latino" (*Conv.* 1.7). Not only did Dante lack a knowledge of the *Iliad* and *Odyssey*, but not even the *Ilias Latina* was available to him, and he shows no evidence of having read his period's "historical" sources for the Trojan War,

218. Hollander, *Allegory in Dante's Commedia*, p. 32. In the letter under discussion Dante refers to a passage from Lucan as *scriptura paganorum* (*Ep.* 10.22). Hollander further argues that of the three modes of allegory known to Dante, it was the fourfold scriptural allegory that he strove to imitate (pp. 23–24 and passim). Hollander plays down the importance of the commentators on Virgil in Dante's conception of the *Aeneid* (pp. 96–103), insisting on the primacy of the historic sense in Virgil and the reflection of that priority in the realistic and historical immediacy of the *Commedia*. Hollander's analysis is a sensitive one, and I agree with most of his conclusions, but I would still argue that it was the existence of the allegorizing tradition and the prevalent conception of the surface of the epic narrative as an ahistorical *integumentum* that allowed Dante to situate his own work in the tradition of Homer and Virgil.

219. Summary in G. Martelotti's article "Omero" in the *Enciclopedia Dantesca* (vol. 4, pp. 145–48).

Dares and Dictys.[220] The connection is indeed remote, and when in the *De monarchia* (1.10) the phrase "let there be one ruler" is echoed from the *Iliad* by way of Aristotle, one is reminded of its echoes in the Arabic tradition, likewise no doubt traceable to the last words of *Metaphysics* Λ.[221]

Dante clearly did know a few *Odyssey* stories, but these were easily available in Virgil, and in Dante's mind can at best belong to Homer at second hand. Most of this material is simply absorbed as metaphor into the fabric of Dante's language. This is the case with the Sirens, specifically an image for *cupiditas* in the fifth letter (*Ep.* 5.4), dramatically elaborated as such in the symbolism of the dream that opens *Purgatorio* 19. There Dante is confronted by a hideous hag who, as he looks at her, is transformed into a seductive Siren and then claims to have drawn Ulysses from his course. The apparent deviation from the *Odyssey* story is not surprising and can easily be ascribed either to Dante's ignorance or to a conflation of Circe and the Sirens, but it may equally be understood as creative distortion of the original situation for dramatic effect. What Dante hears in his dream is prefigured in the Sirens' song of *Odyssey* 12, and neither Homer's Sirens nor Dante's can be expected either to advertise their failures or to tell the truth. Indeed, both on the level of imagery and on that of the Siren's motivation, this is the one point in the *Commedia* at which Dante the epic voyager—in dream—stands in the tracks, even in the persona, of his predecessor Odysseus. He hears the same voice sing the same seductive song, adapted to a new listener; for the Siren clearly *takes* Dante for a traveler on the path of Odysseus, and when she brags of having lured the prototype astray, it is to assert her power over her present listener.

Aeneas had followed in Odysseus's footsteps, and now, however distantly, the voyage of Dante repeats that epic quest. Aeneas often expresses his hate for Odysseus, most strikingly when he narrates the voyage past Ithaca:

> We fled past the rocks of Ithaca, Laertes' kingdom,
> and cursed the land that nourished fierce Ulysses

> effugimus scopulos Ithacae, Laertia regna,
> et terram altricem saevi exsecramur Ulixi.
> <div align="right">(<i>Aen.</i> 3.272–73)</div>

220. Martelotti, "Omero," p. 146.

221. The phrase εἷς κοίρανος ἔστω (*Il.* 2.204) had a remarkable popularity among the Arabs (Kraemer, "Arabische Homerverse," p. 261) and is echoed with no indication of its ultimate source by Dante: *malum autem pluralitas principatuum, unus ergo Princeps* (*De mon.* 1.10).

The Ulysses of the *Aeneid* becomes a focus of the Roman poet's ambiva-
lent attitude toward Greek ingenuity.[222] The characteristic Virgilian epithets for Ulysses consistently emphasize his deceitfulness, his seduc-
tiveness, his gift for manipulation through language: he is *pellax* (*Aen.*
2.90), *scelerum inventor* (2.164), and (albeit in a denigrating taunt) *fandi
fictor* (9.602). It is this Odysseus, not Homer's, whom Dante encounters
in the eighth circle of Hell among the evil counselors, and that encounter
is the occasion of a curious and disorienting resolution of the ambiguities of the relationship of the three poems and their protagonists.
Dante's apparently original reworking of the conclusion of Odysseus's
story (*Inf.* 26.90–142) is well known. The disastrous last voyage of this
voracious and restless intellect has been read as a metaphor for the "misguided philosophical Odyssey" of Dante's own experience just after the
death of Beatrice.[223] Odysseus's mistaken and intellectually pretentious
journey, then, has finally taken him no further than this eternal post
near the bottom of Hell, with no hope of passing through with Dante to
redemption (or even, with Virgil, to the brink of redemption). It is with
Aeneas, not Odysseus, that Dante has (though with self-deprecating humility) identified his fictional persona (*Inf.* 2.32), and Aeneas himself is
with Homer and the other virtuous but unbaptized souls (*Inf.* 4.122),
where Virgil must eventually return. The mere fact of the existence of
the "nobile castello" of *Inferno* 4, where the virtuous pagans may enjoy
the pleasure of one another's company and the measure of eternal reward implied therein, is the major structural intrusion of the classical
tradition into the otherwise symmetrically Christian world-system of the
poem, and it provides an abode for Virgil and his protagonist, as well as
for Homer. But Odysseus, the prototype of that protagonist, has become
the scapegoat whose seductive intellectual pretension stands for the failure of a tradition, a shortcoming translated into a vice by the addition of
willful deception.

These, then, are the strata of the tradition into which the *Commedia*
fits. Not even Virgil can stay with Dante beyond the beatific vision of
Purgatorio 30, and his disappearance is one of the most poignant moments in the poem. Homer, for his part, was never more than the sover-
eign spirit of the "bella scola," a fleeting and ill-defined figure, and his
most memorable creation, Odysseus, lies condemned by a verdict that is

222. The seminal study of Odysseus from the *Iliad* to the *Commedia* and beyond is, of course, W. B. Stanford, *The Ulysses Theme.* On Virgil's Ulysses, see
esp. pp. 128–37.

223. Thompson, *Dante's Epic Journeys*, p. 72.

one of the harshest reminders of the distance separating Dante's value system from our own. But it is doubtless true that the condemnation of Odysseus is a self-condemnation on Dante's part, a self-castigation for past error, and so its harshness need not surprise us. If the intellectual pretension of the pagan tradition is condemned to eternal pain, its epic poets are consigned to what bliss they might themselves have wished, and it is clear that it was as the allegorical θεολόγοι of their respective cultures that they succeeded one another, and that it is in this same role that Dante has stepped into their company.

Preconception and Understanding:
The Allegorists
in Modern Perspective

What has been elaborated here is the history of perhaps the most power-ful and enduring of the "strong misreadings" (to use Harold Bloom's term) that make up our cultural heritage. I have avoided any attempt to hold that reading of Homer up against others, to affirm or to deny it, beyond occasional observations on analogies between these ancient in-terpretive critics and those of our own time. My reticence on this score reveals an implicit model of reading with similarities to Bloom's, and no doubt in part derivative from it. Beyond his definition of the poles of in-terpretation as strong and weak misreading, I would add that strategies of power on the level of the definition of sanity intervene to regulate the history of interpretive traditions. At any given moment, in any given in-terpretive community, a range of (mis-)readings of any text is possible, and outside that range lies—if not madness—then at the very least a mode of discourse easily consigned to the categories of the odd, the quirky, the intellectually negligible. Today, the Neoplatonists' reading of Homer is beyond the pale. Its advocates (if indeed it has any) may not be certifiable on this basis alone, but if not, then they owe their *sursis* only to the tenuous and exquisite moment of crisis in literary theory in which we live. For a thousand years, however, their reading had just the op-posite status—it was central to the sane, to the possible range of inter-pretation, and I know of no more compelling criterion of validity.

The heart of this study has been the thesis that this oldest surviving European tradition of interpretive criticism was in part responsible for the birth of developed allegorical literature in late antiquity, and that it formed the background for the next great contribution to the epic tradi-tion, the *Divina Commedia*. This thesis does not depend on our "taking seriously" the interpretive efforts of the Neoplatonic allegorists, nor does it require that we read Dante any differently. If correct, however, it does throw light on the way in which a mode of reading first generated a mode of writing, and then, through the pervasive influence of its claims for the scope of the meaning and intention of early epic, established the conditions for future contributions to that tradition.

But what of the allegorists' efforts themselves? Allegorical interpretation, ancient, medieval, and modern, has a bad reputation in our time. We imagine the allegorists to have been guilty of willful deception in distorting the meaning of texts, imposing foreign ideas upon them, and then compounding their crimes by appealing to those texts as authority for the very ideas they have fraudulently attached to them. But if we cannot "take seriously" the claims we find in Porphyry and in Proclus regarding the meaning of the *Iliad* and *Odyssey*, then we are left with a curious and unsatisfying model of the cultural process in question. "Garbage in" the tradition's computer seems, against all odds, to have generated not "garbage out" but the *Paradiso*.

If we say that in ancient terms "allegorical interpretation" is coextensive with what we are accustomed to call "interpretation" *tout court*, we are left with the same dilemma, for the modern dislike of allegorical interpretation carries over to interpretation of a sort we would not call allegorical. The hostility takes many forms, from the now somewhat dated esthetic polemic of Susan Sontag's famous essay "Against Interpretation" (1964) to the staid disapproval of G. M. A. Grube's discussion of ancient reading quoted earlier.[1] It is interesting that Sontag incorporated into her essay a historical model widespread in classical scholarship, though by now surely discredited, when she claimed that interpretation made its first appearance in "late classical antiquity."[2] This is an idea that has died hard, and classical scholarship has been reluctant to admit that interpretation, which is doubtless as old as reading itself, was every bit as much a part of the intellectual life of classical Athens as it was eight or nine centuries later. This reluctance was eloquently expressed in Hugh Lloyd-Jones's initial resistance to a mid–fourth-century date for the Orphic interpretive papyrus from Derveni.[3] One must be sympathetic to the im-

1. See Preface above.
2. Susan Sontag, "Against Interpretation," p. 5.
3. "Well, if they are right, this is a most sensational fact from the point of view of content," he observed. "Who ever knew that the Greeks were writing commentaries on poetry, and on Orphic poetry at that, as early as the fourth century? . . . it would be exceedingly dangerous if the hypothesis of an early

pulse to keep the classical moment of fifth-century Athens as a haven of clarity and directness, of rational inquiry, in contrast to the intellectual muddle of late Greek philosophy, riddled with dogmatism, theurgy, and long-dead certainties. But if there is much truth in the traditional formulation, there is also a powerful element of myth, particularly in the model of the relationship of reader and text, for all practical purposes the product of the Enlightenment, which we project into classical Athens.

Indeed, the myth is one of the many that we can trace to the Platonic dialogues and their dramatization of the intellectual life of the last years of the fifth century, and specifically to Socrates' rejection, in the *Protagoras*, of the discussion of the meaning of texts from the poets, "whom it is impossible to interrogate about what they are saying."[4] It is this refreshing, rational, no-nonsense approach that is the most natural to us in confronting the problem of interpretation. "Texts don't mean anything, *people* do," we say in effect, and both the strengths and the weaknesses of that position can be traced right to Socrates' equation of the meaning of a text with the intention of its author and to his rejection of interpretation on the grounds that when texts are discussed, "some say the poet meant one thing, some say he meant another, and they go on talking about something they have no power to verify."[5]

We may in general characterize Socrates' position here as the Enlightenment position, and indeed although it may well have been taken by the historical Socrates, and has affinities with the scholarly principles of the Alexandrians, its general application as a hermeneutical principle serving as the basis for a methodology probably does not antedate the Enlightenment. It leaves open only two paths of action. The first is the total rejection of texts as a means to truth (or even to understanding)— Socrates' position here, echoed in Plato's Letter 7. The other, more moderate and practical approach, is the reduction of problems of meaning to

---

date were to be generally accepted without careful consideration of all the difficulties involved." Discussion of the paper of S. G. Kapsomenos, "The Orphic Papyrus Roll of Thessaloniki," *Bulletin of the American Society of Papyrologists* 2 (1964):20. Lloyd-Jones seems to have adjusted his views over two decades, however, and wrote recently with apparent sangfroid, in a review of a new Homer commentary, "The Greeks themselves started to write commentaries on Greek poems as early as the fourth century B.C." (*London Review of Books* 4, no. 16 [1982]:14).

4. οὓς οὔτε ἀνερέσθαι οἷόν τ᾽ ἐστὶν περὶ ὧν λέγουσιν (Plato *Prot.* 347e).

5. [ἐπαγόμενοί τε αὑτοὺς (sc., τοὺς ποιητάς) οἱ πολλοὶ ἐν τοῖς λόγοις] οἱ μὲν ταῦτά φασιν τὸν ποιητὴν νοεῖν, οἱ δ᾽ ἕτερα, περὶ πράγματος διαλεγόμενοι ὃ ἀδυνατοῦσι ἐξελέγξαι (ibid.).

the level of definition and syntax. This goes hand in hand with the assertion that the authors of texts "are quite capable of expressing their meaning clearly" to their audiences.[6] In other words, what we have called the Enlightenment position denies the historicity of the reader and postulates an eternal and unchanging meaning lying behind the text, a meaning coextensive with the intention of the author at the moment of the creation of the text, and either recoverable or unrecoverable, but not in any case subject to significant deterioration or change over time. A text means what the author meant, *or* it means nothing, should that meaning escape us.

But there is an alternative to the Enlightenment position on meaning in texts and its attendant blanket rejection of interpretation. There is a view of the relationship of reader and text within which the efforts of the allegorists can be seen to have been a respectable intellectual endeavor, and not the offenses against reason and truth they have seemed to so many.

The debate on the historicity of the observer and its implications for the methodology of the disciplines whose object is man has its roots in German thought at the beginning of the nineteenth century, with Hegel, Friedrich Schlegel, and Schleiermacher. In Schleiermacher, the problem of comprehension, of understanding a text, is one of the recovery of the original thought, an action made possible by the fundamental harmony of intellects, which transcends time. A similar sense of the relationship of meaning and text can be found in the English Platonist Thomas Taylor's remarks on translating ancient texts: "Since all truth is eternal, its nature can never be altered by transposition, though, by this means, its dress may be varied, and become less elegant and refined. Perhaps even this inconvenience may be remedied by sedulous cultivation."[7]

It would be difficult to find the transparency of language asserted with such assurance since Taylor's time. From the same milieu sprang the thought of William Hazlitt, who generally receives too little credit for his contribution to Romantic hermeneutics. Placing himself in explicit opposition both to German idealism (entering English Romanticism through Coleridge) and to the Platonism of Thomas Taylor's circle, he located *in the observer* the power that renders possible the transcendence of time and the comprehension of texts from an earlier age, a power he called "the sympathetic imagination." Here in the interaction of ideal-

6. G. M. A. Grube, quoted above in the Preface.

7. Thomas Taylor, Introduction to "Concerning the Beautiful" (= Plot. *Enn.* 1.6), reprinted in Raine and Harper, eds., *Thomas Taylor the Platonist*, p. 137.

ism and Hazlitt's peculiar extension of the empiricist tradition of British thought, we find the essence of the problem as it survives today—the recognition of the historicity of the observer as a factor in the interpretation of texts removed in time, and the elaboration of a theory of understanding, of apprehension, to describe that relationship.

The form taken by twentieth-century thought in this area is largely dependent on the work of Wilhelm Dilthey, and his development of the concept of understanding (*Verstehen*) as the distinctive mode of knowledge appropriate to the disciplines concerned with man. Recognizing the historicity of the observer, the human sciences become utterly estranged from the natural sciences on the levels of epistemology and methodology.[8] The latter are left with a pretense to objectivity that, whatever its weaknesses, is largely unaffected by the problem of historicity. The former are left to redefine their goals.

It was with Dilthey that the concept of the "hermeneutical horizon" and the problem of the "hermeneutical circle" entered twentieth-century philosophy, to be developed by Martin Heidegger and reexamined in the context of a general theory of the human sciences by Hans-Georg Gadamer. With Dilthey, the horizon of the observer is for the first time accepted and recognized as a major, legitimate factor in his experience of the past, and the implications of this acceptance are explored. Foremost among these is the paradox that the observer's knowing of himself is continually a factor in his knowing of the past. This circularity extends beyond the comprehension of human phenomena removed in time to those that are contemporary but removed from the observer's "horizon."[9]

It is the contemporary thinkers working in this tradition—and in particular Gadamer and Paul Ricoeur—who can provide us with a theoretical standpoint from which the hermeneutics of the ancient Neoplatonists can be understood sympathetically. Not that Gadamer and Ricoeur have any interest in allegorism as such,[10] but their understanding of the role of commentary and interpretation as a function of the mediation between reader and text can lend to the endeavors of a Porphyry or a Proclus a seriousness that would be lost on the Socrates of the *Protagoras*. Literary criticism as we know it is inseparable from commentary and

8. See Paul Ricoeur, "Expliquer et comprendre," for a summary of the development and some thoughts on reconciliation.

9. On the "hermeneutic circle" and some of its implications, see Paul Ricoeur, "Metaphor and the Main Problem of Hermeneutics."

10. Cf. Hans-Georg Gadamer, "Hermeneutik," col. 1071, on the relationship of the allegorical hermeneutics of Augustine and Thomas to the tasks of modern hermeneutics.

interpretation, and thus requires a theoretical substructure capable of lending legitimacy to these activities. It is not surprising that the influence of Heidegger, Gadamer, and Ricoeur is felt throughout the range of contemporary criticism.

The influence of these ideas on our understanding of the tradition of ancient literature has, however, been minimal. What we have called the Enlightenment model of the relationship of reader to text has survived almost unscathed in the study of ancient literature. Voices of protest have been raised,[11] and have inspired a substantial backlash against methodological innovation.[12] The present situation would seem to be one of creative polarization within a field that has for too long taken refuge in a static and largely unexamined methodology.

It is not my intention here to champion methodological innovation—indeed, such a polemic would be inappropriate in a study that is itself quite conservative in method. But I do want to suggest that the tradition of Dilthey, Heidegger, and Gadamer can help us to see the value of the interpreters of other periods (including the efforts of the allegorists).

There is one passage of Gadamer's *Wahrheit und Methode*, explicitly dependent on Heidegger, that seems to me especially relevant. In it, Gadamer elaborates on Heidegger's discussion of the hermeneutic circle and the problem of prejudices (*Vorurteile*). The model of the comprehension of texts developed here is based on Heidegger's ideas on the "fore-structure of understanding" (*die Vorstruktur des Verstehens*):

> The person who is trying to understand a text is always carrying out an act of projection. He projects before himself a meaning of the text as a whole just as soon as a first meaning is perceived in the text.

11. See the studies in *Arethusa* 10 (1977) and 15 (1982), the latter honoring Jean-Pierre Vernant. The French have been more adventurous in this area than the Germans and Anglo-Saxons, and the work of Vernant and Marcel Detienne has broken new ground. For German philology and its relationship to advances in hermeneutical theory, see the articles in H. Flashar et al., eds., *Philologie und Hermeneutik im 19. Jahrhundert*. These studies examine the period that forms the background to what Flashar in his introduction describes as a contemporary "Zurückhaltung, z. T. sogar Skepsis gegen Theorie und Methode innerhalb der klassischen Philologie." Terry Eagleton's observation is clearly germane: "Hostility to theory usually means an opposition to other people's theories and an oblivion of one's own" (*Literary Theory*, p. viii). Gadamer's own work on Plato and his influential work on methodology have had some influence among students of classical antiquity. See the papers in *Contemporary Hermeneutics and Interpretation of Classical Texts* (Ottawa: University of Ottawa Press, 1981).

12. See, for example, R. L. Fowler in *Classical Views*, n. s., 1 (1982):77–81, with H. J. Westra's response in a later issue of the same volume, pp. 381–82.

> Even this first meaning emerges only because in reading the text he has definite anticipation of a certain meaning. In the working out of such a projection, constantly and freely revised according to what is revealed in the process of further penetration into the meaning, lies understanding what is there.[13]

This model of the understanding of texts finds a suggestive analogy in recent discussions of the psychology of speech. In practice, our aural comprehension depends largely on the projection of meanings appropriate to the situation, against which we test the sounds we actually hear. Thus the entire process of comprehension becomes a breaking-down of preconceived ideas, an essentially destructive process by which the meaning of the text (or of the spoken sentence) realizes itself in our consciousness by displacing and modifying our preconceptions. Jean-Paul Sartre expressed the principle in more general terms in *Qu'est-ce que la littérature*, asserting that the meaning of a text is a collaborative act involving the text itself and the consciousness of the reader.

The consequence of this is, of course, that texts have meaning only in terms of readers, or, more specifically, in terms of the expectations of readers, which determine their apprehension of texts. And this in turn underlies our interest in ancient readings, however divorced from our own perception of the possible meanings of the text in question. We know next to nothing of the experience of texts in antiquity before Plutarch, and little before Porphyry. But what we can reconstruct of these early readings, of the encounters of these readers and their prejudices with texts we still possess, can open up new vistas in intellectual history.[14] Instead of viewing Porphyry as a falsifier of Homer, wrong from the start and essentially useless to us, we can view the reading of the *Odyssey* he gives us as a remarkable opportunity to see a *whole Odyssey*. This is not a text in search of a reader but a text *with* meaning, appre-

---

13. Gadamer, *Wahrheit und Methode*, 2nd ed., p. 251; in (anon.) translation, *Truth and Method*, p. 236. The translation above is my own.

14. Even if we are reluctant to take this sort of position on the positive value of ancient interpretive texts, we must nevertheless accept their monitory value. Cf. Anne Sheppard's comments on Proclus on Plato: "On the whole Proclus is not to be despised as an expositor of Plato's meaning and the recognition that he brings certain preconceptions about theurgy and about traditional Greek religion to his understanding of his authoritative text should put us on the alert for preconceptions which we in our turn may be foisting on Plato" (*Studies*, p. 110). I take it that the principal difference between Sheppard's position and mine is that I doubt the possibility, indeed the desirability, of removing our own preconceptions from their legitimate role in the reading of texts.

hended and brought to life by the experience of a reader of the late third
century—one ideally suited to communicate to us the quality of the intellectual life of his time.

What this last argument amounts to is a plea for a methodologically
enlightened *Rezeptionsgeschichte* of ancient texts, dealing fully with the
implications of the model of apprehension and meaning we have found
in Gadamer and Sartre, and holding that the *Iliad* has had as many
meanings as it has had readers. Proclus lies roughly halfway between
our own moment in history and that which produced the Homeric
poems. Dante lies halfway between ourselves and Proclus. By halving
again and again, we reach Chapman, then Thomas Taylor, then the hey-
day of analytic criticism of the Homeric poems late in the nineteenth
century. By this Eleatic process we demonstrate simultaneously the necessary (if illusory) impossibility of our own apprehension of Homer and
the ultimate dependence of that apprehension on all previous readings,
however tendentious they might appear in isolation.

APPENDIX I

An Interpretation of the Modest Chariclea
from the Lips of Philip the Philosopher

This translation is based on Hercher's text (see "Works Cited: Ancient Authors"), but I have incorporated some of the emendations and remarks of August Brinkmann ("Beiträge zur Kritik und Erklärung des Dialogs Axiochos," p. 443, n. 1). The marginal numbers refer to the pages of Hercher's edition.

382   One day I was going out the gate of Rhegium that leads toward the sea, and when I had reached the spring of Aphrodite, I heard a voice shouting and calling me by name. When I turned around to see where it was coming from, I saw Nikolaos the royal scribe running down toward the sea with Andreas, Philetas's son. They were both very dear friends, and I decided to give up my walk and go to meet them.

        When we came together, Nikolaos said with a gentle smile, "I'm surprised at you. Are you so indifferent that you allow unbridled tongues to attack the words of wisdom? Around the outer gates of the temple there is a great encampment of lovers of literature reading Chariclea's book, and most of them are treating it scornfully and subjecting it to mockery and ridicule. Lover of Chariclea that I am, I am hurt by this and, by your wisdom, I entreat you not to let the modest girl be insulted, but rather to call to her defense 'your wit and your gentleness' [*Od.* 11.202–3] and to show these babbling quacks that the story of Chariclea is beyond all reproach!"

383   "That's a strange demand, my friend," I said, "going to winter for spring flowers and to hoary old age for the play-

things of childhood. We left these things behind, the milk, as it were, of our infant education, when we reached the philosophic time of life and went on to live in the temples of divine truth. At this point, we have been drawn away from them to the specific forms and language of the philosophy that fits our time of life. Descriptions and tales of love are in harmony with youth and early manhood. Neither gray old souls nor infant souls experience this divine love, but only those of young men and of men in the prime of life, if we can put our faith in the mystical song that goes,

> Therefore do the virgins love thee
> [Song of Sol. 1.3],

since this is the only age of man that has room for the arrows of love. Well, since the sage said, 'Even graybeards play, but the games are solemn,' let us play our part in the solemn mode and venture a bit beyond the meditations of the philosopher and turn to the erotic palinode.[1] Even Socrates the wise, who was contemplative in every other respect, still, sitting in the shade of the chaste-tree with lovely Phaedrus, amused the young man with talk of love. Let us do it, both for your sakes and for the sake of truth herself!"

We went off and found our friends in a throng before the gates of the temple, waiting for us. After the appropriate prayers to the virgin goddess, I spoke to them, sitting in a low chair right next to the threshold of the temple gate, and began thus:

"This book, my friends, is very much like Circe's brew: those who take it in a profane manner, it transforms into licentious pigs, but those who approach it in a philosophical way, in the manner of Odysseus, it initiates into higher things. The book is educational and teaches ethics by mixing the wine of contemplation into the water of the tale.

"Since the human race is divided into male and female and there are independent capacities for good and evil in each, the book shows us both, one beside the other, bearing witness to the virtue and vice of each sex, and displaying serious men in Calasiris, Theagenes, and Hydaspes, and serious women in

384

---

1. This entire passage refers to Plato's *Phaedrus*, where Socrates evokes the story of Simonides' palinode to Helen in order to explain the necessity of his delivering a second speech to apologize for slandering love (242e–243b).

Persina and Chariclea. It presents more women and less men as famed for evil since there is more evil dispersed among the race of women. Calasiris teaches you reverence for the divine and how you must turn aside the plots of enemies and rightfully avoid criminal violence, while defending yourself against those who adopt it, and how to use falsehood as you would use a drug, when you are determined to come to the aid either of friends or of yourselves, neither harming your neighbor nor pledging a falsehood in violation of an oath, but rather how to manage your words with wisdom and to be careful and pleasing in your speech—this, along with every kind of thoughtfulness, for he is very graceful in what he says, very judicious in his acts, and very resourceful in difficulties and misfortune. He also teaches self-restraint in fleeing Rhodopis, as does Knemon fleeing the illicit love of Demainete. Most of all, however, Theagenes and Chariclea are models of self-restraint, he by acting with restraint toward the woman he loves and refusing to give in to Arsace, who is insanely in love with him, either when she fawns on him or when she has him whipped. For her part, Chariclea was so clothed in self-restraint that she avoided intercourse with her lover even in dreams and fantasies.

"Let these two also be a fine example to us with regard to justice, when they judge wealth taken from the spoils of battle inviolable, and let Hydaspes be a similar example, defeating the enemy by bravery and good fortune, while he defended those near to him out of justice. The lovers themselves likewise demonstrate bravery, constantly falling upon bitter fortune, yet never allowing their spirits to be dragged down or exhibiting slavish behavior. Thus the book has been shown to be what we may call an archetypal portrait of the four general virtues.[2]

"In presenting those who live blameworthy lives, it both puts upon evil the name it deserves and describes the end to which it leads. For the story itself cries out! The very letters all but speak! If someone scorns justice and contrives to accumulate a surfeit of undeserved wealth, the misfortunes of Trachinus and Pelorus and the shepherds will win him over. If someone is contriving trickery against his neighbor, let him consider

385

2. That is, εὐσέβεια ("reverence"), σωφροσύνη ("self-restraint"), δικαιοσύνη ("justice"), and ἀνδρεία ("bravery").

Thisbe with the sword of Thamyris driven through her, and Cybele herself who brewed her own destruction, and the fulfillment of what Hesiod said:

He who contrives evil for another contrives evil for his own heart

[*Op.* 265].

Likewise, if some woman should wish to deceive her husband, let her consider the loves of Arsace that ended in her shameful strangling. If one should become a conspirator against kings, like Achaemenes, he may not escape the Ethiopian spear, and do not be forgetful like Oroöndates, lest you be shamefully defeated. Rather, even when you are treated unjustly, be content with the anomalies of chance and bear them nobly, suffering with Theagenes and Chariclea, so that your end may be rich and prosperous.

"Thus our discussion has led us within the gates of the story as we have articulated its capacity for moral instruction,[3] and lifted off the maiden's resplendent robe (in which she had been clothed on account of those who contrive against her), revealing the holy chiton beneath. Now it is time for this as well to take wing and for her beauty to be revealed without intermediary!

"Chariclea is a symbol of the soul and of the mind that sets the soul in order, for 'fame' [κλέος] and 'grace' [χάρις] are (respectively) mind, and soul united with it. Moreover, this is not the only reason that her name is a synthesis. It is also because the soul is united [συντίθεται] with the body and becomes a single substance with it. You can understand this more clearly
386   if you count the elements of the name and establish their number as 7, or 70, or 700.[4] Since the seventh is a secret number, virgin and august [σεπτός] among numbers, as the language of the Italians explains [by giving it the name *septem*], it is fitting that the meaning of 7 is maintained on the levels of monads,

3. This translation for ὁ λόγος . . . ἠθοποιῶν (385.23), though it goes beyond anything sanctioned by LSJ, seems the only possible sense here.
4. Χαρίκλεια can be read as having seven letters only by the unlikely expedient of ignoring the repeated letters. The name does in fact have seven *different* letters, two of which are repeated. More important, however, the cumulative numerical value of the letters of the name is 777.

decads, and hecatontads. The reverent and the perfect are indicated by 700, the soul itself by 70, causing that which is tripartite to be brought into order by the four perfect virtues, since four decads *plus* three decads equals 70. Seven itself represents the body, to which mind is attached, which holds in the middle of the soul the pentad of the senses and the matter and form through which it came to be.

"Chariclea was born among the Ethiopians, for man comes forth out of the invisible as if out of darkness into the light, and proceeds to life in this world as she is taken to Greece. Charicles, the active life, raises her, teaching her to assault the passions with her arrows and to be the handmaiden of bravery and self-restraint—that is, of Artemis, for Artemis is both an archer and a virgin. If these two (Charicles and Chariclea) have virtually the same name, do not be disturbed at this: practical virtue is likewise fitting for the soul itself and procures grace and fame for it.

"However, when she has left the yoke of oxen that has borne her and, bearing her torch, she has reached the temple and catches sight of Theagenes, she forgets everything and entirely engulfs the one she longs for, silently, in her soul. Understand what this riddle is saying to you! When the soul transcends the material dyad, she catches sight of the mind that lies outside of us and that approaches the knowledge of the divine. This leads her upward to the contemplation of her true family and seems lovely to her, and takes up the torch of desire, injecting into her the love of the highest wisdom. Filled with this love and drunk with a sober drunkenness—carried away, so to speak, by love— she scorns her former habits, utterly unmindful of her body, and her thought tends only toward her beloved. Thus, carried off by the one she desires, she rushes to grasp her primal nobility of birth, and she who had previously been serious and scorned love throws herself willingly at Theagenes.

"Artemis does not prevent her being carried away, but holds back when she sees her virgin temple-servant receiving the wound of love. Old Calasiris escorts the bride, orderly in word and deed. This would be the teacher who draws the soul to the good and leads it to initiation into the knowledge of the divine, and he will be a good counselor in practical things, leading the soul in a state of calm through the salt sea and the waves of life.

If Trachinus, the harsh [τραχύς] rebellion of the emotions, plots against her, the good counsel of Calasiris will stand against him.

"How long will he be her fellow traveler and companion? Until she passes through the Egypt of ignorance. Her teacher will leave her when she has already advanced and escaped the sea and forgotten the plots of thieves, since the soul rejoices in conversing in private with her beloved.

"Carnal pleasure [ἡ ἡδονή ἡ σαρκική] in the form of Arsace plots against her, with Cybele for her pimp, representing the senses, who conceives the weapons for the assaults,[5] showers logic with arrows, and draws contemplation to herself in order to debauch the thoughts of the mind. Here let the strong will be made yet tougher! Let it be cast into the fiery furnace of temptation! The ruby [παντάρβη] will keep her unblemished, for the 'ruby' is that which 'fears all' [τὸ πᾶν ταρβοῦσα] or 'is afraid' and hints at the fear of god, since god is all things [τὸ πᾶν]. If the pimp brews up a destructive plot of false accusation, she, rather, will be destroyed: those who plot against others become the destroyers of themselves. Cybele will die brewing the drug. Arsace will be deprived of her cure and die by the noose. The anguish of the wicked plottings will drive Achaemenes insane, and so he will be killed.

"Spear in hand, the soul will advance toward her own country and be put to trial by fire—for 'the fire shall try every man's work of what sort it is' [1 Cor. 3.13]—and, radiant . . ."[6]

388

5. The pun in προσβολῶν (387.21), which means both "assaults" and "embraces," is not easily rendered in English.

6. The preserved text breaks off at this point.

APPENDIX II

Proclus's Commentary on the
Timaeus of Plato, 1.341.25–343.15

This translation of a small portion of Proclus's commentary on the *Ti-maeus* is indebted at a number of points to A. J. Festugière's translation of the entire work (see "Works Cited: Ancient Authors"). Jowett's transla-tion of the *Timaeus* text has been used for the sake of providing standard equivalents for some of the basic terminology. I have italicized repeated key words, giving the original Greek at the first occurrence, and retain-ing the same translation throughout, even at the expense of awkward-ness. The goal is to retain the coherence of Proclus's argument as far as possible. In some cases, italics have been used to indicate the presence of a key term even in instances where there has been a change in the part of speech in the Greek (e.g., *permanent* = βέβαιος [adj.] in line 4, but *per-manent* quality = τὸ βέβαιον [noun] in line 22). The numbers in paren-theses indicate the pages of Diehl's edition.

(341)   ". . .and in speaking of the copy and the *model* [παράδειγμα], we may assume that *words* [λόγοι] are akin to the matter they describe; when they relate to the *lasting* [μόνιμον] and *perma-nent* [βέβαιον] and *intelligible* [μετὰ νοῦ καταφανές], they ought to be *lasting* and *unalterable* [ἀμετάπτωτοι] and as far as their
(342)   nature allows, *irrefutable* [ἀνέλεγκτοι] and *invincible* [ἀνί-κητοι]—nothing less" [Plato *Tim.* 29b].
          Earlier, [Plato] called the *model* "*eternal*" [ἀεὶ ὄν] and "*un-changing*" [κατὰ ταὐτὰ ἔχον] and "*grasped by intellection*" [νοή-σει περιληπτόν], and here he calls it "*lasting*," using that term

in place of *eternal*, "*permanent*," using that term in place of *unchanging*, and "*intelligible*" in place of the other expression, *grasped by intellection*. As far as the *words* concerning them are concerned, he calls them *lasting* in order, by using the same term in both instances, to show their resemblance to the *things* [πράγματα] they represent; he calls them *unalterable* so that they will represent the *permanent* quality of the *things*, and *irrefutable*, so that they may imitate that which is *grasped by intellection* and proceed *systematically and wisely* [ἐπιστημονικῶς]. For, if the *words* are going to be appropriate to intelligibles, they must have the qualities of being highly perfected and closely fitted, since they concern *things* that have these qualities. For, just as the *knowledge* [γνῶσις] of eternal things is *unalterable*, so also is the *word*, since it [i.e., the *word*] is this same *knowledge*, *explicated* [ἀνειλιγμένος]. And since this *word* goes forth into plurality, and has a composite nature, and for this reason falls short of the unity and *indivisibility* of the *thing*, he calls the *thing* "*lasting*" and "*permanent*" and "*intelligible*" in the singular but uses plurals to describe the *lasting, permanent*, and *irrefutable words*. And, though there is a resemblance between the *model* and the *word*, there is also a dissimilarity, and the latter is greater, for only the word "*lasting*" was applied to both, and otherwise different terms were used. And although the *systematic and wise word* cannot be refuted in the context of our *knowledge*—for nothing in us is more powerful than *systematic wisdom*—it may be refuted by the *thing* itself, as being unable to grasp the *thing*'s nature as it is and falling short of its indivisibility, and for this reason Plato added the phrase, "as far as their nature allows." For this *systematic wisdom* is irrefutable on the level of souls, but *mind* [νοῦς] refutes it, for *mind* alone can express that which is, as it is; *systematic wisdom* is secondary, and *explicates* the *indivisible* and grasps the simple by synthesis. Then, the *imagination* [φαντασία] refutes *sense impression* [αἴσθησις] for the latter knows through experience, by combination and separation, and *imagination* is free of that. *Opinion* [δόξα] in turn refutes *imagination* because *imagination* knows by shape and form, and *opinion* is above these. And *systematic wisdom* refutes *opinion* by knowing independently of causal rea-

(343)

soning, which *systematic wisdom* has the primary function of confirming. And finally, as has been said, *mind* refutes *systematic wisdom*, because the latter, as it proceeds, makes division in the thing known, but *mind* seizes it in its entirety along with its cause. Only *mind*, then, is *invincible*. *Systematic wisdom* and the *word* that belongs to *systematic wisdom* are dominated by *mind* according to its *knowledge* of that which is.

APPENDIX III

A Sampling of
Proclus's Use of Homer

This appendix indicates in tabular form the references to the books of the *Iliad* and *Odyssey* in four of the major works of Proclus.

		In Rep.[1]	In Tim.[2]	In Crat.[3]	Theol. Plat.[4]
Iliad	1	X	X	X	
	2	X	X	X	
	3	X	X	X	X
	4	X	X	X	X
	5	X	X	X	X
	6			X	
	7		X	X	X
	8	X	X		
	9	X	(x)*	X	
	10				
	11	(x)*			
	12				
	13		(x)*	X	
	14	X	X	X	
	15	X	X	X	
	16	X	X		
	17	X	(x)**	X	
	18	X	X	X	X
	19	X	X	X	
	20	X	X	X	
	21	X	X	X	
	22	X	(x)*		
	23	X			
	24	X		X	

1. Both the *index auctorum* of Festugière's annotated translation of the *Republic* commentary and that of Kroll's Teubner text have been used. The latter index is somewhat more conservative. Where they do not agree, I have given the entry in parentheses. "(x)*" indicates a reference recognized by Festugière but not by Kroll, "(x)**" one recognized by Kroll but not by Festugière.

2. The same system has been used here, incorporating both the statistics from Festugière's translation of the *Timaeus* commentary and those from Diehl's Teubner text.

		In Rep.[1]	In Tim.[2]	In Crat.[3]	Theol. Plat.[4]
Odyssey	1	x	x		
	2	(x)**	(x)*		
	3	x		x	
	4	x		x	
	5	(x)*	x	x	
	6	x	x		
	7				
	8	x	(x)*		x
	9	x			
	10	x			x
	11	x	x	x	
	12	x	x	x	
	13	x	x	x	
	14	x	x	x	
	15	(x)*			
	16	(x)*		x	
	17	x		x	
	18				
	19	x	x	x	x
	20	x	x		
	21				
	22		(x)**		
	23				
	24	x		x	

3. This table is based on the *index auctorum* of Pasquali's Teubner text.

4. This table is based on the *indices auctorum* of the first three volumes of Saffrey and Westerink's Budé edition of the *Platonic Theology*. The final volumes had not appeared at the time of writing, and the statistics are therefore incomplete, and my own search for the references in the final books has doubtless left some of them undetected.

APPENDIX IV

The History of the Allegory
of the Cave of the Nymphs

The eleven lines of the *Odyssey* containing the description of the cave dedicated to the nymphs near which Odysseus awakens in Ithaca (*Od.* 13.102–12) are the subject of the most elaborate surviving example of Neoplatonic allegorical interpretation of Homer. Porphyry states repeatedly in his essay that the interpretation he is presenting is not a new one, giving credit for the core of the exegesis twice to Cronius (*De ant.* 2,3), once to Numenius (*De ant.* 10), once to Numenius and his associates (*De ant.* 34), and once to Numenius and Cronius together (*De ant.* 21). Furthermore, Porphyry is not the only source permitting us to trace the essentials of the mystical allegory of the cave back to the second-century Neopythagoreans. Proclus, in discussing "How one must conceive the entry of the soul into the body and its departure thence" (Πῶς δεῖ νοεῖν τὸ εἰσιέναι καὶ ἐξιέναι ψυχὴν ἀπὸ σώματος, Proclus *In Rep.* 2.125–28) discusses Numenius's understanding of the matter—not without a note of contempt—and refers to Numenius's use of Homer in support of his bizarre doctrine (Num. fr. 35 = Proclus *In Rep.* 2.128.26–130.14 and 2.131.8–14; see above, ch. 2B).

Another major source tapping the same tradition, Macrobius's *Commentary on Scipio's Dream*, 1.12, probably predates Proclus by a generation, but this elaborate astrological account of the relationship of the soul to the body and the cosmos makes only general reference to Homer.[1]

---

1. With reference to the Tropics of Cancer and Capricorn: *has solis portas physici vocaverunt* (Macrob. *In somn. Scip.* 1.12). These *physici* must include Homer, for both Porphyry and Proclus identify him as the source of the expression (cf. William Harris Stahl's annotated translation of Macrobius's commentary, p. 133,

Furthermore, the extent of Macrobius's debt to Numenius has been extremely difficult to assess. Macrobius mentions Numenius by name once
in the *Saturnalia* (Num. fr. 54 = Macrob. *Sat.* 1.17.65) and once in the
Commentary (Num. fr. 55 = Macrob. *In somn. Scip.* 1.2.19), and it has
been evident to all scholars who have examined the problem since the
pioneering work of Armand Delatte (*Etudes sur la littérature pythagoricienne*, p. 129, n. 1) that Macrob. *In somn. Scip.* 1.12 is to some degree
dependent on a tradition going back to Numenius. The extent of the
Numenian content and the position and importance of Porphyry as mediator between Numenius and Macrobius are, however, matters of dispute.[2] Jacques Flamant has offered the most recent contribution to the
debate, including a very valuable summary of the views of earlier scholars.[3] His interesting conclusion is that Macrobius utilized *not* the surviving Porphyrian version of the material but another, now lost, from the
same author's commentary on the *Republic*. Porphyry, then, would be the
intermediary, but in an unexpected way, and "l'ensemble du chapitre 12,
à quelques additions ou interprétations près, peut être attribué à Numénius."[4] Flamant's conclusion is built on Félix Buffière's assertion that
Numenius's original exegesis must have been aimed at reconciling the
Republic and the Homeric poems,[5] and so would have been utilized by
Porphyry when writing on each of these works. Though not absolutely
compelling, this argument is sufficiently plausible to serve as a working
explanation.

---

n. 2). Macrobius goes on to attribute the doctrine in question to "the divine
wisdom of Homer in the description of the Ithacan cave."

2. On the earlier history of the debate, including Franz Cumont's suggestion
that Macrobius's source was Numenius's lost Περὶ ἀφθαρσίας ψυχῆς, see Henri-
Charles Puech, "Numénius d'Apamée et les théologies orientales au second siècle," p. 747, n. 4, and the references therein.

3. Flamant, *Macrobe*, pp. 546–65. Summary of earlier views in n. 92 on p. 549.
The idea of Macrobius's dependence on the lost *Republic* commentary of Porphyry goes back to Karl Mras, *Macrobius' Kommentar zu Ciceros Somnium* (1933),
cf. Courcelle, *Les Lettres grecques en occident*, pp. 23–24.

4. Flamant, *Macrobe*, p. 562. The conclusion is essentially that reached a few
years earlier by Herman de Ley, *Macrobius and Numenius*, esp. p. 63. Pépin ("La
Fortune du *de antro nympharum* de Porphyre en occident," p. 530) rejects this as a
conjecture founded on a conjecture and argues plausibly that Macrobius worked
directly from the essay on the cave of the nymphs.

5. Buffière, *Mythes d'Homère*, pp. 442–44; cf. Flamant, *Macrobe*, p. 552 and
n. 105.

The traceable history of the allegory of the cave of the nymphs runs roughly as follows:

Numenius and Cronius→Porphyry→Macrobius→Latin Middle Ages

~ 175　　　　　　　　　　~ 275　　~ 430

→Proclus

~ 460

It is certainly possible that, had we direct access to the account of Numenius and Cronius, they would provide us with earlier sources. However, in the absence of any reference to this allegory either in Heraclitus or in Ps.-Plutarch, one must respect Buffière's suggestion that the interpretive tradition had not emphasized this passage when those two compendia were compiled.[6] Unfortunately, neither of these two works can be dated with precision.[7] Heraclitus mentions no datable author later than the second century B.C. and Buffière's *terminus ante quem* of A.D. 100 is based entirely on negative internal evidence—the absence of any mention in Heraclitus of the Pythagorean mystical exegesis current from at least the time of Plutarch. This argument is useless for our purposes because any attempt to use it to date the origin of the cave allegory would invariably lead to circular reasoning. The same is true of Buffière's conclusions regarding a *terminus ante quem* for Ps.-Plutarch. The *absence* of mention of the cave of the nymphs and the generally low level of mystical allegory lead Buffière to assert that "à l'époque où elle [sc., *La Vie et Poésie d'Homère*] fut rédigée, l'exégèse néopythagoricienne avait à peine pris son essor: sans doute attendait-elle encore la venue de son coryphée, Numénius (iie moitié du second siècle après J.-C.)."[8] Other scholars—no more convincingly, it is true—have argued for dates as late as the third century and even attempted to attribute the work to Porphyry.

There is a single further shred of information on the history of the allegorical interpretation of *Od*. 13.102–12 in the B scholion on *Od*. 13.103, and it is primarily with this scholion that I wish to deal here. The scholion is fragmentary, the latter parts apparently misplaced from another passage or passages, and reads as follows:

6. Cf. Buffière's comments in his edition of Heraclitus's *Homeric Allegories*, pp. xxvii–xxix, on the lacuna in Heraclitus's treatment of the *Odyssey* and on the historical relationship of the two works to the development of the allegory of the cave.

7. Cf. Buffière's comments in his edition of Heraclitus, pp. ix–x, and, on Ps.-Plutarch, in his *Mythes d'Homère*, pp. 72–77.

8. Buffière, *Mythes d'Homère*, p. 77.

103 *cave sacred to the nymphs*] The passage is allegorical and says "cave" for *world*, "nymphs" for *souls*, "bees" for the same, and "men" for *bodies*, and the two gates it calls "the exit of bodies" (i.e., birth) and "the entrance of souls," by which nothing at all of corporeal nature enters, but only souls, for they are immortal. Whence it also says "olive tree," whether because of the victor's wreath or because of the . . . that is, the nourishment . . . The reed is a kind of rush. The bushy plant is also a kind of rush [?]. "Inaccessible" is the opposite of "accessible." ἴσαν, which means "know," is conjugated thus: [a list of forms follows].

103 ἄντρον ἰρὸν Νυμφάων] ἀλληγορικῶς λέγει ἄντρον τὸν κόσμον, νύμφας τὰς ψυχάς, τὰς αὐτὰς καὶ μελίσσας, καὶ ἄνδρας τὰ σώματα. δύο δὲ θύρας τὴν τῶν σωμάτων ἔξοδον, ἤτοι τὴν γένεσιν, καὶ τὴν τῶν ψυχῶν εἴσοδον, ἐν ᾗ οὐδὲν τῶν σωμάτων εἰσέρχεται, μόναι δὲ αἱ ψυχαί. ἀθάνατοι γάρ εἰσι, ὅθεν καὶ ἐλαίαν φησί, ἢ διὰ τὸν νικητικὸν στέφανον, ἢ διὰ τὸ . . . ὅ ἐστι τὴν τροφήν . . . [n. 14: sequuntur in B duo scholia futilia et ab hoc loco plane aliena, alterum σχοῖνος τὸ βροῦλον (cf. schol. ε 463) · σχῖνος δὲ τὸ θαμνῶδες φυτόν. βάτος κατ' ἀντίφρασιν ἡ ἄβατος. alterum, τὸ ἴσαν, τὸ ἐγίνωσκον, κανονίζεται οὕτως · (κτλ)]. *Schol. in Od.*, vol. 2, p. 562, with n. 14.

The obviously corrupt text is given here in its entirety to emphasize the fact that the first portion, cited by Buffière,[9] is not an independent and complete statement. The corrupt portion of the text begins *before* the scholiast has finished dealing with the description of the cave and its surrounding landscape. Dindorf points out that the first of the two misplaced scholia that follow the second lacuna seems relevant to *Od.* 5.463, and it is interesting that there is a broad similarity between that passage (Odysseus's arrival on the Phaeacian shore) and the present one. However, the second part of that same scholion explains a word (ἄβατος) that does not occur in the Homeric *corpus*, though it might possibly have some relevance to the latter part of the description of the cave (*Od.* 13.109–12).

Building his argument on the first part of the scholion, Buffière deduced the existence of an earlier exegesis of the cave passage, antedating and in some ways anticipating Numenius,[10] an interpretation with elements both of a Platonic model of the cosmos, in which souls pass underground after death, and of the later allegory given full exposition by Porphyry.

Buffière was not the first to see in this scholion evidence for an inde-

9. Ibid., p. 449 and n. 42.
10. Ibid., pp. 449–53.

pendent tradition of allegorical interpretation of the passage. In 1915, Armand Delatte made the same assumption and went on to suggest that one might trace the interpretation to the school of Philolaus,[11] the Pythagorean contemporary of Socrates. The same scholar believed that Theagenes of Rhegium (fl. 525 B.C.) showed Pythagorean influence, and hence that the earliest surviving traces of allegorical interpretation could be brought under the general rubric of Pythagoreanism.[12] Buffière has good grounds for rejecting Delatte's theory of a source for the interpretation in the school of Philolaus, but he retains the belief that this fragmentary scholion transmits a pre-Numenian reading of the passage, which he dates (again depending on the silence of Plutarch and Ps.-Plutarch) to the period separating Plutarch from Numenius (roughly A.D. 120–50).[13]

But what is the basis for the assumption that this scholion represents an independent interpretation of the passage? If we examine the elements of the scholion one by one, we find that the claim that the cave = the world is consistent with what we find in Porphyry, as are the claims that the nymphs = souls and that the bees = souls. That the word "men" is said to refer to "bodies" is perhaps more properly Homeric than Pythagorean and recalls the usage of *Iliad* 1.3–4, where the "souls" of the dead heroes are described as going to Hades, while "they themselves" (i.e., their corpses) remain on the battlefield.

The most serious problem in the scholion arises in the treatment of the "doors" of the cave. The one—clearly that on the north—is described by the scholiast as an "exit of bodies" or "birth," whereas the southern one is an "entrance of souls." The reader is left with the paradox that apparently bodies never *enter* this world and, even less satisfactorily, souls never *leave* it. Moreover, it is at this point that the scholiast and Porphyry seem to diverge.

Buffière's solution is to claim that the scholiast "se place dans la perspective de l'autre monde."[14] The northern gate remains that of birth, and the "bodies" are said to "exit" because they are in fact infant, embodied souls *leaving* the Platonic underworld to reenter this world. This explanation has at least the merit of recognizing the problem posed by the apparent reversal of "entrance" and "exit," but it is hardly a satisfy-

11. Delatte, *Littérature pythagoricienne*, p. 130. See also Burkert, *Lore and Science*, p. 367, n. 94.
12. Delatte, *Littérature pythagoricienne*, p. 130; cf. Burkert, *Lore and Science*, p. 297, n. 67, and Detienne, *Homère, Hésiode, et Pythagore*, p. 67, n. 2.
13. Buffière, *Mythes d'Homère*, p. 452, n. 46.
14. Ibid., p. 450. Cf. Delatte, *Littérature pythagoricienne*, pp. 129–30.

ing solution, particularly in view of the word καταιβαταί at *Od.* 13.110, applied to the northern gate. If this scholion in fact retains the world-model of Plato, and specifically of the myth of Er, how then can the infant souls "descend" *from* the underworld?

Buffière's conclusion seems to depend upon complete dissociation of the scholion from the text upon which it comments. Were the north gate not explicitly a "path down" or "descent" into the cave, it would be easy to believe that the scholiast imagined souls "exiting" from the underworld by it to enter their lives on the surface of the world. In view of the wording of the passage, however, it seems impossible to maintain that this was the scholiast's intention. (That the second, or southern, gate is the scholiast's "entrance of souls" is guaranteed by the explanatory phrase, "by which nothing at all of corporeal nature enters, but only souls, for they are immortal," which is a paraphrase of *Od.* 13.111–12, describing the southern gate.)

Homer's text does not tell us whether the southern gate is a "descent" or not, specifying only that the northern one is a downward path. The entire idea that one gate is exclusively an entrance and the other exclusively an exit is foreign to Homer, who seems to be saying simply that men come and go through one hole and gods through the other, though, not at all surprisingly, the description focuses on how men enter the cave and specifies that they do *not* enter by way of the "more divine" gate. Both the scholiast and Porphyry, however, leave us with the idea that the northern gate is primarily an entrance (for men) and the southern one an exit (for souls, which have left their bodies behind in this world).

There is nothing in the scholion, then, that is in obvious and unavoidable contradiction with the ideas transmitted by Porphyry concerning the passage. There is no obvious reason why the scholiast should have described the cave from the opposite perspective from that adopted by Homer, and it is tempting to believe that the words ἔξοδος and εἴσοδος have simply been switched. The scholiast will simply have been misled by the word ἐσέρχονται in line 112 and turned the "path of immortals" into an entrance.[15] The fragmentary sentence on the olive tree that follows the observations on the cave itself in the scholion refers to one idea present in Porphyry's essay—the olive crown of victory—and seems also to share with Porphyry some sort of observation on the olive tree as a sort of nourishment. Whatever the source of the reversal of the words

15. The account of this aspect of the problem in Porphyry's essay itself is far from clear, and the text has required emendation. See especially *De ant.* 72.11, and compare the solution of the Buffalo editors.

"entrance" and "exit," it seems clear that this scholion, like many of the B scholia,[16] is close enough to Porphyry that it may in fact be derived from him.

Burkert (who does not mention Buffière's work and may have been unaware of his conclusions based on the scholion) has reassessed Delatte's conclusions on the literature of Pythagoreanism and rejects his idea that the B scholion represents an independent tradition of interpretation with the casual remark that "the difference between this and Porphyry is probably a mistake of the scholiast rather than a reflection of an independent tradition."[17] A careful examination of the scholion suggests that such a mistake is very likely, particularly in view of the corruption and disruption of the text and of the possibility that the confusion arises from the Homeric passage itself.

The minor, but problematical, divergences between the scholion and Porphyry could, of course, have another meaning: they could, as Delatte and Buffière claimed, represent two independent traditions of interpretation. Even in this case, however, reasons for dating the scholiast's version before that of Numenius are lacking. At some moment in history some commentator—whether Numenius or someone else—must have insisted, for the first time, that the passage was a mystical allegory. Thereafter, any expositor could repeat the idea, often no doubt confusing the details. The frequency of references to Numenius as the source is suggestive, but not conclusive.

In the final analysis, it seems more prudent to base a conclusion not on the unresolved conflicts between the scholiast's version and Porphyry's, but rather on the large number of shared elements that the scholiast might have drawn from Porphyry himself or from some other proximal source tapping the tradition of Numenius.

If the scholion does indeed represent only a garbled account of the Numenian version of the allegory, then we may conclude that there is no remaining evidence for any interest in the cave of the nymphs on the part of commentators demonstrably anterior to Numenius. It would, in any case, be no surprise to find that this ingenious Neopythagorean and his friend Cronius were the original assemblers of the entire allegory, which touched the imaginations of philosophers and poets from their own contemporaries to William Blake.

16. See Hermann Schrader's comments in Porph. *Quaest. hom.*, ed. Schrader, vol. 1, pp. 363–68, and also note (p. 86, line 11) his indication that he considered the B scholion on *Od.* 13.103 to be connected to Porphyry.
17. Burkert, *Lore and Science*, p. 367, n. 94.

WORKS CITED

ANCIENT AND MEDIEVAL AUTHORS

Ancient authors are normally cited in the footnotes and parenthetical references in the text by means of standard abbreviations. These are those listed in the *Oxford Classical Dictionary*, supplemented where necessary by those from LSJ or by others made up for the purpose. References include designations of the traditional divisions of the text: e.g., book and line for Homer; book (where relevant), Stephanus page, and page-division for Plato; *Ennead*, essay, and paragraph for Plotinus. In many cases, line numbers have been added for convenience, after the other designations, and for certain works, including the commentaries of Proclus, the volume, page, and line number of the modern text are used to locate citations and references.

Because some of the ancient texts discussed are not easily available and have seldom been edited, it has seemed most convenient to attach a list of some of the editions actually cited. Moreover, where reference has been made to the comments of a modern editor or scholarly translator, the annotated edition or translation in question may be located through the following list. Some familiar series are designated in brief form (e.g., Loeb, OCT, etc.). This list is far from exhaustive and is intended primarily to clarify references that might otherwise be troublesome. Most Christian authors are cited from the series *Die griechischen christlichen Schriftsteller der ersten Jahrhunderte* (= GCS), from the *Sources chrétiennes* editions (= SC), or from Migne's *Patrologia Graeca* (= PG) or *Patrologia Latina* (= PL).

Dubiously attributed texts and pseudepigrapha are alphabetized under the name of the author to whom the text has been attributed, following any authentic works occurring in this list.

Aristotle. *Metaphysics*. Edited with commentary by W. D. Ross. Oxford: Oxford University Press, 1924.

———. *Poetics*. Translated with an introduction and notes by Gerald F. Else. Ann Arbor: University of Michigan Press, 1967.

Ps.-Aristotle. [*Liber de causis*.] *Die pseudo-Aristotelische Schrift über das reine Gute, bekannt unter dem Namen Liber de causis*. Edited by Otto Bardenhewer, 1882. Reprint. Frankfurt: Minerva, n.d.

———. *Liber de pomo*. Edited by Marianus Plezia. *Eos* 47 (1954): 197–217. Also note *The Apple; or, Aristotle's Death*, translated with an introduction by Mary F. Rousseau. Medieval Philosophical Texts in Translation, no. 18. Milwaukee: Marquette University Press, 1968.

Aristoxenus. [*Fragments*.] *Die Schule des Aristoteles, ii: Aristoxenos*. Edited by Fritz Wehrli. Basel: Benno Schwabe, 1945.

Augustine. *The City of God Against the Pagans*. Edited by George E. McCracken, W. M. Green et al. London and Cambridge, Mass.: Heinemann and Harvard University Press (Loeb), 1957–72.

[Bernard Silvestris.] *The Commentary on the First Six Books of the Aeneid of Vergil Commonly Attributed to Bernardus Silvestris*. Edited by Julian Ward Jones and Elizabeth Frances Jones. Lincoln: University of Nebraska Press, 1977.

Boethius. *Philosophiae consolationis libri quinque*. Edited by Karl Büchner. 2nd ed. Heidelberg: Carl Winter, 1960.

Calcidius. *Timaeus a Calcidio translatus commentarioque instructus*. Edited by J. H. Waszink. Corpus Platonicum Medii Aevi: Plato Latinus, vol. 4. London and Leiden: Warburg Institute and Brill, 1962. Reference is also made to *Platonis Timaeus interprete Chalcidio cum eiusdem commentario*. Edited by Johann Wrobel. Leipzig: Teubner, 1876.

Certamen: See Homer, below.

Dante. *Tutte le opere*. Edited by E. Moore and Paget Toynbee. Oxford: Oxford University Press, 1904. All citations are from this edition with the following exception:

———. *Epistolae*. Edited by Paget Toynbee. Oxford: Oxford University Press, 1920.

[Demetrius of Phaleron.] *De elocutione*. Edited by W. Rhys Roberts, 1902. Reprint. Hildesheim: Georg Olms, 1969.

Ps.-Dionysius Areopagites: Quotations are from PG, with the following exceptions:

———. *Divine Names* and *Mystical Theology*. Reference is made to the translation with introduction by John D. Jones. Medieval Philosophical Texts in Translation, no. 21. Milwaukee: Marquette University Press, 1980.

———. *Epistles*. See "Works Cited: Modern Authors" under Ronald F. Hathaway for both text and translation.

————. *La Hiérarchie céleste*. Edited by Günter Heil with introduction by René Roques and notes by Maurice de Gandillac. SC no. 58. Paris: Editions du Cerf, 1958.

Dunchad. *Glossae in Martianum*. Edited by Cora Lutz. APA Philological Monographs, no. 12. Lancaster, Pa.: American Philological Association, 1944.

Eusebius. *Preparatio Evangelica. Eusebius' Werke, 8er Band*. Edited by Karl Mras. GCS vol. 43, parts 1 and 2. Berlin: Akademie-Verlag, 1954–56.

Eustathius. *Commentarii ad Homeri Iliadem / Odysseam . . . ad fidem exempli Romani editi*. 7 vols. Leipzig: Weigel, 1825–28.

Favonius Eulogius. *Disputatio de somnio Scipionis*. Edited and translated by Roger-E. van Weddington. Collection Latomus, no. 27. Brussels: Latomus, 1957.

Fulgentius. *Opera*. Edited by Rudolph Helm. Leipzig: Teubner, 1898.

Heliodorus. *Les Ethiopiques*. Edited by R. M. Rattenbury and T. W. Lumb and translated by J. Maillon. 3 vols. Paris: Les Belles Lettres (Budé), 1935–43. Reference is also made to *Heliodori Ethiopica*, edited by Aristides Colonna. Rome: Typis regiae officinae polygraphicae, 1938.

Heraclitus. *Allégories d'Homère*. Edited and translated by Félix Buffière. Paris: Les Belles Lettres (Budé), 1962.

[Hermes Trismegistus.] *Corpus Hermeticum*. Edited by A. D. Nock and translated by A.-J. Festugière. 4 vols. Paris: Les Belles Lettres (Budé), 1945–54.

Hermias. *In Platonis Phaedrum Scholia*. Edited by P. Couvreur, 1901. Reprint. Hildesheim: Georg Olms, 1971.

Homer. All citations are from *Opera*, edited by Thomas W. Allen. 5 vols. Oxford: Oxford University Press (OCT), 1902–12. The lesser Homerica, lives, and *Certamen* are in vol. 5. Reference is also made to *The Iliad*, edited by Walter Leaf. 2nd ed. 1900–1902. Reprint. Amsterdam: Hakkert, 1971. See also *Chapman's Homer*, edited by Allardyce Nicoll. Bollingen Series, vol. 41. New York: Pantheon, 1956. The Homeric scholia are cited from the following editions: *Scholia Graeca in Homeri Iliadem*. Edited by Hartmut Erbse. Berlin: De Gruyter, 1969–77. Reference is occasionally made to the edition by Wilhelm Dindorf. 4 vols. Oxford: Oxford University Press, 1875–77. *Scholia Graeca in Homeri Odysseam*. Edited by Wilhelm Dindorf. 2 vols. Oxford: Oxford University Press, 1855.

Julian. *Works*. Edited and translated by Wilmer Cave Wright. 3 vols. London and New York: Heinemann and Macmillan (Loeb), 1913–23.

Lucretius. *De rerum natura libri sex*. Edited with apparatus and notes by Cyril Bailey. Oxford: Oxford University Press, 1947.

Lydus, Ioannes. *De mensibus*. Edited by R. Wuench, 1898. Reprint. Stuttgart: Teubner, 1967. References are to page and line of this edition.

Macrobius. *Commentarii in somnium Scipionis. Opera*, vol. 2. Edited by I. Willis. Leipzig: Teubner, 1970. Reference is also made to *Commentary on the Dream of*

Scipio, translated with introduction and notes by William Harris Stahl. New York: Columbia University Press, 1952.

——. *Les Saturnales*. Edited with translation and notes by Henri Bournecque. Paris: Garnier, n.d. [1937].

Magical Papyri (Greek). *Die griechischen Zauberpapyri*. Edited by K. Preisendanz. 2 vols. Stuttgart: Teubner, 1972–73.

Marinus. *Vita Procli*. Edited by J.-F. Boissonnade. Appended to *Diogenis Laertii de clarorum philosophorum vitis . . .* , edited by C. Gabriel Cobet. Paris: Didot, 1850.

Martianus Capella. *De nuptiis Philologiae et Mercurii*. Edited by Adolphus Dick. Leipzig: Teubner, 1925. For glosses, see Dunchad, above.

Musaeus. *Hero and Leander*. Edited by Thomas Gelzer and translated by Cedric Whitman. Appended to recent printings of Callimachus, *Aetia . . .* , edited and translated by C. A. Trypanis. Cambridge, Mass., and London: Harvard University Press and Heinemann (Loeb), 1975.

Numenius. *Fragments*. Edited and translated by E. Des Places. Paris: Les Belles Lettres (Budé), 1973. Reference is also made to E.-A. Leemans, *Studie over den Wijsgeer Numenius van Apamea met Uitgave der Fragmenten*. Académie royale de Belgique, Mémoires, Classe des Lettres, 27, part 2 (1937).

Olympiodorus. *In Platonis Phaedonem Commentaria*. Edited by William Norvin, 1913. Reprint. Hildesheim: Georg Olms, 1968.

Oracles Chaldaïques. With a selection of ancient commentaries. Edited and translated by E. Des Places. Paris: Les Belles Lettres (Budé), 1971.

Origen. All citations are from the GCS or SC editions. Reference is also made to *Contra Celsum*, translated with an introduction and notes by Henry Chadwick. Cambridge: Cambridge University Press, 1953.

[Orpheus.] *Orphica*. Edited by E. Abel, 1885. Reprint. Hildesheim: Gerstenberg, 1971. Reference is also made to *Orphicorum fragmenta*. Edited by Otto Kern. Berlin: Weidmann, 1922.

[Philip the Philosopher.] Τῆς Χαρικλείας ἑρμήνευμα τῆς σώφρονος ἐκ φωνῆς Φιλίππου τοῦ φιλοσόφου. Edited by R. Hercher. *Hermes* 3 (1869): 382–88. See also the version in Colonna's edition of Heliodorus.

Philo. *Works*. Edited and translated by F. H. Colson and G. H. Whittaker. 10 vols. with 2 supplementary vols., the latter edited by Ralph Markus. London and New York (later Cambridge, Mass.): Heinemann and G. P. Putnam's Sons (later Harvard University Press) (Loeb), 1929–62. Philo's *De providentia*, preserved for the most part only in Armenian, is published with Latin translation in *Philonis Judaei sermones tres hactenus inediti*, edited by Johannes Baptista Aucher (= Mkrtich^c Aukerian). Venice: Press of the Coenobitic Armenian Fathers in the Island of San Lazzaro, 1822. There is a complete German translation of Aucher's Latin in the seventh volume of *Philo von Alexandria: Die Werke in deutscher Übersetzung*, edited by Leopold Cohn, et al. 7 vols. Berlin: De Gruyter, 1909–64.

Plato. All citations are from *Opera*, edited by John Burnet. 5 vols. Oxford: Oxford University Press (OCT), 1900–1907. Reference is also made to *Plato's Repub-*

lic, edited with notes and essays by B. Jowett and Lewis Campbell. 3 vols. Oxford: Oxford University Press, 1894.

Plotinus. *Opera*. Edited by Paul Henry and Hans-Rudolf Schwyzer (*editio maior*). 3 vols. Paris: Desclée et Brouwer, 1951–73. The *editio minor* of the same editors is the new OCT (1964–82), which incorporates some new readings and has occasionally been used in the present study. Reference is also made to the edition with translation by Emile Bréhier. 6 vols. in 7. 3rd ed. Paris: Les Belles Lettres (Budé), 1956–63.

Plutarch. *Moralia*. Edited by F. C. Babbitt et al. 15 vols. London and New York (later Cambridge, Mass.): Heinemann and G. P. Putnam's Sons (later Harvard University Press) (Loeb), 1927–69.

Ps.-Plutarch. *The Life and Poetry of Homer*. In *Opera*, edited by F. Dübner. 5 vols. Paris: Didot, 1855–57. The most recent version, in *Moralia*, edited by G. N. Bernardakis, vol. 7 (Leipzig: Teubner, 1896), makes minor improvements on Dübner's text. Reference is also made to E. Clavier's French translation in vol. 23 of *Oeuvres de Plutarque*, translated by Jacques Amyot with notes and observations by G. Brotier and J.-F. Vauvilliers. New ed., corrected and augmented by E. Clavier. 25 vols. Paris: Cussac, 1801–5.

Porphyry. *De antro nympharum*. In *Opuscula selecta*, edited by August Nauck. Leipzig: Teubner, 1886. Reference is also made to *The Cave of the Nymphs in the Odyssey*, a revised text with translation by Seminar Classics 609 (Arethusa Monographs, no. 1. Buffalo: State University of New York, 1969), and to *Porphyry on the Cave of the Nymphs*, translated with introduction and notes by Robert Lamberton. Barrytown, N.Y.: Station Hill, 1983.

———. *Life of Plotinus*. In vol. 1 of both of the Henry and Schwyzer editions of the *Enneads* of Plotinus.

———. Περὶ ἀγαλμάτων. Fragments collected by Joseph Bidez in his *Vie de Porphyre* (see "Works Cited: Modern Authors").

———. Πρὸς Μαρκέλλαν. Edited with introduction, translation, and notes by Walter Pötscher. Philosophia Antiqua, vol. 15. Leiden: Brill, 1969.

———. *Quaestionum Homericarum ad Iliadem / Odysseam Reliquiae*. Edited by Hermann Schrader. 2 vols. Leipzig: Teubner, 1880–90. Reference is also made to *Quaestionum Homericarum liber I*, edited with introduction by A. R. Sodano. Naples: Giannini, 1970.

Proclus. *Commentary on the First Alcibiades of Plato*. Edited by L. G. Westerink. Amsterdam: Nijhoff, 1954. Note that this and the other commentaries of Proclus are referred to in the text and notes by volume (where relevant), page, and line of the modern editions listed here. In most instances, there are no traditional divisions of the texts fine enough to be useful in locating passages.

———. *Elements of Theology*. Edited with introduction, translation, and commentary by E. R. Dodds. 2nd ed. Oxford: Oxford University Press, 1963.

———. *Hymns*. Several editions are mentioned in the text but the best is that of Ernest Vogt. Wiesbaden: Otto Harrassowitz, 1957.

———. *In Platonis Cratylum commentaria*. Edited by G. Pasquali. Leipzig: Teubner, 1908.

———. *In Platonis Parmenidem commentaria*. In *Opera inedita*. Edited by V. Cousin, 1864. Reprint. Hildesheim: Georg Olms, 1961.

———. *In Platonis Rem publicam commentarii*. Edited by G. Kroll. 2 vols., 1899–

1901. Reprint. Amsterdam: Hakkert, 1965. Reference is also made to *Commentaire sur la République*, translated with notes by A. J. Festugière. 3 vols. Paris: Vrin, 1970.

———. *In Platonis Timaeum commentaria*. Edited by E. Diehl. 3 vols., 1903–6. Reprint. Amsterdam: Hakkert, 1965. Reference is also made to *Commentaire sur le Timée*, translated with notes by A. J. Festugière. 5 vols. Paris: Vrin, 1966–68.

———. *In Primum Euclidis elementorum librum commentarii*. Edited by G. Friedlein. Leipzig: Teubner, 1873. Reference is also made to *A Commentary on the First Book of Euclid's Elements*, translated with notes by Glenn R. Morrow. Princeton: Princeton University Press, 1970.

———. *Théologie platonicienne*. Edited and translated by H. D. Saffrey and L. G. Westerink. Paris: Les Belles Lettres (Budé), 1968–in progress.

Prudentius. *Works*. Edited by M. Lavarenne. 4 vols. Paris: Les Belles Lettres (Budé), 1943–63.

Rhetorical Texts (Greek). *Rhetores Graeci*. Edited by Leonard Spengel et al. 16 vols. Leipzig: Teubner, 1856–1931.

Sallustius. *Concerning the Gods and the Universe*. Edited and translated by A. D. Nock, 1926. Reprint. Hildesheim: Georg Olms, 1966.

Stobaeus, Ioannes. *Eclogarum physicarum et ethicarum libri duo*. Edited by August Meinecke. Leipzig: Teubner, 1860–64.

Stoicorum veterum fragmenta. Collected and edited by Joh. von Arnim. 4 vols. Leipzig: Teubner, 1905–24.

Theosophies (Greek). *Fragmente griechischer Theosophien*. Edited by Hartmut Erbse. Hamburg: Hansischer Gildenverlag, 1941.

MODERN AUTHORS

Alexandre, Monique. "La Culture profane chez Philon." In *Philon d'Alexandrie*. Colloques nationaux du C. N. R. S. Paris: C. N. R. S., 1967.

Armstrong, A. J. *The Architecture of the Intelligible Universe in the Philosophy of Plotinus*. 1940. Reprint. Amsterdam: Hakkert, 1967.

———, ed. *The Cambridge History of Later Greek and Early Medieval Philosophy*. Cambridge: Cambridge University Press, 1967. (Here abbreviated CHLGEMP.)

Athanassiadi-Fowden, Polymnia. *Julian and Hellenism: An Intellectual Biography*. Oxford: Oxford University Press, 1981.

Auerbach, Erich. *Mimesis*. Berne: A. Francke, 1946. More easily available is the translation by Willard Trask. Princeton: Princeton University Press, 1953.

Babut, Daniel. *Plutarque et le Stoïcisme*. Publications de l'Université de Lyon. Paris: Les Belles Lettres, 1969.

Bartelink, G. J. M. "Homerismen in Nikolaos Mesarites' Beschreibung der Apostelkirche in Konstantinopel." *Byzantinische Zeitschrift* 70 (1977): 306–9.

Basilikopoulou-Ioannidou, Agni. Ἡ Ἀναγέννησις τῶν γραμμάτων κατὰ τὸν ιβ΄ αἰῶνα εἰς τὸ Βυζάντιον καὶ ὁ Ὅμηρος. Athens: Ἐθνικὸν καὶ Καποδιστριακὸν Πανεπιστήμιον Ἀθηνῶν, Φιλοσοφικὴ Σχολή, 1971.

Beierwaltes, Werner. "Das Problem der Erkenntnis bei Proklos." In *De Jamblique à Proclus*. Entretiens sur l'antiquité classique, no. 21. Vandoeuvres-Geneva: Fondation Hardt, 1974.

———. *Proklos: Grundzüge seiner Metaphysik.* Frankfurt: V. Klostermann, 1965.

Benton, Sylvia. "Excavations in Ithaca, iii: The Cave at Polis, i." *The Annual of the British School at Athens* 35 (session 1934–35, publ. 1938): 45–73.

———. "Excavations in Ithaca, iii: The Cave at Polis, ii." *The Annual of the British School at Athens* 39 (session 1938–39, publ. 1942): 1–51.

Beutler, Rudolf. "Numenios (9)." P-W supplementary vol. 7 (1940): 664–78.

———. "Proklos." P-W 23.1 (1957): cols. 186–247.

Bidez, Joseph. *Vie de Porphyre, le philosophe néoplatonicien.* 1913. Reprint. Hildesheim: Georg Olms, 1964.

Bloch, Herbert. "The Pagan Revival in the West at the End of the Fourth Century." In *The Conflict Between Paganism and Christianity in the Fourth Century*, edited by A. Momigliano. Oxford: Oxford University Press, 1963.

Blumenthal, Henry J. "Plutarch's Exposition of the *De anima* and the Psychology of Proclus." In *De Jamblique à Proclus*. Entretiens sur l'antiquité classique, no. 21. Vandoeuvres-Geneva: Fondation Hardt, 1974.

Bolgar, R. R. *The Classical Heritage and its Beneficiaries.* Cambridge: Cambridge University Press, 1963.

Bouché-Leclerc, A. *Histoire de la divination dans l'antiquité.* 4 vols. Paris: Leroux, 1879–82.

Boyancé, Pierre. *Le Culte des Muses chez les philosophes grecs: Etudes d'histoire et de psychologie religieuses.* Bibl. des Écoles françaises d'Athènes et de Rome, fasc. 141. Paris: E. de Boccard, 1937.

———. "La 'Doctrine d'Euthyphron' dans le *Cratyle*." *Revue des études grecques* 54 (1941): 141–75.

———. "Echo des exégèses de la mythologie grecque chez Philon." In *Philon d'Alexandrie*. Colloques nationaux du C. N. R. S. Paris: C. N. R. S., 1967.

———. "Etymologie et théologie chez Varron." *Revue des études latines* 53 (1975): 99–115.

———. "Les Muses et l'harmonie des sphères." In *Mélanges dédiés à la mémoire de Félix Grat*. Paris: E. de Boccard, 1946.

Bréhier, Emile. *Les Idées philosophiques et religieuses de Philon d'Alexandrie.* Paris: Picard, 1908.

Brinkmann, August. "Beiträge zur Kritik und Erklärung des Dialogs Axiochos." *Rheinisches Museum*, n.s., 51 (1896): 441–45.

Browning, Robert. "Homer in Byzantium." *Viator* 6 (1975): 15–33.

Buchheit, V. "Homer bei Methodius von Olympos." *Rheinisches Museum*, n.s., 99 (1956): 17–36.

Buffière, Félix. *Les Mythes d'Homère et la pensée grecque.* Paris: Les Belles Lettres, 1956. See also "Works Cited: Ancient Authors" under Heraclitus.

Burkert, Walter. *Lore and Science in Ancient Pythagoreanism.* Translated by Edward Minar, Jr. Cambridge, Mass.: Harvard University Press, 1972. This English translation represents a somewhat revised version of the German original, prepared by the author in collaboration with the translator, and is therefore more useful than the original work, *Weisheit und Wissenschaft: Studien zu Pythagoras, Philolaos und Platon.* Nuremberg: Hans Carl, 1962.

Butlin, Martin. *The Paintings and Drawings of William Blake.* New Haven: Yale University Press, 1981.

Cameron, Alan. "The Date and Identity of Macrobius." *Journal of Roman Studies* 56 (1966): 25–38.

Carcopino, Jérôme. *La Basilique de la Porte Majeure.* Paris: L'Artisan du Livre, 1926.

———. *De Pythagore aux apôtres: Etudes sur la conversion du monde romain.* Paris: Flammarion, 1956.

Carne-Ross, D. S. "The Means and the Moment." *Arion* 7 (1968): 549–57.

Christiansen, Irmgard. *Die Technik der allegorischen Auslegungswissenschaft bei Philon von Alexandrien.* Beiträge zur Geschichte der biblischen Hermeneutik, no. 7. Tübingen: Mohr, 1969.

Ciaffi, Vincenzo. *Fulgenzio e Petronio.* Turin: Giappichelli, 1963.

Cilento, Vincenzo. "Mito e poesia nelle *Enneadi* di Plotino." In *Les Sources de Plotin.* Entretiens sur l'antiquité classique, no. 5. Vandoeuvres-Geneva: Fondation Hardt, 1957.

Clark, Mary T. "The Neoplatonism of Marius Victorinus the Christian." In *Neoplatonism and Early Christian Thought: Essays in Honor of A. H. Armstrong,* edited by M. J. Blumenthal and R. A. Markus. London: Variorum, 1981.

Clifford, Gay. *The Transformations of Allegory.* London: Routledge and Kegan Paul, 1974.

Comparetti, Domenico. *Virgilio nel medio evo.* 1872. Reprint. Florence: La Nuova Italia, 1943.

Coulter, James A. *The Literary Microcosm: Theories of Interpretation of the Later Neoplatonists.* Columbia Studies in the Classical Tradition, no. 2. Leiden: Brill, 1976.

Courcelle, Pierre. *Les Lettres grecques en occident, de Macrobe à Cassiodore.* Paris: E. de Boccard, 1948.

———. "Quelques symboles funéraires du néo-platonisme latin: Le Vol de Dédale, Ulysse et les Sirènes." *Revue des études anciennes* 46 (1944): 65–93.

Crombie, I. M. *An Examination of Plato's Doctrines.* 2 vols. London: Routledge and Kegan Paul, 1962.

Cumont, Franz. *Etudes syriennes.* Paris: Picard, 1917.

———. *Recherches sur le symbolisme funéraire des Romains.* Paris: Geuthner, 1942.

Curtius, Ernst Robert. *European Literature and the Latin Middle Ages.* Translated by Willard R. Trask. Bollingen Series, no. 36. New York: Pantheon, 1953.

Dahiyat, Ismail M. *Avicenna's Commentary on the Poetics of Aristotle.* Leiden: Brill, 1974.

Dalsgaard Larsen, Bent. "Jamblique dans la philosophie antique tardive." In *De Jamblique à Proclus.* Entretiens sur l'antiquité classique, no. 21. Vandoeuvres-Geneva: Fondation Hardt, 1974.

———. *Jamblique de Chalcis, Exégète et philosophe.* Thesis. 2 vols. Aarhus: Universitetsforlaget, 1972.

DeLacy, Phillip. "Plato and the Intellectual Life of the Second Century A.D." in *Approaches to the Second Sophistic*, edited by Glen W. Bowersock. University Park, Pa.: American Philological Association, 1974.

——. "Stoic Views of Poetry." *American Journal of Philology* 69 (1948): 241–71.

Delatte, Armand. *Etudes sur la littérature pythagoricienne*. Bibl. de l'Ecole des hautes études, fasc. 217. Paris: Champion, 1915.

De Lubac, Henri. *Exégèse médiévale, les quatre sens de l'écriture*. 2 vols. Paris: Aubier, 1959–61.

Des Places, Edouard. See "Works Cited: Ancient Authors" under Numenius.

Detienne, Marcel. *Homère, Hésiode, et Pythagore*. Collection Latomus, vol. 57. Brussels: Latomus, 1962.

De Vogel, C. J. "The Sōma-Sēma Formula: its Function in Plato and Plotinus Compared to Christian Writers." In *Neoplatonism and Early Christian Thought: Essays in Honor of A. H. Armstrong*, edited by M. J. Blumenthal and R. A. Markus. London: Variorum, 1981.

Dillon, John. "Ganymede as the Logos: Traces of a Forgotten Allegorization in Philo?" *Classical Quarterly* 31 (1981): 183–85.

——. *The Middle Platonists*. London: Duckworth, 1977.

Dodds, E. R. "Numenius and Ammonius." In *Les Sources de Plotin*. Entretiens sur l'antiquité classique, no. 5. Vandoeuvres-Geneva: Fondation Hardt, 1957. See also "Works Cited: Ancient Authors" under Proclus.

Dörrie, Heinrich. "Die griechischen Romane und das Christentum." *Philologus* 93 (n.s. 47) (1938): 273–76.

——. "Zur Methodik antiker Exegese." *Zeitschrift für die neutestamentliche Wissenschaft und die Kunde der älteren Kirche* 65 (1974): 121–38.

Dronke, Peter. *Fabula: Explorations into the Uses of Myth in Medieval Platonism*. Mittellateinische Studien und Texte, vol. 9. Leiden: Brill, 1974.

Else, Gerald F. See "Works Cited: Ancient Authors" under Aristotle.

Ensslin, W. "Praetextatus (1)." P-W 22.1 (1954): cols. 1575–79.

Fergusson, Francis. *Dante*. New York: Macmillan, 1966.

Ferwerda, R. *La Signification des images et des métaphores dans la pensée de Plotin*. Groningen: J. B. Wolters, 1965.

Festugière, A. J. See "Works Cited: Ancient Authors" under Proclus.

Feuillatre, E. *Etudes sur les Ethiopiques d'Héliodore*. Paris: Presses universitaires de France, 1966.

Finsler, G. *Homer in der Neuzeit von Dante bis Goethe*. 1912. Reprint. Hildesheim: Georg Olms, 1973.

Flacelière, Robert. "La Théologie selon Plutarque." In *Mélanges de philosophie, de littérature et d'histoire ancienne offerts à Pierre Boyancé*, edited by J.-P. Boucher et al. Rome: Ecole française de Rome, 1974.

Flamant, Jacques. *Macrobe et le néoplatonisme latin à la fin du ive siècle*. Etudes préliminaires aux religions orientales dans l'empire romain, vol. 58. Leiden: Brill, 1977.

Flashar, Hellmut, Karlfried Grunder,, and Axel Horstmann, eds. *Philologie und Hermeneutik im 19. Jahrhundert*. Göttingen: Vandenhoeck & Ruprecht, 1979.

Fortin, Ernest L. "Christianity and Hellenism in Basil the Great's Address *Ad adulescentes."* In *Neoplatonism and Early Christian Thought: Essays in Honor of A. H. Armstrong,* edited by M. J. Blumenthal and R. A. Markus. London: Variorum, 1981.

Fowden, Garth. "The Pagan Holy Man in Late Antique Society." *Journal of Hellenic Studies* 102 (1982): 33–59.

Frank, Erich. *Plato und die sogenannten Pythagoreer: Ein Kapitel aus der Geschichte des griechischen Geistes.* Halle: Niemayer, 1923.

Friedl, Ansgar Josef. *Die Homer-Interpretation des Neuplatonikers Proklos.* Inaugural dissertation. [Würzburg]: Dittert [1932?].

Gadamer, Hans-Georg. "Hermeneutik." In *Historisches Wörterbuch der Philosophie,* edited by Joachim Ritter. Darmstadt: Wissenschaftliche Buchgesellschaft, 1971–. In progress.

———. *Wahrheit und Methode: Grundzüge einer philosophischen Hermeneutik.* 2nd ed. Tübingen: Mohr, 1965. Translation of the first edition: *Truth and Method.* New York: Seabury, 1975.

Gelzer, Thomas. "Die Epigramme des Neuplatonikers Proklos." *Museum Helveticum* 23 (1966): 1–36. See also "Works Cited: Ancient Authors" under Musaeus.

Gersh, Stephen. *From Iamblichus to Eriugena: An Investigation of the Prehistory and Evolution of the Pseudo-Dionysian Tradition.* Studien zur Problemgeschichte der antiken und mittelalterlichen Philosophie, vol. 8. Leiden: Brill, 1978.

Goldschmidt, Victor. "Théologia." *Revue des études grecques* 63 (1950): 20–42.

Grube, G. M. A. *The Greek and Roman Critics.* London: Methuen, 1965.

———. "How Did the Greeks Look at Literature?" In *Lectures in Memory of Louise Taft Semple, 2nd Series, 1966–70,* edited by C. G. Boulter et al. Norman: University of Oklahoma Press for the University of Cincinnati, 1973.

Hadot, Pierre-Henri. "Fragments d'un commentaire de Porphyre sur le Parménide." *Revue des études grecques* 74 (1961): 410–38.

———. "Ouranos, Kronos, and Zeus in Plotinus' Treatise Against the Gnostics." In *Neoplatonism and Early Christian Thought: Essays in Honor of A. H. Armstrong,* edited by M. J. Blumenthal and R. A. Markus. London: Variorum, 1981.

Hagendahl, Harald. *Augustine and the Latin Classics.* Studia Graeca et Latina Gothoburgensia, vol. 20. Acta Universitatis Gothoburgensis. Göteborg: Almqvist and Wiksell, 1967.

Hahn, Reinhardt. *Die Allegorie in der antiken Rhetorik.* Inaugural dissertation. Tübingen, 1967.

Haller, Robert S., ed. *Literary Criticism of Dante Alighieri.* Lincoln: University of Nebraska Press, 1973.

Halliday, William Reginald. *Greek Divination: A Study of its Methods and Principles.* London: Macmillan, 1913.

Harmon. A. M. "The Poet κατ' ἐξοχήν." *Classical Philology* 18 (1923): 35–47.

Hathaway, Ronald F. *Hierarchy and the Definition of Order in the Letters of Pseudo-Dionysius.* The Hague: Nijhoff, 1969.

Havelock, Eric A. *Preface to Plato.* Cambridge: Cambridge University Press, 1963.

Hay, David M. "Philo's References to Other Allegorists." *Studia Philonica* 6 (1978–80): 41–75.

Heisermann, Arthur. *The Novel Before the Novel.* Chicago: University of Chicago Press, 1977.

Henry, Paul. *Plotin et l'occident: Firmicius Maternus, Marius Victorinus, Saint Augustin et Macrobe.* 1934. Reprint. Dubuque: Wm. C. Brown Reprint Library, [1965?].

Herington, C. J. "Homer: A Byzantine Perspective." *Arion* 8 (1969): 432–34.

Herzog, Reinhardt. *Die allegorische Dichtkunst des Prudentius.* Zetemata, Heft 42. Munich: C. H. Beck, 1966.

Hollander, Robert. *Allegory in Dante's Commedia.* Princeton: Princeton University Press, 1969.

Huxley, G. L. *Greek Epic Poetry from Eumelos to Panyassis.* Cambridge, Mass.: Harvard University Press, 1969.

Igal, J. "La Génesis de la inteligencia en un pasaje de las *Eneades* de Plotino (v, 1, 7, 4–35)." *Emerita* 39 (1971): 129–57.

Jaeger, Werner. *The Theology of the Early Greek Philosophers.* Gifford Lectures, delivered 1936. Oxford: Oxford University Press, 1947.

Jolivet, Jean. "La Philosophie médiévale en occident." In *Histoire de la philosophie,* edited by Brice Parain, vol. 1. *Encyclopédie de la Pléiade.* Paris: Gallimard, 1969.

Jones, J. W., Jr. "Allegorical Interpretation in Servius." *Classical Journal* 56 (1960–61): 217–26.

Jowett, Benjamin and Lewis Campbell. See "Works Cited: Ancient Authors" under Plato.

Kahl, W. "Cornelius Labeo." *Philologus,* supplementary vol. 5 (1889): 717–807.

Kapsomenos, S. G. " Ὁ ὀρφικὸς πάπυρος τῆς Θεσσαλονίκης." Ἀρχαιολογικὸν Δελτίον 19 (1964): 17–25.

Kindstrand, Jan Fredrik. *Homer in der zweiten Sophistik.* Uppsala: Acta Universitatis Upsaliensis, 1973.

Kirk, Geoffrey S., and J. E. Raven. *The Presocratic Philosophers.* Cambridge: Cambridge University Press, 1962.

Klibansky, Raymond. *The Continuity of the Platonic Tradition During the Middle Ages, I: Outline of a corpus platonicorum medii aevi.* London: Warburg Institute, n.d. [1950?—completed 1937].

Kraemer, Jörg. "Arabische Homerverse." *Zeitschrift der deutschen morgenländischen Gesellschaft* 106 (1956): 259–316.

Kroll, W. "Ein neuplatonischer Parmenideskommentar in einem Turiner Palimpsest." *Rheinisches Museum* 47 (1892): 599–627.

Lamberton, Robert. See "Works Cited: Ancient Authors" under Porphyry.

Leemans, E. A. See "Works Cited: Ancient Authors" under Numenius.

Lesky, Albin. *Geschichte der griechischen Literatur.* 2nd ed. Bern and Munich: Francke, 1963.

Lévêque, Pierre. *Aurea Catena Homeri: Une Etude sur l'allégorie grecque.* Annales littéraires de l'Université de Besançon, vol. 27. Paris: Les Belles Lettres, 1959.
Lévy, Isidore. *Recherches sur les sources de la légende de Pythagore.* Paris: Leroux, 1926.
Lord, George deF. *Homeric Renaissance.* New Haven: Yale University Press, 1956.

Margolin, Jean-Claude. "Aspects du surréalisme au xvi⁰ siècle: Fonction allégorique et vision anamorphotique." *Bibliothèque d'humanisme et renaissance* 39 (1977): 503–30.
Markus, R. A. "St. Augustine on Signs." *Phronesis* 2 (1957): 60–83.
Marrou, Henri-Irenée. *Saint Augustin et la fin de la culture antique.* 4th ed. Paris: E. de Boccard, 1958.
Mastandrea, Paolo. *Un Neoplatonico Latino: Cornelio Labeone.* Leiden: Brill, 1979.
Morrow, Glenn R. See "Works Cited: Ancient Authors" under Proclus.
Mountfort, J. F., and J. T. Schultz. *Index rerum et nominum in Scholiis Servii et Aelii Donati Tractorum.* Cornell Studies in Classical Philology, vol. 23. Ithaca, N.Y.: Cornell University Press, 1930.
Mras, Karl. *Macrobius' Kommentar zu Ciceros Somnium: Ein Beitrag zur Geistesgeschichte des 5. Jarh. n. Chr.* Sonderausgabe aus den Sitzungsberichten der preussischen Akademie der Wissenschaften, phil.-hist. Klasse, 1933, no. 6. Berlin, 1933.
Müller, Konrad. "Allegorische Dichtererklärung." P-W, supplementary vol. 4 (1924): cols. 16–22.

Nicoll, Allardyce. See "Works Cited: Ancient Authors" under Homer.

Oldfather, William Abbott. "Lokrika: Sagensgeschichtliche Untersuchungen." *Philologus* 67 (n.s. 21) (1908): 411–72.
O'Meara, John J. "Augustine and Neo-platonism." *Recherches augustiniennes* 1 (1958): 91–111.

Pépin, Jean. *Dante et la tradition de l'allégorie.* Conférence Albert le Grand, 1969. Montreal: Institut d'études médiévales, 1970.
———. "La Fortune du *de antro nympharum* de Porphyre de occident." In *Plotino e il Neoplatonismo in Oriente e in Occidente.* Problemi attuali di scienza e cultura, quad. no. 198. Rome: Accademia nazionale dei Lincei, 1974.
———. *Mythe et allégorie: Les Origines grecques et les contestations judéo-chrétiennes.* 2nd ed. Paris: Etudes augustiniennes, 1976.
———. "Plotin et les mythes." *Revue philosophique de Louvain* 53 (1955): 5–27.
———. "Porphyre, exégète d'Homère." In *Porphyre.* Entretiens sur l'antiquité classique, no. 12. Vandoeuvres-Geneva: Fondation Hardt, 1965.
———. "Remarques sur la théorie de l'exégèse allégorique chez Philon." In *Philon d'Alexandrie.* Colloques nationaux du C. N. R. S. Paris: C. N. R. S., 1967.
———. "Saint Augustin et la fonction protreptique de l'allégorie." *Recherches augustiniennes* 1 (1958): 243–86.
Perry, Ben E. *The Ancient Romances.* Sather Lectures, vol. 37. Berkeley and Los Angeles: University of California Press, 1967.
Peters, F. E. *Aristoteles Arabus: The Oriental Translations and Commentaries on the*

Aristotelian Corpus. New York University Department of Classics, Monographs on Mediterranean Antiquity, no. 2. Leiden: Brill, 1968.

Pézard, André. *"La rotta gonna": Gloses et corrections aux textes mineures de Dante*. 3 vols. Florence and Paris: Sansoni and Marcel Didier, 1967–79.

Pfeiffer, Rudolph. *History of Classical Scholarship from the Beginnings to the End of the Hellenistic Age*. Oxford, Oxford University Press, 1968.

Pötscher, Walter. See "Works Cited: Ancient Authors" under Porphyry.

Praechter, Karl. *Die Philosophie des Altertums*. Part I of Friedrich Ueberweg and Karl Praechter, *Grundriss der Geschichte der Philosophie*. 12th ed. Berlin: Mittler, 1926.

———. "Richtungen und Schulen im Neuplatonismus." In *Genethliakon Carl Robert*. Berlin: Weidmann, 1910.

———. "Syrianos." P-W 4a2 (1932): cols. 1728–75.

Puech, Henri-Charles. "Numénius d'Apamée et les théologies orientales au second siècle." In *Mélanges Bidez*. Annuaire de l'Institut de philologie de d'histoire orientales, vol. 2. Brussels: Secrétariat de l'institut, 1934.

Rabuse, Georg. "Saturne et l'échelle de Jacob." *Archives d'histoire doctrinale et littéraire du moyen age* 45 (1978): 7–31.

Rahner, Hugo. "Das Christliche Mysterium und die heidnischen Mysterien." *Eranos-Jahrbuch* 11 (1944): 347–449. Translated as "The Christian Mystery and the Pagan Mysteries" in *Papers from the Eranos Yearbooks*, edited by Joseph Campbell, vol. 2. New York: Pantheon, 1955.

———. *Griechische Mythen in christlicher Deutung*. Zurich: Rhein-Verlag, 1957.

Raine, Kathleen. *Blake and Tradition*. A. W. Mellon Lectures in the Fine Arts. Princeton: Princeton University Press, 1968.

———, ed., with George Mills Harper. *Thomas Taylor the Platonist: Selected Writings*. Princeton: Princeton University Press, 1969.

Raven, J. E. *Plato's Thought in the Making*. Cambridge: Cambridge University Press, 1965.

Richardson, N. J. "Homeric Professors in the Age of the Sophists." *Proceedings of the Cambridge Philological Society* 201 (1975): 65–81.

Ricoeur, Paul. "Expliquer et comprendre." *Revue philosophique de Louvain* 75 (1977): 126–47. Translation in *The Philosophy of Paul Ricoeur: An Anthology of His Work*, edited by Charles E. Reagan and David Stewart. Boston: Beacon Press, 1978.

Rist, J. M. *Plotinus: The Road to Reality*. Cambridge: Cambridge University Press, 1967.

Rohde, Erwin. *Der griechische Roman und seine Vorläufer*, 1876. 4th ed. Reprint. Darmstadt: Wissenschaftliche Buchgesellschaft, 1960.

Rosán, Laurence J. *The Philosophy of Proclus*. New York: Cosmos, 1949.

———. "Proclus." In *The Encyclopedia of Philosophy*, edited by Paul Edwards, vol. 6. New York: Macmillan, 1967.

Rosenthal, Franz. *Das Fortleben der Antike im Islam*. Zurich: Artemis, n.d. [1965?].

Ross, David. *Plato's Theory of Ideas*. Oxford: Oxford University Press, 1951.

Rudolph, Kurt. *Gnosis*. Translated and edited by Robert McLachlan Wilson. San Francisco: Harper and Row, 1983.

Russell, D. A. *Plutarch*. London: Duckworth, 1972.

Rusten, Jeffrey S. "Interim Notes on the Papyrus from Derveni." *Harvard Studies in Classical Philology* 89 (1985): 121–40.

Sandmel, Samuel. *Philo of Alexandria*. Oxford: Oxford University Press, 1979.
———. "Philo's Knowledge of Hebrew: The Present State of the Problem." *Studia Philonica* 5 (1978): 107–12.
Sandy, Gerald N. "Characterization and Philosophical Decor in Heliodorus' *Ethiopica*." *Transactions of the American Philological Association* 112 (1982): 141–67.
Sandys, John Edwin. *A History of Classical Scholarship*. 3 vols. Cambridge: Cambridge University Press, 1908.
Schrader, Hermann. "Telephos der Pergamener ΠΕΡΙ ΤΗΣ ΚΑΘ ΟΜΗΡΟΝ ΡΗΤΟΡΙΚΗΣ." *Hermes* 37 (1902): 530–81. See also "Works Cited: Ancient Authors" under Porphyry.
Seznec, Jean. *The Survival of the Pagan Gods: The Mythological Tradition and its Place in Renaissance Humanism and Art*. Bollingen Series, no. 38. New York: Pantheon, 1953.
Sheppard, Anne D. R. *Studies on the 5th and 6th Essays of Proclus' Commentary on the Republic*. Hypomnemata, Heft 61. Göttingen: Vandenhoeck and Ruprecht, 1980.
Shorey, Paul. *The Unity of Plato's Thought*. 1903. Reprint. [no loc.]: Archon, 1968.
Simonsuuri, Kirsti. *Homer's Original Genius: Eighteenth-Century Notions of the Early Greek Epic (1688–1798)*. Cambridge: Cambridge University Press, 1979.
Smith, Macklin. *Prudentius' Psychomachia: A Reexamination*. Princeton: Princeton University Press, 1976.
Sontag, Susan. "Against Interpretation." In *Against Interpretation and Other Essays*. New York: Farrar, Straus & Giroux, 1966.
Stahl, William Harris. See "Works Cited: Ancient Authors" under Macrobius.
Stanford, William Bedell. *The Ulysses Theme: A Study in the Adaptability of a Traditional Hero*. 2nd ed. Oxford: Blackwell, 1963.
Stewart, J. A. *The Myths of Plato*. 1904. Reprint. London: Levy, 1960.
Susemihl, Franz. *Geschichte der griechischen Literatur in der Alexandrinerzeit*. Leipzig: Teubner, 1891.

Tarán, Leonardo. *Academica: Plato, Philip of Opus, and the Pseudo-Platonic Epinomis*. Memoirs of the American Philosophical Society, vol. 107. Philadelphia: American Philosophical Society, 1975.
Tate, J. "The Beginnings of Greek Allegory." *Classical Review* 41 (1927): 214–15.
———. "On the History of Allegorism." *Classical Quarterly* 28 (1934): 105–15.
———. "Plato and Allegorical Interpretation." *Classical Quarterly* 23 (1929): 142–54.
Taylor, A. E. *A Commentary on Plato's Timaeus*. Oxford: Oxford University Press, 1928.
Thesleff, Holger. *An Introduction to the Pythagorean Writings of the Hellenistic Period*. Acta Academiae Aboensis Humaniora xxiv, 3. Abo: Abo Akademi, 1961.
———. *The Pythagorean Texts of the Hellenistic Period*. Acta Academiae Aboensis Humaniora xxx, 1. Abo: Abo Akademi, 1965.
Thomas, Emile. *Essai sur Servius et son commentaire sur Virgile*. Paris: Ernest Thorin, 1880.

Thompson, David. *Dante's Epic Journeys*. Baltimore: Johns Hopkins University Press, 1974.
Tigerstedt, E. N. *The Decline and Fall of the Neoplatonic Interpretation of Plato*. Commentationes Humanarum Litterarum, no. 52. Helsinki: Societas Scientiarum Fennica, 1954.
———. *Interpreting Plato*. Uppsala: Almqvist and Wiksell, 1977.
Tollinton, R. B. *Clement of Alexandria: A Study in Christian Liberalism*. London: Williams and Norgate, 1914.
Trouillard, Jean. "L'Activité onomastique selon Proclos." In *De Jamblique à Proclus*. Entretiens sur l'antiquité classique, no. 21. Vandoeuvres-Geneva: Fondation Hardt, 1974.
———. "Le Merveilleux dans la vie et la pensée de Proclos." *Revue philosophique de la France et de l'étranger* 163 (1973): 439–52.
———. "Le Néoplatonisme." In *Histoire de la philosophie*, edited by Brice Parain, vol 1. *Encyclopédie de la Pléiade*. Paris: Gallimard, 1969.

Ullmann, Manfred. *Die arabische Überlieferung der sogenannten Menandersentenzen*. Abhandlungen für die Kunde des Morgenlandes, vol. 34, no. 1. Deutsche morgenländische Gesellschaft. Wiesbaden: Franz Skiner, 1961.

Van Winden, J. C. M. *Chalcidius on Matter: His Doctrine and Sources*. Philosophia antiqua, vol. 9. Leiden: Brill, 1959.

Wallis, R. T. *Neoplatonism*. London: Duckworth, 1972.
Walzer, Richard. *Greek Into Arabic: Essays on Islamic Philosophy*. Oriental Studies, no. 1. Cambridge, Mass.: Harvard University Press, 1962.
Waszink, J.-H. "Porphyrios und Numenios." In *Porphyre*. Entretiens sur l'antiquité classique, no. 12. Vandoeuvres-Geneva: Fondation Hardt, 1965.
Weinstock, Stefan. "Die platonische Homerkritik und seine Nachwirkung." *Philologus* 82 (1926–27): 121–53.
Wenrich, J. E. *De Auctorum Graecorum versionibus et commentariis Syriacis Arabicis Armeniacis Persicisque*. Leipzig: Vogel, 1842.
Wetherbee, Winthrop. *Platonism and Poetry in the Twelfth Century: The Literary Influence of the School of Chartres*. Princeton: Princeton University Press, 1972.
Wolfson, Harry Austryn. *Philo*. Cambridge: Harvard University Press, 1947.
Wüst, Ernst. "Pantomimus." P-W 18b2 (1949): cols. 833–69.
Wytzes, J. *Der letzte Kampf des Heidentums in Rom*. Etudes préliminaires aux religions orientales dans l'empire romain, vol. 56. Leiden: Brill, 1977.

Ziehen, L. "θεολόγος." P-W 5a2 (1934): cols. 2031–33.

ANCIENT AND MEDIEVAL PASSAGES CITED

On the format of citations, especially from later authors, see p. 325. More familiar works are referred to by English title, less familiar ones by Latin title.

Acts of the Apostles		*Rhetoric*	
17.34	244	1405b	203
Alcaeus		Ps.-Aristotle	
frs. 18, 19	145	*Liber de causis*	
Anacreon		11	241
fr. 75	145	*Liber de pomo*	
Anaxagoras		370–72	241
fr. B12	97	Augustine	
Anth. Lyr. Gr.		*City of God*	
7.75	69	2.14	16, 260
Apuleius		3.2	259
De deo Socratis		4.10, 26, 30	260
24	233	5.8	261
Metamorphoses		6.5	260
9.13	233	7.16	260
Archilochus		7.26	261
fr. 54	145	8.5	260
Aristotle		8.26	257
Metaphysics		9.7	98, 233, 260, 261
A 983b	11, 24, 252	9.10	91
A 987a	41	9.15	260
A 989b–990a	43	10.10	227
B 1000a	28	10.13	258
E 1026a	23	10.14	257
Λ 1071b	28	10.15	169, 259
Poetics		10.21	259
1447a	188	10.26	257
1459b	223	11.19	257
1460a	188	13.21	257

INDEX OF GREEK TERMS

A few Greek words appear in the original in the text, because they are technical terms or otherwise resist satisfactory translation. Equivalents are offered here for the more important of these.

GENERAL INDEX

Procopius of Gaza, 160
Prometheus, 103–4
Proteus, viii, 17, 37, 172, 226–27
Prudentius, x, 145–48, 158, 283, 290
Ps.-Dionysius, 232n270, 246–47
Ps.-Plutarch, 11n27, 14, 20n52, 36n125,
    41, 110, 112–13, 118, 251–53, 268,
    320, 322
Pythagoreanism, ix, 2, 9, 15, 19, 21, 237,
    238; allegorical interpretations in,
    31–43, 73–75, 115, 178, 270–72,
    320–24; doctrine of souls in, 73–74,
    101–2, 118–19, 271; Philolaus as
    source on, 28; sects in, 36; use of
    Plato's myths by, 38, 128. *See also*
    Numenius; Platonism; Plotinus; Por-
    phyry; Proclus

Rahner, H., 242, 243
Raphael, 8–9
Renaissance, x, 1, 9, 10, 146, 186n81,
    223, 234, 240
Rhea, 213–14
Rhetoric, 20, 40, 57, 187, 193, 201, 268,
    273
Richard of St.-Victor, 287
Ricoeur, P., 302
Romances, Greek, 148–53, 157, 160
Ross, D., 165
Rufinus, 263

Sallustius, 139–43, 148, 171, 188
Sappho, 176
Sarpedon, 215n214
Satire, 55, 58–59, 220–21, 275, 286
Saturnalia of Macrobius. *See* Macrobius
Schlegel, F., 301
Schleiermacher, F., 301
Scholia on Homer, ix, 20, 32, 38, 52, 94,
    112, 114, 194n124, 198, 219, 254,
    320–24
School of Chartres. *See* Chartres,
    School of
Schrader, H., 108, 110
Scipio, dream of (in Cicero's *De re pub-
    lica*): commentary by Favonius Eu-
    logius, 272–73; commentary by
    Macrobius, 66, 71, 249, 269–73, 289,
    318–19
Second Sophistic, 57, 193, 201
Seneca, 13

Servius, 224n246, 250, 262–64, 269–70, 282
Severus, 84
Sheppard, A., 185n77, 190–91, 200,
    201n150, 208n180, 210n189, 214–15,
    247, 304n14
Sibyl, 248
Simonides, 29
Sirens, 7, 10, 37, 52, 230–32, 243, 275,
    281, 295
Skylla, 51
Socrates: attitudes toward myth and po-
    etry, 23, 25, 102, 124, 140, 180–85,
    196, 197, 237, 243; condemnation of
    Homer by, 16–19, 70, 100, 124, 153–
    54, 172–73, 182–85, 196–97, 198,
    215–16, 260; etymological specula-
    tions and, 38–39, 165–66, 214; in
    text of Philip the Philosopher, 307;
    on uses of texts, 21, 159, 252, 300–1;
    as voice of Plato, 64–65. *See also* Plato
Sodano, A. R., 108
Solon, 176
Sontag, S., 299
Sophistic, Second. *See* Second Sophistic
Spercheios, 18
Speusippus, 34, 39
Stesichorus, 195–96
Stobaeus, 42, 109, 113–15
Stoicism, ix, 13–14, 21, 40–41, 56, 94,
    109, 251, 260n105; allegorical inter-
    pretation in, 25, 81, 143, 164n5,
    210n191, 219, 260, 265–66; as source
    for Philo's allegorizing, 45–51, 75–76;
    theology in, 26, 261
Strabo, 24, 26–27, 121, 122, 138
Structuralism, 201
Styx, The. See Porphyry
Suda, 64n66, 176, 177
Symmachus, 263, 267–68
Synesius, 144n1
Syrianus, 134, 164n5, 176–77, 197–98,
    200, 206, 208, 210, 244

Tate, J., 2
Taylor, T., x, 301–2
Telemachus, 7n13
Telephus of Pergamon, 16
Tethys, 252
Thales, 252
Theagenes and Chariclea. See Heliodorus;
    Philip the Philosopher

Designer: Leigh McLellan
Compositor: G&S Typesetters, Inc.
Text: 10/13 Palatino
Display: Palatino
Printer: Edwards Brothers, Inc.
Binder: Edwards Brothers, Inc.